AF600578

THE CATHOLIC UNIVERSITY OF AMERICA
STUDIES IN CANON LAW
No. 54

THE VOW *of* POVERTY

A DISSERTATION

Submitted to the Faculty of Canon Law of the Catholic University of America, in partial fulfillment of its requirements for the Degree, Doctor of Both Laws

BY

SIDNEY JOSEPH TURNER, C.P., J.U.L.
(*of the Province of St. Paul of the Cross.*)

The Catholic University of America
Washington, D. C.
1929

Nihil Obstat:

WILLIAM T. CAVANAUGH, C.P., J.U.D.
Censor Deputatus

Imprimi Permittitur:

STANISLAUS GRENNAN, C.P.
Praep. Provincialis
Union City, N. J., die 10 Aprilis, 1929

Nihil Obstat:

VALENTINE SCHAAF, O.F.M., J.C.D.
Censor Deputatus

Imprimatur:

✠ MICHAEL J. CURLEY
Archiepiscopus Baltimorensis
Washingtonii, die 11 Aprilis, 1929.

THE SIGN PRESS, *Union City, N. J.*

Dedication

Dedicated with esteem and gratitude to the
Very Reverend Stanislaus Grennan, C.P.,
Provincial of the Province of St. Paul of the Cross.

CONTENTS

FOREWORD

Observance of evangelical Poverty belongs to the essence of the Religious State. On this account it is ever and always an important factor in the life of Religious Institutes and their members. Hence the canonical regulation of the practice of poverty is of concern to the Religious Superiors and subjects as well as their confessors.

The primary purpose of this dissertation is to explain the present canonical legislation concerning the observance of evangelical poverty. As preparation for the interpretation of the Code relative to this subject the available anterior legislation was consulted. In studying the historical development of the law, notes were taken of whatever data (found in the legislation of Religious Institutes and the General Law), which might prove interesting or helpful to others interested in this phase of the Religious Life.

The writer avails himself of this opportunity to express his gratitude to his friends and the Faculty of Canon Law at the Catholic University of America for their helpfulness during the past three years.

BIBLIOGRAPHY

Sources

A. Civil

Alabama Code of 1928, Charlottsville, Va., 1929.
Alaska, the Compiled Laws of the Territory of (1913), Washington, 1913.
Arizona, the Revised Statutes of (1913), Phoenix, 1913.
Arkansas, A Digest of the Statutes of (1919), Little Rock, 1919.
Basilicorum Libri LX, 7 vol. ed. G. G. E. Heimbach, Lipsiae, 1883.
British Columbia, the Revised Statutes of (1924), Victoria, 1924.
Bürgerliches Gesetzbuch, Leipzig, 1927.
California, the Codes of, 4 vol. (ed. James M. Kerr), San Francisco, 1920.
Civil Code of Lower Canada, the, Montreal, 1867.
Code Civil annote d'apres la doctrine et la jurisprudence (Griolet-Verge-Bourdeaux, ed. 21), Paris, 1921.
Code Civil de la Province de Quebec, Montreal, 1905.
Code Civil Portugais (1868), Paris, 1894.
Codex Legum Antiquarum, Francofurti, 1613.
Codigo Civil Bolivia (1910), Santiago de Chile.
Codigo Civil de la Republica de Chile, Valparaiso, 1912.
Codigo Civil Colombiano (ed. 5) Bogota, 1923.
Codigo Civil de la Republica de Ecuador, Neueva York, 1889.
Codigo Civil de la Republica de Nicaragua, 1904.
Codigo Civil Republica de Panama, Barcelona, 1817.
Codigo Civil de la Republica de el Salvador (ed. 5) San Salvador.
Colorado, the Compiled Laws of (1921), Denver, 1922.
Connecticut, the General Statutes of (1918), Hartford, 1918.
Corpus Iuris Civilis; Institutiones, recognovit P. Krueger; Digesta, recognovit Th. Mommsen, retractavit P. Krueger, Vol. I, Berolini, 1922; *Codex Justinianus, recognovit et retractavit P. Krueger,* Vol. II, Berolini, 1915; *Novellæ, recognovit R. Schoell, opus Schoelli morte interceptum absolvit G. Kroll,* Vol. III, Berolini, 1912.
Delaware, Revised Statutes of the State of (1915), Wilmington.
District of Columbia, Code (1924), Washington, 1925.
Florida, the Compiled General Laws of (1927), Atlanta, 1929.
Georgia, Code (1926).
Grotze Ausgabe, Das allgemeine burgerliche Gesetzbuch fur das Raisertum Osterreich, Wien, 1922.
Hawaii, Revised Laws of (1925), Honolulu.
I Cinque Codici, Napoli, 1922.
Idaho, the Compiled Statutes of (1919), Boise.
Illinois, Statutes of the State of (1927), Chicago, 1927.
Indiana, Annotated Statutes (1926), Indianapolis, 1926.
Iowa, Code of (1927).
Kansas, Revised Statutes of (1923), Topeka, 1923.
Leges Nationum Germanicarum, Tomus I, *Leges Visigothorum,* Lipsiae, 1802.

Les Codes Belges et les Lois Speciales les plus usuelles en vigueur en Belgique, Bruxelles, 1925.
Louisiana Revised Code (1870).
Maine, the Revised Statutes of the State of (1917), Augusta.
Manatoba, the Revised Statutes of (1902), Winnipeg, 1903.
Maryland, the Annotated Code of the Public General Laws of (Bagley), Baltimore, 1924.
Massachusetts, the General Laws of the Commonwealth of (1921), Boston, 1921.
Michigan, the Compiled Laws of the State of (1915), Lansing.
Minnesota, Mason's Statutes (1927), St. Paul, 1927.
Mississippi, Annotated Code (1927), Indianapolis, 1927.
Missouri, the Revised Statutes of the State of (1919), Jefferson City.
Montana, the Revised Codes of (1921), San Francisco, 1921.
Nebraska, Compiled Statutes of the State of (1922), Columbia, Mo., 1922.
Nevada, Laws of (1912), Carson City.
New Hampshire, the Public Laws of the State of, Manchester.
New Jersey, Compiled Statutes of (1910), Newark, 1911.
New Mexico, Statutes Annotated (1915), Denver, 1915.
New York, Cahill's Consolidated Laws of (James J. Cahill), Chicago, 1923.
Nova Scotia, Revised Statutes of (1923), Halifax, 1923.
North Carolina, Consolidated Statutes of, Raleigh, 1920.
North Dakota, the Compiled Laws of the State of (1913), Rochester, N. Y., 1914.
Ohio, Throckmorton's 1929 *Annotated Code of,* Cleveland, 1929.
Oklahoma, Compiled Statutes (1921), Ardmore, 1922.
Ontario, Revised Statutes of (1927), Toronto, 1927.
Oregon, Laws (1920), San Francisco, 1920.
Pennsylvania, Digest of Penn. Statute Law (1920), St. Paul, Minn., 1921.
Porto Rico, Compilation of the Revised Statutes and Codes of, Washington, 1913.
Rhode Island, General Laws of, Pawtucket, 1923.
South Carolina, Code of Laws of (1922, Columbia, 1922.
South Dakota, Revised Code (1919), Pierre S. Dak. 1919.
Tennessee, Shanon's Code of (1918).
Texas, Somplete Statutes of (1928), Kansas City, 1928.
Theodosiani Libri XVI cum Constitutionibus Sirmonianis et Leges Novellae ad Theodosianum pertinentes, (ed. Krueger, Th Mommsen, P. M. Meyer, 3 vol. Berolini, 1905.
Utah, the Compiled Laws of the State of, (1917), Salt Lake City.
Vermont, General Laws (1917), Montpellier.
Virginia, the Code of (1924), Charlottsville, 1924.
West Virginia, Code. 1916.
Wisconsin, Statutes, 1927.
Wyoming, Compiled Statutes (1920), Sheridan, 1920.

B. Canonical

Acta Apostolicae Sedis, Romae, 1909.
Acta Capituli Generalis Ordinis Praedicatorum, Romae (7 iunii 1862).

Acta Capitulorum Generalium Ordinis Praedicatorum, I (1220-1303), recensuit B. M. Reichert, Romae 1898 in *Monumenta Ordinis Praedicatorum Historica,* Tomus III.

Acta et Decreta Concilii Plenarii Baltimorensis II, Baltimoriae, 1868.

Acta et Decreta Concilii Plenarii Baltimorensis III, Baltimoriae, 1886.

Acta et Decreta Sacorum Consiliorum Recentiorum (*Collectio Lacensis,* 7 vol., Friburgi Brisgoviae 1897).

Acta Leonis XIII Pontificis Maximi, Romae 1881-1905.

Acta Ordinis Minorum vel ad Ordinem quoque modo pertinentia, Quaracchi, 1882.

Acta Pii IX Pontificis Maximi, Romae 1854.

Apostolica Diplomata sive Pontificia Privilegia Fratrum Discalceatorum Ordinis Beatissimae semperque Virginis Mariae de Monte Carmelo, Matriti, 1700.

Biblia Sacra, Vulgatae Editionis, (ed. Hetzenauer), Ratisbonae, 1904.

Bullarium Benedicti Papae XIV, 13 vol. Mechlin, 1827.

Bullarium, Diplomatum, et Privilegiorum, Sanctorum Romanorum Pontificum, editio . . . auspicante Cardinali Francisco Gaude, 24 vol. Augustae Taurinorum, 1858-1872.

Bullarium Ordinis Fratrum Minorum S. Francisci Capucinorum seu Oraculorum . . . qua a S. Sede Apostolica pro Ordine Capucino emanarunt, 9 vol. Romae, 1740-1884.

Bullarium Ordinis Praedicatorum sub auspiciis SS. D. N. D. Benedicti XIII, 7 vol. Romae, 1759-.

Bullarii Romani Continuatio Summorum Pontificum, 19 vol. Prati, 1756-1892.

Codex Iuris Canonici, Romae, 1917.

Collectanea in usum Secretariae Sacrae Congregationis Episcoporum et Regularium, Romae, 1885.

Collectanea S. Congregationis de Propaganda Fide seu Decreta, Instructiones, Rescripta, pro Apostolicis Missionibus, 2 vol. Romae, 1907.

Concilia Provincialia Baltimori, habita ab anno 1829 usque ad annum 1849, Editio altera, Baltimore, 1851.

Concilii Tridentini Actorum, Pars Sexta, Complectens Acta Post Sessionem Sextam (XXII), *usque ad finem Concilii* (17 sept. 1562-4 dec. 1563). Collegit, Edidit, Illustravit, Stephanus Ehses, Friburgi, Brisgoviae, 1924.

Corpus Iuris Canonici, editio Lipsiensis secunda post Aemelii Ludovici Richteri curas ad librorum manuscriptorum et editionis Romanae fidem recognovit et adnotatione critica instruxit Aemelius Friedberg, 2 ed. 2 vol. Leipsic, 1922.

Decretum No. 49. 877, S. C. EE et RR, 10 iunii 1902.

Fontes Juris Canonici Codicis, 4 vol. Romae, 1923-1926.

Magnum Bullarium Romanum, Cherubini Laertius, Luxemburgi, 1727-1740.

Monumenta Selecta Juris Regularis tum Seraphici quum Communis, Ad Claras Aquas 1913.

Normae secundum quas S Cong. Episcoporum et Regularium procedere solet in approbandis novis Institutis votorum simplicium, Romae, 1901.

Theasaurus Resolutionum Sacrae Congregationis Concilii, Romae, 1700-1908.

C. Religious Legislation.

Codex Regularium, Holstenius, 5 vol. Augustae Vindelicorum, 1759.

Constitutiones Canonicorum Regularium Congregationis Sanctae Crucis Collimbriensis, Olisipone, 1784.

Constitutiones Congregationis Clericorum Regularium Marianorum, sub titulo Immaculatae Conceptionis Beatissimae Virginis Mariae, Romae, 1927.

Constitutiones et Regulae Congregationis Missionarium Oblatorum Sanctissimae et Immaculatae Virginis Mariae (1928), Romae, 1928.

Constitutiones Fratrum S. Ordinis Praedicatorum, Parisiis,, 1886.

Constitutiones Fratrum S. Ordinis Praedicatorum inchoatae in Capitulo Generali Provincialium, Romae celebrato A. D. 1924, Romae, 1925.

Constitutiones Societatis Verbi Divini, Steyl, 1910.

Constitutiones Societatis Verbi Divini, Steyl, 1922.

Constitutiones Sororum S. Ordinis Praedicatorum, Parisiis, 1886.

Constitutiones of the Sisters of Penance of the Third Order of Saint Dominic, forming the Congregation of the Most Holy Rosary of the United States of America, Wisconsin, 1884.

Constitutiones Ordinis Eremitarum S. Augustini, Romae, 1895.

Constitutiones Urbanae Ordinis Minorum Conventualium, S. P. Francisci auctoritate VII Pontificis Maximi Explanatae, Mechilinae, 1880.

Constitutio totius Ordinis Canonicorum Regularium Ordinis Sancti Augustini (*Bul. Rom.* pp. 425 sq.).

Constitutiones Monachorum Syrorum Maronitarum Ordinis Sancti Antonii Abbatis Congregationis Montis Libani, (*Bul. Rom.* XXIII, pp. 328 sq.).

Constitutiones Ordinis Fratrum Beatissimae Virginis Mariae de Monte Carmelo, Romae, 1927 (non approbata).

Constitutiones Ordinis S. Mariae de Mercede, (*Bul. Rom.* XX, pp. 232 sq.)

Constitutions of the Third Order of St. Francis of the Immaculate Conception, Little Falls, 1893.

Constitutions, Soeurs de la Charite de L'Hospital General de Montreal, Ditis Communement "Soeurs Grisis", Montreal, 1917.

Constitutions of the Congregation of the Sisters of the Adoration of the Most Precious Blood, O'Fallon Mo. 1919.

Constitutions of the Association of Franciscan Sisters of the Sacred Heart of the Third Order of St. Francis at Joiliet, Ill.

Constitutions of the Sisters of St. Joseph, New York.

Constitutions et Regles de la Congregation des Soeurs de Charite erige sous le titre et la protection de Notre Dame du Bon et Perpetuel Secours, Rome, 1882.

Constitutions and Rules of the Sisters of St. Joseph of Peace.

Constitutions of the Sisters Servants of the Immaculate Heart of Mary, Immaculate, Penn. 1925.

Constitutions of the Congregation of the Holy Cross, Le Mans, 1859.

Constitutions of the Society of Mary, Dayton, 1910.

Constitutions de la Congregation de Saint Basil, Lyons, 1878.

Constitutiones Presbyterorum Societatis Marie, Augustae Turinorum, 1823.

Constitutions de la Congregation des Soeurs de Sainte Croix.

Constitutions of the Religious of Our Lady of Charity of the Good Shepherd of Angers, Rome, 1836.

Constitutions of the Religious of Our Lady of Charity of the Good Shepherd of Angers, Roehampton, 1898.

Costituzioni delle Suore Terziarie Figlie Di D. Franceso, Quaracchi, 1916.

Coutumier de la Societe de Marie ou Recueil des Coutumes et des regles de la direction. Bar-le Duc. 1893.

Customs, Book of, for the use of the Sisters Servants of the Immaculate Heart of Mary, Immaculate 1928.

Declarations on the Rule of Our Holy Father St. Benedict and the Statutes of the American Cassinese Congregation, 1926.

Directory of the Sisters of the Incarnate Word, Texas, 1926.

Regel und Constitutionen fur die Schwestern des Diritten Ordens des Hl. Franziskus von Assisi M. C. bei St. Francis Wisconsin, Milwalkee, Wis. 1901.

Regula S. Pachomii (Migne, P. L. XXIII, 61-68).

Regula S. Basilii Fusius Tractatae (Migne P. G. XXXI, 389 sq.).

Regula S. Basilii Brevius Tractatae (Migne, P. G. XXXI, 1037 sq.).

Regula sive Doctrina monastica veterum testimonia Orsiensi (Migne, P. L. CIII, 453 sq.).

Regula ad Monachos [Caesarius of Arles] (Migne, P. L. LXVII, 1099 sq.).

Regula ad Virgines [*Caesarius of Arles*] (Migne, P. L. LXVII, 1107 sq.).

Regula SS. Pauli et Stephani (Migne, P. G. LXVI, 949 sq.).

Rule of Our Most Holy Father Saint Benedict, Birmingham, 1844.

Regula Sancti Columbani (Migne, P. L. LXXX, 209 sq.).

Rule of St. Carthage (Irish Ecclesiastical Record, XXVII [1910] 4th. series).

Regula S. Isadori [Hispaniae] (Migne, P. L. CIII, 557 sq.)

Regularium Concordia (Migne, P. L. CIII, 1057 sq.)

Rule of Saint Chrodegang, London, 1916.

Regula S. Augustini (Migne, P. L. XXXII, 1381 sq.).

Rule of St. Augustine (for women) Roehampton, 1898.

Regula Sancti Francisci (*Bul. Franc.* I, 15).

Regula S. Clarae a beato Francisco traditae (*Bul. Rom.* III, 570 sq.).

Regula S. Clarae a P. Urbano mitigatae (*Bul. Rom.* III, 709 sq.).

Regula et Constitutiones Generales Fratrum Minorum, Ad Claras Aquas, 1922.

Regula et Constitutiones Fratrum Discalceatorum Ordinis B. V. M. de Monte Carmelo, Romae, 1906.

Regula et Constitutiones Fratrum Beatissime Virginis Mariae de Monte Carmelo, Romae, 1904.

Institutum Societatis Jesu, Volumen secundum. *Examen et Constitutiones Decreta Congregationum Generalium Formulae Congregationum,* Florentinae, 1893.

Rules of the Society of Jesus, Washington, 1839.

Le Vraye Regle de S. Benoist, Paris, 1628.

Rules of the Brothers of the Christian Schools, New York, 1865.
Rules and Constitutions for the Congregation of Discalced Clerks of the Most Holy Cross and Passion of our Lord Jesus Christ, Baltimore, 1870.
Rule of St. Francis with the Constitutions of the Institute of the Sisters of the Third Order of St. Francis (Philadelphia Foundation), Glen Riddle, Philadelphia, 1925.
Rules and Constitutions of the Friends of Mary at the Foot of the Cross, Cincinnati, 1896.
Rules and Constitutions of the Sisters of Mercy, Baltimore, 1892.
Rules and Constitutions of the Religious Sisters of Mercy of the Archdiocese of Baltimore, Baltimore, 1925.
Rules and Constitutions of the Sisters of the Presentation, Dublin, 1881.
Regula T. Ordinis S. Francisci (AAS, XIX (1927) 363 sq.).

II. Authors.

ASs.-Acta Sanctorum . . . collegit, digestit, illustravit Iohannes Bollandus S. J. Godefiriedus Henschius . . . 54 vol. Antwerp, 1643-1853.
Abbeloos, J. B., *De Consuetudine in Jure Canonico*, Louvain, 1888.
Adeney, Walter F., *The Greek and Eastern Churches*, New York, 1908.
Aertnys, Jos., C. SS. R., *Theologia Moralis*, 2 vol. 7 ed. Paderbornae, 1906.
Aertnys, Jos., C. SS. R., *Theologia Moralis*, (Ed. undecima-C. A. Damien C. SS. R.), 2 vol. Augustae Taurinorum, 1928.
Alenconiensis Eduardus, O. M., Cap., "Thomas de Celano", *St. Francisci Assisiensi vita et miracula*, Romae, 1906.
Allard, Paul, *Saint Basile*, Paris, 1820.
Allies, Thomas W., *The Monastic Life*, London, 1896.
Alphonsus, St., *Theologia Moralis* (ed. Leonardus Gaude) 3 vol. Romae, 1905.
Alston, G. Cyprian, *Rule of St. Benedict* (Cath. Ency.).
Altauer, Berthold, *Die Bexienhungen des hl. Dominikus zum hl. Franziskus* in Franziskanische Studien, IX (1922) 1-28.
Altauer, Berthold, *Die Armutsidee des hl. Dominikus*, in Theologie und Glaube, XI (1919) 405-417.
Alzog, John, *History of the Church*, translated by Rev. F. J. Pabisch and Rt. Rev. Thomas S. Byrne, 3 vol., New York, 1874.
Amelineau, E., *La Geographie de L'Egypte A L'Epogue Copte*, Paris, 1893.
Amelineau, E., *Memoires publics par Les Members de la Mission Archiologique Francais au Caire*, Tome Quartrieme (*Monuments pour servir a Histoire de L'Egypte Chretiene aux IVe et Ve siecles*), Paris, 1888.
Amelineau, E., *Oeuvres de Schenoudi, Texte Copte et Traduction Francais*, Paris, Vol. I (1907), Vol. II (1914).
Amelineau, E., *Vie de Schenoudi*, Paris, 1889.
Amos, Sheldon, *The History and Principles of the Civil Law of Rome*, London, 1883.

Angelus, a SS Corde, O. C. D., *Manuale Juris Communis Regularium et Specialis Carmelitarum Discalceatorum,* Gandea, Vander Scheldon, 1899.

Antonelli, Ferdinandus, O, F. M., *De Re Monastica in Diologis S. Gregorii Magni* (Antonianum, II [1927] 401 sq.).

Antonelli, Ioannes C., *Tractatus novissimus et absolutissimus de tempore legale,* Venetiis, 1692.

Antonius a SS. Spiritu Sancto, O.D.C., *Directorium Regularium,* Lugduni, 1670.

Appeltern, Victorinus, *Compendium Praelectionum Juris Regularis,* (ed. alt. adm. R. P. Piati Montani) Parisiis, 1913.

Arndt, Augustin S. J., *Die Kirchlichen und Weltichen Rechtsbestimmungen für Orden und Kongregationen,* Paderborn, 1919.

Arregui, Antonio S. J., *Summarium Theologiae Moralis,* ed 7. Bilbao, 1922.

Aryinhac, H., *Penal Legislation in the New Code of Canon Law,* New York, 1920.

Aryinhac, H., *General Legislation in the New Code of Canon Law,* New York, 1923.

Augustine, St., *Confessionum* (Migne, P. L. III, 354 sq.).

Augustine, St., *Epistola CCXI* (Migne P. L. XXXIII, 960 sq.).

Augustine, St., *Sermo CCCLV* et *Sermo CCCLVI* (Migne, P. L. XXIX, 1570, 1575.).

Augustine, St., *De Moribus Ecclesiae Catholicae et de Moribus Manachorum* (Migne P. L. XXXII, 1339).

Augustine, St., *De Civitate Dei* (Corpus Scriptorum Ecclesiasticorum Latinorum, Vol. XL, Vindebonae).

Augustine, Charles, *A Commentary on the New Code of Canon Law,* 8 vol. St. Louis, 1918-1922.

Augustine, Charles, *Rights and Duties of Ordinaries,* St. Louis, 1924.

Augustine, Charles, *Canonical and Civil Status of Catholic Parishes,* St. Louis, 1926.

Baart, Peter, *Legal Formulary,* New York, 1898.

Baart, Peter, *The Tenure of Catholic Church Property in the United States of Amerika,* Marshall, Mich., 1900.

Bacchus, F. J., *Eastern Monasticism before Chalcedon* (Cath. Ency.).

Bachofen, A., *Compendium Juris Regularium,* New York, 1903.

Badii, Caesare, *Ius Canonicum Comparatum cum edictis legum Civilium de re ecclesiastica,* Romae, 1925.

Bakalarczyk, R.,*De Novitiatu,* Washingtonii, 1927.

Ballay, Ferdinandus, *Quaestiones quaedam de votis simplicibus,* (AkkR, XVII [1867] 3-43).

Ballerini, A., *Opus Theologicum Morale in Busembaum Medullam,* absolvit, edidit, Dominicus Palmeiri, 7 vol. Prati, 1898-1901.

Balleriniorum, *Disquisitiones de antiquis Collectionibus et Collectoribus canonum,* (Migne, P. L. LXIV, 752).

Balmes, Milaire, O. M. I., *Les Religieux a Voeux Simples,* Bruxelles, 1923.

Balthasar, C., *Geschiche des Armutsstreites im Franziskanerorden bis zum Konzil von Vienne,* Münster, 1911.

Barbossa, Augustino, *Iuris Ecclesiastici Universi, Libri Tres,* Lugduni, 1634.

Barbossa, Augustino, *De Officio et Potestate Episcopi*, Lyons, 1656.
Barbossa, Augustino, *Collectanea Doctorum in Concilium Tridentinum*, Lugduni, 1660.
Bardenhewer, O., *Patrology* translated from the second edition by Thomas J. Shahan, St. Louis, 1908.
Bargilliat, M., *Praelectiones Juris Canonici*, 2 vol. Parisiis, 1907.
Barker, Ernest, *The Dominican Order and Convocation*, Oxford, 1903.
Bartholi, J. B., *Institutiones Juris Canonici*, Ausugii, 1749.
Bartlett, J. C., *The Tenure of Parochial Property*, Washington, 1926.
Bartsherer, Giles, *Tyrocinium Religiosum*, Revised and translated by Vincent Huber, O. S. B., Beatty, 1903.
Bastien, P. O. S. B., *Directoire Canonique a l'usage des Congregations a Voeux simples*, 3 ed. Maresdous, 1923.
Batiffol, Pierre, *History of the Roman Breviary*, translated by Atwell Ballay, New York, 1903.
Baumer, Dom., *Geschichte des Breviers*, Friedburg, 1895.
Baviera, J., *Fontes Juris Romani Antejestiniani*, Florentiae, 1908.
Beijersbergen, H. S. J., *De nieuwe Codex en de Religieuzen* (Nederlandshe Katholieke Stemmen, XXI [1921] 172-184; 33-347).
Bellarminus, Robertus, *Opera Omnia*, De Monachis, 7 vol. Parisiis, 1897.
Belogey, J. J. Martinus, *De Consuetudine*, Locogiaci, 1893.
Benedict XIV, *De Synodo Dioecesana*, Roma, 1806.
Benedict XIV, *Institutiones Ecclesiasticae*, Prati, 1844.
Benedict XIV, *Quaestiones Canonicas et Morales in materiis ad Sacram Concilii Congregationem spectantibus a Benedicto XIV expositas et discussas, dum munus secretari eiusdem Congregationis obiret.* Prati, 1845.
Benedict XIV, *De Servorum Dei Beatificatione et Beatorum Canonizatione*, Prati, 1843.
Berliere, U., *Revue Benedictine*, Maresdous.
Bernardini, Philip, *Peter's Pence, Catholic University and Foreign Mission Collections* (American Ecclesiastical Review, LXXIX [1928] 15-23).
Besse, J. M., *Les Moines d'Orient Anterieurs au Concile de Chalcedoine*, Paris, 1900.
Besson, J., *Nouvelle Revue Theologique*, XLV (1918) 709.
Bibliotheca Maxima Veterum Patrum . . . a Margarino de la Bigne edita, ed. Lugdunensi, 1677.
Biederlack-Führich, *Praelectiones de Jure Regularium*, Oenopitente, 1919.
Bihl, Michael, O. F. M., *Order Friars Minor*, (Cath, Ency.).
Bihl, Michael, O. F. M., *Fraticelli* (Cath. Ency.).
Biner, Joseph P., *Apparatus Eruditionis ad Jurisprudentiam praesertim Ecclesiasticam*, Friburgi, 1754.
Bingham, Joseph, *The Antiquities of the Christian Church*, 2 vol. London, 1856.
Bizzarri, Andreas, *Collectanea in usum Secretariae Sacrae Congregationis Episcoporum et Regularium*, edita Romae, 1885.
Blair, D. Oswald Hunter, *The Rule of St. Benedict*, Friedburg, Baden, 1907.

Blat, Albertus, *Commentarium Textus Codicis Juris Canonici,* 6 vol., Romae, 1921-1927.
Boak, Arthur E. R., *A History of Rome to 565,* New York, 1923.
Bonal, A., SS., *Institutiones Canonicae,* 2 vol., Lugduni, 1898.
Bonaventura, S., *Opera Omnia,* 10 vol., Quaracchi, 1882-1902.
Bordonus, Fr., *Tractatus de Professione Regulari,* Mediolani, 1635.
Boudinhon, A., *Les Congregations Religieuses a Voeux Simples* (Le Canoniste Contemporain, XXV [1902] Paris).
Bouix, D., *Tractatus de Jure Regularium,* 2 ed. 2 vol., Bruxellis, 1867.
Bouix, D., *Tractatus de Judiciis Ecclesiasticis,* 2 vol., Paris, 1885.
Bouvier, John, *Bouvier's Law Dictionary,* 3 vol., Kansas City, 1914.
Bouuaert-Simenon, *Manuale Juris Canonici,* Gandae, 1924.
Brandys, M., O.F.M., *Kirchliches Rechtsbuch,* Paderborn, 1920.
Brown, Brendan Francis, *The Canonical Juristic Personality with special reference to its status in the United States of America,* Washington, 1927.
Bruck, H., *Lehrbuch der Kirchengeshicte,* Maintz, 1902.
Bucceroni, Januario S. J., *Institutiones Theologiae Moralis,* ed. 4, 2 vol., Romae, 1900.
Buckland, W. W., *A Text Book of Roman Law,* Cambridge, 1921.
Bund, Willis J. W., *The Celtic Church of Wales,* London, 1892.
Burchardus, *Decretum* (Migne, P. L. CXL.).
Busembaum, H., *Medulla Theologiae Moralis,* Petavii, 1746.
Butler, A. J., *Ancient Coptic Churches of Egypt,* Oxford, 1884.
Butler, E. C., *Benedictine Monachism,* London, 1919.
Butler, E. C., *Monasticism* (Encyclopedia Britanica).
Butler, E. C., *Monasticism* (Cambridge Medieval History).
Butler. E. C., *The Lausiac History of Palladius,* 2 vol., Cambridge, 1898.
Cadoux, Cecil J., *The Early Church and the World,* Edinburgh, 1925.
Callaey, F. O. M. C., *The Third Order of St. Francis,* translated by John M. Lenhart, O .M., Cap., Pittsburgh, 1926.
Cambridge Medieval History, New York, 1912.
Campbell, Thomas, J. S. J., *The Jesuits, 1534-1921,* New York, 1921.
Cange, Adrien, *Le Code de Droit Canonique,* 2 vol., Paris, 1928.
Canonical Legislation concerning Religious, Authorized English Translation, Rome, 1919.
Cappello, Felix M., *De Visitatione SS Liminum et Dioeceseon,* 2 vol., Romae, 1913.
Carlyle, A., *Community of Goods,* (Dictionary of the Apostolic Church).
Carriere, Jos., *De Justitia et de Jure,* Parisiis, 1839.
Catechism of the Religious Profession, Translated from the French and revised in conformity with the New Code of Canon Law, Metuchen, 1919.
Catholic Encyclopedia, 16 vol., New York, 1907-1914.
Ceravegna, S. J., *De Societatis Jesu Paupertate,* Prati, 1892.
Chelodi, J., *Jus de Personis,* editio altera a Sac. Ernesto Bertagnolli, Tridenti, 1927.
Chelodi, J., *Jus Poenale,* Tridenti, 1925.
Choupin, Lucien, *Nature et Obligations de l'Etat Religieux,* Paris, 1923.

Cicognani, H., *Ius Canonicum,* Romae, 1925.
Cicognani, H., *Commentarium ad Primum Librum Codicis,* Romae, 1925.
Cimitier, F., *Pour etudier le Code de Droit Canonique,* Paris, 1927.
Clark, W. K. Lowther, *The Lausiac History of Palladius,* London, 1918.
Clark, W. K. Lowther, *St Basil the Great,* A Study in Monasticism, Cambridge, 1913.
Clark, W. K., *The Ascetic Works of St. Basil,* London, 1925.
Cocchi, Guidus, *Commentarium in Codicem Juris Canonici,* 9 vol., Turin, 1924-1927.
Cogliolo, Pietro, *Manuale Fonti del Diritto Romano,* 2 ed., Torino, 1911.
Concina, Danielis, O. P., *Disciplina Apostolico-Monastica,* Venetiis, 1769.
Conventual Order of St. Dominic and its Development in England, By a Dominican of Stone. Cincinnati, 1923.
Cotel-Jombart-McCabe, *Catechism of the Vows,* New York, 1924.
Coulton, G. G., *Five Centuries of Religion,* Cambridge, Vol. I, 1923, Vol. II, 1927.
Craisson, L. Abbe, *Des Communautes Religieuses a Voeux simples legislation canonique et civil,* Paris, 1869:
Craisson, D., *Manuale Totius Juris Canonici,* ed. 4, 4 vol. Pictavii, 1875.
Creusen, J. S. J., *Religieux et Religieuses d'apres le Droit Ecclesiastique,* ed. 13, corrige et augmentee, Bruxelles, 1924.
Currier, C. W., *History of Religious Orders,* New York, 1896.
Cuthbert, Fr, O. S. F. C., *St. Francis and Poverty,* New York, 1910.
Cuthbert, Fr., O. S. F. C., *Life of St. Francis of Assisi,* New York, 1914.
Cyclopedia of Law and Procedure, 40 vol., New York, 1912.
D'Angelo, Sosius, *De Aequitate in Codice Juris Canonici* (Appolin aris I [1928] 363 sq. Periodica XVI [1927] 210 *).
D'Angelo, Sosius, *Ius Digestorum,* Taurini,, 1928.
D'Annibale, J., *Summula Theologiae Moralis,* Mediolani, 1881.
Da Tortona, Andrea D., *Catechismo della Prima Regola di Santa Chiara,* Ferrara, 1882.
David, G. S. M., *The Religious State,* Revised and Enlarged by A. verny, S. M., Lyon, 1927.
Davison, E. S., *Some Forerunners of St. Francis Assisi,* New York, 1907.
De Angelis, P. C., *Praelectiones Iuris Canonici,* 3 vol., Romae, 1876.
De Borbone, Stephanus, O. P., *Annecdotes historiques legends et apoloques tires de recueil inedit d'Etienne de Bourbon, Dominicain de XIIIe siecle,* Paris, 1877.
De Brabandere, J. C. L., *Compendium Juris Canonici et Juris Canonico-Civilis,* 2 vol., Bruges, 1866.
De Buck-V. Tinnebrorck, *Examen Historicum et Canonicum Libri R. D. Verhoeven,* Bibliopolas, 1847.
Decretum Gratiani Emendatum et Novationibus Illustratum, Romae, 1862.
Deferrari, R. J., *St. Basil,* The Letters, London, 1926.

De Franchis, Laurenti-Pasqualigi Zarhariae, *Controversiae inter Episcopos et Regulares,* Romae, 1656.
De Grafiis, J., *Decisionum Aurearum Casuum Conscientiae,* 2 vol. Venetiis, 1500.
Dehey, E. T. *Religious Orders of Women in the United States,* Chicago, 1913.
De Hemptienne, D. J., *L'Ordre de Saint Benoit,* 2 ed. Lille, 1924.
De Journal Rouet, M. J. S. J.,*Enchiridion Patristicum,* Friburgi in Br. 1922.
Delatte Abbot Paul, *A Commentary on the Rule of St. Benedict,* New York, 1921.
De Labriolle, Pierre, *History and Literature of Christianity from Tertullian to Boethius,* Translated by H. Willson, New York, 1925.
De Luca, Card.,*Annotationes ad SS. Concilii Tridentini,* Matriti, 1783.
De Lugo Ioannes, S. J., *Disputationes Scholasticae et Morales,* ed. 9 Parisiis, 1869.
De Meester, A., *Juris Canonici et Juris Canonico-Civilis Compendium,* 3 vol., Brugis, 1921-1927.
De Meester, Placidus, O. S. B., *De Monachismo apud Graecos et Slavos post saeculum nonum,* (CpR, VIII [1927] 302 sq.).
Denifle, H. O. P., *Die Konstitutionen des Predigerordens vom Jahre* 1228 (Archiv für Litteratur, I [1885]).
Denziger-Bannwart, *Enchiridion Symbolorum,* Friburgi in Br. 1922.
De Oronsoro Pedro, *Manual Serafico o Libro de la Vida de Las Frayles Menores,* Mexico, 1779.
Devine, Pius C. P., *The Life of St. Paul of the Cross,* New York, 1886.
Devoti, Ioannes, *Institutiones Canonicarum,* 3 vol., Leodii, 1860.
Diana Antonius, *Resolutiones Morales,* Venetiis, 1647.
Dictionaire d'Archiologie Chretienne, Paris, 1907.
Dictionary of the Apostolic Church, ed. James Hastings, New York, 1916.
Dillon, William, *Bequests for Masses for the Souls of Deceased Persons,* Chicago, 1896.
Doheny, W. J. C. S. C., *Church Property,* Modes of Acquisition, Washington, 1927.
Döllinger, J. J., *A History of the Church,* Translated by Ed. Cox, London, 1840.
Donaldson, James, *The Apostolic Constitutions,* Edinburgh, 1870.
Donatus, Hy., O. P., *Rerum Regularium Praxis Resolutoria,* 4 vol., Coloniae Agripinae, 1675.
Duchesne, L., *Origenes du Culte Chretien,* Paris, 1908.
Duchesne, L.,*L'Histoire Ancienne de l'Eglise,* 2 vol., Paris, 1907.
Dudden, F. H., *Gregory the Great,* His Place in History and Thought, London, 1905.
Dunford, David, *Roman Documents and Decrees,* London, 1906-1914.
Droste, Francis, *Canonical Procedure in Disciplinary and Criminal Cases of Clerics,* Edited by Sebastian G. Messmer, New York, 1887.
Eckenstein, L., *Woman under Monasticism,* Cambridge, 1896.

Egger, Augustine, O.S.B., *Das Neue Ordensrecht für die religiosen Gewossenschaften mit einfachen Gelubden,* Freidburg, im Br., 1919.
Eichman Eduard, *Lehrbuch des Kirchenrechts,* Paderborn, 1926.
Eichman Eduard, *Das Sträfrecht des Codex, Juris Canonici,* Paderborn, 1920.
Encyclopedia Britanica, ed. 11, New York, 1910.
Encyclopedia of Religion and Ethics, Edited by J. Hastings, New York, 1916.
Encyclopedia of Universal Knowledge, New York, 1928.
Encyclopedia Universale Illustrada, Europeo-Americana, 35 vol., Barcelona.
Espelage, B. Theo., *Aggregation of Tertiary Religious Institutes,* Washington, 1926.
Eusebii, Pamphili, Ecclesiasticae Historiae, Parisiis, 1678.
Ehrle, Franz, S.J., *Die Briefsammlung des F. Angelus de Clareno* (Archiv für Litteratur und Kirchengeschicte, I [1885], 559).
Fagnanus, Prosperus, *Commentarium in Librum Decretalium,* Venetiis, 1695.
Fanfani, Lud., O.P., *De Jure Religiosorum,* ed. 2, Romae, 1925.
Feasey, H. J., *Monasticism,* Edinburgh, 1908.
Felder, H., O.M.Cap., *The Ideals of St. Francis of Assisi,* Translated by Berchmans Bittle, O.M.Cap., New York, 1925.
Ferraris, F. L., *Prompta Bibliotheca Canonica, Juridica, Moralis, Theologica, necnon Ascetica, Polemica, Rubristica, Historica,* 9 vol., Romae, 1885-1892.
Ferreres, Joannes, B.S.J., *Compendium Theologiae Moralis,* 2 vol., Barcinone, 1925.
Ferreres, Joannes, *Institutiones Canonicae,* Barcinone, 1920.
Ferreres, Joanes, *Las Religiosas segun disciplina del nuevo Codigo,* ed. 5, Madrid, 1920.
Ferreres-Mach, *Razon y Fe,* Madrid, 1900.
Ford, Ed. H., *Benedict of Nursia* (Cath. Ency.).
Fortescue, Adrian, *The Greek Fathers,* London, 1908.
Fortescue, Adrian, *The Orthodox Eastern Church,* London, 1907.
Fortescue, Adrian, *Eastern Monasticism* (Cath. Ency.).
Fortescue, Adrian, *The Uniate Churches,* London, 1923.
Freriks, C. A., *Religious Congregations in their External Relations,* Washington, 1916.
Funk, F. X., *Patres Apostolici,* 2 vol., Tubingae, 1901.
Funk, F. X., *Manual of Church History,* London, 1914.
Garcia, N. H., *De Beneficiis Ecclesiasticis,* 2 vol., Venetiis, 1618.
Gardiner, Ed. G., *The Dialogues of St. Gregory the Great,* Boston, 1911.
Gaselle, Stephan, F.R.S.L., *Transaction R. S. L.,* vol. 33, Cambridge.
Gasquet, Abbot, O.S.B., *English Monastic Life,* New York, 1905.
Gautrilet, F. X., *Traite de l'etat Religieux,* 2 vol., Paris, 1846.
Gearin, Michael, C.SS.R., *The Confessor and the Vow of Religious Poverty* (American Ecclesiastical Review, LXI [1919] 136 ff.).
Genicot, Ed., S.J., *Institutiones Theologiae Moralis,* 2 vol., Louvanii, 1902.

Genicot, Ed., S.J., *Institutiones Theologiae Moralis,* ed. 10, 2 vol., I, Salsmans, S.J., recognovit, Bruxelles, 1922.
Gennari, Casmirus Card., *Il Monitore Ecclesiastico,* Roma.
Gibson, Edgar, *A Select Library of Nicene and Post Nicene Fathers of the Christian Church,* 2nd series, New York, 1894.
Giraldus, Ubaldus, *Expositio Juris Pontificii,* 2 vol., Romae, 1829.
Golden, F. H., *Parochial Benefices in the New Code,* Washington, 1921.
Goyeneche, S. C. M. F., *De Transitu ad Aliam Religionem* (Commentarium pro Religiosis, I [1920] and II [1921].
Goyheneche, L'Abbe, *Cours Elementaire de Droit Canonique,* Paris.
Graham, H., *The Early Irish Monastic Schools,* Dublin, 1923.
Graham, R., *Medieval England,* Edited by H. W. C. Davis, Oxford, 1927.
Grandclaude, E., *Jus Canonicum,* 3 vol., Parisiis, 1882.
Grenier, W. E., O.M.Cap., *The Asceticism of St. Francis,* Washington, 1927.
Grisar, Hartman, *History of Rome and the Popes in the Middle Ages,* edited by Luigi Cappadelta, London, 1912.
Grützmacher, Georg, *Die Bedentung Benedhtsvon Nursia und Ziener Regle in der Geschichte des Mönchtums,* Berlin, 1892.
Grützmacher, Georg, *Pachomius und das alteste Klosterleben ein Beirag zur monchengeschichte,* Freiburg im Br. 1896.
Guggenberger, A., *A General History of the Christian Era,* 3 vol., St. Louis, 1900.
Gury-Ballerini, *Theologiae Moralis,* ed. 15, Romae, 1907.
Gwatkin, H. M., *Early Church History to A. D.* 313, 2 vol., London, 1909.
Haddan, A. W., and W. Stubbs, *Councils and Ecclesiastical Documents relating to Great Britain and Ireland,* 3 vol., London, 1869-1871.
Hall, Fred. M., *Legal Forms,* Chicago, 1925.
Hannah, Ian, *Christian Monasticism,* London, 1924.
Harduin, Jean, S.J., *Acta Conciliorum et Epistulae, Decretales ac Constitutiones Summorum Pontificium,* 12 vol., Parisiis, 1714-1725.
Harnack, Adolph, *Dögmengeschichte,* III, Freiburg, im Br. 1897.
Harris, Dr., *The Four Books of Justinian's Institutes,* London, 1814.
Hastings, James, *Encyclopedia of Religion and Ethics,* 12 vol., New York, 1918-1922.
Hauck, Albert, *Kirchengeschichte Deutchlands,* Leipzig, 1913.
Hefele, J. C., *History of the Christian Councils from the Original Documents,* 7 vol., Edinburgh, 1895-1896.
Heimbucher, Max., *Die Orden und Kongregationen der Katholichen Kirche,* 2 ed., 2 vol., Paderborn, 1907.
Heinrich, Sr., *The Canonesses and Education in the Early Middle Ages,* Washington, 1924.
Helyot, Pierre, *Histoire des Ordres Monastiques Religieux et Militaires et des Congregations Seculieres de l'un et de l'autre sexe qui ont ete establies jusqu' a present* a Paris 1714-1719.
Herwegen, I.O.S.B., *Der Heilige Benedikt Ein Charakterbild,* Dussendorf, 1917-1919.
Hilarius, Parisiensis, O.M.Cap., *Liber Tertii Ordinis S. Francisci Assisiensis,* Paris, 1888.

Hill, Travers O'Dell, *English Monasticism,* London, 1867.
Hilling, Nicholaus, *Interpretatio Codicis Juris Canonici,* Friburgi in Br. 1925.
Hoffmann, Eberhard, *Das Konverseninstitut des Zisterzienserordens,* Friburgi in Schweitz, 1905.
Holzapfel, Heribert, *Manuale Historiae Ordinis Fratrum Minorum,* Freiburg, 1909.
Huddleston, G. Roger, *Monasticism* (Cath. Ency.).
Hughes, L., *The Christian Church in the Epistles of St. Jerome,* London, 1923.
Hughes, P., *The Canons Regular of Premontre* (Irish Ecclesiastical Record, XIX [1922], 131).
Humphrey, W., S.J., *Elements of the Religious Life,* London, 1895.
Iglesias, A., O.F.M., *Liber Vitae seu Regulae S. Francisci Exposito* auctore P. Kiliano Kazenberger, O.F.M., Ad Claras Aquas, 1926.
Ilg, John, O.F.M., *An Explanation of the Rule of the Friars Minor in accordance with the Declarations of the Supreme Pontiffs and the Expositions of the Approved Authors,* Illinois, 1927.
Instructions on the Vows for the Use of the Brothers of the Christian Schools (from the French of the First Edition), Tours, 1892.
Iwiens, H. M., *Les Freres Precheurs,* Paris, 1905.
Jacobili, L., *Vita della B. Angelina,* Bologna, 1659.
Jaffe, Phil., *Regesta Pontificum Romanorum,* 2 ed., Lipsiae, 1881.
Jansen, P. Jos., O.M.I., *Ordensrecht,* ed. 2, Paderborn, 1920.
Jardi, A., O.F.M., *El Derecho de las Religiosas,* ed. 2, Vich, 1927.
Jarre, Cyrillus, O.F.M., *De iis qui Vicariatum vel Praefecturam Apostolicam Sede Vacante vel Impeditae regunt* (Antonianum, III [1928]).
Jenks, Ed., *Law and Politics in the Middle Ages,* London, 1919.
Jewish Encyclopedia, New York, 1906.
Jombart, E. J., *Les Moniqles a Voeux Simples* (Nouvelle Revue Theologique, LI [1924], 276-277).
Jungmann, Bernardus, *Dissertationes Selectae in Historiam Ecclesiasticam,* 7 vol., Ratisbonae, 1880-1888.
Kaufmann, Kohler, *Essenes* (Jewish Ency.).
Kazenberger, Killian, O.F.M., *The Book of Life,* Patterson, 1905.
Keller, Ch., *Mass Stipends,* Washington, 1925.
Kinane, J., *Nuns and Sisters* (Irish Ecclesiastical Record, XII [1918]).
Kirch, C., S.J., *Enchiridion Fontium Historiae Ecclesiasticae Antiquae,* ed. 4, Friburg in Br. 1923.
Kirchenlexicon, Welter und Welt's, 2 ed., 12 vol., Freiburg im Br. 1882-1901.
Klekotka, Peter J., *Diocesan Consultors,* Washington, 1920.
Knabenbauer, J., *Cursus Scripturae Sacrae,* Nov. Test. Pars I, Evangel. secundum S. Matthaeum, Pars II, Parisiis, 1893.
Koch, Hugo, *Virgines Christi* (Text und untersuchungen zür geschicte der Altchristlichen Liereatur, vol. XXXI), Leipzig, 1907.
Koeniger, H. M., *Grundriz einer Geschichte des katholichen Kirchenrechts,* Koln, 1919.
Konings, A., C.SS.R., *Theologia Moralis,* ed. 7, 2 vol., New York.

Kraus, F. H., *Real Encyklopadie der christlichen Alterthumer,* 2 vol., Freiburg im Br. 1882-1886.

Krynicki, Wladyslaw, *Ks Dzieje Kosciola Powsechnego,* Wlaclawek, 1908.

La Croix, Claudius, *Theologia Moralis,* Colonae, 1739.

Ladeuze, Paulinus, *De Instituto Coenibitico Sancti Pachomii,* Louvain, 1898.

Lambermond, H. C., O.P., *Der Armutsgedanke des hl. Dominikus und seines Ordens,* Zwolle, Holland, 1926.

Landry, Ch., *La Mort Civile des Religieux,* Paris, 1900.

Lanslots, D. I., O.S.B., *Handbook of Canon Law for Congregations of Women under Simple Vows,* ed. 4, New York, 1910.

Lanslots, D. I., *Handbook of Canon Law for Congregations of Women under Simple Vows,* New York, 1919.

La Regula dei Fratri Minori, Breve Commento ad uso speciali dei novizi e dei nuovi professi, ed. 4, Quaracchi, 1915.

Larraona, A., C.M.F., *De Paupertate Simplici* (Commentarium pro Religiosis, I [1920] and II [1921]).

Laymann, Paulus, *Theologia Moralis,* ed. 9, Moguntiae, 1723.

Leage, R. W., *Roman Private Law,* London, 1924.

Leclerq, H. L., *L'Afrique Chretienne,* 2 vol., Paris, 1904.

Lega, M., *De Delictis et Poenis,* Romae, 1910.

Lega, M., *De Judiciis,* Romae, 1902.

Lehmkuhl, A., *Theologia Moralis,* 2 vol., Friburgi in Br. 1910.

Leipoldt, Johannes, *Schenute von Atripe und die Entstehung des National Aegyptischen Christentums,* Leipzig, 1903.

Lemmens, Leon, O.F.M., *Opuscula S. Patris Francisci Assisiensis,* Ad Claras Aquas, 1904.

Lessius, S.J., *De Justitia et Jure,* Louvanii, 1606.

Leurenius, Petrus, S.J., *Forum Ecclesiasticum,* Venetiis, 1729.

Lightfoot, J. B., *The Apostolic Fathers,* Part I, St. Clement of Rome, London, 1890.

Lijdsmann, B. C., *Der Neue Codex und das Testament der Ordensleute* (Theologisch-praktische Quartalschrift, LXXIII [1920], 336-347).

Lillie, A., *The Influence of Buddhism on Primative Christianity,* London, 1893.

Lincoln, Ch. Z., *The Civil Law and the Church,* New York, 1916.

Linderbauer, Benno, O.S.B., *S. Benedicti Regula Monachorum Herausgegeben und Philologisch Erklart,* Metten, 1922.

Lingard, John, *The History and Antiquities of the Anglo-Saxon Church,* 2 ed., 2 vol., London, 1899.

Logeman, H., *The Rule of St. Benedict,* London, 1888.

Lombardi, Carolus, *Institutiones Juris Canonici Privati,* Romae, 1901.

Lopez, Felipe de Jesus, O.F.M., *De Novitiatu,* Washingtonii, 1918.

Lucidi, Angelus, *De Visitatione Sacorum Liminum Instructio S. C. Concilii,* ed. 3, 3 vol., Romae, 1883.

MacCaffrey, James, *History of the Catholic Church from the Renaissance to the French Revolution,* 2 vol., 1917.

McCaffrey, R. O. C., *The White Fathers,* Dublin, 1926.

Machean, W. H., *Christian Monasticism in Egypt to the Close of the fourth century,* London, 1920.

McNeil, Th., *Religious of Diocesan Right,* Washington, 1924.
Mackeldy, F., *Handbook of the Roman Law,* Translated and edited by Moses A. Dropsie from the 14th German Edition, Philadelphia, 1883.
Mackensie, Lord, *Studies in Roman Law,* Edinburgh, 1862.
McCormick, R. E., *Confessors of Religious,* Washington, 1926.
Malan, S. C., *The Calendar of the Koptic Church,* London, 1873.
Makee, Ch., *Institutiones Juris Ecclesiastici tum Publici tum Privati,* Romae, 1897.
Mandic, Dominicus, O.F.M., *De Protoregula Ordinis Fratrum Minorum,* Mostar, 1923.
Mandonnet, Pierre, F.F., O.P., *Order of Preachers* (Cath. Ency.).
Mann, Horace K., *Lives of the Popes in the Early Middle Ages,* London, 1922.
Mannock, P., *The Origin and Progress of Religious Orders,* London.
Maranus, P., *Sancti Patris Basilii Caesareae Cappadociae Archiepiscopi, Opera Omnia quae extant,* 3 vol., Parisiis, 1839.
Marc-Gesterman, *Institutiones Morales,* Romae, 1920.
Marin, Abbe, *Les Moines de Constantinople,* Paris, 1897.
Marmion, C., O.S.B., *Christ the Ideal of the Monk,* St. Louis, 1926.
Maroto, P., *Institutiones Juris Canonici,* 3 ed., 2 vol., Romae, 1921.
Marsot, Abbe, *Petit Traite Practique des Voeux et de l'etat Religieux,* ed. 15, Paris, 1923.
Martigney, M. L., *Dictionaire des Antiquities Chretiennes,* Paris, 1877.
Marx, J., *Lehrbuch der Kirchengeschichte,* ed. 4, Trier, 1908.
Massebieau, L., *Le Traite de la Vie Contemplative* (Revue de L'Histoire des Religions XVI).
Matulewicz, Georgius, *Constitutiones Congregationis Clericorum Regularium Marianorum,* Romae, 1927.
Malot, S.J., *De Ordinibus et Congregationibus Religiosis,* Louvanii, 1888-9.
Meynial, Ed., *The Legacy of the Middle Ages,* edited by G. C. Krump and E. F. Jacob, Oxford, 1927.
Michael, Emil, *Geschichte des Deutschen Volkes Seit dem Dreizenhnten Jährundert bis zum Ausgang des Mittelalters,* Freiburg im Br. 1897.
Michaelicka, W. C., O.S.B., *Judicial Procedure in the Dismissal of Clerical Exempt Religious,* Washington, 1923.
Migne, *Patrologia Latina.*
Migne, *Patrologia Graeca.*
Miller, Newton T., *Founded Masses* according to the New Code of Canon Law, Washington, 1926.
Mochegiani, Peter, O.F.M., *Jurisprudentia Ecclesiastica,* Ad Claras Aquas, 1904.
Moeller, Ch., *The Military Orders* (Cath. Ency.).
Moffatt, James, *Essenes* (Ency. of Rel. and Ethics).
Molina, Jud., S.J., *De Justitia et Jure,* Moguntiae, 1658.
Montalambert, Count de, *The Monks of the West,* 5 vol., Boston, 1872.
Monthon, Jos. P., *Traite sur L'Etat Religieux,* Paris, 1922.
Montalvo, Th., *Glossa Fundamentalis Statutorum Cismontanae Familiae Ordinis Minorum,* 2 vol., Matriti, 1740.
Monumenta Ordinis Fratrum Praedicatorum Historica, Romae, 1906.

Moricca, U., *Gregorii Magni Dialogi Libri IV*, Roma, 1924.
Morin, Germain, O.S.B., *The Ideal of the Monastic Life,* Chicago, 1914.
Morison, B. D., *St. Basil and His Rule,* A Study in Early Monasticism, London, 1912.
Mortier, O.P., *Histoire des Maitres Generaux de l'Ordre .des Freres Precheurs,* 5 vol., 1903-1911.
Muirhead, J., *Historical Introduction to the Private Law of Rome,* Revised and edited by Henry Goudy, 2 ed., London, 1899.
Müller, Karl, *Die Waldenser und ihre einzelne Grippen,* Gotha, 1886.
Müller, Michael, *The Religious State,* Baltimore, 1872.
Murphy, F. X., *Clerks Regular* (Cath. Ency.).
Napier, S., *The Old English Version of the Enlarged Rule of Chrodegang together with the Latin Original,* London, 1906.
Natalis, Alex., *Historia Ecclesiastica,* 8 vol., Ferrariae, 1761.
Navarrus (Azpilcuetae Martinus) *Concilia et Responsa,* Lugduni, 1594.
Neale, J. M., *A History of the Eastern Church,* London, 1847.
Nebreda, Eulogio, *De Loci Ordinariorum Iuribus Circa Pia Legata,* Romae, 1920.
Neuberger, J. Nich., *Canon* 6, Washington, 1927.
Noldin, H., S.J., *Summa Theologiae Moralis,* 3 vol. Oenipotente, 1922.
Noval, J., O.P., *De Ratione Corrigendi et Puniendi sive in Judicio sive Extra, Jure Codicis Juris Canonici* (Jus Pontificium, II, III).
O'Connor, John B., *St. Dominic* (Cath. Ency.).
Official Catholic Directory, New York, 1928.
Ojetti, B., *Synopsis Rerum Moralium et Juris Ponticium,* ed. 3, 4 vol., Romae, 1912.
Oliger, *Rule of St. Francis of Assisi* (Cath. Ency.).
Orth, Clement, O.M.C., *A History of the Approbation of Religious Institutes,* Washington, 1925.
Ott, Mich., *Benedict of Nursia* (Ency. of Universal Knowledge).
Ott, Mich., *Schenute* (Cath. Ency.).
Pallottini, S., *Collectio omnium conclusionum et resolutionum quae in causis propositis apud Sacram Congregationem Cardinalium S. Concilii Tridentini interpretum prodierunt ab eius institutione anno* 1564 *ad annum* 1860, 17 vol., 1868-1893.
Papi, Hector, *Religious in Church Law,* New York, 1924.
Papi, Hector, *Religious Profession,* New York, 1918.
Parsons, R., *Studies in Church History,* 6 vol., New York, 1910.
Passerinus, Petrus, *De Hominum Statibus et Officiis Inspectiones Morales ad ultimas septem quaestiones secundae secundae Divi Thomae,* 3 vol., Lucae, 1732.
Peeters, P., *Analecta Bollandiana,* vol. XXV, Bruxelles.
Pellizarius, F. S., *Tractatio de Monialibus,* Romae, 1741.
Pennacchi, Jos., *Commentaria in Constitutionem "Apostolicae Sedis,"* 2 vol., Romae, 1910.
Petra, Vinc. Card., *Commentaria ad Constitutiones Apostolicas,* 5 vol., Venetiis, 1729.
Piatus, Montensis, O.M.Cap., *Praelectiones Juris Regularis,* ed. 2, vol. 2, Tornaci, 1898.

Pichler, Vito, *Jus Canonicum*, 2 vol., Venetiis, 1741.
Pierron, J. B., *Die Katholichen Armen*, Freiburg im Br. 1911.
Pignatellus, Jacobus, *Consultationes Canonicae, 7* vol., Romae, 1668.
Piontek, C., *De Indultu Exclaustrationis necnon Secularizationis*, Washingtonii, 1926.
Pirhing, Enericus, S.J., *Jus Canonicum in V Libros Decretalium*, 4 vol., Venetiis, 1759.
Platus, Hieronymus, S.J., *De Bono Status Religiosi*, 3 vol., Romae, 1590.
Polaccus, Georgius, *Vacationum Epidimialium*, Pars Prima, sive pro paupertate Regulari et pro decreto Sacrae Congregationis contra Regulares alloquentes Moniales collectanea, Venetiis, 1621.
Pollard, W. R., *Rosminians* (Cath. Ency.).
Pollen, J. H., S.J., *The Society of Jesus* (Cath. Ency.).
Pollen, J. H., S.J., *St. Ignatius* (Cath. Ency.).
Poste, Ed., *Gai Institutiones*, Oxford, 1904.
Pourrat, P., *Christian Spirituality from the time of our Lord till the Dawn of the Middle Ages*, 2 vol., London, 1922.
Preus, Arthur, *The Fortnightly Review*, St. Louis, 1894.
Preuschen, Erwin, *Mönchtum und Sarapiskult* (Jahresbeiricht, Darmstadt), Abhandlung 30s Darmstadt Winter, 1899.
Prichard-Nasmith, *The History of Roman Law* from the text of Ortolan's *Histoire de la Legislation Romaine et Generalisation du Droit*, ed. 1870, London, 1871.
Prima Regola della Madre S. Chiara trodotta in Italiano con annotazione, Quaracchi, 1918.
Prümmer, Dominicus, O.P., *Jus Regularium Speciale*, Friburgi in Br. 1907.
Prümmer, Dominicus, O.P., *Manuale Juris Canonici*, ed. 3, Friburgi in Br. 1922.
Prümmer, Dominicus, O.P., *Manuale Theologiae Moralis*, 3 vol., Friburgi in Br. 1923.
Radin, Max, *Handbook of Roman Law*, St. Paul, Minn., 1927.
Raus, J. B., *De Sacrae Obedientiae Virtute et Voto*, Lugduni, 1923.
Raus, J. B., *Institutiones Canonici*, Lugduni, 1923.
Raus, J. B., *Der heilige Alfons von Liguori, die Manuscriptenfrage und die neuesten römischen Entscheidungen* (Theologisch-praktische Quartalschrift LXXI [1921], 356 sq.).
Rauschen, *Jährbücher der christlichen Kirche unter dem Kaiser Theoldosius den Grossen*, 1897.
Ravelet, Armand, *Blessed John Baptist de la Salle*, Paris, 1888.
Reiffenstuel, F. Anacletus, *Jus Canonicum Universum*, 5 vol. Antverpiae, 1743.
Reinmann, Gerald J., *The Third Order Secular of St. Francis*, Washington, 1928.
Repertorum Juridicum Ecclesiasticum (1918-1924), Romae, 1925.
Retzbach, J., *Die Verbindlichkeit formloser letzwiller Verfügungen zu frommen Zwecken noch dem alten und neuen Kirchenrecht*, Freiburg im Br. 1917.
Revellout, E., *Revue d'Histoire des Religions*, Vol. VIII, Paris.

Robinson, Pascal, *The Rule of St. Clare and its Observances in the light of early documents,* Philadelphia, 1912.

Robinson, Pascal, *The Writings of St. Francis,* Philadelphia, 1906.

Rodericus, F. E., *Quaestiones Regulares et Canonicas,* 3 vol. Salamanticae, 1689.

Rosedale, H. G., *St. Francis of Assisi according to Brother Thomas of Celano,* London, 1904.

Rotarius, Thomas F., *Theologia Moralis Regularium,* 3 vol. Venetiis, 1735.

Rudge, F. M., *Humiliati* (Cath. Ency.).

Sabatier, Paul, *Speculum Perfectionis seu S. Francisci Assissiensis Legenda Antiquissima,* Paris, 1898.

Sabatier-Houghton, *Life of St. Francis of Assisi,* New York, 1909.

Sabetti-Barrett, *Compendium Theologiae Moralis,* New York, 1929.

Saier, Salesius M., O.S.M., *Statistiches von den katholischen Orden und Kongregationen* (Theologisch-praktische-Quartalscrift, LXV [1912], 356 sq.).

Saint-Jure, R. J., S.J., *The Religious,* 2 vol., New York, 1882.

Salmanticenses, *Collegii Salmanticensis Cursus Theologiae Moralis,* 6 vol., Venetiis, 1764.

Salucci, Raffaele, *Il Diritto Penale,* Subiaco, 1926.

Sanchez, Cordubensis, *Opus Morale in Praecepta Decalogi,* Antverpiae, 1631-1637.

Santi, F., *Praelectiones Juris Canonici,* ed. 3, 5 vol., Ratisbonae, 1898.

Schaaf, Philip, *History of the Christian Church,* 7 vol., New York, 1907.

Schaaf, Valentine, O.F.M., *The Cloister,* Washington, 1921.

Schäfer, T., O.M.Cap., *Compendium de Religiosis,* Munster, 1927.

Schiweitz, Stephan, *Das Morgenlandesche Mönchtum,* Maintz, 1904.

Schmalzgrueber, F., S.J., *Jus Ecclesiasticum Universum,* 12 vol., Romae, 1843-1845.

Schrörs, H., *Das Charaketerbild des heiligen Benedikt von Nursia und seine Quellen* (Zeitschrift für katholische Theologie, XLIV [1921], 169-207).

Schwetz, J. J., S.M., *The Origin of the Teaching Brotherhoods,* Washington, 1918.

Scriptores Ordinis Praedicatorum, I, II, Quetif-Echard, Lut. Paris, 1719.

Sebastianelli, G., *Praelectiones Juris Canonici,* 3 vol., 1905-1906.

Seraphicae Legislationis Textus Originales, Ad Clares Aquas, 1897.

Severus, Sulpitius, *Vita Sancti Martini* (Corpus Scriptorum Ecclesiasticorum Latinorum).

Sherman, C.P., *Roman Law in the Modern World,* New Haven, 1922.

Sisters of Charity of St. Vincent de Paul, Translated from the French by a Priest of the Mission, Emmitsburg, 1927.

Slater, Thomas, *A Manual of Moral Theology,* 2 vol., New York, 1908.

Sleutjes, M. O., F.M., *Commentarius in Constitutiones Generales Fratrum Minorum,* Ad Claras Aquas, 1915.

Smith, I, Greg., *Christian Monasticism from the fourth to the ninth century of the Christian Era,* London, 1892.

Smith, Richard T., *The Church in Roman Gaul,* New York.

Smith, S. B., *Elements of Ecclesiastical Law,* 3 vol., New York, 1889.

Smith, S. B., *The New Procedure in Criminal and Disciplinary Causes of Ecclesiastics in the United States,* New York, 1888.

Snow, Abbot, O.S.B., *St. Gregory the Great, His Character and Work,* Revised by Dom. Roger Huddleston, London, 1904.

Sole, Iacobus, *De Delictis et Poenis,* Romae, 1920.

Sozomen, *The Ecclesiastical History,* Walford Edition, London, 1885.

Sporer, Patritius, *Tomi Tres Theologiae Moralis Super Decalogum,* Salisburgi, 1711.

Spreitzenhoefer, Ernest, *Die Entwicklung des alten Mönchthums in Italien von seiner ersten Anfängen bis zum Auftreten des H. Benedikt,* Wien, 1894.

Spuche, Galiano, *De Origine et Institutione Veri Monachatus,* Matriti, 1696.

Stadtmüller, Raphael, O.P., *Das neue Ordensrecht,* Dülmen, 1919.

St. Hilpich, O.S.B., *Die Quellem zum Charakterbild des heiligen Benedikt* (Zeitschrift fur katholischen Theologie, XLIX [1925], 358-386).

Steiger, A. P., S.J., *De Propagatione et Diffusione Vitae Religiosae,* (Periodica, XIII [1925], Brugis).

Steck, F. B., O.F.M., *The Glories of the Franciscan Order,* Illinois, 1919.

Stutz, Urich, *Der Geist des Codex Iuris Canonici,* Stuttgart, 1918.

Suarez, Franciscus, S.J., *Opera Omnia,* Parisiis, 1859.

Tamburinus Asc., *De Jure Abbatum et Aliorum Praelatorum Episcopis Inferiorum,* Lugduni, 1640.

Tanquerey, Ad. SS, *Synopsis Theologiae Moralis et Pastoralis,* 3 vol., Tournai, 1904.

Taunton, Ethelred, *The Black Monks of St. Benedict,* 2 vol., London, 1897.

Taylor, Osborn H., *The Medieval Mind,* 2 vol., London, 1912.

Telch, Carolus, *Epitome Theologiae Moralis,* Oenipotente, 1914.

Theodorus a Bied-Brig, *Manuale Practicum Juris Disciplinaris et Criminalis Regularium,* Romae, 1902.

Thomas, de Celano, *Tractatus Primus super Vitam Sancti Francisci de Assisi, scriptus* circa 1229, apud Rosedale H. G., London, 1904.

Thomas, St., *Summa Theologica,* Romae, 1886.

Thomas, St., *Summa Contra Gentiles,* Romae, 1882.

Thomassinus, L., *Vetus et Nova Disciplina Ecclesiae circa Beneficia et Beneficiarios,* Venetiis, 1730.

Thompson, A. H., *English Monasteries,* Cambridge, 1913.

Tiffany, Walter C., *Handbook of the Law of Person and Domestic Relations,* St. Paul, 1909.

Tillemont, L., *Memoires pour servir a l'Histoire Ecclesiastique des six premiers siecles,* Venise, 1733.

Toso, Al., *Commentaria Minora ad Codicem Juris Canonici,* Fiferni Triburini, 1921.

Tosti, D. Luigi, *Della Vita di San Benedetto,* Montecassino, 1892.

Trienekens, Isadorus, O.F.M., *Vota et Praecepta Regulae Fratrum Minorum,* Ad Claras Aquas, 1909.

Tschpert, O.M.Cap., *Religious Profession,* Washington, 1918.

Van den Borne, Fidentius, O.M.Cap., *Die Anfänge des Franziskanischen Dritten Ordens* (Franziskanische Studien, Beiheft VIII), Münster, 1925.

Vechiotti, Septimi M., *Institutiones Canonici,* Taurini, 1886.

Verhoeven, Marianus, *De Regularium et Saecularium Clericorum Juribus et Officiis,* Louvanii, 1846.

Vermeersch, A., *Questiones de Justitia,* Brugis, 1901.

Vermeersch, A., *De Religiosis,* 2 vol., Vrugis, 1907.

Vermeersch, A., *Poverty* (Cath. Ency.).

Vermeersch, A., *Religious* (Cath. Ency.).

Vermeersch, A., *Periodica de Religiosis et Missionariis Supplementa et Monumenta,* 18 vol., 1905.

Vermeersch, A., *Theologiae Moralis, Principia-Responsa-Concilia,* 4 vol., Brugis, 1926-1927.

Vermeersch-Creusen, *Epitome Juris Canonici,* Brugis, 1924.

Vicente, Felice, C.M.F., *Recentia Instituti,* Segoviae, 1916.

Vidal, P., *Notio Delici in Jure Codicis* (Jus Pontificium, II [1922], 99 sq.).

Villecourt, Louis, O.S.B., *Le Rite Copte de la Profession Monacle,* Roma, 1910.

Villier, M., S.J., *Exemplar Ideale Monasticum et Sacerdotale in Oriente Usque ad Saeculum Nonum* (Commentarium pro Religiosis, VIII [1927], 196 sq.).

Visosevic, J., O.S.Bas., *De Disciplina Monastica apud Catholicos Ritus Graeco-Slavici* (Commentarium pro Religiosis, VIII [1927], 210 sq.).

Von der Burg, J. J., *Opera Omnia Beati Patris Francisci Assisiatis,* Coloniae, 1849.

Vromant, G., *De Bonis Ecclesiae Temporalibus,* Louvain, 1927.

Wadding, Lucas, O.F.M., *Annales Minorum,* 15 vol., Romae, 1731-1736.

Walter, F., *Lehrbuch des Kirchenrechts aller christlichen Confessionen,* Bonn, 1854.

Warren, F. E., *The Liturgy and Rites of the Celtic Church,* Oxford, 1881.

Wasserschleben, *Die Irische Kanonsammlung,* Giessen, 1874.

Waterworth, J. W., *The Canons and Decrees of the Council of Trent,* London, 1848.

Weber, N. A., *Waldenses* (Cath. Ency.).

Weldon, Bennet, O.S.B., *Chronological Notes containing the Rise, Growth and Present State of the English Congregation of the Order of St. Benedict.* Drawn from the Archives of the said Congregation at Douay in Flanders, Dieulwart in Lorraine, Paris in France, and Lamspung in Germany where are preserved the Authentic Acts and Original Deeds, 1707, London, 1881.

Wernz, Franciscus, S.J., *Jus Decretalium,* 6 vol., Romae, 1906-1913.

Wilpert, J., *Die Gottgeweihten Jungfrauen in den ersten Jährhunderten Kirche,* Freiburg im Br. 1892.

Wolter, Maurus, O.S.B., *Praecipua Ordinis Monastici Elementa,* Brugis, 1880.

Workman, Herbert B., *The Evolution of the Monastic Ideal,* London, 1913.

Wouters, H. G., *Historiae Ecclesiasticae Compendium,* 2 vol., Neapoli, 1871.
Woywod, S. O., F.M. *A Practical Commentary of the Code of Canon Law,* 2 vol., New York, 1925.
Zaplotnik, I. L., *De Vicariis Foraniis,* Washingtonii, 1927.
Zallinger, Jac. Ant., *Institutiones Juris Ecclesiastici,* Romae, 1823.
Zimmerman, M. O., C.D., *Carmelite Order* (Cath. Ency.).
Zitelli, Zepherino, *Apparatus seu Compendium Juriș Ecclesiastici,* Romae, 1907.
Zöckler, D. O., *Askese und Mönchenthum,* Frankfurt, 1897.
Zoega, Georgius, *Cathologus Codicum Copticorum Manuscriptorum,* Anastatischer Neudruck der Originaluasgabe 1810, Leipzig, 1908.
Zollmann, Carl, *American Civil Church Law,* New York, 1917.
Zollmann, Carl, *American Law of Charities,* Milwaukee, 1924.

PERIODICALS

Acta Sanctae Sedis, 41 vol., Romae, 1865-1908.
American Ecclesiastical Review, 80 vol., Philadelphia, 1889-1929.
Analecta Bollandiana, vol. XXV, Bruxelles.
Analecta Ecclesiastica, Romae, 1893.
Antonianum, Romae, 1926.
Annuario Pontificio, Romae (1915).
Apollinaris, Romae, 1928.
Archiv für katholisches Kirchenrechts, Maintz, 1857.
Archiv für Litteratur-und kirchengeschicte des Mittelalters, Berlin, 1885.
Archivum Franciscanum Historicum, Quaracchi, 1908.
Commentarium pro Religiosis, Romae, 1920.
Fortnightly Review, The, St. Louis, 1894.
Franziskanische Studien, Beiheft VIII, Munster, 1925.
Homeletic and Pastoral Monthly, New York, 1900.
Il Monitore Ecclesiastico, Roma, 1888.
Ilustracion del Clero, Madrid, 1909.
Jus Pontificium, Romae, 1921.
Irish Ecclesiastical Record, Dublin, 1892-1912, 4th series.
Le Canoniste Contemporain, Paris, 1877.
Netherlandsche Katholieke Stemmen, Brugis, 1900.
Nouvelle Revue Theologique, Tournai, 1856.
Periodica de re canonica et morali utilis praesertim Religiosis et Missionariis, Brugis, 1905.
Razon y Fe, Madrid, 1900.
Revue Benedictine, Maresdous, 1886.
Revue d'Histoire Ecclesiastique, Louvain, 1899.
Revue d'Histoire des Religions, Paris, 1898.
Sal Terrae, Satandier, 1912.
Tesoro del Sacerdote, Barcelona, 1920.
Theologie und Glaube, Paderborn, 1908.
Theologisch-praktische Quartalschrift, Linz, 1832.
Zeitschrift fur katholische Theologie, Innsbruck, Rauch, 1876.

INTRODUCTION

THE VOW OF POVERTY

Notion, Definition and Species

Poverty, in general, is characterized by a lacking of riches. It may be voluntary or involuntary according as the lacking of riches was willed or not willed. Poverty, in itself, is an indifferent thing, being neither good nor bad. Involuntary poverty may even prove to be an incentive towards vice, rather than a means towards virtue.

Poverty may be considered good in so far as it is useful to remove the obstacles which may stand in the way of spiritual perfection.[1] Voluntary poverty was frequently used by the ancients for the purpose of making themselves independent from the fleeting things of earth.[2] Well known among these were the Greek philosophers who lived in voluntary poverty.[3] But how conceited were these Greeks in reputing themselves to be above the vulgar crowd![4] Buddhism also taught the renunciation of property as being advantageous for restraint of human desires. Many of their religiously inclined people even practiced community of goods voluntarily.[5] Nor was the Hebrew

1. Cf. S. Thomas, *Contra Gentiles,* lib. III, c. 133; Suarez, *Opera Omnia,* Vol. XV, *De Religione,* tract. VII, lib. 8, c. 2, n. 6; Bucceroni, *Institutiones Theologiæ Moralis,* II, 75, n. 31.

2. Vermeersch, "Poverty" (*Cath. Ency.* XII, 324).

3. E.g. Zeno, casting his all into the sea, exclaimed, "Oh Fortune I thank thee for returning me to my Philosphical mantle." (Oratio XLVII, cf. Platus, *De Bono Status Religiosi,* Vol. I, p. 78; Mannock, *Origin and Progress of Religious Orders,* p. 82). Crates, moved entirely by his judgment and will, not being influenced by a storm, as had been Zeno, threw a large sum of gold into the sea, in order to become a better philosopher (St. Jerome, *Epis.* XIII; Platus, *ibid.;* St. Thomas, *Summa,* II, 2, quaes. 126, art. 3, ad. 3). Seneca said: "If thou wilt have thy mind free from trouble, thou must be either poor, or like the poor" (Cf. Platus, *ibid.;* Mannock, 1 c.).

4. Recall for example the notorious incident of Diogenes trampling on the property of Plato.

5. Cf. Lillie, *The Influence of Buddhism on Privitime Christianity,* pp. 106-107. The tenth precept of the novices, among the Chinese

Religion without members who as individuals and as communities appreciated the value of voluntary poverty as an agency for spiritual progress.[6] And the Son of God counseled voluntary poverty as a means towards the attainment of supernatural perfection, in this life, and eternal bliss in Heaven. "Si vis perfectus esse, vade, vende omnia quae habes et da pauperibus, et veni, sequere me."[7] Only the poverty as counseled by Christ is the concern of this dissertation.

The question naturally arises, "what poverty is required for the state of perfection?" Since cupidity, vain glory and excessive solicitude are the obstacles which riches place in the path of perfection,[8] the renunciation that is essential and strictly required, is the abandonment of all superfluous things, not that it is absolutely necessary to renounce the ownership of all property but a man must be contented with whatever is necessary for his own use. Then only is there a real detachment sufficient to mortify

---

Buddhist novices forbids them to touch gold or silver and the second precept of the female novices forbids them to possess anything as their own. (Vermeersch, "Poverty" (*Cath. Ency.*, XII, 324).

6. Spuche, *De Origine et Institutione Veri Monachatus,* Pars II, Diss. 4, nn. 1-4, who contends that voluntary poverty among the Jews was not practiced under vow. The Essenes and the Therapeutæ were Jews (Cf. Massebieau, *Le traite de la Vie Contemplative,* in *Revue de L'Histoire des Religions,* XVI (1987), 170-198, 284-319; Conybeare, *Philo about the Contemplative Life,* pp. 53, 206; who led a community life very similar to that practiced by the Christian monks. Community of goods and voluntary poverty were most strictly observed. "They do not treasure up gold nor silver, nor do they acquire large tracts of land in an eager desire for income but they only make provision for the absolute necessities of life. They are almost the only people who remain absolutely detsitute of money and possessions by use and wont, rather than by any lack of prosperity, yet they are esteemed wealthy for they consider that to be frugal and contented is, as indeed it is, ample abundance." (Philo, *Quod omnis probus liber,* § 12, *Apology for the Jews* excerpted in Eusebius, *Praeparatio Evangelica,* VIII, 11, ed. E. H. Gifford, in *Encyclopaedia of Religion and Ethics,* V, 397; Kaufmann, "Essenes," *Jewish Encyclopedia,* V, p. 277; Moffatt, "Essenes," *Encyclopedia of Religion and Ethics,* V, pp. 396-401; Josephus, *Wars of the Jews,* Book II, c. 8, n. 3, *Antiquities of the Jews,* Book XVIII, c. 1, n. 5, in Whiston edition; Feasy, *Monasticism,* pp. 18-20.

7. Matt. XIX, 21.

8. St. Thomas, *Summa, Theologica,* II, 2, quaes. 186, art. 8.

9. Cf. Vermeersch, "Poverty" (*Cath. Ency.*, XII, pp. 324-325).

the love of riches, to cut off vain glory and to free from the excessive care for temporal property.[9]

From the words of Christ, it is readily gathered that when He counseled poverty, He also counseled permanence in the position of a person voluntarily poor.[10] This stability is effected by means of a vow. In some sense then it may be said that Christ implicitly counselled a vow of poverty.

The Code itself does not define the vow of poverty. But a *vow* is, according to the Code, a deliberate and free promise made to God concerning something possible and better.[11] In general a vow of *evangelical poverty* may be defined as a promise made to God of a certain constant renunciation of temporal goods in order to follow Christ.[12] Such a vow may be made by a person living outside a Religious community and may have its limitations relative to the renunciation of property, according to the will of the vowing. If a vow is made in the presence of a legitimate ecclesiastical Superior and is accepted by him in the name of the Church, then it is a *public* vow, [13] e.g., as is done in Religious Institutes of men and women. If a vow of poverty is accepted by a legitimate ecclesiastical Superior acting in the name of the Church, it is a *public vow of poverty*. Other vows of poverty are private, e.g., the vow made by the Daughters of Charity. The public vow of poverty, as is made in Religious Institutes today is well described as that whereby the individual promises God the renunciation of exterior property or riches which the legislation of the Institute prescribes as the matter of the vow.[14] Public vows of Religious are classified according to the time they are to endure. If the vows are made for only a limited time, e.g., one or three years, they are known technically as *temporary* vows. If the vows are intended to endure as long as the vowing person lives, they are

---

10. Humphrey, *Elements of the Religious Life*, p. 182.

11. "Votum, idest promissio deliberata ac. libera Deo facta de bono possibili et meliore, ex virtute religionis impleri debet" canon 1307, § 1.

12. Vermeersch, *De Religiosis*, Vol. I, n. 237, p. 158.

13. "Votum est publicum, si in nomine Ecclesiæ a legitimo Superiore ecclesiastico acceptetur; secus privatum." canon 1308, § 1.

14. Cf. Vermeersch, *Theologiæ Moralis Principia-Responsa-Concilia*, III, n. 125, p. 112.

called *perpetual* vows. Perpetual public vows are further classified into solemn and simple. *Solemn* vows are those which the Church acknowledges as being solemn. Other public perpetual vows, as well as temporary vows are technically known as *simple*. What has been said concerning vows in general, applies to vows of poverty. Moreover, since in each Institute, the vow of poverty is professed according to what the legislation of the Institute prescribes as the matter of the vow of poverty, the vow made in each Institute may be considered different and may be designated rightly according to the name of the Institute in which it is made, e.g., the Franciscan vow of poverty, the Dominican vow of poverty.[15]

15. Cf. Marsot, *Petit traite practique des Voeux et de l' etat Religieux,* pp. 215-216.

N. B.—The conventional ascetical literature, the *Normae,* cc. IX, X, and many authors treat of the *virtue* of poverty. Cf. Gury, II, n. 155; Pejska, pp. 132-133; Ferreres, II, n. 211. Other authors maintain that a special virtue of poverty does not exist. Cf. Suarez, vol. XV, tract. 7, lib. 8, c. 2, n. 6; Vermeersch, *De Religiosis,* I, n. 253; "Poverty," (*Cath. Ency.* XII, 325); *Theologiae Moralis,* III, n. 134; Slater, I, 648; Schäfer, pp. 396-397; Bucceroni, II, n. 31. Riches and their possession are in themselves something indifferent. Voluntary restraint as regards property seems to belong to the virtue of temperance or can pertain to other virtues contingent on the motive behind its practice. But certainly there is such a thing as the *spirit* of poverty to which pertains interior acts relative to possessions, e.g., detachment from disorderly affection concerning temporalities, etc.

CHAPTER I.

DEVELOPMENT OF VOW OF POVERTY IN THE LEGISLATION OF RELIGIOUS INSTITUTES

ART. I. THE OBSERVANCE OF EVANGELICAL POVERTY UNTIL THE THIRD CENTURY

(*a*) *Evangelical Poverty of the Apostles and Jerusalem Converts*

THE Savior of the world did not prohibit the possession of private property, as some heretics thought,[1] nor did He condemn the ownership of wealth.[2] Nevertheless, it is true that He indicated material riches as dangers to the supernatural perfection of man.[3] Moreover, by example[4] and, by word[5] He counselled His disciples to practice voluntary poverty.[6]

---

1. Cf. Suarez, *Opera Omnia,* Vol. XV, tract. 7, lib. 8, cc. 1-2; E. G. Peligaans, Cf. S. Aug. (*Epis.* 89 & 106) who says Fraticelli held this doctrine; Rotarius, *Theologia Moralis Regularium,* Tomus, I, lib. 1, c. 5, n. 15.

2. Vermeersch, *Quaestiones de Justitia,* n. 210.

3. "Iesus autem dixit discipulis suis: Amen dico vobis, quia dives difficile intrabit in regnum coelorum. Et iterum dico vobis: Facilius est camelum per foramen acus transire, quam divitem intrare in regnum coelorum." (Matt. XIX, 23-24); "Et circumspiciens, Iesus ait discipulis suis: Quam difficile qui pecunias habent, in regnum Dei introibunt! Discipuli autem obstupescebant in verbis eius. At Iesus rursus respondens ait illis: Filioli, quam difficile est, confidentes in pecuniis in regnum Dei introire! Facilius est, camelum per foramen acus transire, quam divitem intrare in regnum Dei" (Marc. X, 23-25); cf. Luc. XII, 16 sq.; Luc. XVIII, 24-25.

4. "Et dicit ei Iesus: Vulpes foveas habent, et volucres coeli nidos: filius autem hominis non habet ubi caput reclinet" (Matt. VIII, 20); cf. Luc. IX, 58; I, Tim. VI, 8. Repudiating temporal wealth Christ spontaneously chose poverty at His birth, during His youth, and in His public ministry accepting His maintenance from others. Christ, says St. Bonaventure, was poor in His origin, poor in the progress of His Life and poor at the end of it. Cf. *Apol. Pauper.* c. 13, n. 7; vide etiam opus VI, *De Perfectione vitæ ad Sorores,* c. 3, n. 2 sq.; Wolter, *Praecipua Ordinis Monastici Elementa,* pp. 241-242; Schäfer, *De Religiosis,* p. 5; McNeil, *Religious of Diocesan Right,* p. 9. Cf. Ioannes XXII, const. *Cum inter nonnullos,* 13 nov. 1323 (c. 4, *de verborum significatione,* tit. XIV, in Extravag. Ioan. XXII)

The Apostles heeded the Master's counsel, as the Scriptures testify.[7] Some theologians have maintained that the Apostles obligated themselves to the observance of voluntary poverty by vow.[8] Yet, it remains to be shown that the fine theological reasoning begets moral certitude in this matter.

Some of the converts of Jerusalem, at least, for a time, observed the counsel of the Savior.[9] How long this practice continued is not known, as we have no authentic record of their observance of "community of goods" being perpetuated. The letter of Pope Urban I exhorting the clerics of Jerusalem to persevere in the "common life"[10] is a forgery.[11]

Denzinger-Bannwart, *Enchiridion Symbolorum* § 494 (419), "Cum inter nonnullos viros scholasticos saepe contingat in dubium revocari, utrum pertinaciter affirmare, Redemptorem nostrum ac Dominum Iesum Christum eiusque Apostolos in speciali non habuisse aliqua nec in communi etiam, haereticum sit censendum, diversa et adversa etiam sentientibus circa illud: Nos, huic concertationi finem imponere cupientes assertionem huiusmodi pertinacem—cum Scripturae sacrae, quae in plerisque locis ipsos nonnulla habuisse asserit, contradicat expresse, ipsamque Scripturam sacram, per quam utique fidei orthodoxæ probantur articuli, quoad praemissa fermentum aperte supponat continere mendacii, ac per consequens, quantum in ea est, eius in totum fidem evacuans, fidem catholicam reddat, eius probationem adimens, dubiam et incertam—deinceps erroneam fore censendam et haereticam, de fratrum nostrorum concilio hoc perpetuo declaramus edicto. Rursus in posterum pertinaciter affirmare, quod Redemptori nostro praedicto eiusque Apostolis, iis quae ipsos habuisse Scriptura sacra testatur, nequaquam ius ipsis utendi competierit, nec illa vendendi seu donandi ius habuerint aut ex ipsis alia acquirendi, quæ tamen ipsos de praemissis fecisse Scriptura sacra testatur seu ipsos potuisse facere supponit expresse; cum talis assertio ipsorum usum et gesta evidenter includat in praemissis non iusta: quod utique de usu, gestu seu factis Redemptoris nostri Dei Filii sentire nefas est, sacræ Scripturæ contrarium et doctrinæ catholicæ inimicum: assertionem ipsam pertinacem, de fratrum nostrorum consilio, deinceps erroneam fore censendam merito ac haereticam declaramus." For a reconciliation of this with Nicolaus III, *Exiit qui seminat seminare* (*Monumenta Selecta* pp. 14 sq.); cf. Natalis, *Hist. Eccles.* (saec, XII et XIV) disc. 11, art. 1.

5. "Ait illi Iesus: Si vis perfectus esse, vade, vende quæ habes, et da pauperibus, et habebis thesaurum in coelo: et veni sequere me." (Matt. XIX, 21.) Cf. Montalvo, *Glossa Fundamentalis Statutorum Cismontanae Familiae Ordinis Minorum,* Vol. I, p. 233; De Oronsoro, *Manual Serafico o Libro de la Vida de los Frayles Menores,* p. 45; Marc. X. 21; Luc. XVIII, 22; "Sic ergo omnis ex vobis, qui non renunciat, omnibus, quae possidet, non potest meus esse discipulus." (Luc. XIV, 33); "Nolite possidere aurum, neque argentum, neque

(*b*) *Virgins*

During the first three centuries of the Christian Era, there were Virgins in the Church.[12] Certainly at the beginning of the third century, they were recognized as a distinct class among the Faithful,[13] and at the end of this century there were many Virgins living together in colonies.[14] Some of these persons voluntarily disposed of their property and conformed their lives to the evangelical counsel of poverty.[15]

---

pecuniam in zonis vestris: non peram in via, neque tunicas, neque calceamenta, neque virgam." (Matt. X, 9-10); Cf. Rotarius, Tomus, I, lib. 1, c. 5, n. 14; Orth, *Approbation of Religious Institutes,* p. 2; Nicholas III, const. *Exiit qui seminat,* 14 Aug. 1279, 2 (*Monumenta Selecta,* pp. 19-20).

6. Matt. X, 9-10; "Vendite quae possidetis, et date eleemosynam. Facite vobis sacculos, qui non veterascunt, thesaurum non deficientem in coelis: quo fur non appropriat, neque tinea corrumpit. Ubi enim thesaurus vester est, ibi et cor vestrum erit." (Luc. XII, 33-34); Suarez, o.c. Vol. XV, tract. 7, lib. 8, c. 2, n. 14; Biner, *Apparatus Eruditionis ad Jurisprudentiam praesertim ecclesiasticam,* Pars VII, p. 567; Concina, *Disciplina Apostolica-Monastica,* p. 2; Rotarius, Tomus, I, lib. 1, c. 5, nn. 8 sq.; Zallinger, *Institutiones Iuris Canonici,* lib. III, tit. 31, de reg. p. 32:

7. "Tunc respondens Petrus, dixit ei: Ecce nos reliquimus omnia et secuti sumus te: quid ergo erit nobis?" (Matt. XIX, 27); Bouix, *Tractatus de Iure Regularium,* Vol. I, p. 148.

8. S. Augustin. *De Civitate Dei.* lib. XVII, c. 4; S. Thomas, *Summa Contra Gentiles,* II, 2, q. 88. art. 4, ad 3; Suarez, Vol. XV, tract. 7, lib. 3, c. 2, nn. 9 sqq.; Pelagius, *De Planctu Ecclesiæ,* II, c. 56 apud Platus, lib. II, c. 20; Rodericus *Quaestiones Regulares et Canonicæ,* Tomus, I, quaes. 1, art. 1; Platus, *De Bono Status Religiosi,* lib. II, c. 20, pp. 410-413; Mannock, *Origin and Progress of Religious Orders,* p. 8; Müller. *The Religious State,* pp. 8-11; cf. Verhoeven, *De Regularium et Saecularium Clericorum Juribus et Officiis,* c. 1, § 1, n. 1, p. 2; cf. De Buck V-Tinnebroeck, *Examen Historicum et Canonicum libri R. D. Verhoeven,* pp. 32 sq.

9. Acta, II, 44-45; IV, 33; IV, 34-37; V, 1-10; Cf. S. Augustin. *In Psalm.* CXXXII, 2-3; Bellarminus, *De Monachis,* Opera Omnia, t. 7, c. 5; Platus, lib. II, c. 21, pp. 413 sq; cf. Carlyle, *Dictionary of the Apostolic Church,* Vol. I, pp. 236-237.

10. Mansi, *Sacrorum Concilliorum Nova et Amplissima Collectio,* II, 751; cf. etiam I. *Cor* 16; II Cor. VIII, 12; *Rom.* XV, 26; I *Tim,* VI.

11. Cf. Jaffe, *Regesta Pontificum Romanorum,* p. 13; Maroto, *Institutiones,* n. 60; Cicognani, *Ius Canonicum,* p. 260; Ayrinhac, *General Legislation on the New Code of Canon Law,* n. 19.

12. I Cor. VII; Acta, XXI, 9; S. Clem. I, *"Epis ad Cor."* c. 38 (Funk, *Patres Apostolici,* Vol. I, pp. 148-149); Hermas, *Pastor,* lib. 3, *Simil. IX,* c. 29 (Funk l. c. pp. 626-627); S. Ignatius, *Epis. ad Poly-*

(c) *The Ascetics*

Another primeval form of the Religious Life, was that of the ascetics who strove heroically to attain Christian sanctity.[16] Sometimes they lived in solitude outside the cities and villages.[17] And it is recorded, that some of these devout people, divested themselves of their property and bestowed it upon the Church and the poor.[18]

---

carp. c. 5 (Funk, 1. c. pp. 292-293); *ad Smyrneos,* XIII (Migne, *Patrologia Graeca,* VI, 350); Athenagoras, *Legatio pro Christianis,* c. 33 (Migne, o. c. VI, 936); De Journel, *Enchiridion Patristicum,* pp. 67-68; Clement. Alex. *Paedigogus,* lib. I, c. 7 (Migne, o. c. VIII, 311); *Stromata,* lib. III, c. 1 (Migne, o. c. VIII, 1103); Origin, *In Levit. Hom.* III, n. 4 (Migne o. c. XII, 428); Tertullian. *Apologeticus,* c. 9 (Migne *Patrologia Latina,* I. 327); *De cultu Fem.* II, 9 (Migne, P. L. I, 1325-1327); *De Virg. Veland.* c. 10 (Migne, P. L. II, 905-906); Cf. Bayllay, *De Votis Simplicibus, quae Votis Solem. Praemittuntur* AkkR. XVII (1867) 13; De Buck-Tinnebroeck, c. 2, n. 8, pp. 44 sq., Steiger, *Periodica,* XIII (1925), p. (37); Parsons, *Studies in Church History,* Vol. VI, 520; Battifol, *History of the Roman Breviary,* p. 4; Schaaf, *The Cloister,* 10; Döllinger, *History of the Church,* II, 286; Koch, *Virgines Christi,* Texte und untersuchungen zur geschicte der Altchristlichen Literatur, XXXI (1907) 59 sq.), Schäfer, p. 10: Heinrich, *The Canonesses,* p. 4.

13. Origin, *In Num. Hom.* II, n. 1 (Migne, P. G. XII, col. 591); Tertullian, *De exhort. cast.* II (Migne, P. L. II, col. 957); *Constitutiones Apostolorum,* lib. I, c. 57; Cf. Maroto, *Institutiones,* n. 42; Schiweitz, *Vorgeschichte des Mönchtums oder das Aescetentum der drei ersten christlichen Jährhunderten,* AkkR, LXXVIII (1898) 19; Vermeersch, *De Religiosis,* Vol. I (Supplementum I, pp. 4-5); Cf. Schiweitz, *Das Morgenländesche Mönchtum,* Vol. I, p. 16; Schäfer, p. 11.

14. S. Athanasius, *Vita Sancti Antonii,* c. III (Migne, P. G. XVI, col. 844); cf. De Buck-Tinnebroeck, c. II, n. 9, p. 47; Vermeersch, *De Religiosis,* Vol. I (Suppl. I, p. 4). The Canonesses were the direct successors of the Virgins (Roloff, *Lexicon der Pädagogik,* II, 1082; Heimbucher, *Das Kanonissen-Institut,* Heinrich, p. 4).

15. S. Cyprian, *De Habit. Virg.* c. 7 (Migne, P. L. IV, col. 446); S. Ambrose, *De Virg. I,* c. 2 (Migne, P. L. XVI, col. 206); S. Greg. Nazian. *De Vita S. Greg. Thau.* (Migne, P. G. XLVI, col. 908). Cf. Suarez, Vol. XV, tract. 7, lib. 8, c. 7, n. 10 sq.; De Buck-Tinnebroeck, c. II, n. 8, pp. 46-47.

16. Cf. Justin, *Apol.* I, 7, Migne (P. G. VI, col. 350, 374); Clemens, Alex. *"Quis dives salvetur?"* (Migne, P. G. VIII, col. 651); Origin, *In Matt. Homil.* 15 (Migne, P. G. XIII, col. 1294); S. Cyprian. *De Habitu Virg.* c. 11 (Migne P. L. IV, col. 461; Athenagoras, *Legat. pro Christ.* n. 33 (Migne, P. G. VI, col. 966; S. Greg. *Hom. XXXII in Evangel.* (Migne, P. L. LXXVI, 123); Tertullian, *De Patientia,* c. 1 (Migne, P. L. I, col. 1371; Martigney, *Dictionaire des Antiquities Chretiennes,* p. 61; Döllinger, II, 270. Christian monasticism was

ARTICLE II. THE OBSERVANCE OF EVANGELICAL POVERTY IN EASTERN MONASTICISM

(*a*) *The Antonians*

During the Decian Persecution (249-251),[19] many of the ascetics fled to the desert, and there is reason to believe that some of them remained in the wilderness after the occasion of their life of solitude had disappeared.[20] St. Anthony (251-356) profoundly impressed by the text: "If thou wilt be perfect, go sell what thou hast, and give it to the poor . . . and come follow Me,"[21] considered it as addressed to himself.[22] At once he disposed of his property and became an ascetic. About 305 A. D. he assumed the spiritual direction of a colony of ascetics who had gathered around his hermitage at Pispir.[23] The Egyptian character, with its inborn tendency to asceticism and mysticism, was tinder for the spark of monasticism enkindled by Anthony.[24] Within the life time of its founder, Christian monasticism became what it has been ever since, viz.: one of the outstanding features of the Catholic Church.

---

not derived from an imitation of the Serapis (as Preuschen, *Mönchtum und Sarapiskult*, p. 30; and Weingarten, in Herzog, *Real-Encyl.* v. *Moenchtum* or Buddhism (as was conjectured by Hilgenfeld in *Zeitschrift f. wiss. Theol.* XXI, p. 148 sq.) or Neoplatonism, Cf. Brück, *Lehrbuch der Kirchengeschichte*, § 3, n. 6, sq. § 72, n. 1, sq.; Schiweitz, *Vorgeschichte des Mönchtums*, AkkR, LXXVIII (1898) 8 sqq.; Knabenbauer, *Commentarium in Evangelium* sec. Matt. II, p. 158 sq.; Heimbucher, *Die Orden und kongregationen der Katholichen Kirche*, Vol. I, p. 15 sq.; apud Wernz, *Ius Decretalium*, III, p. 266, n. (63); Schäfer, pp. 10-11; cf. Ladeuze, pp. 168-172; Kraus, Real-Encyklopädie der christlichen Alterthumer, *Asceten.*

17. S. Athanasius, *Vita Sancti Antonii*, c. 3 (Migne, P. G. XXVI, 844); Machean, *Christian Monasticism in Egypt to the Close of the Fourth Century*, p. 68.

18. Acta, II, 44; IV, 34 sq.; Eusebius, *Historia Ecclesiastica*, III, c. 37 (Migne, P. G. XX, col. 288); VI, c. 3 (Minge, P. G. XX, col. 530); *Vita Sancti Cypriani* (Migne, P. L. III, col. 1543, 1483-1484; Vermeersch, *De Religiosis*, Vol. I, Suppl. I, p. 5; Suarez, Vol. XV, tract. 7, lib. 8, c. 1, 2, n. 17; Schiweitz, AkkR, LXXVIII (1898) 324 sq.; Wernz, III, p. 267, n. (73); Feasy, *Monasticism*, p. 24.

19. Wernz, III, p. 268.

20. Bingham, *The Antiquities of the Christian Church*, Book VII, c. 1, sect. 4; Gwatkin, *Early Church History to A. D.* 313, Vol. I, p. 245; Wernz, III, p. 268; Schäfer, p. 11; Vermeersch, *De Religiosis*, I (Suppl. I P. 6).

21. Matt. XIX, 31.

How quickly monasticism spread, may be seen from the fact that at Nitria alone there were five thousand monks.[25]

Anthony did not compose a written Rule.[26] Nor did the Antonian monks have the "common life" as we know it today.[27] Nor were they obligated to the ascetical practices of the community by any other bond than that of a voluntary disciple to his master. Anthony exhorted his disciples to practice voluntary poverty.[28] With them the renunciation of property should be as absolute as possible.[29] Yet perforce of necessity, they had to retain the dominion use and usufruct of some property.[30] In general it may be said that their observance of poverty demanded a life of privation, especially as regards the superfluities which the wealthy enjoyed.[31]

(*b*) *The Pachomian Monks*

Saint Pachomius[32] (292[33]-346[34] A. D.) having learned the ascetical life from Palemon, a hermit, retired to Tabennessis, near Denderah, in southern Egypt (315-320 A. D.) and founded the first cenobitical monastery.[35] However,

---

22. *Vita S. Antonii*, n. 14 (Migne, P. G. XXVI, col. 833); Villier, *Exemplar Ideale Monasticum*, CpR, VIII (1927), p. 198.

23. Clark, *Lausiac History of Palladius*, p. 23; Neale, *A History of the Eastern Church*, pp. 107, 110.

24. Machean, p. 70.

25. Rufinus, *Hist. Monch.* cc. 2-3 (Migne, P. L. XXI, col. 407-433); Heimbucher, Vol. I, p. 112; Gaselle, *Transaction R. S. L.* p. 11; Feasy, p. 32.

26. Boak, *A History of Rome to* 565, p. 399.

27. McNeil, *Religious of Diocesan Right*, p. 4.

28. *Vita S. Antonii*, nn. 16, 45 (Migne, P. L. CIII, col. 425, 427).

29. Among the early leaders in Christian monasticism we find similar examples, e.g. Abbot Agathon used to say: "Own nothing which it would grieve you to give to another." Macarius in discovering a thief carrying off his few articles of furniture, pretended to be a stranger and assisted the thief. Another monk, who owned only a copy of the Gospels, rejoiced after he had sold it and had given the price away, saying: "I have sold the very book that bade me sell all I had." Huddleston, "Monasticism," (*Cath. Ency.* X, 460).

30. Rotarius, Tomus, II, lib. 3, c. 1, n. 6; Suarez, Vol. XV, tract 7, lib. 8, c. 7, nn. 4-6.

31. In 1732, a Religious Institute which traced its origin to these monks, received the papal approbation of their Constitutions. Chapter III of these regulations declared: "Monachum convenit nihil omnio

the oft quoted incident of the angelical assistance in the establishment of the Tabennessiot monastery, viz., the dictation of the *Rule* is today considered to be only a legend by leading authorities on early monastic life.[36]

There are two *Rules* attributed to Saint Pachomius. The Jeromian[37] version is probably not authentic, in its entirety,[38] yet it is considered to represent the regulations that prudence and experience dictated to Pachomius in the fourth century.[39] The Palladian version is authentic[40] and represents the regulations obtaining when he visited the Thebaid, a few years after the death of the Tabennesiot Saint.[41]

The dominant note of the Pachomian (although confined to narrower limits) as well as the Antonian communities, was the ideal of surpassing the rest of the brethren in feats of penance.[42] Hence resulted that fanatical

---

possidere." Cf. *Constitutiones Monachorum Syrorum Maronitarum Ordinis Sancti Antonii Abbatis Congregationis Montis Libani* (*Bullarium Romanum Continuatio,* XXIII, n. 56, p. 328).

32. Roswede (Migne, P. L. LXXIII, 271; *Acta Sanctorum,* 14 maii, III, 295.

33. Montalambert, *The Monks of the West,* Vol. I, p. 197; Ladeuze, *De Instituto Coenibitico Sancti Pachomii,* p. 241; Hughes, *The Christian Church in the Epistles of St. Jerome,* p. 39; Kirch, *Enchiridion Fontium Historiæ Ecclesiasticæ Antiquæ,* p. 455, n. 784.

34. Leipoldt, *Schenute von Atripe und die Entstehung des National Aegyptischen Christentums,* p. 36; Bacchus, "Christian Monasticism before Chalcedon" (*Cath Ency.* X, 465); Heimbucher, Vol. I, p. 107; Koeniger, *Grundriz einer Geschichte des Katholichen Kirchenrechts,* p. 24; Kirch, p. 455, n. 784.

35. Ladeuze, p. 241; Butler, *Historia Lausiaca,* Vol. II, p. 206; Butler, "Monachism," *Cambridge Mediaeval History,* and *Ency. Britnanica;* Thompson, *English Monasteries,* p. 2. Previous to this Aotas had attempted a similar foundation but it had been a failure. Cf. Tillemont, *Memoires pour servir a l'Histoire Ecclesiastique des six premiers siecles,* Vol. VII, p. 176; Machean, p. 91; Duchesne, *Histoire d'Anciene,* Vol. II, p. 498.

36. Ladeuze, p. 257; Steiger, *Periodica, XIII* (1925) p. 56.

37. Migne, P. L. XXI, col. 61-68.

38. Benedict of Aniane (Migne, P. L. CIII, col. 416); Smith, "Pachomius," *A Dictionary of Christian Biography;* Cabrol, *Encyclopedia of Religion and Ethics,* Vol. VIII, p. 585; Steiger, l. c.; Fortescue, "Eastern Monasticism" (*Cath. Ency.* X, p. 468).

39. Machean, p. 98; Steiger, *Periodica,* XIII (1925), p. (56).

40. Butler, *Historia Lausiaca,* Vol. I, p. 236; Cf. Chapter XXXVIII, *Historia Lausiaca* (Migne, P. L. LXXIII, col. 1337-1338; Kirch, nn. 784-788).

41. Pachomius died May 9, 346. At the time of his death, he ruled nine monasteries for men and two for women. Cf. Tillemont,

desire to make records in austerities, which frequently led to extravagances and ridiculous eccentricities.[43]

Nowhere in the biographies or the Rules of Pachomius is there indication of an express vow of poverty, made on the occasion of entrance into a community.[44] That the Pachomians made no vow of poverty seems clear from the fact that when the Superiors had to reprimand a subject they never made any kind of reference to a monk's covenant with God.[45] Nevertheless the Pachomian observances of the evangelical counsel have wrought a mighty influence on the practice of the vow of poverty in Religious Institutes.

An applicant for admission to the community, was required to prove that he contemned the faculty of ownership.[46] Cassian, describing how this rule was fulfilled, related: "They inquire whether he is contaminated with a single coin clinging to him."[47] Without the Superior's permission, no one could keep in his cell anything other than his personal clothing and the mat used for sleeping.[48] If a monk left a community to join another, he could take nothing with him except what he needed for daily use.[49] Articles, permitted to the monks for private use, ought not to be exchanged with a fellow monk.[50] It was prohibited to retain anything on deposit for anyone.[51] Gifts could not be accepted without the Superior's permission.[52] If a monk lost anything, he was to be publicly corrected

---

VII, 176; *Vita S. Pachomii*, n. 28 (Migne, P. L. LXXIII, p. 248): Zöckler, *Askese und Mönchenthum*, p. 208; Schaaf, p. 12. The women followed practically the same Rule as the men. Cf. Villicourt, *Le Rite Copte de la Profession Monacle*, p. 6; Butler, *Hisoria Lausiaca*, Vol. II, pp. 96-97; Clark, *The Lausiac History of Palladius*, pp. 116 ff.

42. *Hist. Monch.* c. III, Jerome's Preface to *Regula Pachomii* (Migne, P. L. XXIII, col. 62); *Vita S. Pachomii*, n. 14; *Historia Lausiaca*, n. 38 (32); Hannah, *Christian Monasticism*, p. 19; Butler, *Historia Lausiaca*, Vol. I, p. 238; Gasquet, *English Monastic Life*, p. 5; Machean, p. 105; Villier, CpR, VIII (1927) 197.

43. Butler, *Historia Lausiaca*, Vol. I, p. 238; Feasy, p. 29.

44. Steiger, *Periodica*, XIII (1925) p. (48); Clark, *St. Basil the Great*, p. 37; Leclerq, *Dictionaire d'Archeologie chretienne*, "Cenobitism," n. 1116.

45. Leclerq, 1. c.; Ladeuze, p. 282.

46. R. 49.

47. *Inst.* IV, c. 3.

48. R. 81, 82, 88, 114; Cf. Migne, P. L. XXIII. cc. 63-64

49. R. 83.

50. R. 97.

51. R. 113.

52. R. 106.

before the altar;[53] and if he broke anything through a lack of due care he was to receive a public correction.[54] Even at this early date it was a principle that whatever profit arises from the labor of a monk belongs to the Institute and not to the individual Religious.[55]

(c) *The Schenoudian Monks*

Within recent years much interest has been focused on Schenute. His influence on the monasticism of his time seems to have been great,[56] but his importance, as regards the subsequent history of the Religious Life, was small. By some authors he is considered to have exacted express formal vows on the occasion of entrance into his community.[57] Other savants do not share this opinion.[58]

Not later than 371 A. D., [59] the Koptic Monk, Schenute,[60] Schenoudi or Sinuthius (330 or 340[61]-July 1, 451 or 452[62]) entered the cenobitical monastery, Dier Al Abiad,[63] of Bgol, near Aklimin, Egypt, where the Rule

---

53. R. 131.

54. R. 132.

55. Cassian, *Inst.* IV, n. 14: "It was considered a great offence if there drops from the mouth of a monk such an expression as "my book," "my tablets," "my pen," "my coat," or "my shoes," and for this he would have to make satisfaction by a proper penance if by accident some such expression escaped his lips through thoughtlessness or ignorance." Cf. *Inst.* IV, n. 13; *Regula sive Doctrina Veterum Testimonia Orsiensi,* cc. 21, 22, 27 (Migne, P. L. CIII, col 461-464).

56. Cf. *Memoires publics par les Membres de la Mission Archiologue Francais, au Caire,* Tomus IV, p. 230.

57. Leipoldt, pp. 106-113; Peeters, *Analecta Bollandiana,* XXIV (1905), p. 406; Piontek, pp. 18-22; Revillout, *Revue d'Histoire des Religious,* Tomus, VIII, p. 109; Ott, "Schenute," *Cath. Ency.* XIII, 527; Heimbucher, Vol. I, p. 113 (seems).

58. Amelineau, *Oevres,* cxlix; ibid, *Vie de Schenute,* p. 44; Ladeuze, pp. 114-115; Workman, *The Evolution of the Monastic Ideal,* p. 127; Besse, *Les Moines d'Orient Anterieurs au Concile de Chalcedoine,* p. 139; Leclerq, "Cenobitisme," *Dictionaire d'Archiologie Chretienne,* n. 3117; *Memoires publics par les Membres de la Mission Archiologique Francais au Caire,* Tomus, IV, pp. 234 sq.; Zoega, *Cathologus Codicum Copticorum Manuscriptorum,* p. 375, N. CLXXXI; Vermeersch, "Religious" (*Cath Ency.* XII, 751).

59. Schaaf, p. 15; Ott, 1. c.

60. Revillout, o. c. pp. 401-467; 543-581; Leipoldt, *Corpus SS. Christ. Orient. Schrift.* c. II, iil.

61. Ladeuze, *Revue d'Histoire Ecclesiastique,* Tomus VII, pp. 76-83; Machean, p. 110; Piontek, p. 18.

62. Besse, p. 85.

63. Amelineau, *Geographie,* p. 21; *Oevres,* p. XV, LIII.

was fundamentally the Pachomian.[64] In the course of time, especially when Schenute became abbot, a more strict observance was introduced.[65] Many of the Tabennessiot monks submitted themselves to his regime.[66] Convents of women also came to acknowledge his jurisdiction.[67]

Among the Schenoudian manuscripts, pertaining to the Religious Life, those dealing with observance of poverty are the most numerous. However, modern study of the fragments of the Schenoudian manuscripts, has not established with historical certitude, that Schenuti introduced either an implicit or explicit vow of poverty. On entering the monastery, the postulant abandoned all his possessions.[68] So rigid was the concept of evangelical poverty among the Schenoudian monks that whoever retained as his own, even a grain of wheat, thereby proved himself to be an enemy of the community.[69] They could not as individuals, dispose of the fruit of their labors,[70] nor could they give presents of any value.[71]

(*d*) *The Basilian Monks*

A more perfect form of the cenobitical life, was developed under the guidance of St. Basil the Great[72] (329[73]-

64. *Memoires publics par les Members de la Mission Archiologique Francaise au Caire,* Tomus, IV. p. 235; Ladeuze, *De Instituto Coenibitico Sancti Pachomii,* p. 206; Machean, p. 112.

65. Schaaf, p. 15.

66. Grützmacher, *Pachomius und das alteste Klosterleben ein Beirag zur mönchengeschichte,* p. 114; Leipoldt, p. 158.

67. Leclerq, o. c. n. 3117; Amelineau, *Oevres,* p. clxix; Besse, p. 139; Ladeuze, pp. 114 sq.

68. Zoega, N. CCXXXII.

69. Zoega, N. CCXII.

70. Zoega, N. CCIV et N. CCXII.

71. Zoega, N. CCXII. It has been computed that about the year 450 A. D. one-half the adult population of Egypt, excluding Alexandria, were monks and nuns: "in some parts of the country there were villages in which were no full grown persons who were not monks and nuns." Gaselle, p. 11. Cf. St. Aug. *De Moribus Ecclesiae Catholicae et de Moribus Mönachorum,* I, 31; Rufinus, *De Vita Patro.* lib. II, cc. 5, 7, 18.

72. Marianus, *Opera Omnia S. Patris Basilii Caesareæ,* Tomus, III, pp. xxxvii-ccliv; Hergenroether, *Handb. d. allg. K.,* Tomus I, pp. 444 sq.

73. Morison, *St. Basil and His Rule,* p. xii; Clark, *St. Basil the Great,* p. 20; Venables, "Basil", *A Dictionary of Christian Biography,*

379[74]). Having made an intimate study of the various types of monasticism, obtaining in Egypt, Palestine,[75] Coelia Syria [76] and Mesopotamia,[77] he returned to Pontus near Neo Caesarea about 358,[78] and organized a community of ascetics. Unfortunately, we do not possess the code of rules (if ever such existed), nor a record of the customs which regulated the daily routine of the Cappadocian's monks. The most fruitful source of historical data concerning their observance of poverty, is the *Regulae Fusius Tractatae*[79] and the *Regulae Brevius Tractatae.*[80] Both of these writings are reputed to be authentic.[81] They are collections of advices given to monks, seeking St. Basil's counsel on matters relating to the asectical life.

From these questions and answers, we learn that Basil required his prospective subjects to make a formal profession of chastity. As regards this profession, Basil taught: "A man who dedicates himself to God, and then springs away to another form of life, has committed a sacrilege, for he has stolen himself away and robbed God of his votive offering."[82] Some authors opine that this profession, constituted monastic vows.[83] Undoubtedly, it did produce a perpetual obligation to remain a monk; but, why at this early date, the profession of merely chastity, constituted a vow of poverty, is not evident. It did

---

Vol. I, p. 282; Montalambert, I, p. 201; Clark, *The Ascetical Works of St. Basil,* p. 13; Currier, *History of Religious Orders,* p. 77; Allard, *Saint Basile,* p. 5.

74. Rauschen, *Jährbucher der christlichen Kirche unter dem Kaiser Theodosius den Grossen,* p. 456; *Encyclopedia, Universal Illustrada,* Vol. VII, p. 1062; Montalambert, Vol. I, p. 201; Morison, p. xii; Clark, *St. Basil the Great,* p. 26; Allard, p. 149; Vermeersch, *De Religiosis,* Vol. I (Suppl. I, p. 32); De Journal, n. 911; Kirch, p. 354. Women also followed the Rule of Basil, cf. Clark, *St. Basil the Great,* p. 117.

75. Vita S. Hilarion (Migne, P. L. XXIII, 24); Tillemont, VII, p. 563. Allard, *Saint Basile,* p. 38.

76. Theoderet, *Historia Ecclesiastica,* Migne, P. G. LXXXII, col. 1190-1411; Adeney, *The Greek and Eastern Churches,* pp. 158-159.

77. Zöckler, p. 182.

78. Curran, p. 77; Tillemont, IX, p. 31; *Ency. Univer. Illust.* Vol. VII, p. 1064.

79. Migne, P. G. XXXI, col. 389 sq.

80. Migne, P. G. XXXI, col. 1037 sq.

81. Garnier (Migne, P. G. XXXI, col. 1641); Deferrari, *St. Basil, The Letters,* xxi; Morison, p. 17.

82. *Reg. Fus. Tract.* n. 14; Cfr. *Epis.* CCXVII, canon 60.

create an obligation to observe the evangelical poverty practiced in the community. This was a natural consequence of being a monk. But was every observance attached to the monastic life, the object of a specific vow? Why, then, do authors consider poverty as having been vowed?

Most difficult indeed is it to determine how the Basilian monks practiced evangelical poverty. Our principal source of information is not a monastic Rule, in the ordinary sense of that term, but merely the replies given to individual monks, seeking advice from their Spiritual Father.

Clearly Basil states, that private possession of property is not lawful.[84] Private property is not an evil in itself, but it distracts the soul from the service of God.[85] Nevertheless, Basil's personal conduct presents facts, which are difficult to reconcile with the ideal. After his travels, it is true, he renounced his property.[86] In Letters XXXVI and XXXVII he declared, "We have nothing of our own." Yet his brother, Saint Gregory Nazianzen, describes him as a man who ungrudgingly spent his money on the poor, even before he became a priest, and most of all, in the time of the famine . . . and afterwards did not hoard what remained to him.[87]

Maranus explains Gregory's words, by supposing that about the time of the famine, Basil had acquired property by his mother's death.[88] Clark has a different interpretation. He is of the opinion, that Basil probably sold his personal possessions, when he became a monk, and gave the proceeds to the poor; but to dispose of his share of the family property was not so easy.[89] Letter XXXVII shows, that Basil did retain or acquire some rights over the family property, at least as regards administration. In

83. Helyot, *Histoire des Ordres Monastiques Religieux, etc.*, Tomus I, c. 18, p. 175; Montalambert, Vol. I, p. 204; Piontek, p. 23; Brueck, Vol. I, p. 215; Clark, *St. Basil the Great*, pp. 107-109; Butler, *Benedictine Monachism*, p. 122; David, *The Religious State*, p. 265.

84. *Reg. Brev.* n. 85; Reg. Fus. n. 8.

85. *Reg. Brev.* n. 2.

86. Cf. Greg. Naz. *Oration*, n. 43 and n. 60; *Letter* CCXXIII of Basil.

87. St. Greg. Naz. *"In Eunom."* 1, n. 10.

88. *Vita S. Basilii*, IV. n. 2.

89. Clark, *St. Basil the Great*, p. 45.

Letter III, he complains bitterly of an attack on his property that had disturbed him. Hence it seems, that St. Basil did not consider himself as inhabile to private property, after becoming a monk. However, we can be sure that whatever income accrued to him was dedicated to God and expended on works of charity.

Again, it seems as though property could be acquired by the monks from their patrimony. "It is necessary that relatives should give to those who have embraced the Religious Life their income and retain none of it, lest they incur the judgment passed on sacrilege.[90] The monk may distribute his property in person, if he is able to do so wisely.[91] Yet the acts of distribution, ought not to be done in the presence of the brethren, lest it be an occasion of envy to those who have none to distribute. If a monk was incapable of prudently bestowing his property, he ought to choose someone fitted for such an undertaking.[92] It was left to the judgment of the Superior as to whether a gift should be accepted by a subject.[93] Sometimes monks made contributions to the coenobia, but Basil did not want such persons to receive special consideration on that account.[94] In writing to the assessors of taxes, Basil stated that the monks: "if their life was consistent with their profession, possess neither money nor bodies; for the former is spent on behalf of the needy."[95] He also declared that if a monk retained his property, he must pay taxes on it.[96]

90. *Reg. Brev.* 185.
91. *Reg. Fus.* 8.
92. *Reg. Brev.* 187.
93. *Reg. Brev.* 304 et 305.
94. *Reg. Brev.* 308.
95. *Epis* 284.
96. *Reg. Brev.* 94. Basil permitted ascetics to live in his cenobium even though they intended to remain there only temporarily. Perhaps the seeming mitigations were addressed to these subjects and not to his monks who had made perpetual profession. Among the Greco-Slavs today there is a flourishing Congregation of Basilian monks. They make the equivalent of our simple perpetual vow of poverty before their solemn profession. Cf. Visosevic, O. S. Bas., *De Disciplina Monastica apud Catholicos Ritus,* CpR, VIII (1927), p. 210 sq.; De Meester, "De Monachismo apud Graecos et Slavos post Saeculum Nonum," CpR, VIII (1927) 309-311; Fortesque, *The Uniate Churches,* pp. 124-134. *The Orthodox Eastern Church,* pp. 354-360, gives an interesting picture of the subsequent history of the Basilian monks. The original monasticism of Palestine (Migne, LXXXII, col.

ARTICLE III. EVANGELICAL POVERTY IN WESTERN RELIGIOUS INSTITUTES

(*a*) *Earliest Western Monasticism*

In Gaul, the earliest European monasticism had its greatest expansion.[97] About 373 A. D. Saint Martin became the leader of a gathering of hermits near Poitiers.[98] The concept of monasticism there obtaining was but a reproduction of the Antonian system.[99] Concerning the practice of evangelical poverty among the Martinian monks we have no reliable information.

In Southern France, Saint Honoratus founded the famous monastery of Lerens, in 410 A. D. At Marseilles, 413-416, John Cassian founded two monasteries.[100] Throughout this part of France, the Pachomian ideal was the norm of monastic life. However, as regards the observance of poverty serious abuses soon arose. Against these, Cassian inveighs strongly: "We carry about our own keys and trampling under foot all feeling of shame and disgrace which should spring from our profession, we are not ashamed to wear rings with which to seal what we have stored up and in whose case not merely boxes and baskets but not even chests and closets are sufficient for those things which we collect or which we reserved when we forsook the world: and who sometimes get so angry over trifles and mere nothings to which we lay claim as if they were our own, that if any one dares to lay a finger on any of them, we are so filled with rage against him, that we do not keep the wrath of our heart from being expressed on our lips and in bodily excitement."[101]

1339-1342), Syria(Theodoret, *Hist. Eccl.*, Migne, P. G. LXXXII, col. 1190, 1411; Adener, pp. 157-158) ; Mesopotamia (Zöckler, p. 182), Persia and Arabia (Migne, P. G. IXXIX, col. 590, 694), or Armenia (Migne, P. G. XXXVII, col. 1471), contributes nothing of general interest to the history of the vow of poverty.

97. Butler, *Benedictine Monachism,* p. 18.

98. Sulphitius Severus, *Vita Sancti Martini,* n. 10 (*Corpus Scriptorum Ecclesiasticorum Latinorum,* Vol. I, pp. 119 sq.).

99. Butler, *Historia Lausiaca,* Vol. I, p. 244; Graham, *Mediaeval England,* p. 55.

100. Le Labriolle, *History and Literature of Christianity from Tertullian to Boethius,* p. 423.

101. *Inst. IV,* n. 15; Gibson, *Ante and Post Nicene Fathers,* p. 189; Smith, *The Church in Roman Gaul,* p. 245.

The first monastic Rule of Western monasticism was that of Caesarius of Arles (470-542)[102] His Rule for monks required them to sell their property or donate it to their parents or the monastery before entering the community, if it was possible to do so legally. If a prospective monk was too young to perform such an act when he entered, or if he received his patrimony after Profession, he must as soon as possible dispose of the property and reserve nothing to himself.[103] His Rule for Virgins was worded somewhat more exactingly. "They must reserve nothing in their power which they may seem to possess or administer, as the Lord said, If thou wilt be perfect, go sell what thou hast, Matt. XIX. Everyone of you that doth not renounce all he possesseth, cannot be my disciple, Luke XIV, 23, I say venerable daughters that a nun who has possessions can not have perfection."[104]

Of early Spanish monasticism little is known. However, we can be sure there were Iberian monks and nuns as early as the fifth century. Euric who reigned from 464-484 legislated that if clerics, monks and nuns died intestate, not having relatives up to the seventh degree, the church which they served would vindicate their "substance."[105] By a positive disposition of law at a later period it may be seen that the term "church" in Visigothic legislation, comprised monasteries of men and women.[106]

We have little certain knowledge of Celtic monasticism before the sixth century[107] other than that it was Egyptian in its general characteristics.[108] Saint Columban

---

102. Schaaf, p. 20.

103. *Regula ad Monachos,* cc. 1, 47 (Migne, P. L. LXVII, col. 1099-1104); Thomassinus, *Vetus et Nova Disciplina Ecclesiæ,* Pars III, 2, 43, 8.

104. *Regula ad Virgines,* c. 4 (Migne, P. L. LXVII, col. 1107), Eckenstein, *Woman under Monasticism,* p. 48.

105. *Codicis Euriciani Fragmenta,* CCCXXXV (*Monumenta Historica Germanica Leges,* Sectio I, t. 1, p. 27.

106. *Leges Visigothorum,* IV, 5, 6 (*Monumenta Historica Germanica, Leges,* Sectio I, t. 1, pp. 204-205). In 636 St. Isadore of Spain formulated a Rule for Monks, in which he ordered that no one was to have anything as his own, but all things were to be held in common after the example of the Apostles (Migne, P. L. XIII, col. 557). The civil law of Spain recognized monks and nuns as capable of making a will.

107. Butler, *Benedictine Monachism,* p. 19.

108. Warren, *The Liturgy and Rites of the Celtic Church,* p. 56; Baumer, *Geschichte des Breviers,* p. 163.

(543-615)[109] did not write a monastic Rule, properly so called.[110] What is known as the *Rule of St. Columban* is more properly an anthology of exhortation than legislation. It was never used to any great extent in Ireland and Wales.[111] Chapter IV stated that not only to have but even to will to have superfluous things was damnable.[112] The Irish *Rule of St. Carthage,* declared that it was the duty of monks not to have private property or goods of great value.[113]

There is good authority for the statement that there were cenobites as well as hermits in Italy before the visit of Saint Athanasius and his companions in 339.[114] However, we can still trust the tradition that these men, Athanasius and the Antonian monks, were prime factors in the establishment of Italian monasticism.[115] Soon after the middle of the fourth century there appeared in the principal cities monasteries of men. The numbers of virgins increased under the mighty influence of St. Ambrose.[116] Worthy of mention, in view of later developments of the Religious Life, is Eusebius of Vercelli, who with his clerics practiced the "common life."[117] Another important factor in the development of Italian monasticism was the reading of *The Lives of the Fathers of the Desert.*[118] Yet it must be admitted that even at the end of the fourth

109. Pourrat-Mitchell-Jacques, *Christian Spirituality,* Vol. I, p. 256; McCormick, *Confessors of Religious,* p. 11.

110. Bund, *The Celtic Church of Wales,* pp. 166-167.

111. Gasquet, p. 11; Butler, *Benedictine Monachism,* p. 11.

112. Migne, P. L. CIII, col. 557; LXXX, col. 209 sq.

113. F. "The Duties of Monks," (*Irish Ecclesiastical Record,* XXVII [1910] 4th series). Primitive Scottish monasticism was modeled on the Pachomian. Bede says the little property they enjoyed was common to all and poverty was considered the surest guardian of virtue (Lingard, *The History and Antiquities of the Anglo-Saxon Church,* Vol. I, pp. 182-183).

114. S. Aug. *De Moribus Ecclesiæ,* I, 33, 70 (Migne, P. L. XXXII, col. 1139-1140; Grisar, *History of Rome and the Popes in the Middle Ages,* Vol. III, p. 5; Spreitzenhofer, *Die Entwicklung des alten Mönchtums, in Italien,* p. 5; Willpert, *Die Gottgeweihten Jungfrauen in den ersten Jährhunderten Kirche,* p. 32; Schaaf, p. 19.

115. Cf. Schäfer, p. 12; Devoti, *Institutionum Canonicum,* Tomus, I, tit. 9, n. 4 footnote; Butler, *Benedictine Monachism,* p. 19.

116. S. Ambrose, *De Virginibus,* II, 6, 7, 15, 16, 66, 67; Pourrat, Vol. I, p. 144.

117. S. Ambrose, *Epis.* LXIII, c. 66; *Epis.* LXXXII, *Ad eccle. Vercel.* p. 254; *Sermo,* LVI; Spreitzenhofer, pp. 13-17; Bingham, Book VII, 1, 4.

century Italian monasticism remained somewhat amorphous in character and "prone to many of the diseases of hysterical subjectivism."[119] During the following century, information about it is meager. Perhaps it is best described as an eclecticism drawn from *The Lives of the Fathers of the Desert,* the Rules of Macarius, Basil, Serapion, the Institutes and Conferences of Cassian.[120]

Saint Augustine of Hippo (354-430) organized community life among the clergy of his African diocese.[121] Speaking of their manner of living, the illustrious Bishop said: "To no one . . . is it lawful to have anything as his own."[122] He was much grieved because one of his clerics presumed to make a last testament.[123] The practice of Gospel poverty was a requisite condition for membership in his community.[124] Yet these Augustinian clerics did not make a vow of poverty. In a letter the Saint wrote to a convent of nuns, he prescribed that the prospective subjects should surrender their property to the community when they became formal members of it.[125] All property of the members should be common.[126]

118. S. Augustin, *Confessionum,* VIII, 6 (Migne, P. L. XXXII, col. 354 sq.).

119. Spreitzenhofer, pp. 88 sq.; Gasquet, p. 6; Workman, p. 134.

120. Butler, *Benedictine Monachism,* p. 17. During the days of primitive western monasticism several other Rules were composed but their enactments do not warrant special mention here. The Rule of St. Benedict supplanted them all. Cf. *Regula SS. Pauli et Stephani,* c. XXIII (Migne, P. L. LXVI, col. 649 sq.; *Regula Monachorum* of St. Fructuosius, cc. VI, VIII (Migne, LXXXVII, col. 1104 sq.; *Concordia Regularium,* of Benedict Aniane for other Rules (Migne, CIII, col. 1057 sq.).

121. Leclerq, *L'Afrique Chretienne,* Vol. II, pp. 70-77; Steiger, *Periodica,* XIII (1925) p. (88).

122. *Sermo,* CCCLV, c. 11, n. 1 (Migne, P. L. XXXIX, col. 1570); cf. *Epis.* CLVII, *ad Hilarion,* c. 4, n. 39.

123. *Sermo,* CCCLV ut supra.

124. *Sermo,* CCCLVI, n. 14 (Migne, P. L. XXXIX, col. 1579); *ibid.* n. 3 (Migne, P. L. XXXIX, col. 1575); *Sermo,* CCCLV, c. 1, n. 2 (Migne, P. L. XXXIX, col. 1569-1570).

125. *Epis.* CCXI, n. 5 (Migne, P. L. XXXII, col. 960); Thomassinus, Pars I, lib. III, c. XLII, n. 10.

126. *Rule of St. Augustine for Women,* cc. III, IV. Documents have been educed to show that Christian monasticism existed in England before the advent of St. Augustine of Kent. Hadden and Stubbs, *Councils and Ecclesiastical Documents Relating to Great Britain and Ireland,* Vol. I, pp. 113 ff. Weldon, *Chronological Notes,* p. 11, doubts the evidence as being reliable. At least as early as 597 the Benedictine Rule came to England from St. Gregory's monastery

(*b*) *The Rule of St. Benedict*

The Rule [127] of St. Benedict [128] (480-543) [129] was written probably at Monte Cassino[130] towards the end of the Patriarch's life.[131] Although in every respect it can not be called original (it manifests a familiarity with the monastic literature of the time) yet it is so perfectly composed that it has been justly described "a monument of the legislative art, remarkable alike for its completeness, its simplicity and its adaptability to all times." It was destined to produce a revolution rather than a new development in Christian monasticism.

St. Benedict's conception of evangelical poverty was: "We are all children of God, and remaining minors for all eternity. We live in our father's house, the house of God. All the possessions of the monastery are His[132] and He dispenses to us what we need by the hands of the Abbot, His representative. *We are poor not when we are in want of all things and suffer from scarcity but when we have nothing in our possession save what the Abbot has given us or permitted us to keep.* The Abbot is re-

in Rome. Graham, *Mediaeval England,* pp. 346-347; Weldon, pp. 11-13; Gasquet, p. 214; Taunton, *The Black Monks of St. Benedict,* pp. 3-4; Lingard, pp. 182-183; Thompson, p. 4; Hill, *English Monasticism,* p. 113.

127. Linderbauer, *S. Benedicti Regula; Monachorum Herausgegeben und philögish erklärt;* Logeman, *The Rule of St. Benedict,* pp. 1-118; Grutzmacher, *Die Bedeutung Benedhtsvon Nursia,* §4 for its authenticity. For those who follow this Rule, cf. Steiger, *Periodica,* XIII (1925), p. (79) sq.; Wernz, III, p. 269 sq.

128. Tosti, *Della ita di S. Benedetto; Dialogues of St. Gregory the Great,* II; Concerning the historical value of the Diologues consult, Moricca, *Gregori Magni Dialogi,* Libri IV (*Fonti la storia d'Italia,* N. 57); Herwegen, *Der heilige Benedikt;* Schrörs, "Das Charakterbild des heiligen Benedikt von Nursia und seine Quellen," in *Zeitschrift für katholische Theologie,* XLIV (1921) 169-207, challenged the historical value of the Dialogues. St. Hilpich, "Die Quellen zum Charakterbild des heiligen Benedikt," in *Zeitschrift für katholische Theologie,* XLIX (1925), 358-386, offers a worth while reply to Schrörs. Cf. Antonelli, "De Re Monastica in Dialogis S. Gregorii Magni," *Antonianum,* II (1927), 402.

129. Dudden, *Gregory the Great,* pp. 162, 168; Snow, *St. Benedict,* p. 11; Steiger, *Periodica,* XIII (1925), p. (79).

130. De Hemptienne, *L' Ordre de Saint Benedict,* p. 70; Butler, *Benedictine Monachism,* pp. 161-162; Ford, "Benedict of Nursia [probably] (*Cath. Ency.* II, 471); Alston, "The Rule of St. Benedict [probably] (*Cath. Ency.* II, 436).

131. Butler, *Benedictine Monachism,* p. 162.

132. Cf. Doheny, *Church Property,* p. 19.

sponsible to God for both what he refuses and what he gives. Yet each individual should help him to fulfill the role of guardian by reducing his requirements."[133]

St. Benedict deliberately eliminated austerity as it had been understood and practiced heretofore. Besides this negative element he introduced a positive one, viz., the replacement of rivalry in ascetical achievement by the immersion of individualism in community observance.[134] Again his aim seems to have been to keep the bodies of his monks in a healthy condition by means of decent clothing, sufficient food and ample sleep in order that they might be fit for the performance of the Divine Office.[135]

The observance of evangelical poverty was not expressly promised or vowed in the solemn formula used at a monk's Profession. But, when a novice made his Profession, he thoroughly understood what obligations he was assuming as regards the observance of poverty; for the Rule prescribed that candidates be familiarized with the Benedictine mode of life. The profession of stability, however, involved not only perseverance in the monastery until death but also in the observance of the Rule[136] in which, regulation concerning poverty was conspicuous.

---

133. Delatte, *A Commentary on the Rule of St. Benedict,* pp. 248-249; Yet Marmion, *Christ the Ideal of the Monk,* pp. 191-208, merely stresses renunciation of property and dependence on the Abbot for everything. *The Declarations on the Rule of Our Holy Father St. Benedict and the Statutes of the American Cassinese Congregation* (1926), n. 32, in interpreting the founder's ideal for these modern monks state: "Gold watches with or without chains are not allowed under any pretext whatever."

134. Butler, *Historia Lausiaca,* Vol. I, p. 256.

135. "Whereas the Egyptian ascetics reduced the use of food to a minimum, some of them eating but twice or thrice in a week and to whom parched vegetables with salt and oil, three olives and two prunes and a fig were a "sumptuous repast" (Cassian, *Collationes,* viii, 1), St. Benedict prescribed a reasonable amount of food (Chap. XXIX). As to clothing the habits were to be warm and not too old (Chap. LV), which was in great contrast to the Egyptian monk's, as the Abbot Pambo wanted them to be so poor that if left on the road, no one would be tempted to take them (*Apophthegmata,* Migne, P. G. LXV, col. 369). As to sleeping accommodations the Egyptians frequently used a mat or a stone for a pillow, the Abbot John being unable to mention without shame the fact that he found a blanket in a monk's cell (Cassian, *Collationes,* XIX, 6); but Benedict allowed not only a blanket but also a coverlet, a mattress and a pillow to each monk (Chap. LV, Alston, "The Rule of St. Benedict," (*Cath. Ency.* II, 439).

"If he has any property (speaking of the novice to be professed) let him either first bestow it on the poor or by a solemn deed of gift, make it over to the monastery, keeping nothing for himself, as knowing that from this day forward he shall have no power even over his body."[137] When the donation was made to the monastery, the legal formalities required by the civil statutes had to be observed so that the intention of the donor was clearly defined and the support of the law assured, the monastery being thus safeguarded against judiciary procedure for dispossession.[138]

When nobles and people of wealth offered their infants[139] to God as monks, besides the other promises the parents had to make on behalf of the child, they had to: "promise under oath that they will never, either themselves or through an intermediary, or in any way whatever, give him anything or the means of having anything. Or else if they are unwilling to do this, and desire to offer something as an alms to the monastery for their advantage, let them make a donation to the monastery, reserving to themselves, if they so wish the usufruct. And so let every way be blocked that the child may have no expectation, by which he may be misled and perish (which God forbid) as we have learned by experience, may happen."[141]

"The vice of private ownership is to be cut off by the roots. Let no one presume to give or receive anything, without the Abbot's permission, nor to keep anything as their own." "But let them hope to receive all that is necessary from the Abbot of the monastery."[141] "Let all things be common to all. . . . But if anyone be found to indulge in this most baneful vice [private possession] and after one or two admonitions does not amend, let him be subjected to correction.[142] Slovenliness or negligence

136. Cf. Martene, *Commentarius in Regulam S. Patris Benedicti,* ad caput LVIII, following the most ancient commentators on the Rule.

137. Chapter LVIII.

138. Delatte, p. 404.

139. Cf. Blair, *The Rule of St. Benedict,* p. 205.

140. Chapter LIX.

141. "Quanta severitate haec ordinatio servabatur exempla quaedam Dialogorum clare demonstrat. (II, 19), S. Benedictus severe reprehendit monachum qui a sanctimonialibus feminis contra praeceptum mappulas acceperat." Chapter LIV; cf. Antonelli, *Antonianum,* II (1927), 430.

142. Chapter XXXIII; Cf. Chapters LIV, LV and LVIII; vide

in the use of monastic property was an offence liable to the discipline of the Rule.

(c) *The Canons Regular*

There are not wanting authors of weight claiming an Apostolic origin for this form of the Religious Life.[143] Caesar Benvenuti educes much testimony to prove that from the beginning of the Church, till the twelfth century, there had always been the practice of clerics living together after the example of the Apostles.[144] Pope Benedict XII in his Preface to the Constitutions of the Canons Regular confirms this opinion.[145] Moreover, when a controversy arose between the Canons and the Monks, with regard to precedence, the question was settled by Pius V in favor of the Canons on account of their Apostolic origin.[146] It is interesting to note also that Code of Canon Law following the practice based on the decision of Pius V declares that the Canons have the same right today.[147]

The clergy serving in large churches and living in the same household were from ancient times known as Canons.[148] The "common life" revived by Eusebius of Vercelli and St. Augustine of Hippo spread throughout Europe.[149] In 763 the Bishop of Metz, Chrodegang, composed a Rule for the clergy living with him.[150] This Rule did not prohibit clerics from retaining the property they

---

Coulton, *Five Centuries of Religion,* Vol. I, p. 214; Women obtained Rules based on the Rules for men. Cf. Butler, *Benedictine Monachism,* p. 335; *La Vraye Regle de S. Benoist* and the Constitutions bearing on the chapters mentioned in connection with the Rule for men. Infantile Professions were in later years abolished and in recent years poverty came to be expressly vowed. Cf. Helyot, Vol. V, p. 17; VI, 307-397; *Kirchenlexicon,* II, p. 335.

143. Allaria, "Canons and Canoneses Regular" (*Cath. Ency.,* III, 389-390); Natalis, *Historia Ecclesiastica,* T. VII, c. 7, n. 7, p. 163; De Buck-Tinnebroeck, pp. 32 sq.

144. Allaria, 1 c.; cf. Zaplotnik, *De Vicariis Foraniis,* p. 2.

145. *Ad Decorem Ecclesiæ,* 15 maii 1339 (*Bul. Rom.* IV, p. 425).

146. Allaria, 1. c.

147. Canon 491 § 1.

148. Gasquet, p. 222; cf. Humphrey, *Elements of Religious Life,* p. 329 for origin of term "Canon"; Currier, 165.

149. Cf. *Constitutiones Canonicorum Regularium Congregationis Sanctae Crucis Collimbriensis,* P. L., 1; Hughes, *Irish Ecclesiastical Record,* XIX (1922) 131.

150. *Rule of Chrodegang;* Mansi, *Sacrorum Concilliorum Nova et Amplissima Collectio,* XIV, 313 sq.; Harduin, *Acta Concilliorum, IV,* 1181.

had possessed before they became clerics nor from acquiring the free will offerings that might be extended to them.[151] In 1059, a Roman Synod enacted that clerics living a community life must hold in common all that comes to them from their churches.[152]

About this time there was composed the so-called *Rule of St. Augustine*.[153] It embodied the teachings of the Saint as revealed in his writings.[154] Regulating the observance of evangelical poverty we find the prescription: "Let no one call anything his own but all things be common among you."[155] However, it was the mind of the legislator that distinctions should be made in the manner of treating individuals for we read: "Let food and clothing be distributed to each by the Superior but not equally to all because not all are of the same constitution, but to each according to his need."[156] Persons who had been accustomed to the better things in life and who would find the ordinary Religious food, clothing and bedding injurious to their constitutions could have allowances made for them in such things.[157]

From the eleventh century many Orders of Canons arose,[158] all following the Rule of St. Augustine but each having its own compilation of Constitutions. Benedict XII on May 15th, 1339, issued a Papal Constitution, *Ad decorem Ecclesiae,* also known as the *Constitutio totius Ordinis Canonicorum Regularium Ordinis S. Augustini.* The only legislation to be found here relative to the observance of poverty, is the action to be taken against those guilty of peculia practices. The Pope enumerates some of the ways in which peculia had been obtained. He then enacts, that those having peculium, publicly or secretly, if they are specially and "nominatim" admonished by the Superior, they must within a month restore to the com-

151. Cf. Workman, p. 257.

152. S. Lateran, c. 4 (Mansi, XIX, 897-898); Natalis, Vol. VII, c. 7, art. 7, p. 163 sq.

153. Migne, P. L. XXXII, col. 1381 sq.; cf. *Cath Ency.,* Index Volume, XVI, pp. 141-142, 290 for Institutes using the Augustinian Rule.

154. *Epis.* CCXI; *Sermo,* CCCLV et CCCLVI.

155. Chap. III.

156. Chap. IV.

157. Chap. VIII.

158. Cf. Steiger, *Periodica,* XIII (1925), pp. (89)-(98); David, pp. 275-276.

mon fund the property they had been retaining as their own, under penalty of being "ipso facto" inhabile to the office of prior or administrator, or to a benefice. Superiors were authorized to dispense such delinquents when they reformed and restored the peculia. Each year at the annual chapter Superiors were to warn Religious having peculia to place it in the common fund.[159]

(*d*) *The Mendicant Friars*

At the beginning of the thirteenth century there was firmly established among Religious, a new practice relative to evangelical poverty, viz. inability to possess property even in common. The Benedictine and Augustinian, as well as the other Institutes which had adopted their Rules, practiced the evangelical counsel of poverty by the personal renunciation of property on the part of individuals; the Institutes, as corporate entities, had always possessed property in common.[160] In the course of time the older Institutes had become enormously wealthy and had assumed an important civil,[161] political,[162] and social[163] status in Europe.[164] "As a result of this state of affairs, the complaints against the enormous wealth of

---

159. *Bul. Rom.*, IV, p. 458; Cf. cc. 4, 5, X, *de statu monach. et canon reg.*, III, 35; Heimbucher, I, 391 sq.;

160. S. Bonaventuræ, *De Paupertate Evangelica,* q. 2, art. 2, Opera Omnia, V. 136.

161. Cf. Coulton, II, pp. 34-65.

162. Cf. Mabillon, *Annales Ordinis S. Benedicti,* Vol. V, p. 555; VI, 124; Dugdale-Caley, *Monasticon Anglicanum,* Vol. IV, p. 28 b; for some examples; cf. Coulton, II, pp. 34 sq.

163. Cf. Coulton, II, pp. 1, 18-33.

164a. From the tenth century on, there had been several noteworthy attempts on the part of reformers to bring these Religious Institutes back to the state of poverty and simplicity which would be more conformable to their profession as Religious. The most powerful effort was that conducted by the Cistercians in the twelfth century. This reform aimed directly at eliminating extravagance in the household, and insisted on personal labor, contrary to the prevailing system of renting lands to tenant. But this system of personal management, which meant cheap labor and as a natural consequence high profits, again led to the rapid enrichment of the Institutes. (Cf. Hoffman, *Das Konverseninstitut des Zisterzienserordens,* p. 27; Felder, *The Ideals of St. Francis,* pp. 94-95.)

164b. Berthold von Regenburg, *Predigen* (ed, Pfeiffer-Strohl) Vol. I, pp. 93, 393); De Vitry, *Historia Occidentalis* (ed. 1596), c. 5, pp. 272 sq.; Desiderius, *De Miraculs S. Benedicti,* in Bibli. Max. Patrum, Lugd. Vol. XVIII, pp. 839 sq.; Davison, *Some Forerunners of St. Francis of Assisi,* p. 13; Felder, p. 95.

the Religious and the feudal clergy became louder and more vehement in the twelfth century." In 1173, Peter Waldes nobly began his attempt to reform the practice of evangelical poverty among the Religious.[165] After a decade of nearly futile activity, as an advocate of total renunciation of property[166] his movement degenerated into heresy.[167]

The Franciscans

St. Francis of Assisi, profoundly impressed by the texts, "If thou wilt be perfect, go sell what thou hast and give it to the poor, and thou shalt have treasure in Heaven and come follow Me,"[168] "Do not possess gold or silver or money in your purses,"[169] understood these words literally and forthwith based his life on them.[170] Companions joined him in his practice of evangelical poverty,[171] and on April 16, 1209, the Franciscan Order was founded.[172] Innocent III orally approved the Order in the same year.

---

165. *Chronicon Laudunense*, (*Monumenta Germanica Historica*, Vol. XXXVI, p. 447); Etinenne de Bourbon, *Anecdotes Historiques* (1877), pp. 290 sq.; Sabatier-Houghton, *Life of St. Francis of Assisi*, pp. 37-39; Weber, "Waldenses," (*Cath. Ency.*, XV, n. 258), Coulton, II, pp. 109-11.

166. Müller, *Die Waldenser und ihre einzelne Gruppen*, p. 7 ff.

167. The Waldenses who returned to the Church, i.e., the "Catholic Poor Men" of France and the re-united Lombards of Italy, retained the principle of absolute poverty after their conversion (Pierson, *Die katholischen Armen*, pp. 173-176, Felder, p. 453), but had little influence and disappeared after a few years. There were other precursors of St. Francis, especially the Humiliati, who in some measure prepared the way for his coming. Cf. Berliere, *Revue Benedictine*, XXVII (1911), 413, where is redacted the study of L. Zanoni *Gli Hulmiliati;* Rudge, "Humiliati" [*Cath. Ency.*, VII, p. 542]; Coulton, II, pp. 107-133; cf. Van Den Borne, *Die Anfänge des Franziskanischen Dritten Ordens* [Franziskanische Studien, Beiheft VIII, p. 67]; Reinmann, *The Third Order Secular of St. Francis*, pp. 17-20).

168. Matt. XIX, 23.

169. Matt. X, 9.

170. Eduadus Alenconiensis, Thomas de Celano, *St. Francisci Assisiensis Vita et Miracula*, Legenda II, n. 12; Thomas de Celano, *Tractatus Primus super Vitam Sancti Francisci de Assisii* (Rosedale version), pp. 36-47; Ferraris, *Prompta Bibliotheca, Supplementum*, p. 393; Robinson, "St. Francis of Assisi," (*Cath. Ency.*, VI, 222); Greiner, *The Asceticism of St. Francis*, p. 14; Cuthbert, *Life of St. Francis*, pp. 41, 49, 55, 135 for further details; Felder, 97 sq.

171. Cf. *Testamentum*, in Opuscula S. Patris Francisci Assisiensis (Böhmer, p. 37; Lemmens, 79); Feder, 97-98; 121-122.

The First Order consists of three separate bodies, the Friars Minor, the Conventuals, and the Capuchins. All three observe the so-called Second Rule of St. Francis,[173] yet each body has its own set of Constitutions which differentiate their mode of life.

The ideal of St. Francis relative to evangelical poverty may be tersely described: *"total renunciation of earthly things, and the greatest moderation in the use of these things."*[174] The renunciation of property, he demanded absolutely and unconditionally; to possess anything in person or in common, was incompatible with his ideal." The moderation in the use of things was to be governed by the conditions under which the individual Franciscan as well as the Order, were to perform their functions.[175]

The sixth chapter of the Rule (1223) establishes: "The brethren shall appropriate to themselves neither a house nor place nor anything. . . . And as pilgrims and strangers in this world . . . let them go confidently for alms."[176] Chapter IV forbade the Friars to receive coins or money, either themselves or through an interposed person.[177] By virtue of this legislation: "His subjects could not have in common or in particular, any right,

---

172. Mandic, *De Protoregula Ordinis Fratrum Monorum,* p. 22; Steck, *Glories of the Franciscan Order,* p. 1.

173. Approved by Honorius III, bulla *"Solet annuere,"* 29 nov. 1223, (*Bullarium Franciscanum,* I, 15); Cf. Sabatier, p. 252 ff.

174. Felder, p. 94.

175. Felder, pp. 118-119. "In consequence of the manifold, inevitable needs that arose, a development in this regard could not be avoided even during the life time of the Saint and more so in later years."

176. Translation from Ilg, *An Explanation of the Rules of the Friars Minor,* p. 8; Cf. Felder, pp. 142 ff.

177. The new status of money achieved tremendous importance about the time Francis began his Order. Poets and preachers of the thirteenth century depict in somber colors the evil results of the new system of economics which had just arisen, (Felder, pp. 120-121); Scheel, *Der Begriff des Geldes in seiner historisch-ökonomischen Entwicklung,* in *Jahrbücher für Nationalökonomie und Statistik,* VI, (1866), 12-29; Lotsz, *Die Lehre vom Ursprung des Geldes,* o. c. LXII (1894), 337-359; Michael, *Geschichte des deutschen Volkes seit dem dreizehnten Jährhundert bis zum Ausgang des Mittealters,* I, pp. 136-144; Felder, p. 457; Thomas de Celano, II, n. 65; cf. Nicholas III, const. *Exiit qui seminat,* 15 aug. 1278, art. VI (*Monumenta Selecta,* p. 25); Innocent XI (const. *Solicitudo,* 20 nov. 1679, n. 2 (*Monumenta Selecta,* p. 60); declared that the *civil* handling of money as well as the *physical* handling was prohibited; Felder, pp. 121 ff.

dominion, usufruct, right of use, to any temporal thing but only the simple actual use, always dependent on the free will of the owner conceding the use of the thing, which is revocable at pleasure."[178] But of course the individual was to be furnished with the use of whatever was necessary, for food, clothing, the divine worship and study.[179]

In 1226 the Friars on the mission in Morocco received a dispensation from the Holy See permitting them to have money to use, as long as the necessity of such a practice obtained.[180] In the course of the centuries similar dispensations became more frequent on account of the constantly increasing commercial use of money.[181] In September of the year 1230, a papal authentic interpretation was given to this Order making possible the appointment of a "nuntius" who could receive money from benefactors and in the latter's name spend it in behalf of the Friars or confide it to a spiritual friend for imminent wants.[182] Innocent IV allowed the Friars to have recourse to this "nuntius" not only for necessities but for things useful and convenient.[183] This same Bull declared that all things in the use of the Friars belonged to the Holy See unless the donor reserved the ownership to himself. The office of procurator or Apostolic Syndic was instituted in 1247.[184]. It

---

178. Kazenberger, *The Book of Life or a Brief Literal Exposition of the Holy Rule of the Seraphic Father, St. Francis,* p. 154; Cf. Nicholas III, const. *Exiit qui seminat,* 14 aug. 1279, art. II, n. 3, (*Monumenta Selecta,* p. 30).

179. Nicholas III const. *Exiit qui seminat,* 14 aug. 1279, art. III, n. 5 (*Monumenta Selecta,* p. 22; c. 3, *de verb. signif.* V, 12 in. VI°).

180. Honorius III, bulla, *Ex parte vestra,* 17 martii 1226 (*Bul. Rom.* III, pp. 418-419; *Bul. Franc.* I, 26, 25). The Dominicans under similar circumstances received a similar dispensation.

181. Felder, p. 129. "Today this commercial use has become so common and so general that the Order simply could not exist nor carry on its work properly without such dispensation."

182. Greg. IX, bulla, *Quo elongati* (*Bul. Franc.* I, 68); Cf. Fagnanus, *Commentaria in Librum Decretalium,* II, de probat. c. in praesentia; Oliger, "Rule of St. Francis" (*Cath. Ency.,* VI, 212).

183. Bulla, *Ordinem vestrum,* 14 nov. 1245 (*Bul. Franc,* I, 400; *Bul. Rom.,* III, pp. 520-521); cf. Clem. V, bulla, *Exivi de paradiso,* 6 maii 1312, art VII, n. 2 (*Monumenta Selecta,* p. 49; c. 1, *de verb. signif.,* V, 11, *in Clem.*).

184. Innocent IV, bulla, *Quanto studiosius,* 19 aug. 1247 (*Bul. Franc.* I, 487).

was the Syndic's duty to act in the name of the Holy See as the civil administrator of the property in the use of the Friars. Martin IV greatly extended the powers of this agent, especially in regard to lawsuits.[185]

In 1260, during the Generalate of Saint Bonaventure, an express vow of poverty was annexed to the Franciscan formula of profession. This is the first record we have of poverty being expressly vowed (in the modern sense of the term) by Religious.

John XXII, the noted canonist, declared that since according to Roman Law, in many things, the use could not be separated from the property, he renounced the proprietorship of goods on the part of the Holy See and forbade the appointment of an Apostolic Syndic.[186] The former state of affairs was restored to the Observants by Martin V in 1438.[187]

The Conventuals

Although until 1517, those who professed the Rule of St. Francis constituted but one body, yet within the Order, as is well known, there had been, even from the days of the Founder, a division of spirit due to the desire of some to mitigate the rigor of poverty.[188] As the years rolled on, the line of demarkation, between those who wished for dispensation and the Observants, grew more apparent. So it was by no means a total surprise when Tridentine legislation these Religious owned property, as an Institute.[191] In 1568, Pius V endeavored to impose on this Order a stricter observance of poverty and the "common life." He perpetually deprived these Leo X constituted the former into a separate Institute,[189] known as the Conventuals.[190]

---

185. Bulla, *Exultantes in Domino,* 18 ian. 1283 (*Bul. Franc,* III, 501); cf. c. 3, *de verb. signif.* V, 12, in VI°; c. 1, *de verb. signif.* V, 11, *in Clem.;* cf. Ehrle, *Archiv. für Litteratur- und Kirchengeschichte,* VI, 1890) 55.

186. Bulla, *Ad conditorem canonum,* 8 dec. 1322 (*Bul. Franc,* V, 233); cf. Bihl, "Fraticelli" (*Cath. Ency.,* VI, 247); Lombardi, *Institutiones Iuris Canonici Privati,* Vol. I, p. 431, declares that the opinion of John XXII about the separability of dominion and the use of things, as held by this illustrious canonist, was certainly the less probable opinion in these matters.

187. *Amabiles fructus,* I nov. 1428 (*Bul. Franc.* VII, 712).

188. Cf. Robinson, "Conventuals," (*Cath. Ency. IV,* 345).

189. Bulla, *Ite et vos,* 29 maii 1517 (*Bul. Rom.,* V, n. 27, p. 692);

From the concessions of the Roman Pontiffs and the Trindentine legislation these Religious owned property, as an Institute.[191] In 1568, Pius V endeavored to impose on this Order a stricter observance of poverty and the "common life." He perpetually deprived these Religious, as individuals, of the dominion, use and usufruct, as well as the private detention, of all property, movable and immovable, no matter how it had been acquired. Furthermore, he declared all privileges, dispensations, permissions and indults for private gardens, houses, money and other things, even if given because of old age, sickness, assistance of parents, dowers for sisters, etc., even if given by previous Pontiffs, even if granted "ex certa scientia," etc., were expressly revoked and were to have no further effect. He commanded the Superiors under holy obedience to have all the aforesaid things made "common property" and henceforth everything was to be "common" and indivisible, even though an established custom had previously obtained to the contrary. All money, even that acquired "intuitu personae," was to be brought to the Superior within twenty-four hours.[192] The Superiors of the Order immediately enacted statutes in conformity with the will of the Pope and these were approved papally in July of the same year.[193] Urban VIII, promulgated in 1628, a set of newly formed Constitutions known as "Constitutiones Urbanae Ordinis Fratrum Minorum S. F. Conventualium," which were observed down to the formulation of the Code.[194]

By their profession, the Conventuals vow to observe the Rule of St. Francis in accordance with the Urban Constitutions. "It would therefore be no less false than

---

Bihr, "Friars Minor, Order of" (*Cath. Ency.*, VI, 284), claims that John XXII introduced Conventualism, or "community of goods" into the Franciscan Order.

190. For the origin of the term Conventuals, cf. Robinson, "Conventuals" (*Cath. Ency.*, IV, 344-345).

191. The Council (Sess. XXV, *de regularibus*, c. 3) declared that all Institutes, except the Friars Minor and the Capuchins, could have property in common.

192. Bulla, *Ad extirpandos cupidæ*, 8 iun, 1568 (*Bul. Rom.*, VII, n. 27, pp. 676-678).

193. Pius V, *Illa nos cura*, 3 iulii 1568 (*Bul. Rom.*, VII, n. 104, p. 693).

194. Cf. Chapters IV, t. 2 and VI, t. 1 (for the administration of goods).

unjust to regard the Conventuals as less observant of the obligations contracted by their profession than the Friars Minor and Capuchins, since they are not bound by either of the latter."[195]

The Capuchins

Another division in the ranks of the Franciscans occurred in 1528 when the Capuchins were papally recognized as a separate organization within the Order.[196] The Capuchins drafted a set of regulations, known as the *"Constitutiones Albanicae."* Herein it was declared that the "proprietorships (of the houses) must always be vested in the municipality or the donor, who may turn the Friars out at will, etc." They were permitted to receive food as alms," however, "they were never to lay in a store of food but to depend on daily alms. At the utmost, they might receive sufficient food to last three days and rarely for a week." Concerning all property, it was established: "No other Syndic shall there be for us save Christ, our Lord, and our procurator and protector shall be the most blessed Virgin, Mother of God: and our deputy shall be our Blessed Father Francis: but all other procurators, we absolutely reject."[197]

Poor Clares

The date of the foundation of the Poor Clares or Second order of St. Francis is considered to be March 18, 1212.[198] Francis gave to Clare a "Form of Life."[199] Yet from the earliest days of this Institute, the houses in different places did not always follow the same Rule.[200] St. Clare received her muchly desired "Privilegium Paupertatis" a few days before her death. Herein it was enacted: "Since, therefore, you have asked for it, we confirm by

195. Robinson, "Conventuals" (*Cath. Ency.*, IV, 345).

196. Clem. VII, bulla, *Religionis zelus*, 3 iui, 1528 (*Bul. Rom.*, VI, p. 113 sq.) ; Paul. III, *Exponi nobis*, 25 aug. 1536 (*Bul. Rom.*, VI, p. 239). As to whether or not the problem of poverty occasioned the separation of the Capuchins, cf. Hopzapfel, *Geschichte des Franziskanerordens*, p. 613; Wadding, *Annales Minorum*, ad an. 1525, XI, 12,

197. Cuthbert, "Capuchin" (*Cath. Ency.*, III, 321).

198. Robinson, *Rule of St. Clare*, p. 8.

199. *Opuscula Sancti Patris Francisci* (1904), p. 75; Robinson, *The Writings of St. Francis* (1906), p. 77.

200. Oliger, *Archivum Franciscanum Historicum*, V (1912), 416; Robinson, p. 26; Coulton, II, pp. 159 ff.

Apostolic favor your resolution of the loftiest poverty and by the authority of these present letters grant that you may not be constrained by anyone to receive possessions."[201] Innocent IV confirmed the legislation of the Poor Clares in 1253.[202] The Rules for these women contained practically the same observance of poverty as had been given to the men; the chief exception was that the nuns were permitted to have enough land for the necessities of their convent.[203] Later, Pope Urban IV approved of a mitigated Rule for some of these nuns.[204] According to this Rule the Order was permitted to receive, have and retain revenues and property in common.[205] Individuals, of course, like other Religious at this time, were obliged to live "sine proprio."[206]

The Third Order Regular

As early as the thirteenth century there was a tendency among some of the secular Tertiaries to unite in community life.[207] At first no vows were professed. Towards the close of the fourteenth century some professed a solemn vow of obedience.[208] The Congregations of Tertiaries in Belgium and the Netherlands were allowed by Boniface IX to profess the solemn vows of chastity and obedience. It is to be noted that they did not solemnly profess poverty. Clerics could hold their benefices with the permission of their Superiors, *"cum Regula dicti Tertii Ordinis abdicationem proprietatis non contineat."*[209] In order to remove the divergency of Rules,

---

201. Robinson, "Clare of Assissi," (*Cath. Ency.*, IV, 5).
202. Const. *Solet annuere,* 9 aug. 1253 (*Bul. Rom.*, III, p. 570 sq.).
203. Chapters II, IV, VIII.
204. Const. *Beata Clara,* 18 oct. 1264, (*Bul. Rom.*, III, pp. 718 sq.).
205. Chapter XXI.
206. Chapter I.
207. Reinmann, p. 71.
208. Reinman, p. 71; Wadding, *Annales Minorum,* ad. an. 1397, IX, n. 31, p. 444; ad an. 1435, X, n. 18, p. 238 sq. The first known Tertiary nuns were founded at Foligno in 1397. (Jacobili, *Vita della B. Angelina*); Benedict XIII, bulla, *Paternæ Sedis Apostolicæ,* 10 dec. 1725 § 1 (*Bul. Rom.*, XXII, p. 296); cf. *Etudes Franciscaines,* XXV, p. 296.
209. Hilarius Parisiensis, *Liber Tertii Ordinis, S. Francisci Assisinsis,* p. 56; Boniface, IX, bulla. *His quae divini,* 18 ian, 1401

among the Tertiaries living in community and the practices contingent on such diversity,[210] on January 20, 1521, Leo X formally erected them into a Religious Institute. The Bull of erection contained a Rule which was adaptable to both men and women.[211] Chapter III of this Rule required the profession of a solemn vow of poverty. Pius V in 1568 enacted that these Religious should not have property even under pretext of privilege, dispensation, apostolic permission or even an established custom against the vow or from any other cause. Whatever is received privately or even "intutitu personae" must be common and indivisible to all the Religious. Money or anything else, if concealed from the Superior, is to be considered as theft and punished as such.[212]

The Dominicans

In 1203, Dominic Guzman first conceived his idea of founding a Religious Institute. Passing through Toulouse, he was greatly affected by the havoc the Albigensian heresy was working there. From this sight there arose the inspiration to combat heresy and to spread the Gospel to the ends of the world by preaching.[213] On December 22, 1216, he obtained formal approbation from the Holy See for his Order.[214] And as he had once been a Canon

(Wadding, *Annales Minorum,* ad. an. 1397, IX, n. 44, pp. 462 sq.); Reinmann, p. 72.

210. Reinman, p. 72; Alijardi, CpR, II (1921), 382; Maroto, CpR, VIII (1927), 421, says that in 1413 Tertiaries in Flanders made three Solemn Vows.

211. Leo X, bulla, *Intera caetera,* 20 ian. 1521 (*Seraphicæ Legislationis Textus Originales,* pp. 287-297); cf. Holzapfel, *Manuale historiae Ordinis Fratrum Minorum,* § 125; cf. the new Rule for Franciscan Tertiaries, Pii XI, const. *Rerum condicio,* 4 oct. 1927 (AAS, XIX [1927], 361-367); *Homeletic Monthly,* XXVIII (1928), pp. 424-429.

212. Pius V, *Ea est.* 3 iulii 1568 (*Bul. Rom.,* VII, p. 681). For an account of this branch of the Franciscans after the Council of Trent, consult Maroto, *Annotationes,* CpR, VIII (1927), 423-424; Alijarde, *Super Tertio Ordine Regulari S. Francisci,* CpR, II (1921), 382, III (1922), 16-20.

213. Cf. O'Connor, "St. Dominic" (*Cath Ency.,* V, 108).

214. Honorius III, bulla, *Religiosam vitam* (*Bul. Rom.* III, pp. 309-310).

215. Denifle, *Die Konstitutionen des Predigerordens vom Järre* 1228 (*Archiv für Litteratur- und Kirchengeschichte,* I (1885), 172

Regular, it was not surprising that he adopted the Augustinian Rule and drew much from the Premontre Constitutions for his own.[215]

The poverty of the Dominicans is as original as that of the Franciscans.[216] Francis chose his form of poverty for the sake of his salvation and that he might imitate in his humble way his Divine Master.[217] Dominic and his Order chose poverty that being freed from the care attendant on having possessions, he and his companions might enjoy greater freedom in the pursuit of study and preaching so that their efforts in preaching might be more effective.[218] The Dominicans adopted their poverty not from a love of poverty but for the sake of the Apostolate.[219]

From the beginning, St. Dominic had resolved to eliminate all appearance of luxury as an aid to the preaching of the Catholic Faith.[220] The value of such an appearance for the work he intended to accomplish had been branded into his memory from the time when he had beheld at Languedoc the poor results of the missionaries against the efforts of the Albigensian leaders with their rigorous poverty. Yet it was a poverty similar to the Canons of Premontre that was practiced by the Dominicans up till the First General Chapter in 1220.[221]

At Bologna in the May of 1220 the Dominican Order

---

sq.); Barker, *The Dominican Order and Convocation,* p. 11; Steiger, *Periodica,* XIII (1925), p. (99); Iwiens, *Les Freres Precheurs,* p. 17.

216. Cf. Hauck, *Kirchengeschichte Deutschlands,* IV, 387.

217. We must not forget, however, that Francis and his companions renounced all vain things of this world in order to scatter the seed of the word of God everywhere. But this was not the primary idea behind the form of poverty among the Franciscans. (Felder, p. 153).

218. Denifle, *Die Konstitutionen des Predigerordens vom Jahre* 1228 (*Archiv für Litteratur- und Kirchengeschichte,* I [1885], 182); Barker, p. 11.

219. Lambermond, *Der Armutsgedanke des Hl. Dominikus und seines Ordens,* p. 10; Felder, p. 154.

220. Jordan, *Legend. B. Dominici* (*Scriptores Ordinis Praedicatorum* ed. Quetif-Echard, I, 5); De Bourbon, *Anecdotes Historiques,* 79, n. 83; 213, n. 251, Felder, p. 452.

221. As to whether and how far Francis influenced Dominic in the matter of making the Dominican Order incapable of corporate ownership, there is much dispute. It has been said by some that shortly after 1216 when the two founders met in Rome, Dominic decided to have his Order become like the Franciscans. (Cf. Sabatier,

became incapable of owning property even in common. But this poverty was to be only a means to an end and therefore of relative value to the Institute, viz. in so far as it proved an aid towards the conversion of heretics and the preaching of the Gospel. The same conception that Dominic had in this matter was shared by his followers in the thirteenth century as may be seen mirrored in the decrees of the Chapters and the teaching of St. Thomas.

As a result of this complete poverty, in an Order that had dedicated itself to study and preaching rather than to manual labor, begging became a necessity. In the decades following the introduction of the extreme poverty it is noteworthy that many convents strove to acquire property, in spite of the repeated interdicts of General and Provincial Chapters. The reason for this is not hard to discover. Too many mendicant associations had sprung up, begging had fallen into disrepute and as a result the income of the convents was insufficient. It seems that as early as 1244 certain convents owned gardens and other lands in such quantity that an effort had been made to exact tithes from them.[222] The fact that the General Chapters of 1240 and 1242 prohibited changing the General Statutes of the Order woud indicate the hidden tendency towards a modification.[223] Clement IV in a Bull

---

Speculum perfectionis, pp. 75-77; Sabatier-Houghton, p. 219; Felder, p. 452; Tout, *The Political History of England,* 1261-1377, p. 84; Legenda II, pp. 280-282, in Alenconiensis, Thomas de Celano, *S. Francisci Assiensis, Vita et Miracula.* Others say that the incentive to the resolution came from Francis. (Ehrle, *Die Briefsammlung des F. Angelus de Clareno,* in: *Archiv für Litteratur- und Kirchengeschichte,* I [1885], 559). According to Altauer, Francis did not meet Dominic until after 1218 and hence he would not be influenced directly and personally by St. Francis in the change he made. ("Die Armutsidee des) Hl. Dominikus," *Theologie und Glaube,* XI [1919], 405-417); "Die Beziehungen des Hl. Dominikus zum Hl. Franziskus," (*Franziskanische Studien,* IX [1922], 1-28); Lambermond argues well that it can not be claimed from the meeting of the two saints that Dominic got his ideal from Francis ("Der Armutsgedanke," pp. 19-21). The elements of Dominic's idea were derived from the spirit of the times, the influence of Hugolinus, the Albigensian experiences and the desire to be free from the care of much property, so that his Order could devote itself the more to study, preaching and the Apostolate.

222. Innocent IV, bulla, *Qui Deum,* 3 feb. 1244, (*Bull. Ord. Praed.,* I, p. 131); Lambermond, pp. 76-77.

223. Mandonnet, "Order of Preachers" (*Cath. Ency.,* XII, p. 359).

of February 12, 1266, granted the Friars the right to acquire such inheritances as they would have a right to, had they lived in the world. These they could sell or keep as they saw fit.[224] After 1270, at the insistence of third parties, various Bulls were issued setting bounds to the right to beg, and in other ways, the income of the Order was lessened. These Bulls were of very great importance in the removal of the practice of complete poverty in the Order, as they forced it to look for other sources of income, viz. to acquire properties sufficient to support the Order.[225] Mendicancy having become detrimental to the primary purpose of the Order, it had to give way officially to moderate ownership in common, because ownership, under the circumstances, was of greater value for the one great purpose of the Order: "The Salvation of Souls through teaching and preaching."[226] Martin V partially removed the legal impediment to corporate ownership in 1425 and finally Sixtus V, by papal Constitutions of July 1, 1475, and April 13, 1477, entirely removed the capacity to own property in common.[227] "This was one of the causes that quickened the vitality of the Order in the sixteenth century."[228]

It is not without interest to note in this Order the progress of the practice of evangelical poverty. In an Institute which was founded for the refutation and conversion of heretics and the preaching of the Gospel, the use of books was of prime importance. From the very nature of the extreme poverty which was practiced after 1220, there arose the necessity of relying on friends for the books and the other necessities.[229] From the Acts of

---

224. Cf. Lambermond, p. 78 (4); Clement IV, bulla, *Obtenti Divini Nominis,* 12 febr. 1286 (*Bull. Ord. Praed.,* I, p. 470).

225. Cf. Lambermond, p. 81. At the time of the IV Lateran Council a rumor had spread that Gregory X had granted to the Friars Minor and Preachers the right to have property. Ehrle (*Archiv. für Litteratur- und Kirchengeschichte,* II [1886], pp. 301-302).

226. Lambermond, p. 98.

227. Sixtus IV, bulla, *Considcrantes* (*Bull. Ord. Praed.* III, p. 528); Sixtus IV, *Nuper per* (*Bull. Ord. Praed.,* III, p. 550); Goyeneche, *Cours Elementaire de Droit Canonique,* pp. 122 sq. Mortier, *Histoire des Maitres Generaux de l'Ordre des Freres Precheurs,* IV, 495.

228. Mandonnet (*Cath. Ency.,* XII, p. 359).

229. Lambermond, pp. 47, 52.

the General Chapters it is learned that at an early date the Friars could be given permission to receive a limited amount of money,[230] but under extraordinary conditions the presumed permission of the Superior was sufficient for the mere acceptance of the gifts.[231] The primary purpose for which the money was to be spent was the purchase of books.[232] Books could be taken from one house to another in case of transfer.[233] If a Friar was sent from one Province to another for the sake of teaching, he could take his library with him; but if a Religious left the Province to assume an administrative office, he could take with him only a copy of the Bible and his Breviary.[234] When presents of money were accepted they should not be retained for a long time in the possession of the individual but were to be placed on deposit or spent as soon as possible for the purpose for which it had been allowed.[235] The purchase of clothing was forbidden as this necessity was to be obtained from the common supply.[236] In order to safeguard the deposits of money for the individuals, strict regulations were made.[237] Everyone had to render an account of the expenditure of the money he had received; the private to the Conventual Prior, the Conventual Prior to the Prior Provincial, or Visitator, the Prior Provincial to the definitors of the Provincial Chapter and the Master General to the Definitors of the General Chapter. This account could be demanded once or many times a year.[238] Nor were students at the universities exempt from this accounting, for they had to submit their report to the Provincial Prior;[239] it was understood that the money allowed to these students was to be spent for theological books; permission should be specially asked to use the money for other things.[240] The Friars of those days being mortals, it is not astounding when we learn

230. *Acta Capitulorum Generalium Ordinis Praedicatorum,* I, p. 154.
231. *Ibid,* p. 186.
232. *Ibid,* p. 153.
233. Lambermond, p. 50.
234. *Acta Capitularum Generalia,* p. 14; cf. pp. 19, 22, 212, 216.
235. *Ibid.,* p. 256; cf. etiam pp. 8, 197, 223.
236. *Ibid.,* p. 92; cf. 253.
237. *Ibid.,* p. 42; cf. pp. 52, 58, 138, 191, 224, 273.
238. *Ibid.,* p. 108; cf. etiam, 32, 114, 118, 130, 154, 182, 186.
239. *Ibid.,* p. 82.
240. *Ibid.,* p. 169; cf. p. 268.

that the General Chapter found occasion to admonish the priors and visitators to secure the observance of previous Constitutions about individuals carrying money.[241] Property of externs was not to be held on deposit for them, except in the case of books and ecclesiastical "paramentorum.[242]

The knowledge of how poverty was observed in the first century of the existence of the Dominican Order enables us to appreciate better the practices obtaining among these Friars in days nearer to our own time. The Constitutions of 1886, which were of legislative value even to the promulgation of the Code, declared that Superiors could tolerate peculium only with these restrictions: The peculium must be had with at least the implicit permission of the Superior and dependent on his will; the amount must be moderate in quantity relative to the quality of persons, places and times; excessive deposits, not in accord with the state of poverty are to be incorporated in the common fund; it is to be expended with at least the implicit permission of the Superior and used for laudable purposes; moreover, it must be kept on deposit with the convent, except minor sums which are to be spent in a brief time; it must be really on deposit and not merely on paper; special stress is laid on the prohibition of keeping peculum with seculars.[243]

Dominican Nuns

The Second Order of St. Dominic was founded at Prouille in 1206.[244] On March 4, 1218, the Institute was papally approved by Honorius III.[245] The Augustinian Rule for women was to be their guide. In the eleventh chapter of their Constitutions it is stated that to give or receive presents from any man without permission and expression of the person concerned is to be punished as theft.[246]

241. *Ibid.*, p. 76; cf. pp. 148, 164, 262.

242. *Ibid.*, p. 256; cf. 289.

243. *Constitutiones*, D. I., c. XV, dec. VII, nn. 316 sq.; These Constitutiones also positively declared that acts of buying, selling, receiving, retaining, giving, exchanging, depositing, etc., if done without permission were null. Vide. D. I, c. XV, dec. VII, nn. 312 sq.

244. *Acta Sanctorum*, Aug. 1, 401-402; Schaaf, p. 27.

245. Steiger, *Periodica*, XIII (1925), pp. (153)-(154); This Bull could not be located in the *Bull. Ord. Praed.*

Carmelite Order

The date of the foundation of the Carmelite Order has been a matter of discussion from the fourteenth century even to our own day. The historians of the Order attempt to trace its origin to Elias and Eliseus. But modern historians, with Baronius, deny its existence before the latter part of the twelfth century.[247]

While Blessed Albert was Patriarch of Jerusalem, he received the request that he formulate a Rule for the hermits who were living on Mt. Carmel. Previously they had been living separately, but about this time they adopted community life. The Carmelite Rule as drafted by Albert about 1209 was approved by Honorius III in 1226.[248] Innocent IV mitigated this Rule.[249] Both the Discalced and the Calced Carmelites, who became a separate organization in 1593,[250] use the Innocentian mitigation. The Honorian Rule ordained that: "None of the brethren may call anything his own, but all things are common among you."[251] As regards the observance of poverty or "common life," the mitigation of Innocent conceded to the hermits: "Assinos autem sive mulos, prout vestra expostulaverint necessitas, vobis habere liceat, et aliquod animalium sive volatilium, ad nutrimentum."[254]

---

246. *Constitutiones,* pp. 659, 600. In the papal Constitutions of Innocent VII and Eugenius IV, containing the Rule of the Third Order Dominican, no mention was made of the "common life" nor of the observance of poverty. The postulant merely promised, for the honor of God, the Blessed Virgin and St. Dominic, that he or she would observe the Rule until death. (*Constitutiones* O. P., pp. 682 sq.) For further details about this Third Order Secular consult Reinmann, pp. 21-23.

247. Zimmerman, "The Carmelite Order" (*Cath Ency.,* III, 354 ff.; Steiger, *Periodica,* XIII (1925) pp. (164)-(165).) For the Carmelite view consult McCaffrey, *The White Friars,* pp. 14 ff.; Suarez, tract, 9, lib. 2, c. 10, n. 1.

248. Bulla, *Ut vivendi,* 30 ian. 1226 (*Bullarium Carmelitarium,* p. 3 sq.). The Order as such was approved by the Second Council of Lyons, although St. Simon had obtained some sort of approval in 1247 (Zimmerman, *Cath Ency.,* III, 355b).

249. Bulla, *Quae honorem conditoris* as found in the *Bullarium Carmelit.* I, p. 41 sq.

250. Clem. VIII, Bulla, *Pastoralis officio,* 20 dec. 1593, *Bullarium Carmel.* 1, pp. 212-215).

251. Chapter VII in the *"Ut vivendi."*

252. Chapter IX in the *"Quæ honorem conditoris."*

Discalced Carmelites

The Constitutions of the Discalced Carmelites were very careful in their legislation for the preservation of their idea concerning the observance of evangelical poverty. Under no pretext were the brethren permitted to keep even the least thing as their own, or reserve as their own even the use of a thing, whether in the house or out of doors, since all things must be common.[253] Monasteries in large cities and towns were not to have revenues except a moderate amount received for Masses and functions. Inheritances and legacies and donations were never classed as revenues and hence could be accepted in all houses. Houses situated in small towns and outside cities could have revenues if the Praepositus or General Definitors decided that these were necessary. Under certain conditions the Order could contest in court for legacies or inheritances given by testament.[254] It was expressly prohibited to receive, reserve for private use, or give presents, or even exchange anything with a fellow Religious. In the monastery, there must not be anything superfluous or elaborate. Whatever was not in actual use of a Religious must be returned to the common use.[255]

Under no pretext could a Religious retain privately "money to be restored," or distributed in alms; all this must be placed in the custody of the Prior. The Religious were prohibited to ask alms for externs, even for parents or blood brothers, if the amount to be begged was more than "unum aureum," unless the Provincial Definitor had granted special permission. However, under this prohibition did not come the soliciting of alms for the monastery (as was usually done from the pulpit) provided nothing beyond what was necessary was asked.[256] If any one was found guilty of proprietorship, he was "eo ipso" deprived of active and passive voice for the space of two years and besides placed in prison for two months, no dispensation from this being allowable.[257]

253. *Constitutiones* (1906) Pars I, c. III, n. 1.
254. *Ibid*, nn. 2-5; cf. Pars II, c. XVI, n. 5.
255. Pars I, c. III, nn. 6-7.
256. Pars I, c. III, nn. 10-11, 13.
257. *Ibid.* 14.

Calced Carmelites

The Constitutions of the Calced Carmelites regulate the practice of poverty with considerable exactitude.[258] In Chapter VII it is enacted that none of the brethren shall dare to possess as his own what has been granted for his use nor accept nor give anything of value nor exchange anything with one of his brethren. Permission, at least presumed, must be had for the acceptance of anything from seculars. Those things allowed by law for the use of the brethren must not be fine (exquista) but simple and of moderate price. All alms no matter how acquired must immediately be given to the Prior or Procurator. When money is given to the brethren for some definite purpose, if anything happens to be left over, it must be brought immediately to the Superior and not retained for private use. In large cities, the Prior can grant to brethren engaged in the care of souls, permission to retain a small amount of money for transit but this money must be spent for the purpose for which it was given and an account of its expenditure rendered. The Superiors must be careful lest they go beyond the standard of poverty in the building of houses and even as regards the size of the cells. The cells must be uniform and entirely conformable to Religious poverty, and therefore superfluous things, especially such as are redolent of a worldly rather than a Religious spirit are not to be retained in the cells. In conformity with the prescription of the Council of Trent was the penal sanction stated in these Constitutions. "We strictly prohibit lest there be elected to any office anyone who does not exactly observe the 'common life' as regards poverty"; "and if election is made contrary to this statute, it is 'eo ipso' null and void."

Augustinian Hermits

The Augustinian Hermits must not be confused with the Augustinian Canons who have already been considered under the title of Canons Regular. During the twelfth and thirteenth century many associations of hermits were founded, especially in Italy. Among these were the Her-

---

258. Cf. *Regulæ et Constitutiones Fratrum Beatissimæ Virginis Mariæ de Monte Carmelo* (1904), Chapter VII, nn. 86-96.

mits of St. Augustine.[259] These hermits were frequently confounded with other Institutes with the result that ill feeling was increasing. To avoid trouble Alexander merged all the hermits into the one Order of "The Hermits of St. Augustine.[260] The Rule of St. Augustine was to be their guide.

The Constitutions of this Order established more in detail the Augustinian concept of "community of goods." Excepting certain little presents, "munusculis" which with due permission could be retained, whatever was received from parents, benefactors or from stipends for preaching, teaching, the celebration of Mass or any other reason must within twenty-four hours be placed in the hands of the Prior or the administrator.[261] The Prior is to refuse to his Religious, things superfluous, useless and not conformable to Religious poverty; he may allow only what is suitable to the Religious State, useful or necessary, having due regard to the conditions of place, dignity, station, office and age.[262]

* * * * *

These four Orders were called the Mendicants "de iure communi."[263] The Fourth Lateran Council had prohibited the formation of new Orders.[264] Despite this prohibition quite a number of communities were founded, and these merited the condemnation of the Second Council of Lyons which demanded their immediate or gradual extinction. Those which had been established after the

---

259. Innocent IV, *Quoniam*, 26 aprilis 1244 (*Bul. Rom.*, III, pp. 507-509); Alexand. IV, *Iis quæ*, 31 iulii 1255 (*Bul. Rom.*, III, pp. 616-618).

260. Bulla, *Licet Ecclesiæ*, 4 maii 1256 (*Bul. Rom.*, III, pp. 635-636).

261. *Constitutiones Ordiins Erimitarum S. Augustini* (1895), Pars III, c. 1, n. 5.

262. *Ibid*, n. 6; cf. Pars II, caput, VIII, nn. 4-5, for the regulations when simple vows became obligatory as a preparatory exercise before solemn profession.

263. Cf. De Luca-Galiemart, *Sacro Sanctum Oecumenicum Concilium Tridentinum*, p. 624, n. 6. The papal Constitution of Pius V, *Cum indefensæ*, 7 iuli 1571, *declared* the Jesuits to be truly and not fictitiously mendicants. Cf. Wernz, *Ius Decretalium*, III, p. 262; Suarez, *Opera Omnia*, tract. X, lib. 4, cap. 7 sq.; Schmalzgrueber, *Ius Ecclessiasticum Universum*, lib. III, tit. 31, n. 12.

264. c. III (Harduin, VII, 31); Mansi, XXII, 1002) Orth. 18; for reasons of the condemnation, cf. Mocchegiani, *Jurisprudentia Ecclesiastica*. I, 15.

Lateran IV Council were to be abolished immediately; those which had received approval were not to receive new members. The Servites founded in 1223 survived this condemnation. In 1256 the members of this Order were allowed to make a vow of poverty, the violation of which, as regards immovable property, was to bring down on the culprit the curse of Almighty God, of our Lord Jesus Christ, of the Blessed Virgin Mary and of the Saints of God.[265] It was to this Order that the famous decree "Nullus Omnino" was addressed. There will be occasion to refer to this papal document in another part of this dissertation; nor will it be out of place there to recall the details of the Servite vow of poverty in conjunction with the papal enactment.[266]

(e) *The Military Orders*

About the same time that the Mendicants appeared, the greater number of the Military Orders arose. Today there is hardly anything left of them. Their practice of evangelical poverty is of merely historical value as it did not affect in any notable degree the legislation on the vow of poverty as it obtains today.

The Knights Templars, Knights of St. John of Jerusalem, the Teutonic Knights, and the Mercedarians, are regarded as being among the great Military Orders. These made a solemn vow of poverty.[267] The permission of the Holy See permitting the Mercedarians to have an amount of peculium on account of their work is sometimes used as an argument to show that peculium is not "per se" opposed to the vow of poverty.

The landed property of the Knights was free from tithes. During their existence some of these Orders became enormously wealthy. The individual houses were obliged to contribute their revenues to a central treasury, after the deduction of the house expenses. As a result of

---

265. Alex., IV, Const *Deo Grata,* 20 aprilis 1256 (*Bul. Rom.* III, pp. 733-735.

266. For other mendicant Orders cf. David, pp. 279-280.

267. Schaaf, *History of the Christian Church,* Vol. V, Part I, pp. 296, 302, 305; Moeller, "The Military Orders" (*Cath. Ency.,* X, pp. 304 ff. Currier, 209, 211; Teutonic knights swore to renounce all property (according to Currier, 212).

this circulation of wealth, these Orders at times became veritable credit and deposit banks.[268]

(f) The Clerks Regular

The exact date of the appearance of the Clerks Regular in the Church is difficult to determine. Clerks Regular, understood in the sense of priests devoted to the works of the ministry and the practice of the Religious Life, are found in the earliest days of the Christian antiquity.[269] Yet it was not till the sixteenth century that Clerks Regular, in the modern sense of the term, came into being. Just as the peculiar conditions of the time had brought the Mendicants into existence so also the needs of the time occasioned the appearance of the Clerks Regular.[270]

The pioneers in the ranks of the Clerks Regular, as understood in the strictest sense, were the Theatines, in 1524.[271] They were followed by the Clerks Regular of Good Jesus (1526); the Barnabites (1530);[272] the Somaschi (1532);[273] the Society of Jesus (1534);[274] the Clerks Regular of the Mother of God (1583)[275] the Camillians (1584);[276] the Minor Clerks Regular (1588), and the Piarists (1597).[277]

---

268. Cf. Schaaf, o. c., p. 304 Yet if an individual Hospitaler was found in death with money he was subject to the Gregorian punishment for such offenses. (Schaaf, o. c., p. 303; Curzon, XXVII); cf. p. 307, for Minor Military Orders professing a vow of poverty.

269. Many eminent theologians hold that they were instituted by Christ Himself. cf. Murphy, "Clerks Regular" (*Cath Ency.*, IV, p. 52).

270. For the distinction between the Clerks Regular and the Canons Regular cf. Murphy, 1 c.

271. Cf. Holstenius, *Codex Regularium,* V. p. 347; Heimbucher, II, p. 247 sq. They bind themselves first of all to possess nothing in common, but to expect everything from Divine Providence, without asking for anything" (David, p. 282).

272. Approved by Paul III, const. *Dudum,* 25 iul. 1535.

273. Cf. Paul III, const. *Ex iniuncto,* 5 iunii 1540; Holstenius, III, pp. 199 sq.; Heimbucher, II, pp. 259 sq.

274. Campbell, *The Jesuits,* pp. 24, 31; approved Paul III, const. *Regimini* 27 sept. 1540.

275. Approved as a simple Congregation by Clem. VIII in 1593 and finally erected into an Order by Greg. XV, *In supremo,* 3 nov. 1621; cf. Heimbucher, II, pp. 262 sq.

276. Sixtus V, const. *Ex omnibus,* 18 martii 1586 (*Bul. Rom.,* VIII, pp. 669 sq.) as a mere association living a community life without vows; Clem. VIII, const. *Illius,* 21 sept. 1591.

The Society of Jesus

Outstanding among the Clerks Regular is the Society of Jesus. The early Jesuits were not guided by a Rule but by practices introduced by St. Ignatius that were intended to develop into customs.[278] The official collection of legislation in the Society is the *"Institutum Societatis Jesu."* The Second Volume of this Anthology is entitled, *"Examen et Constitutiones, Decreta Congregationum Generalium, Formulae Congregationum."* "The Constitutions as drafted by St. Ignatius and adopted finally by the first congregation of the Society (1558) have never been altered."[279] The text that was in use in the Society shortly before the Code of Canon Law was promulgated was a Latin version prepared under the direction of the third congregation.[280]

In the 1893 edition of the Constitutions it is stated that the "Professed Houses" are not to have real estate.[281] However, "Houses of Probation" and "Colleges" are not incapable of ownership.[282]

Very edifying is the legislation found in the *"Rules of the Society of Jesus,"* a manual of guidance. "All that are under obedience in the Society, must remember that they are to give freely what they have freely received; neither asking nor accepting any reward or alms whereby the masses, confessions or sermons or any other offices, which the Society may according to our Institute exercise, may seem to be recompensed, that we may with greater liberty and edification of our neighbors, go forward in

---

277. Instituted "ad instar" a simple Congregation by Paul V, *Ad ea,* 6 martii, 1617; cf. Clem. IX, const. *Ex iniuncto,* 23 oct. 1663; Greg. XV, const. *In supremo,* 18 nov. 1621 (as an Institute of Solemn Vows).

278. Pollen, "St. Ignatius" (*Cath. Ency.,* VII, p. 640).

279. Pollen, "The Society of Jesus" (*Cath Ency.,* XIV, 81).

280. Pollen, 1 c., p. 82.

281. P. I, C. I, n. 3. Relative to this might be consulted the remark of Biederlack-Führich, p. 180: "quum prater habitationem cum horto, et templo ac hortum suburbanum cum domo conveniente possidere bona immobilia nequeant, hereditate vel legato alia immobilia bona acquirere quidem potuerunt, at ea vendere debuerunt, ut pretium acceptum pro sustentatione adhiberetur. Nunc autem dispositia Sedis Apostolicæ videtur expetenda."

282. Pius V, *Cum indefensae,* 7 iuluii 1571; cf. Wernz, *Ius Decretalium,* III, p. 262, nota (53). Even bona stabilia can be retained; cf. Biederlack-Führich, p. 180.

God's service."[283] Those who were to be admitted into the Society were to dispose of their property before they began to live under obedience in any house or college. If a just cause prevented this being done, at the time of entrance, it had to be done at least before the vows of a "coadjutor" were made.[284] This disposal ought to be made in favor of the poor rather than relatives. However, if relatives of the prospective Jesuit were poor, the Superior should appoint someone or a number of men to judge whether the relatives should benefit by the disposal of the property rather than other poor people.

After two years of probation had been completed, the novice (if destined for the priesthood) could become a Scholastic by professing simple vows. The vow of poverty, professed by these Religious, was perpetual only on the part of the vowing.[285] Because the Scholastic might wish to withdraw from the Society or might be dismissed from it before he is fully trained, he retained the dominion but not the usufruct, of the property previously possessed, until the General decided it should be abdicated.[256] If the Scholastic proved himself worthy, he was permitted to become either a "Coadjutor" by the profession of simple perpetual vows or a "Professed Father" by the profession of solemn vows. The vow of poverty professed by the "Co-

---

283. *The Rules of the Society of Jesus,* p. 17, n. 27; cf. *Constitutiones,* P. I, C. I, n. 3; P. I, C. 4, n. 27; P. 4, C. 7, n. 3; 15, n. 4; 17 F; P. 6, C. 2, nn. 7-8; P. 7, C. 4, B; P. 10, C. 5.

284. Greg. XIII, Const. *Quanto fructuosius,* 1 febr. 1583, § 3 (*Fontes,* n. 150); P. I, C. 4, n. I. As regards the novices and the renunciation of benefices the first general congregation, canon 1 declared that they could retain them (modo tamen sit simplex et residentiam non exigat) not only during the two year's novitiate but even after simple vows, even to profession of the "coadjutor." (Bouix, *Tractatus de Iure Regularium,* Vol. I, p. 593); Cf. Pichler, *Ius Canonicum,* lib. III, tit. 35, p. 452.

285. Simple vows, perpetual only on the part of the vowing, enabled the General to dismiss a subject for a reasonable cause according to the constitutions as the Constitution of Greg. XIII, *Quanto fructuosius,* 1 febr. 1583, § 2 (*Fontes,* n. 150) expressly stated. The constitution of Gregory XIII, *Ascendente Domino,* 25 maii 1584, § 7 (*Fontes,* n. 153) was very explicit on this. Cf. De Luca-Gallemart, p. 622, n. 22.

286. Campbell, p. 33. A scholastic is not inhabile to private property; hence if he becomes the beneficiary of a will, he can receive the property but he needs permission of a superior for its licit acceptance. Biederlack-Führich, p. 180.

adjutor" entailed inability to acquire property even by heredity.[287] The solemn vow of the "Professed Fathers" like the other solemn vows of poverty professed in other Institutes effected that the vowing became incapable of owning property. The Professed Fathers made an additional simple vow whereby they obliged themselves never to act or consent, in any way, so that, what the "Constitutions" determined concerning poverty should be changed; except when for a just cause, arising from necessity, poverty might be made more restricting.[288] In the "common rules"[289] it is stated: "None must have money in their own custody; and in another's keeping, neither money nor anything else." In the "Rules of the Temporal Coadjutors,"[290] it is declared: "they must be very careful never to take anything for themselves, or give, lend, or send to others, or do anything of this kind, without the express leave from the Superior; especially "reliquaries, crosses, agnus dei's and such like: and they must persuade themselves that they may in such things grieviously offend against their vow."[291] Vincent Caraffa declared that a Superior can not validly give a permission to a subject for peculium.[292]

ARTICLE IV. LEGISLATION OF SIMPLE VOW INSTITUTES REGARDING EVANGELICAL POVERTY

Shortly after the Council of Trent, Pius V outlawed all communities not professing solemn vows.[293] Although canonically non-existent, many of these condemned societies continued to exist, as a matter of fact (cf. Larraona,

---

287. P. 6, C. 2, n. 12; cf. Schmalzgrueber, lib. III, tit. 35, n. 6; Biederlack-Führich, p. 180. If an inheritance or legacy is left to a formed coadjutor or a professed father, if it is decided the property was really left to the house or college, it is accepted as such; if the property came "intuitu personæ" the testament is invalid on that point and recourse is had to the Holy See for the disposition of the property.

288. *Constitutiones* (1893), p. 146; cf. P. 6, C. 2, A. This is a private vow. (Vermeersch, *Epitome,* I, n. 681.)

289. *The Rules of the Society of Jesus,* p. 35.

290. I.e. the non clerical members of the Society.

291. Cf. *The Rules of the Society of Jesus,* pp. 103-104.

292. Cf. Vermeersch, *De Religiosis,* Vol. I, n. 276, p. 179.

293. A detailed account of the canonical vicissitudes of simple vow Institutes until their welcome into the ranks of Religious will be given in the historical sketch of the canonical legislation regulating the observance of evangelical poverty.

CpR, I (1920) pp. 47-48). As early as 1617 Pius V canonically recognized the Poor Clerks of the Mother of God of Pious Schools. During the next century other Institutes of men having but simple vows were approved by the Holy See. In 1760 the Holy See even refused to permit the Passionists to make solemn vows, although such permission had been granted to several Congregations in the preceding century. It is also worthy of note, that several solemn vow Institutes obtained permission of the Holy See to make only simple vows in the future.

During the past century numerous simple vow Institutes appeared in the Church.[294] Not only have they offered successful help to their members in the attainment of personal sanctity but they have rendered invaluable service to the Church in the work of the salvation of souls. Just before the Code was promulgated, the number of Religious in the sixty-six *papally* approved simple vow Institutes outnumbered the Regulars in the thirty-three solemn vow Institutes.[295]

As regards the practice of evangelical poverty in these simple vow Institutes there was great diversity.[296] It is beyond the scope of this sketch to give in detail an account of how evangelical poverty was observed in all the Institutes of simple vows. However, in view of the fact that the Code conceded to Institutes which had legislation contrary to the common law (in the matters of capacity to retain ownership and to acquire ownership after profession, as well as the administration, use and usufruct of such property) the right to retain their private legislation even after the code, it will not be out of place to take cognizance of some of this private legislation.

---

294. During the seventeenth and eighteenth centuries in France alone there sprung up fifty Sisterhoods within less than one hundred and fifty years. (Revelet, *Blessed John Baptist de la Salle*, pp. 76 ff.; Schuetz, *The Origin of Teaching Brotherhoods*, p. 20.

295. Saier, "Statiches von den katholischen Orden und Kongregationen" (*Linzer theologisch praktische Quartalschrift*, LXV [1912]. 356 sq.). Above and beyond the number of Religious in the *papally* approved simple vow Institutes were the thousands of Religious in the simple vow Institutes which enjoyed only *episcopal* approval.

296. There was one aspect in which all these Institutes were alike, i.e., the capacity of the community as such to possess property.

(a) Capacity of Ownership

It is quite clear that the members of the Congregation of Poor Clerks of the Mother of God of Pious Schools *lost entirely their capacity of ownership.* Their legislation made it impossible for the Religious to acquire property as individuals, under any title whatsoever.[297] Very explicit was the legislation governing the Lorretto Sisters: "Holy poverty as practiced in the Society of Lorretto consists in this: that no Sister as such shall own anything absolutely in her own name, no matter how inconsiderable this object may seem to be . . . should anything be given to her, she must at once transfer it to the Superior, who may do with it as she thinks fit, but always for the benefit of the Society."[298] The Constitutions of the Sisters of St. Joseph[299] prescribed: "To keep their vow of poverty, the Sisters should effectually give up all their goods by leaving them to their relatives or to the poor or by resigning them to the Superiors of the Congregation."[300] "Their vow of poverty disqualifies them from having a right to anything and consequently . . . should they have accepted anything they must place it at the disposal of the Superior to be employed as she sees fit" . . . "All those who receive an inheritance are bound to resign it immediately into the hands of the Superior who shall dispose of it as of any other property belonging to the house. It is therefore prohibited to any Sister who may receive an inheritance, property or goods, to dispose of it or them, in whole or part, for themselves, for their friends or other persons whomsoever, without the express

297. Paul V, const. *De ea* (*Bul. Rom.*, XII, pp. 383-384). This Congregation afterwards became an Order.

298. *Rules and Constitutions of the Friends of Mary at the Foot of the Cross,* Chapter III; cf. *Constitutions for the Religious of Our Lady of Charity of the Good Shepherd of Angers* (1836), const. XVIII, for similar legislation; also *Regel und Constitutionen für die Schwestern des Dritten Ordens des Hl. Franzistus von Assisi bei St. Francis Wisconsin* (1901) p. 9.

299. An Institute founded by the Bishop of Puy, France, March 10, 1651.

300. *Constitutions of the Sisters of St. Joseph,* P. III, C. 1. "If a Sister should leave the Institute, whatever property, real or personal, the Sister brought with her must be returned to her by the Superior who received such property, minus the interest" (p. 1, c. 2).

permission of the Superior. The infraction of this vow shall be considered an injustice."[301]

It can not be too strongly stressed that the legislation of Institutes of simple vows must be carefully weighed before conclusions are derived. From a cursory reading of the Constitutions of the Sisters of Mercy, it would not be difficult to make a Judgment that these Sisters had as little capability as a Regular relative to property. Their legislation, having declared that the Sisters of Mercy before they enter to Congregation, "have renounced all property in earthly things," prescribes, "They shall not give or receive any present without the permission of Mother Superior: when with her permission they receive any present either from their relatives or from others, it must be considered as received not for the private use of the individual but for that of the community."[302] Yet, one of older and representative members of the community offered the information that with the permission of Mother Superior, it was possible for a subject to give to a relative the amount of a legacy or an inheritance amounting to $500.00 or more, which may have come to the subject.

Unique, indeed, was the status of the members belonging to the "Societas a charitate nuncupata," the Institute founded by Rosmini in 1828 and approved by the Holy See in 1838. The members were required to have "the will to practice every grade of poverty." Its form of poverty permitted the retention of bare ownership in the eyes of the civil law but each member had to be ready to surrender even that ownership at the call of obedience.[303]

(*b*) *Capacity to Acquire*

It may be safely said that usually when the capacity to acquire after profession was denied in the Constitutions, the power even to retain what had been possessed before profession was also taken away. Some institutes permit-

301. Part III, c. VII.

302. *Rules and Constitutions, The Sisters of Mercy* (1892), Chapter 5; *The Rules and Constitutions of the Institute of the Religious Sisterhood of the Presentation of the Ever Blessed Virgin Mary,* Chapter III, contained the same regulations about poverty as was quoted concerning the Sisters of Mercy.

303. Cf. Pollard, "Rosminians," (*Cath. Ency.*, XIII, p. 200), for further details concerning the concept Rosmini had of evangelical poverty.

ted the Religious to retain the radical dominion of the property owned before profession but restricted the capacity to acquire property after profession. Thus the legislation of the "Bon Secours" having declared the Religious capable of acquiring property by inheritances after profession, declares it to be an act of proprietorship to accept anything for personal use unless permission has been obtained for it.[304] The Marianists were expressly prohibited to accept personal gifts; all presents must be accepted for the community or chapel.[305] Other Institutes left the Religious unrestricted in the matter of acquiring property after profession. There is an instance of this in the Congregation of the Holy Cross whose Constitutions declared that the Religious : "preserve the right of keeping that which they had previous to their profession and of accepting that which might afterwards be granted to them in any way whatever."[306]

In a class by itself, as regards acquirement of property after profession was the legislation of the Basilians, a Congregation that received the "Decretum Laudis" in 1837. The members of the Institute professed a perpetual vow of poverty which only the Holy See could dispense. In the formula of profession, the aspirant having expressed the vows he had made, added referring to the vow of poverty: "the last is to be understood, however, in the sense that I may not without an express permission, retain anything of my revenues, from whatever source they may come, except those of the preceding year, according to the specifications of the Constitutions."[307] The Constitutions declared that the brethren were not to keep anything except what they had received in the past year, unless the Superior should grant a dispensation for a definite period of time in order that a member might be able to promote a good

304. *Constitutions et Regels de la Congregation des Soeurs de Charite, etc.*, c. 4, art. 5.

305. *Constitutions of the Society of Mary,* Chapter III. This Congregation permitted its members to retain the radical dominion of the property owned before profession.

306. *Constitutions of the Congregation of the Holy Cross,* n. 101. The Little Sisters of Charity of the Sorrowful Mother, could acquire property after profession, by donation, legacy or by testament, S. C. EE et RR, dec. 20, 1884 (*Fontes,* n. 1939).

307. *Constitutions de la Congregation de Saint Basil,* p. 32. The Canadian branch of this Institute, since 1922, have legislation like that in the Code.

work, he might have in view.[308] The members of the Congregation who were not priests received from the Institute annually three hundred francs; the priests receiving two hundred francs a year. Whatever revenue arose from labor or industry *which had been obligatory* belonged to the Institute; but whatever came from other sources, "casuel" belonged to the individual.[309] At the beginning of November, each member had to make a declaration that he had spent all his income, beyond what he had received during the past or present year.[310]

Finally there may be quoted the legislation of the Sisters of the Holy Cross which declared: "Professed Sisters are not permitted to refuse legacies which may come to them personally or an inheritance for the Congregation but they shall be required to ask the advice of Mother General."[311]

(c) *Use and Usufruct and Administration of Private Property After Profession*

In those Congregations which permitted the Religious to own private property while they were members of the Institute, there was more or less adequate legislation for the provision of this private property. Some Institutes almost lacked legislation.[312] Indeed, to all Institutes the legislation contained in the Code is a great blessing.

---

308. P. 17.

309. P. 28. The brethren were expressly forbidden to speculate, e.g., to play the market (les operations de bourse) or in a word, whatever might even remotely give them the appearance of "exchange speculators." Under this prohibition the procurators of the Congregation were also included. It was likewise forbidden to become a guarantor of a note, to borrow, to contract debts by purchase, or credit or otherwise, unless small sums were involved with a time limit of twenty-four hours (pp. 37-38).

310. P. 29.

311. *Constitutions de la Congregation des Soeurs de Sainte Croix*, n. 102.

312. *The Constitutions of an Association of Franciscan Sisters of the Sacred Heart of the Third Order of St. Francis at Joliet, Illinois,* merely interdicted the use and administration of the property of the novices, postulants and Professed Sisters to the individuals owning it. (Chapter II § 1) Somewhat similar legislation obtained in the *Constitutions of the Third Order Regular of the Sisters of St. Francis of the Immaculate Conception,* Chapter II, § 1, n. 1, where it was stated that the administration and use were prohibited to the Religious who must so dispose of them so that they could be regained if the Religious left the Institute.

Passionists were required to renounce the proceeds of their property in favor of whomsoever piety or charity might suggest.[313] If the person to whom the usufruct had been ceded, died during the life time of the Religious, he had the right to favor some one else with it; this second cession being governed of course by the regulation that governed the first. The Holy See declared that while the usufructuarius remained alive, the Religious of this Congregation could not revoke the usufruct even if a just cause obtained and the Superior General approved of it.[314]

The Constitutions of the Redemptorists prescribed: "Quoniam Congregationis sodalis suorum bonorum proprietatem semper retinet, de iis disponere poterit in utilitatem suorum coniunctorum: quod si non fecerit in horum beneficium, id facere debebit in beneficium Congregationis."[315] From this regulation it was not certain that the Religious could dispose of the usufruct. The Sacred Congregation of Bishops and Regulars, in a decree of July 2, 1841, declared that the Italian members of the Institute could abide by the declarations of the General Chapter of 1764, viz. they could dispose of the usufruct in favor of relatives within the fourth degree of consanguinity or affinity according to the canonical mode of computation; or in favor of their own soul or in any use but with permission of the Superior. On June 1, 1852, the

313. Clement, XIV, *Salvatoris D. N. J. C.*, 21 Nov. 1769 (*Bull. Rom. Continuatio*, XVII, pp. 111 sq.); Lucidi, *De Visitatione*, II, n. 320; *Rules and Constitutions for the Congregation of Discalced Clerks of the Most Holy Cross and Passion of Our Lord Jesus Christ* (1870), Chapter XIII.

314. S. C. EE et RR, declaratio 15 sept. 1837, Bizzarri, *Collectanea in usum Secretariæ Sacræ Congregationis Episcoporum et Regularium*, pp. 74-75). Bizzarri commenting on this decision said that when difficulties arise concerning the disposal of property after profession, they are to be solved by a sedulous study of the approved Constitutions and Statutes of the individual Institute, since there is no regulation of common law covering such problems. The Passionists had no express legislation for the administration and usufruct of their private property, it being supposed that the Religious would entrust the administration and cede the use, to the usufructuarius. Institutes which employed the Bizzarrian formula could revoke their cession of the usufruct, if they obtained Apostolic permission (Bizzarri, p. 806).

315. § 1, n. 8 apud Lucidi, II, n. 321.

Holy See declared the same enactment applicable to members of the Congregation outside of Italy.[316]

The Christian Brothers had to abandon the usufruct of their property to their parents or the Institute.[317] In other Institutes the administration of the property had to be given to the Superioress.[318] The Institutes which used the Bizzarrian formula could dispose of the use and usufruct in favor of whomsoever they pleased.[319] It was also the practice in some Institutes to furnish the Religious with a formula to be filled out when the provision was made for the property while the individual remained a Religious. The following is an example:

"Je soussigné . . . (*nom et prénoms*), déclare céder par cet acte à . . . (*indiquer ici si la cession se fait à la Société de Marie ou à un parent ou a une autre personne*), l'administration, l'usufruct et l'usage de tous mes biens consistant en . . . (*détailler ici la nature de ces biens*). Je fais cette cession, à titre purement gratuit. (*On peut mettre a la place de cette derniere phrase:* Je fait cette cession a la charge par le destinataire d'accomplir telle ou telle bonne oeuvre.) J'entends faire cette cession pour tout le tenps que je demeurrai lie à la Société de Marie par les voeux de religion.

Toutefois, ma volunta est que cet acte de cession soit en temps révocable a mon gré *au for exterieur,* en sorte qu'on ne puisse jamais devant la loi et les tribunaux civilis réclamer de moi la continuation de cette cession au dela du moment òu il m'aura plu de la révoquer. Je reconnais neanmoins que je ne puis en conscience, *au for intérieur,* user de ce droit de révocation tant que subsisteront mes voeux, à moins que je n'en obtienne l'autorization du Saint-Siége.

Fait a . . . le . . . 18 . . . "[320]

---

316. Lucidi, II, n. 321.

317. *Rules and Constitutions of the Brothers of the Christian Schools,* Chapter XIX, n. 1.

318. *Constitutions of the Hand Maids of Charity* § 1, c. 9 (Luccidi, II, n. 323); *Le Religiose dell' Istuto di Verona sotto il titolo delle Sorelle Minime della Carita di Maria Addolorata,* S. C. EE et RR., *Veronen.* 20 dec. 1844 (*Fontes,* n. 1939).

319. *Constitutiones Presbyterorum Societatis Mariæ,* n. 41 (Bizzarri, p. 806); cf. same source for other Congregations using same formula.

320. *Coutumier de la Societe de Marie,* p. 243.

(*d*) *Disposal of Property After Death*

Some Institutes had no provision in their legislation for the disposal of the private property of a Religious after his death. But in many Institutes there was a custom permitting the Religious to make a will.[321] Institutes having the Bizzarrian formula were permitted to make a will. Among the Passionists it was not customary to draft a testament. Instead, there was positive legislation declaring that when a Religious died, leaving property, it was to be considered as having been left by will to those who had a claim on it by law.[322] The Sisters of St. Francis of Assisi, in Wisconsin, had rather exact legislation. Should a Sister become seriously ill, not having as yet made over (by will) to the community, property which might come to her, she was obliged to remedy the omission.[323]

(*e*) *The* Normae *of* 1901

During the latter part of the nineteenth century, Pius IX and Leo XIII were called upon to approve the numerous simple vow Institutes which had sprung into existence on account of the needs of the times. The events of the nineteenth century had directed the attention of the Holy See to the wants of simple vow Religious. The many problems that had been placed before the Sacred Congregation in charge of the affairs of Religious had shown the necessity of more perfect legislation for the Institutes to be approved in the future. In 1901, the Holy See published the "Normae" which it was accustomed to follow in the approval of the legislation of new Institutes of simple vows. The norms for the observance of evangelical poverty were as follows:[324]

---

321. *Constitutions of the Sisters of St. Joseph,* Part III, c. VII.

322. *Rules and Constitutions,* Chapter XIII.

323. "Wenn eine Schwester schwer erkranken sollte, und das ihr zukommende Vermögen noch nicht an die Gemeinschaft gabracht hat, so macht sie ein Testament zum Wohle der Genossenschaft." (*Regel und Constitutionen,* p. 9).

324. Previous to these Norms, the so-called Bizzarrian formula had been used in formulating the legislation of new Institutes. As regards poverty, the formula stated: "Professi in hac instituto dominium radicale, uti aiunt, suorum bonorum retinere poterunt, sed eis omnino interdicta est eorum administratio, et redituum erogatio atque usus. Debent propterea ante professionem cedere, etiam private, administrationem, usufructum, et usum, quibis eis placuerit, ac eiiam suo

"Art. 113. Per votum simplex paupertatis, sorores[325] renunciant iure licite disponendi de re quacumque temporali sine venia legitimorum Superiorum.

Art. 114. Prohibitum est sororibus, retinere per seipsas administrationem bonorum suorum quorumcumque.

Art. 115. Propterea ante primam votorum emissionem disponere debent de usu et usufructu redituum vel fructuum bonorum suorum, quo modo ipsis placuerit, et etiam, si ita pro earum arbitrio existimaverint, in favorem sui Instituti.

Debent etiam ante prima vota cedere administrationem suorum bonorum personae vel personis sibi bene visis; et, si libere velint, etiam proprio Instituto praemonito et acceptanti.

Art. 116. Cessio administrationis, usus et ususfructus vim amplius non habebit in casu egressus ab Instituto; quin immo apponi poterit condicio quod sit quandocumque revocabilis.

Art. 117. Revocatio autem, et etiam mutatio horum actuum cessionis licite fieri nequit durantibus votis sine licentia moderatricis generalis.

Art. 118. Dispositio de usu et usufructu et designatio administratoris, de quibus supra, fieri possunt per actum sive publicum sive privatum.

Art. 119. Professae retinent dominium radicale bonorum suorum immo ipsis prohibetur se abdicare hoc

---

instituto, si ita pro eorum libitu existimaverint, Huic vero cessioni apponi poterit conditio, quod sit quandocumque revocabilis; sed professus hoc iure revocandi in conscientia minime uti poterit, nisi accedente Apostolicæ Sedis placito. Quod etiam dicendum erit de bonis, quae post professionem titulo hereditario eis obvènerint. Poterunt vero de domino, sive per testamentum, sive de licentia tamen Superioris generalis, per actos inter vivos libere disponere, quo ultimo eveniente casu, cessabit concessio ab eis facta quoad administrationem, usufructum, et usum; nisi eam concessionem tempore eis beneviso firmam voluerint, non obstante cessione dominii. Professis autem vetitum non est ea proprietatis acta peragere de licentia Superioris, quæ a legibus praescribuntur.

Quidquid professi sua industria, vel intutitu Societatis acquisierint non sibi adscribere, aut reservare poterunt; sed haec omnia inter communitatis bona refundenda sunt, ad communem societatis utililtaem" (Bizzarri, *Collectanea,* p. 806).

325. What was said concerning Sisters was to be applied in the cases of men, unless otherwise was stated. Cf. Vermeersch, *De Religiosis,* II, p. 366.

dominio radicali ante professionem votorum perpetuorum per actus inter vivos.

Art. 120. Convenit tamen, ut omnes et singulae, antequam vota temporanea primo emittant, de suis bonis praesentibus et futuris per testamentum omnino libere disponant.

Art. 121. Ut sorores in perpetuum professae licite se spoliare possint dominio radicali omnium bonorum suorum per actus inter vivos, requiritur licentia Apostolicae Sedis.

Art 122. Sorores professae tum ad faciendum, tum ad mutandum testamentum indigent venia Apostolicae Sedis: attamen in casibus vere urgentibus sufficiet licentia vel Ordinarii, vel Moderatricis Generalis, vel etiam, si aliter fieri nequit, Superiorissae localis.

Art. 123. Sororibus vetitum non est, ea proprietatis acta peragere quae a legibus praescribuntur, de licentia tamen moderatricis generalis; et si casus urgeat, moderatricis localis.

Art. 124. De bonis quae sororibus post emissa vota quocumque legitimo titulo obvenerint, ipsae debent, vel respective possunt, disponere iuxta normas hactenus statutas circa bona quae ante primam professionem possidebant.

Art. 125. De dote Instituto allata sorores nullo modo disponere possunt.

Art. 126. Quidquid sorores post emissa vota, industria sua vel intuitu Instituti acquisiverint, non possunt sibi adscribere vel reservare; sed ea omnia communitatis bonis adiudicanda sunt ad communem Instituti vel domus utilitatem.

Art. 127. Omnia in Instituto communia dicantur et sint quoad supellectilem victum, et vestitum. Congruit tamen singulis, in communi custodia, sed separatim servare et distribuere vestes stricti usus personalis.

Art. 128. Supellex qua sorores, permittentibus superioribus, utuntur, paupertati conveniat, nihilque superflui in ea sit, nihil etiam quod sit necessarium iis denegetur."[326]

---

326. *Normæ secundum quas S. Congregationis Episcoporum et Regularium procedere solet in approbandis novis Institutis votorum simplicium.*

CHAPTER II.

CANONICAL LEGISLATION CONCERNING THE OBSERVANCE OF THE VOW OF POVERTY

ART. I. PRE-TRIDENTINE LEGISLATION

(a) *Earliest Canonical Legislation*

What a happy introduction to the canonical history of the vow of poverty would that be, to cite the letter of Pope Clement I[1] commanding the community of Jerusalem to live in evangelical poverty and maintain the "Common Life!" But alas, Gratian has quoted for us only a spurious document.[2] The document of Urban I which has been used by some authors for impressive argumentation is also a forgery.[3]

From the dawn of community life in Christian monasticism, the practice of evangelical poverty was considered an inseparable part of it. Hence when a postulant formally entered a community, he implicitly obliged himself to observe the Gospel counsel as it was understood and practiced in that cenobium. Since withdrawal from the monastic state after Profession was considered unlawful, the monk was obliged to this form of poverty for the remainder of his life. The source of his obligation, in the earliest days of Christian monasticism, was not a vow of poverty, at least not a public one, but merely the natural consequence of being a member of a monastic community.

The Church at first silently observed the formation and development of these monastic institutions, which were mostly the product of laymen. When the inevitable

1. c. 2, C. 12, q. 1.
2. Jaffe, *Regesta Pontificum Romanorum*, p. 3; Lightfoot, *The Apostolic Fathers, St. Clement of Rome*, Vol. I, pp. 414-415; Bardenhewer-Shahan, *Patrology*, pp. 82-83; Ballerinorum, *Disquisitiones de antiquiis Collectionibus et Collectoribus Canonum*, (Migne, P. L. LXIV, col. 752); Maroto, *Institutiones*, p. 65; Cicognani, *Ius Canonicum*, p. 260.
3. c. 9, C. 12, q. 1; Jaffe, p. 13; Maroto, p. 65; Cicognani, p. 60; Ayrinhac, *General Legislation in the New Code of Canon Law*, p. 37; Bartholi, *Institutiones Canonici*, c. 50, p. 438.

frailty of human nature began to assert itself, the Church promptly and carefully applied her jurisdiction in protection of so beneficient an influence on the lives of her fervent children.

Shortly after the foundation of Christian monasticism in France, some of the monks were guilty of hoarding private possessions. The First Synod of Orleans (511) instructed the abbots to take from these monks and spend for the welfare of the community, whatever private property the monks had acquired.[4] Thus we see that peculium in the Western Church is nearly as old as the Religious State, itself.

(*b*) *The Proprietary Rights of Monks and Nuns in Civil Law Before the Middle Ages*

Certainly the Civil Law obtaining at the decline of the Roman Empire, at least from the latter part of Justinian's reign, was an important factor in stabilizing the practice of evangelical poverty in the Religious State. In the early fifth century, Christian monasticism had assumed such proportions that the civil government deemed it necessary to make a special law regulating the possession of property by Religious. In the Theodosian Code, we find a statute dated December 15, 434,[5] dictating that if any monk or nun died intestate, without relatives, and free from property obligations to the State or a patron, whatever property he or she had owned, belonged to the monastery where the Religious lived. However, this Code recognized the ability of Religious to make wills and testaments.[6]

In Justinian Law, it is evident that Religious were capable of receiving inheritances after Profession but if they left the monastery, the property they had received

---

4. c. XIX, (Hefele, *History of the Councils*, IV, p. 91).

5. C. Th. 5, 3, 1; cf. etiam, C. 1, 3, 20; N. 123, 38; c. 9, C. xix, q. 3: Suarez, Vol. XV, lib. 8, 6, 16.

6. During Justinian's reign, the status of the Catholic Religion as the State Religion became fully developed. When we recall the position of bishops in the administration of law (*Constitutio Constantini ab Ablabium* (333), Const. Sirmondiana 1"; C. Th. 1, 27, *"de episcopali definitione;"* C. 1, 4, *"De episcopali audentia,"* and the fact that Justinian believed that the army would succeed and the towns posper, only if monks joined their hands in pure and stainless prayer (N. 133, 5) we need not be surprised at the laws dealing with Religious and their property).

must remain as the possession of the monastery.[7] An Imperial decree in 535, defined more exactly the comprehension of these laws according to the mind of the legislator and declared that if anyone abandons the monastery, "let him know he must render satisfaction to God; whatever he possessed when he entered the monastery, belongs to the monastery and he may take away absolutely nothing."[7] Before a person entered a monastery, he could dispose of his property in whatever way he preferred but once he became a monk, he no longer had dominion over any property in any way. The only exception to this was the case of the married man, who, before entering the monastery, had neglected to give to his wife and children their share of the patrimony. These dependents were not to suffer on account of the omission; and the portion of the patrimony to which they were legally entitled must be granted to them even if Religious Profession has been made.[8] Moreover, what was enacted for men applied to women in similar circumstances.[9]

Several years later, the Emperor, in another decree expatiated on this idea and legislated that if a man or woman had neglected to distribute to their children, their share of the patrimony before becoming a Religious, such an omission could be lawfully supplied after Profession; whatever property remained after this division, belonged to the monastery. If a person had neglected to give to his children what was due to them, and died as a Religious, the law would supply the omission and distribute to them their inheritance.[10]

If a monk transferred to another community after Profession, the property he had formerly possessed must remain in the possession of the community in which he was professed.[11] But if a monk returned to secular life, whatever property he acquired during his absence belonged to the community.[12]

These enactments were enforced in the East, North

7. C. 1, 3, 54 (56); cf. c. 10, C. XIX, q. 3.
7. N. V, 4; Polaccus, *Vacationum Epidimialium,* Pars I, p. 6.
8. N. V, 5; Cf. N. V, 6.
9. N. V, 5.
10. N. CXXIII, 38.
11. N. V, 7; cf. N. LXXVI; Thomassinus, III, 2, 43, nn. 11-13.
12. N. CXXIII, 42.

Africa, parts of Italy and Spain.[13] In the Eastern Empire, they remained on the statute books for a long time but were not incorporated in the "Basilica." In the West, especially in the territory of the Holy Roman Empire, the Justinian Law was the principal part of the Common Law.[14]

Charlemagne made Religious inhabile to private property rights under all circumstances, thus removing the exception obtaining in the Justinian Law: "Whosoever enters a monastery as a monk or nun has no control over his property (the property they had at the time of their profession) although he has children; but all the property the subject justly possessed on the day of entrance belongs to the monastery."[15]

Suarez taught that the inhability of individual Religious in the matter of proprietary rights, obtained universally, as ecclesiastical legislation, only from the time of Justinian.[16] Bouix, admitted as probable, the opinion that Justinian was primarily responsible for the inhability of Religious to have property after Profession.[17] Many authors believe that Justinian formulated these laws about the property of Religious, with the consent of the Roman Pontiff; or the Pope certainly gave his consent either implicitly or expressly to at least the favorable laws.[18] At least so much is certain, all the ecclesiastics lived by the

---

13. Cf. Taylor, *The Mediaeval Mind,* Vol. II, pp. 241, 242, 258; Grisar-Cappadelta, *History of Rome and the Popes in the Middle Ages,* Vol. II, p. 337; Amos, *The History and Principles of the Civil Law of Rome,* p. 419; Muirhead-Goudy, *Historical Introduction to the Private Law of Rome,* p. 403; For Germany, Mackeldy, Dropsie, *Handbook of the Roman Law,* pp. 78 ff; Ortolan-Prichard-Nasmith, *History of Roman Law,* pp. 513 ff.

14. Radin, *Hand Book of Roman Law,* p. 1; Sherman, *The Roman Law in the Modern World,* I, § 12, § 139, § 143; cf. Cigognani, *Ius Canonicum,* pp. 54-55; cf. Meynial, *The Legacy of the Middle Ages,* p. 363.

15. *Capitularia Francorum Regum,* Lib. VI, cc. 108, 110 (Mansi, XVIIb, 941); cf. Lib. V, cc. 329, 330 (Mansi, XVIIb, 905); C. Aquisgranense (739), c. 71 (Mansi, XVIIb, 238).

16. Vol. XV, tract. 7, lib. 8, c. 7, n. 32.

17. Vol. I, p. 482; cf. Carriere, *De Iustitia et de Iure,* Vol. I, n. 203; Wernz, III, n. (370), p. 330; Vermeersch, *Theologiæ Moralis,* Vol. III, n. 381.

18. Cf. Suarez, Vol. XV, lib. 8, c. 7, n. 28; cf. Maroto, CpR, V (1924) 13.

common law, the Law of Justinian—"Ecclesia vivit lege Romana."[19]

(c) *Development of Canonical Legislation Relative to Vow of Poverty*

While Gregory the Great was Pontiff, he labored strenuously to uphold the standard of poverty in the Religious Life. In his letters he declared even the desire to acquire property was notoriously unlawful for a monk.[20] He forbade Religious to acquire, retain or dispose of anything as their own.[21] If Religious had not disposed of their property before their "conversion," all of it belonged to the monastery of which they became members; nor could monks subsequently bequeath anything except by special dispensation obtained from the Pope.

To his agent at Ravenna he wrote: "Be careful to tell our aforesaid brother and fellow bishop to repress most diligently proprietorship in four or five monks of the monastery, which, heretofore he has by no means corrected and let him hasten to cleanse the monastery of such a pest; for if proprietorship is held by the monks there, neither concord nor charity can exist in the community. For what does the habit of the monk signify except contempt of the world? How can they contemn the world who seek after gold in the monastery?"[22]

Rather interesting is the curious case of an Abbess and the will she had made. The will was claimed to be valid because during her term of office she had not worn the Religious habit. Gregory wrote to the Bishop of Cagliari: "It is declared by a clear definition of the law, that those who enter a monastery for the purpose of 'conversion' have no longer the right to make a will but all their goods belong to the monastery . . . the property [of the nun]

---

19. Cf. *Lex Ripuariorum*, LVIII, 1, De Tabulariis (*Codex Legum Antiquarum*, p. 461); Capitulare Ludovici, 55; Ortolan-Prichard-Nasmith, pp. 517 ff.; Shahan, *The Middle Ages*, pp. 101-102; Jenks, *Law and Politics in the Middle Ages*, p. 26.

20. *Epis.* I, 40 (Mansi, IX, 1058); cf. lib. III, 6 (Mansi IX, 1159); Dudden, *Saint Gregory the Great*, Vol. I, p. 178.

21. Snow, *St. Gregory the Great*, p. 202.

22. *Epis.*, XII, 6, (24); cf. Snow, *St. Greg. the Great*, p. 204; *Dialogi*, III, 14; Mann, *Lives of the Popes in the Early Middle Ages*, I, p. 212.

by law manifestly belonged to the place she had entered and over which she had become Abbess."[23]

Very severe was Gregory's treatment of the case of a monk, Justus by name, who had hidden three pieces of gold, which were discovered after the monk's death. Vehemently indignant was the Pontiff on learning of the violation of the vow of poverty. The sentence he passed on that occasion became the norm for other cases down through the centuries. "Nullus ex fratribus se ad eum morientem iungat, nec sermonem consolationis ex cuiuslibet eorum ore (Justus) percipiat . . . cum viro mortuus fuerit, corpus illius cum fratrum corporibus non ponatur, sed quolibet fossam in sterquilinio facite, in ea corpus eius proicite, ibique super eum tres aureos, quod reliquid iactate, simul omnes clamantes: pecunia tua tecum sit in perditione, et sic eum terra operite . . . Quod ita factum est."[24]

In his efforts to eradicate abuses in monasticism Gregory strove to enforce the Rule of St. Benedict.[25] Thus what the Rule of St. Benedict prescribed concerning the observance of poverty and the "Common Life" might be said to be canonized. Numerous national councils, in the three succeeding centuries, decreed that the Benedictine Rule should be enforced in the territory of their jurisdiction.[26] At least from the ninth to the eleventh century, "Benedictine Poverty" ruled the Religious Life in Europe. It was the ecclesiastical or canonical law, as well as the monastic legislation of the Western Church, during this period.[27]

---

23. *Epis.*, IX, x, 7; C. XIX, q. 3; Snow, *St. Gregory the Great*, p. 202.

24. *Dialogi*, IV, 57; C. Londonense, (Mansi, XX, 453-454); C. Pictaviensis, (1078), c. VI, (Mansi, XX, 498); C. Lateran, III, c. X (Harduin, VIb, 1678); C. 6, X, *de statu monach.* III, 35.

25. Cf. Dudden (Vol. I, p. 79) doubts that Gregory ever officially approved the Benedictine Rule as legislation for Christian monasticism.

26. Cf. C. Augustodunense (670), c. XV (Mansi, XI, 124); C. Germanicum (742), c. VII (Hefele, III, 501); C. Liftenense (743-745), c. I (Hefele, III, 501); C. Francofordense (794), cc. XI, XIII, XXIV Hefele, III, 690-691); C. Aquisgranense (802, (Hefele, III, 744); C. Moguntinum (813), c. XI (Hefele, III, 7[illegible]); C. Cabilloniense (813), c. XXII (Hefele, III, 765). In 811, Charlemagne prescribed that an investigation be made to see if all the monks in Gaul observed the Rule of St. Benedict. (*Primum Capitulare* (Mansi, XVII b, 479).

27. Krynichi, Ks *Dzieje Kosciola Powszechnego*, p. 163; De

At the beginning of the eighth century there was compiled the *"Collectio Hibernensis."* Its influence extended far beyond the limits of Ireland and until the twelfth century enjoyed great authority in France and Italy. One of the statutes found in that anthology of legislation declared that a monk who contumaciouly left his monastery and presumed to obtain property should give to the Abbot whatever he had acquired.[28]

In 916 a new development in the legislation concerning the vow of poverty appeared. An Abbot who had been the means of much income to a monastery was elevated to the episcopacy. While a bishop he received a large paternal patrimony. After his death, the monks approached his successor and requested the former Abbot's inheritance. The case was settled in the Council of Altheim, held in the presence of the Emperor Konrad. Whatever the Abbot had received, while he was a mere monk, belonged to the monastery but once the Abbot was elevated to the Episcopacy, he acquired the faculty of acquiring property not for himself personally but for the See over which he presided.[29] As Benedict XIV afterwards interpreted this decision, the Abbot-Bishop now had the right to use and administer the property he had acquired, although he did not own it as his personal property.[30] Burchard (1023) incorporated this decision in his *Collectarium Canonum,*[31] as did Ivo of Chatres in his French Collection.[32] About a century later, Gratian embodied this enactment in his *Concordia Discordantium Canonum.*[33] While the mere presence of this legislation in Gratian's Decretals did not give it any added legislative value for the Whole Church, yet it undoubtedly caused this decision to

---

Hemptienne, *L'Ordre de Saint Benoit,* p. 70; Steiger, *Periodica,* XIII (1925), p. (79), are of the opinion that the Benedictine Rule supplanted all others from the seventh century till the eleventh.

28. Ex Libro, XXXIX, c. VII (Wasserschleben, *Die Irishe Kanonensammlung,* pp. 175-176).

29. *Monumenta Germanica,* LL. 2, p. 560; Mansi, XVIIa and XVIIIa, 332.

30. *Quaestiones Canonicas et Morales,* Q. CCCXXXIX, Vol. I, pp. 436-437); cf. Santi, *Praelectiones Iuris Canonici,* lib. III, tit. 35, n. 10.

31. Migne, P. L., CXL, 615.

32. Migne, P. L., CLXI, 426.

33. c. 1, C. XVIII, q. 1; cf. Glossators, in *"Decretum Gratiani,"* Vol. II, 1585 sq.

be used more frequently in similar cases.[34] Even as late as 1050, a Spanish Council obliged all the Religious under its jurisidiction to follow the Benedictine norm of poverty.[35] At Rome in 1074, a similar canon was formulated.[36] Shortly before this date, in Rome, a statute had been drafted declaring Canons Regular to be incapable of possessing anything as their own.[37] At London in 1075, a synod was held under the presidency of the illustrious Lanfranc, wherein it was decreed that if a monk possessed private property without permission and died before he had obtained absolution, he was not to be buried in a Catholic cemetery.[38]

The Ecumenical Council of 1179, the Lateran III, formulated a canon prohibiting Religious to have peculium.[39] Very determined was the intention of the prelates to stamp out this abuse. They declared that if any one shall have peculium[40] except the abbot had permitted it

---

34. In reviewing the history of canonical legislation concerning the practice of evangelical poverty, it is well to remember that custom can make and unmake laws. Human nature being what it is, in monks as well as other mortals, we are not so surprised to discover many instances of Religious acquiring quasi proprietary rights arising from what had previously been a willful violation of law. This obtained rather frequently in the Middle Ages when the feudal system thrust unworthy incumbents into the place of conscientious Abbots. The commendatory Abbots (Cf. Healy, *The Catholic World* [July, 1923]; MacCaffrey, *History of the Catholic Church from the Renaissance to the French Revolution,* Vol. I, p. 46; Ott, "St. Benedict of Nursia," [*Encyclopedia of Universal Knowledge,* II, 618], for relaxation of monastic discipline due in no small measure to the comendatory Abbots.) of the latter type not only failed to observe the counsel but, by their example, they induced their subjects to follow in their footsteps. Positive legislation, by National and General Councils, was the means used by the Church to combat the abuses and restore the former discipline. Oftentimes the acts of the Councils were but exact repetition of canons formulated in previous Councils. These acts are recorded as they are found, in order that the history and development of the canon law concerning the observance of evangelical poverty may appear in its true perspective.

35. Cf. C. Coyacencis, (Mansi, XIX, 789).

36. c. VII, (Mansi, XX, 399).

37. 1059, c. IX, (Mansi, XIX, 915); cf. c. 2, C. XII, q. 1; c. 4, 7-10, C. XIX, q. 3. This of course meant Canons Regular, as individuals, not as a community.

38. Mansi, XX, 543-454; cf. C. Pictaviensis, (1078), c. VI (Mansi, XX, 498).

39. c. X, (Harduin, VIb, 1678).

for the administration of an office, he must be removed from the communion of the altar. If after the death of a Religious, it was discovered he had died in possession of peculium, and had not repented, the usual suffrages were to be denied to him nor was he to receive burial with the brethren. The Council expressly declared that this canon applied to all Religious.

(*d*) *Solemn and Simple Vows before the Council of Trent*

About this time there appears the distinction between solemn and simple vows.[41] The General Council of 1139, the Lateran II, had stated that it did not consider (censemus) the union of a monk and a woman, though a marriage ceremony had been performed, to be matrimony.[42] The express terms solemn and simple vows are to be found in the legislation of the year 1880.[43] Although the text shows clearly the solemn vows mentioned were those made in Religion, the simple vows there mentioned have no indication of being such as were made in a Religious Institute.

Some authors claim that although the terminology did not appear till this time, the solemn vows existed in the fourth century[44] from custom and in the sixth century were recognized by the Emperor Justinian and the Pontiff Gregory, the Great.[45] Several canonists and theologians

---

40. The peculium here prohibited was that which was possessed independently of the Superior; not that which was held with dependence on the Superior: "Monachi non pretio recipiantur in monasterio, nec peculium permittantur habere. . . . Qui vero peculium habuerit, nisi ab abbate fuerit eo pro iniuncta administratione permissum, a communione removeatur altaris, et qui in extremis cum peculio inventus fuerit, et digne non poenituerit, nec oblatio pro eo fiat, nec inter fratres accipiat seupulturam; quod etiam de universis religiosis praecipimus observari. Abbas autem qui diligenter ista non caverit, officii sui iacturam se noverit incursurum . . . ; cf. Schmalzgrueber, lib. III, tit. 35, n. 12; Concina, c. XII, n. 2; Wernz, III, p. 334 (380).

41. Cf. Gratian, D. XXVII et C. XXVII, q. 1; cf. Ballay, *Archiv für Katholiches Kirchenrechts,* XVII (1867), pp. 3-4.

42. c. VII, (Harduin, VIb, 1209).

43. cc. 3, 4, 6, 7, X, *qui clerici,* IV, 6.

44. Devoti, *Institutionum Canonicarum,* lib. II, tit. 2, sect. 9, § 129; Walter, *Lehrbuch des Kirchenrechts,* p. 662, § 307, n. 7; Richter, *Lehrbuch des kath, und evang. Kirchenrechts,* p. 578 § 268, n. 4.

45. Cf. Sebastianelli, *Praelectiones Iuris Canonici,* II, p. 352; De Angelis, *Praelectiones Iuris Canonici,* Vol. II, lib. III, tit. 31, n. 3.

produce weighty argumentation in an effort to demonstrate that the vows of the early Religious were all simple.[46] Others claim that Solemn vows arose in the eleventh century.[47]

In 1298 Boniface VIII declared: "Quod voti solemnitas ex sola *constitutione Ecclesiae est inventa.*"[48] In the same chapter he also stated that only such a vow can be called solemn which is solemnized by the reception of Sacred Orders or by express or tacit profession made in a Religious Institute approved by the Holy See. Furthermore, Innocent III in the Lateran IV Council of 1215 had prohibited the foundation of any new Religious Institutes and had declared that if anyone desired to become a Religious, he must become a member of one of the approved Orders. Although these enactments did not carry an express nullifying clause, nevertheless canonists judged that it rendered contrary acts null and void because the matter, the reason alleged, and the mode of prohibition sufficiently made known the will of the legislator.[49]

However, new societies were formed. Against these, the Second Council of Lyons in 1274,[50] fulminated a canon reiterating the previous legislation and ordered the new societies to disband. That this applied to all the congregations of men and women desiring to have community life under a rule is evident.[51] In 1318, John XXII declared as canonically non existent all such congregations as the "Poor of Lyons" and the "Beghards."[52] It is cer-

---

Who do not hold this opinion but speak of other authors who do.

46. Cf. Mabillon, *Annales Ordinis Sancti Benedicti*, I. lib. 7, p. 610, apud Bouix, I, pp. 119-120; Freriks, *Religious Congregations*, p. 16; Van Espen and Thomassinus held this opinion according to Bayllay, *Archiv. für Katholichen Kirchenrechts*, XVII (1867), 15.

47. Cf. De Angelis, Vol. II, lib. III, tit. 31, n. 3, who there speaks of such authors.

48. c. 1, *de voto et redempt.* III, 15, in VI°.

49. Mansi, XXII, 1002; c. 9, X *de rel. domibus*, III, 36; Pirhing, lib. III, tit. 36, n. 32; Suarez, Vol. XV, lib. 2, c. 16, n. 10; Angelus, aSS. Corde, II, lib. 3, tit. 31, p. 81; Mocchegiani, *Jurisprudentia Ecclesiastica*, p. 16, n. 17; Bouix, I., p. 178, Orth, 21.

50. c. XXIII (Harduin, VII, 715); c. 1, *de rel. domibus*, III, 17, in VI°; Mansi, XXIV, 76.

51. Petra, Const. IX, Greg. IX, 15 sq.; Piat., Vol. I, p. 21; Suarez, Vol. XV, lib. 2, c. 16, n. 24.

52. C. 1, *de rel. domibus*, tit. 7, *in Extravag. Ioann., XXII;* cf. c. un. *de rel. domibus* III, 11, *in Clem.;* Orth, p. 22; McNeil, 22 ff.

tain that at this date there were, canonically, no Religious who did not belong to one of the approved Orders.[53] Since all these Institutes professed solemn vows it may be concluded that the only vows of poverty made in the Religious Life at this time were solemn.

Many associations of Franciscan and Dominican Tertiaries arose during the fourteenth and fifteenth centuries.[54] Gradually many of these associations adopted the "community life." Some of them professed one or more of the solemn vows but it can not be proven that any of them professed valid simple Religious vows of poverty.[55] It is true that after Julius II had recognized the vows of the Dominican Tertiaries in 1509, doubts arose as to whether they were simple or solemn; but Paul III made it clear that they were solemn.[56] The ultimate conclusion to be drawn from this article is that the first Religious vows of poverty which may be considered valid public simple vows were those professed by Jesuit novices at the completion of their novitiate. The effects of the simple vows of poverty made by the Jesuits have already been seen. Nor did the Council of Trent make any changes in this matter.

(*e*) *Enactments of National Councils in the latter part of the Middle Ages*

The canons of the Councils of the latter part of the Middle Ages offer some points of interest in the history of the vow of poverty. Among other things they afford an insight into some of the problems confronting Superiors in their attempts to secure the observance of evangelical poverty.

The Council of Oxford found it necessary to make very exact proscriptions in regard to the abuse of Religious with solemn vows drafting testaments concerning the

53. Pirhing, lib. III, tit. 36, n. 33; Schmalzgrueber, III, tit. 36, n. 22; cf. Boiux, I, pp. 202 sq.; Lombardi, I, p. 401.

54. Alijard, *Super Tertio Ordine Regulari Francisci,* CpR, II (1921), 381; Callaey-Lenhart, *The Third Order of St. Francis,* pp. 58-59.

55. Cf. Orth, p. 75; Angelus aSS Corde, Vol. II, lib. 3, tit. 31, p. 88; McNeil, p. 15 ("it would seem that prior to the sixteenth century there were no officially approved Congregations").

56. *Exponi nobis,* 26 iulii 1542 (*Bull. Ord. Praed.*, IV, p. 611); cf. Rodericus, Tomus III, quaes. 72, art. 2.

property they possessed with the permission of Superiors. Yet it declared that the practice whereby Superiors holding the property of the community in their own name and at their death making a will concerning it in favor of another member of the community was not to be considered as prohibited by the Council. Such a practice as the latter was morally necessary on account of the fact that the monastic wealth in England at this time was a prey to laics, both magistrates and princes, and this was but a means of protection. Such acts on the part of Superiors was merely an act of administration and not an illicit act of proprietorship.[57] The prelates of this Council were also solicitous about another phase of the observance of evangelical poverty by Religious: "We order that nuns and other women dedicated to Divine worship do not have a silk veil or "peplum," nor dare to wear in the veil silver or gold pins; nor may the monks or Canons Regular have silk belts ornamented by gold or silver." Only consecrated nuns could have rings and they were to be contented with only one. Those who violated this canon were to be admonished and if they did not amend were to be subjected to monastic discipline.[58]

Gregory IX, well understanding the need of the times, incorporated into his Decretals the legislation of a Council held at Rome in 1213 and thus gave universal legislative value to a law which previously enjoyed only local extention: "We strictly prohibit under conjuration of the Divine Judgment that any monk, in any way possess private property; if any one has private property, he must resign the whole of it to the common fund. But if any one, having received the regular previous admonition, is discovered in the possession of private property, he is to be expelled from the monastery nor may he again be received until he has repented according to monastic discipline. If after death this is discovered, it is to be buried with him outside the monastery in a dung hill as a sign of perdition."[59]

---

57. C. Oxoniensis, c. XLVII (Harduin, VII, 126); Cf. c. 2, X, *de testam. et ult.*, Vol. III, t. 26; Thomassinus, III, 2, 49, nn. 1-3. In 1234, Greg. IX made a positive general law prohibiting Religious to make a will. Cf. c. 2, X, *de testam. et ult.*, III, 26.

58. c. XXXVIII, (Harduin, VII, 123); cf. Coulton, II, 52.

59. c. 6, X, *de statu monachorum*, III, 35.

The Council of Rouen forbade monks to give anything to the Abbot for their board and room at a priory and Abbots were forbidden to receive anything on this account.[60] The Religious living under the jurisdiction of this Council were ordered to wear poor clothing prescribed by their Rule and not expensive vesture. Bishops were to be vigilant in this matter, and were to compel the monks to obey this injunction.[61] Several years later another Council held at this place cautioned the bishops to use diligent care lest nuns accumulate private property.[62] Another French Council enacted that no monk could have anything as his own, even if the Abbot gave permission for it; Abbots giving such permissions were to be severely punished.[63] In its efforts to secure an exact fulfillment of the vow of poverty still another French Council repeated the prohibition and punishment promulgated by the Third Latern Council and added: "Let no Religious Superior presume to mitigate this ordination, because abdication of property as the guardian of chastity is so attached to monastic Rules, that even the Supreme Pontiff can not permit indulgence against it."[64]

It seems that one of the abuses that had crept into the Religious Life at this time arose from the practice whereby monks and other Religious held money for the purchase of clothing. To remove the occasion of sin many Councils legislated against the practice.[65]

At a convention held at Capinacium in 1238, the archbishop and his suffragans reiterated the tenth canon of third Lateran Council and its sanction relative to peculium, but expressed some leniency; "If the Abbot or the Superior who received his Profession, humbly and devoutly

---

60. c. XLIII, (Harduin, VII, 189).

61. c. XLI (ibid.).

62. a. (1231) c. XXIX, (Mansi, XXIII, 218).

63. C. Castrum Guntherii, c. XXVI, (Harduin, VII, 195).

64. C. Bitterense, c. XIV (Harduin, VII, 211); cf. Cajetanus, 2. 2, quaes. 188, art. 1; Soto, lib. VII, de justitia, quaes. 1, art. 1 et 3; Navarrus, Comment. 1, de regular, nn. 18, 25-25, apud Bayllay, *Archiv für Katholichen Kirchenrechts,* XVII (1867), 7.

65. C. Biterrense, c. XVI (Harduin, VII, 211-212); C. Turonense (1239), c. XI (Harduin, VII, 325); C. Vallem Guidonis (1242), c. VII (Harduin, VII, 350); C. Coloniense (1260), c. III (Harduin, VII, 525); C. Albiense (1254), c. LII (Harduin, VII, 466); C. Londonense (1268), c. XLII (Harduin, VII, 640).

asks for the Christian burial of the monk who dies in the possession of private property, this dispensation may be granted.[66]

The Council of London in 1268 having prohibited monks and Canons Regular to possess private property, ordered that Religious Superiors should investigate twice a year as to whether the prohibition was being observed. If these Superiors failed in this respect they were "ipso facto" suspended from office.[67]

In France at the beginning of the fourteenth century there had developed a condition which needed the attention of the prelates in the Council of Auscitaneum convened in 1308. The Abbots had a practice of dividing the monastic property among the members of the community. The Council forbad this and declared that such acts were invalid.[68] The bestowal of pensions by the Abbots in favor of their subjects was equally censured.[69] Mendicants who had left their own Order to obtain such proprietary favors in a monastic Order, were to be deprived of what they has acquired.[70]

ARTICLE II. DECREES OF THE COUNCIL OF TRENT RELATIVE TO THE OBSERVANCE OF EVANGELICAL POVERTY

In order that the former discipline of Religious Orders might be promptly restored where it had fallen away, and might be more firmly maintained where it had been preserved, the Council of Trent decreed: "all Regulars, men

66. c. XX (Harduin VII, 320).

67. c. XLI (Harduin, VII, 640). Several other Councils which convened in the thirteenth century also passed enactments concerning the observance of poverty but they do not seem to be of sufficient interest on this point to be quoted in detail. Cf. C. Bituricense (1286), c. XIX (Harduin, VII, 958); cf. etiam, c. 2, X, *de testam et ult. volunt.* III, 26; c. 14, X, *de reg. et trans.*, III, 31; c. 6, X, *de statu monach.* III, 35. Within this period, similar to what the national Councils of the Western Church had ordained concerning the Rule of St. Benedict, the Provincial Council of Nicosiensis, ordained for the Greek and Syrian monks of the Kingdom of Cyprus, viz. that they follow the Rule of St. Basil. Among the parts of that Rule which was signalled out for special care as regards its observance was that pertaining to the renunciation of property. (c. XVI (Harduin, VII, 1716).

68. c. IV, (Harduin, VII, 1282).

69. ibid.

70. c. V, (Harduin, VII, 1282-1283).

and women, shall order their lives in accordance with the prescriptions of the Rule they professed . . . and above all, they shall observe whatever pertains to the perfection of their profession, such as the vows of obedience, poverty and chastity, as also the other vows and precepts . . . which regard the observance of a common mode of living, food and dress."[71]

(*a*) *Peculium*

Very exact were the terms used in the decree striking at peculium. "For no Regular, therefore, whether man or woman, shall it be lawful, to possess or to hold as his own or even in the name of the Institute, any property, movable or immovable, of whatever nature it may be, or in whatever way it may be acquired; but all shall be immediately delivered to the Superior and become incorporated with the Institute. Nor, henceforth shall it be lawful for Superiors to allow any real property (bona stabilia) to any Regular, not even by way of having the usufruct, or the use or administration thereof, or "in commendam." But the administration of the property of the monasteries or of the convents shall belong only to the officials thereof who are removable at the will of the Superiors."

"Let Superiors so allow the use of movables that everything be suitable to the state of poverty which they have professed, and there be nothing therein superfluous. However, nothing necessary shall be denied. . . . But should anyone be discovered (aut convictus est) to possess anything in any other manner, he must be deprived during two years of active and passive voice, and also punished in accordance with the constitutions of his own Rule and Order.[72]

(*b*) *Corporate Ownership*

The Council was not favorably disposed towards the idea of Religious Orders being incapable of owning property in common. Therefore it enacted: "The Holy See grants to all monasteries of men and women and of Mendicants (except to the houses of the Friars called Capuchins

---

71. Sess. XXV, *de regularibus,* c. I; cf. Waterworth on this point for the translation.

72. Chapter II; Cf. Barbossa, lib. I, c. XLIII, n. 73.

and Minor Observants)[73] and even to those in which this is prohibited or was not granted by Apostolic privilege, that henceforth, they may possess real estate (bona stabilia)."

(*c*) *Novices*

To protect perfervid youth from imprudence, a wise and beneficent decree proclaimed: "Profession must not be made in any Institute of men or women, before the completion of the sixteenth year, nor shall anyone be admitted to Profession, who has been under probation for less than a year since the habit was received. A Profession made before is null and induces no obligation to the observance of any Rule or Institute or Order or to any effects whatever."[74] Chapter Sixteen continues: "Further, no renunciation made or obligation assumed before, even though under oath or in favor of any pious object whatsoever, shall be valid, unless it is made with the permission of the bishop or of his vicar, within two months nearest Profession, and it shall not be understood otherwise as having any effect unless the Profession followed thereupon: but if done in any other manner, even with the express renunciation of this privilege, even if under oath, it shall be invalid and of no effect."[75]

"Before the Profession of the Novice, whether male or female, nothing shall be given to the monastery out of the property of the same, either by the parents, relatives, or guardians, under any pretext whatever, except for food and clothing, during the time they are under probation, lest (the said Novice) be unable to leave on this account that the monastery is in possession of the whole or the greater part of his substance and he is not able to recover it easily if he should leave. The Holy Synod commands under pain of anathema on the givers and receivers lest in any way this be done and that everything that was theirs be restored to those who leave before Profession. In order that this may be properly observed, the bishop shall use if necessary ecclesiastical censures."[76]

---

73. Cf. Bizzarri, p. 279, for a decision given 20 iunii 1686.

74. Chapter XV.

75. This decree also stated that it was not the intention of the Council to modify the Rule and practice of the Society of Jesus.

76. Chapter XVI.

(*d*) *Scope of Application of These Decrees*

The phraseology of the decree regulating the application of the foregoing legislation is interesting. "The Holy Synod enjoins that each and everything contained in the preceding decrees be observed in all the convents and monasteries, colleges and houses, of all the monks and Religious whatsoever, as also of all the Virgins and Widows, even though living under the care of the Military Orders, even under the Order (of St. John) of Jerusalem, and by whatever name they may be designated, under whatsoever Rule or Constitutions they may be, or under the care or government of, or in subjection to, union with, or dependence upon, any Order whatsoever, whether Mendicants or Non-Mendicants, or of other Regular monks or Canons of whatsoever kind; any privileges whatsoever, of all and each of the above named, under whatsoever form of words expressed, even those called "mare magnum," even those obtained at their foundation, as also any Rules and Constitutions even though sworn to, and any customs or prescriptions whatsoever to the contrary, even though immemorial. But if there be any Regulars, whether men or women, who are living under a stricter Rule or statutes, the Holy See does not intend to withdraw them from their Institute and observance, except as to the power of possessing real estate in common."[77] This chapter of the twenty-fifth session concludes with instructions intended to secure the execution of the above cited decrees.

ART. III. POST TRIDENTINE LEGISLATION UNTIL THE NINETEENTH CENTURY

(*a*) *Solemn and Simple Vows After Trent*

Shortly after the Council of Trent, Pius V displeased with nuns who were not observing the law of enclosure[78] ordered women with solemn vows to obey the decree of the recent General Council.[79] The tertiaries living the

77. Chapter XXII.

78. Cf. Schaaf, *The Cloister,* pp. 49-50.

79. Sess. XXV, *de regularibus,* Chapter V. One of the chief causes for some of these nuns' failure to keep within the cloister was the fact that their poverty compelled them to go out begging for their sustenance. Cf. Pennacchi, *Commentaria in Constitutionem "Apostolicæ Sedis,"* Vol. I, p. 706.

"common life" without solemn vows[80] were to be persuaded to make solemn vows, and to observe the strict cloister. If they refused they were barred from receiving any more subjects and if, in spite of this latter regulation, they received candidates, then any Profession and Reception of prospective subjects was null and void.[81]

Again in 1568, the celebrated Bull, "Lubricum vitae genus," promulgated by the same Pontiff and addressed to all Institutes not renouncing property nor professing any of the approved Rules, ordered that within twenty-four hours after they received notice of this legislation, they must adopt one of the approved Rules and within a month they must make solemn vows. If they refused to conform to the dictates of this Bull they were to be punished.[82] The mention of these Congregations of men in the latter Bull seems to indicate that the only objection against them was the fact they made only simple vows.[83]

Although the constitution "Lubricum vitae genus," from its wording, included all Institutes, yet, from the sixteenth to the eighteenth centuries, the Holy See approved Institutes of men and without the restricting clause which usually accompanied the official toleration of Institutes of women at a later date, viz. "circa approbationem conservatorii."[84] There can be no doubt about the validity of the vows of poverty professed in these Institutes of men. The

80. Boudinhon, *Le Canoniste Contemporain,* XXV (1902), 361; Orth (p. 28) rightly remarks that the reason Tertiaries were specifically mentioned was the fact that they were the only ones existing at the time. It was the intention of the Pope to abolish all that did not conform to his wishes.

81. Const. *Circa Pastoralis,* 29 maii 1566 (*Bul. Rom.,* VII, p. 447). For the assistance of those in want, the Pope ordained that extern Sisters, who were not permitted to enter the cloister, be commissioned to beg for alms for the nuns; if this means did not suffice, the bishops and other Superiors were to provide in any other suitable manner; the number of nuns in a convent ought not be greater than could be well supported by its income or usual alms. (Cf. Schaaf, 50-51), vide etiam Pius V, const. *Decori,* 1 febr. 1570 (*Fontes,* n. 133).

82. 17 nov. 1568 (*Bul. Rom.* VII, pp. 725-726).

83. Orth, p. 27.

84. e.g. Congregation of Clerks Regular Administering to the Infirm, (Sixtus V, const. *Ex omnibus,* 18 martii 1586 (*Bul. Rom.,* VIII, pp. 669 sq.); Clerks Regular of the Mother of God, Clem. VIII, const. *Ex quo Divina,* 13 oct. 1595 (*Bul. Rom.* X, p. 227); Congregation of Christian Doctrine, Clem. VIII, const. *Exposcit debitum,* 23

obligations arising from these vows were determined by the private legislation of the particular Institute.[85]

Communities of Women Without Solemn Vows

Despite the solemn condemnation merited by so many of these Tertiaries, the legislation of Pius V never attained its full effect, viz. the total abolition of these communities.[86] It is certain many of these communities of Tertiaries continued "de facto" to exist and function even though they were at this time canonical non-entities.[87] These congregations continued to grow in numbers and new ones sprang up in the course of years. Subsequent Popes did not issue explicit decrees against these congre-

---

dec. 1597 (*Bul. Rom.*, X, p. 411 sq.); Congregation of Poor Clerks of the Mother of God of Pious Schools, Paul. V, const. *Ad ea,* 6 martii 1617 (*Bul. Rom.* XII, p. 382); The Congregation of the Mission, Alex. VIII, const. 22 sept. 1655 (*Bul. Rom.* XVI, p. 67); The Congregation of the Most Holy Redeemer, Benedict XIV, brev. *Ad Pastoralis,* 25 febr. 1749 (mentioned in const. of Pii VI, *Sacrosanctum,* 21 aug. 1789 § 2, *Bul. Rom. Continuatio,* X, p. 2111 and in beginning of the *Codex Regularium et Constitutionum* (1895); Congregation of the Passion, Clem. XVI, brev. *Supremi Apostolatus,* 16 dec. 1769 § 3 (*Bul. Rom. Continuatio,* VII, p. 73; Litt. Apos. *Salvatoris D. N. J. C.*, 21 nov. 1769, *Bul. Rom. Continuatio,* VII, pp. 111 sq.).

85. It is worthy of notice that some of the simple vow Institutes became Orders and some of the Orders became Congregations, e.g. Priests Regular of the Mother of God, Greg. XV, const. *In supremo,* nov. 3, 1621 (*Bul. Rom.* XII, p. 608); Clerks Regular of the Mother of God, Greg. XV, const. *In supremo,* nov. 3, 1621 (*Bul. Rom.* XII, p. 608); Clerks Regular of the Mother of God, Greg. XV, const. *In supremo,* nov. 18, 1621 (*Bul. Rom.* XII, pp. 627-628); Hospitalers of St. Joseph, Alex. VII, const. *Sacrosancti,* 8 ian. 1666 (*Bul. Rom.*, XVII, pp. 411 sq.); Hippolitans, Innocent. XII, const. *Ex debito,* 20 maii 1700, § 3, (*Bul. Rom.* XX, 933); Bethlehemites, Clem. XI, const. *Ex debito,* 1 aprilis 1710 (*Bul. Rom.* XXI, p. 385); Portugal Congregation of Discalced Monks of St. Paul the First Hermit, Pius VI, const. *Ex debito,* 3 *febr.* 1784 (*Bul. Rom. Continuatio,* IX, p. 1337); Order of Friars of Penance, Pius VI, const. *Ex debito,* 21 maii 1784 (*Bul. Rom. Continuatio,* IX, p. 1381; Immaculate Conception Marianists, Pius VI, const. *Ex debito,* 27 martii 1787 (*Bul. Rom. Continuatio,* IX, p. 1782); cf. Battandier, *Guide Canonique Pour Les Constitutions des Instituts a Voeux Simples,* p. xii; Bizzarri, pp. 616, 631, 735-737, 487; Saler, *Linzer theologische praktiche Quartalschrift,* LXV (1912) 265; Freriks, *Religious Congregations in Their External Relations,* pp. 21-26; De Angelis, Vol. II, lib. 3, tit. 35, p. 98; [Orth, p. 33, and Larraona, CpR, I (1920), 133 are somewhat inaccurate here.]

86. Cf. Orth, p. 28; Lucidi, II, n. 264; Bouix, I, p. 234; Larraona, CpR, I (1920), 47; Moroto, CpR, VIII (1927) 423; McNeil,

gations, although several expressed a desire that they should observe the intent of Pius V.[88]

Gradually the Holy See came to tolerate these institutions[89] which had only episcopal approval.[90] Benedict XIII even went so far as to say he did not wish to prohibit them.[91] Yet the attitude of the Holy See, a few years later, was such that the Pope nullified the Bull "Pretiosus" of Benedict XIII[92] and thus the state of affairs reverted to that preceding Benedict XIII.[93] In the reign of Benedict XIV the attitude of the Holy See was again that of tolerance.[94] The celebrated Bull concerning the Anglican Nuns expresses the status of the Institutes of women not making solemn vows. "Dictarum vero virginum conservatoria, licet ab Apostolica Sede, ut prefertus, non approbata, ab hac tamen benigne tolerari."[95] After advising the Bishops to treat them kindly, he continues, "Earum vero conservatoria tolerari quidem ab hac eadem Apostolica Sede, sed Institutum ipsum nec approbatum, nec confirmatum esse; obsistentibus sacris canonibus et generali constitutione Sancte Pii V ne religiosae mulierum domus Apostolica confirmatione stabiliantur, quae se perfectae clausurae legibus non obstrinxerit."[96]

---

p. 27; Bachofen, p. 364; Zittelli, P. I, lib. II, p. 422; Vermeersch, *De Religiosis,* I, n. 66.

87. As Benedict XIV taught: "Certum quidem est post decretum etiam eiusdem Pontificis, in multis Italiæ Urbis huiusmodi Tertiarias versari, quae nec solemnia vota concipiunt, nec claus rarum legibus tenentur." (*Institutiones Ecclesiasticæ,* Inst. XXIX, n. 3; CV, nn. 76-77).

88. Orth, p. 29.

89. Cf. Espelage, *Aggregations of Tertiary Religious Institutes,* pp. 2-3.

90. The legate of the Holy See in France, the Cardinal of Vendome, in 1668, speaking of the Rules of the Daughters of Charity (who even today profess only private vows) declared: "We give them all the force that the perpetual and inviolable authority of the Holy See can give and supply all defects, in general and particular, if there be any." Cf. *Sisters of Charity of St. Vincent de Paul,* pp. 43, 49.

91. Bulla, *Pretiosus,* 25 maii 1727 (*Bul. Rom.* XXII, p. 542).

92. Clem. XII, bulla, *Romanus Pontifex,* 31 martii 1732 (*Bul. Rom.* XXIII, 324).

93. Cf. Benedict XIV, *Institutiones Ecclesiasticæ,* Inst. CV, n. 79.

94. Benedict XIV, *Institutiones Ecclesiasticæ,* Inst. XXIX, n. 6.

95. Const. *Quamvis insto,* 30 aprilis, 1749, § 13 (*Bullarium Benedict XIV,* III, p. 54; (*Fontes,* n. 398). The same paragraph said their promises were, at the most, simple vows.

Whatever vows of poverty were made by these simple vow Institutes were regulated by the private legislation obtaining in the respective Institute. There was no general legislation for the simple vow of poverty at this time. The only legislation of a papal character that applied as regards the simple vow of poverty was an occasional rescript given to some of the approved Institutes.[97]

(*b*) *Deathbed Professions and Property Rights*

During the Middle Ages it had happened too frequently that men of wealth at the last moment of their lives made Profession in a Religious Institute. The purpose of this Profession was to avail themselves of the "Second Baptism" and thus enter at once into Heaven; for, long had it been the teaching of divines, that the Religious Profession affected the soul, as regards its previous defilement, after the manner of Baptism. Needless to say this practice not infrequently had ill effects. The deceased, having departed this world as a Religious, his property belonged to the monastery. But, many were the law suits that arose, when the people who would have succeeded to the deceased's property, contested in court for the property in the possession of the Religious.

After the Council of Trent, Pius V granted to the Dominican Nuns a privilege whereby the novices could be admitted to profession when in danger of death, even though the term of the novitiate was not yet completed.[98] This favor was also accorded to many other Institutes.[99] Doubts having arisen concerning the effects of this Profession in regard to the possessions of such a person, Clement VIII declared that the Institute did not thereby obtain any title to the property nor any property rights.[100]

---

96. § 23 of same constitution.

97. Cf. e.g. Bizzarri, pp. 74-75; Lucidi, II, n. 321.

98. *Sumni sacerdotii,* 22 aug. 1570 (*Bul. Rom.* VII, 849).

99. Vermeersch states that the other Orders obtained the privilege only by the "communicatio privilegiorum." *De Religiosis,* Vol. I, p. 129.

100. *Cum ad Regularem,* 19 marti 1603, (*Bullarium Ordinis Praedicatorum* II, p. 370; cf. Fagnanus, III, de regularibus, c. Ad Apostolicam, nn. 32-33. On Nov. 26, 1616, the S. C. Concili decided that when a person had been seduced to enter the Religious Life in order to obtain his property, the profession would be considered valid but the property was to go to the heirs. (Fagnanus, III de regularibus, c. Sicuti nobis, nn. 7-22).

If the novice recovered she could freely leave the Institute.[101]

(c) *Donations Made to Externs*

Since great abuses had arisen in the past from the practice of presenting gifts to influential persons outside the Institute Clement VIII determined to end this once and for all. On June 19, 1594, he issued a constitution forbidding all Religious, except the Military Orders, to make donations. Hospitality was to be admitted within proper limits.[102] Five years later the same Pontiff cautioned Superiors of the Servite Order not to violate the law about the bestowal of gifts.[103] The penalties which the Pontiff prescribed for violations of this law were indeed drastic.[104] Urban VIII modified the law itself to the extent of permitting donations to be made for the sake of gratitude, conciliation or for the obtainment and conservation of benevolences towards the monastery or Religion.[105]

(d) *Peculium After Trent*

Before the Council of Trent, Religious could have peculium with dependence on the Superior for its use. This obtained at least from custom, according to the medieval canonists.[106] Yet it is difficult to mistake the intention of the Council of Trent in prohibiting all forms

101. On Sept. 10, 1912 this privilege of deathbed professions was extended to all Religious Institutes. (AAS, IV [1912] 589.)

102. *Religiosae Congregationes* (*Bul. Rom.* VIII, p. 146; *Fontes*, n. 178).

103. Decr. *Nullus omnino*, 25 iulii 1599, § 21, (*Fontes*, 187.).

104. *Religiosae Congregationes* §§ 7-8; Piat I, pp. 265-266 may be consulted for the interpretation of the application of the penalties contained in this section of the constitution.

105. const. *Nuper a congregatione*, 16 oct. 1640, (*Fontes*, n. 220.).

106. Cf. Suarez, Vol. XV, tract. 7, lib. 8, c. 14, n. 3; Schmalzgrueber, lib. III, tit. 35, n. 12; Bouix, I, p. 515. It had often happened in monasteries of men and women, that the novice in the act of renunciation required of all Religious, donated his property to the monastery but at the same time reserved to himself the revenues thereof. A variation of this custom was to make the act or reservation at the time of Profession. In some places there was the practice of parents and relatives committing property to the monastery, with the proviso that the Superior must grant to the relative in the monastery, the administration of the property so that the revenues could be used by him for an honest purpose. In other places there flourished the surprising monastic stratagem whereby the remuneration

of peculia.[107] However, shortly after the Council, some communities continued their former practices, and some canonists argued that these communities were not acting illicitly, at least if the peculium was on deposit with the Superior and his permission was had for the use of it.[108] Using only the strict letter of the law, the opinion of these canonists was not devoid of all probability.[109] There may have been lacunae in the Tridentine legislation, although the opposite opinion clearly appears to be most probable.[110]

Clement VIII effectually supplemented the Tridentine legislation in his well known decree, "Nullus omnino,"

---

acquired by preaching or teaching and all the other property otherwise acquired was handed over to the Superior with the agreement that a capital be formed therefrom and its revenue be given to the Religious for his necessities. Cf. Fagnanus, III, De statu monachorum, c. Monachi, n. 1 sq.; De Luca-Gallemart, *Annotationes ad SS. Concilium Tridentium,* Discursus XXXIV, nn. 16 sq.; Pius V, bulla, *Ad extirpandos cupidae,* 8 iuni 1567, (*Bul. Rom.* VII, n. 27, pp. 676-678). For papal indults granting other dispensation from the common life, cf. Migne, P. L., IX, 410; *Monumenta Ordinis Fratrum Praedcatorum Historica,* IV, 116.

107. Sess. XV, *de regularibus,* Chapter II; Fagnanus, III, de statu monachorum, c. Monachi, 2 sq.; Schmalzgrueber, lib. III, tit. 35, n. 14; Reiffenstuel, lib. III, tit. 35, n. 6.

108. Cf. Suarez, Vol. XV, tract. 7. lib. 8, c. 14, n. 6; Antonius a Spiritu Sancto, Sect. II, disp. 4, 80 sq.

109. Those who held that the Tridentine law prohibited only peculium possessed independently of the Superior declared: (1) The phrase, "Superiori tradantur conventuque incorporentur" does not militate against dependent peculium because it is had from the goods already incorporated in the community property and is held with the permission of the Superior. (2) Nowhere from the face of the decree, does it appear that the Council of Trent intended to make a new law which did not prohibit dependent peculium. (3) Those asserting that the Council of Trent intended to make a new law should prove it and they have advanced no convincing argument in favor of their contention. cf. Biederlack-Führich, pp. 187-188.

110. The opinion which was more widely received relative to the force and extent of the Tridentine decree adduced this argumentation: (1) The decree positively exacted that property, however acquired may not be possessed or retained by the private Religious; even though the private Religious retained the propetry not in his own name but in the name of the Institute, the decree expressly legislated against such a practice. (2) The decree also stated: "Administratio autem bonorum monasteriorm seu conventuum *ad solos officiales* eorundem ad nutum Superiorum amovibiles pertinent. "What could be plainer? cf. Biederlack-Führich, p. 188. The "Nullus omnino" referred to the decree of Trent as its basis.

addressed to the Servites.[111] Having reiterated the prohibition of the Council, he specifically enumerated and condemned the ways Religious as individuals had been holding property. "Quo Tridentini Concilii decreta de paupertatis voto custodiendo fidelius observentur, praecipitur, ut nullus ex fratribus, etiam si Superior sit, bona mobilia vel immobilia, aut pecuniam, proventus, census, eleemosynas, sive ex contionibus, sive ex lectionibus, aut pro Missis, tam in propria ecclesia, quam ubicumque celebrandis aliove ipsorum iusto labore et quocumque nomine acquisita etiamsi subsidia consanguineorum, aut piorum largitiones, legata aut donantiones fuerint, tamquam propria, aut etiam nomine conventus possidere possit: sed ea omnia statim Superiori tradantur et conventui incorporentur, atqui cum certis illius bonis, reditibus, pecuniis, ac proventibis, confundantur, quo communis inde victus et vestitus omnibus suppeditari possit."

Continuing the same idea the decree declared: that no Superior could grant to these Religious any usufruct, use, administration of "bona stabilia," neither "incommendam" nor in the name of deposit or custody. No dispensation of any Superior or permission for movable or immovable property could excuse these Religious from the penalty which the Council declared would be "ipso facto" incurred by the possessors of private property. This held effective even if the Superior had asserted that he could grant such permissions or dispensations.[112]

Several other interpretations of the Tridentine decrees given at this time by the Holy See leave practically no room for doubt that the Council prohibited even dependent peculium.[113] Yet it was possible that in the course of time that custom could if vested with the due conditions

111. Decr. 25 iulii 1599 (*Fontes,* n. 187); cf. *Bul. Rom.* VII, p. 821 for other legislation on poverty given to this Institute.

112. § 2 of the *Nullus omnino*: cf. etiam. S. C. Concilii, 21 Sept. 1624 § 1, apud Vermeersch, *De Religiosis,* II, p. 318.

113. S. C. Concilii, a. 1586, lib. decreto, 4. p. 114; a. 1601, lib. decreto, 10, p. 11 apud Benedict XIV, *De Synodo Diocesana,* LXIII, c, 12, n. 20; S. C. Concilii 4 iulii, 1602; 12 ian 1603; 17 aprillis 1649; S. C. EE et RR, 7 aprilis 1707; apud Wernz, III, p. 334; cf. Suarez, Vol. XV, tract. 7. lib. 8, c. 14, n. 5-8 sq.; Schmalzgrueber, lib. III, tit. 35, nn. 13-14; Reiffenstuel, lib. III, tit. 35, n. 6; Piat. I, pp. 246 sq. Petra *Const. V, Benedict. XII,* II, n. 28-34; Fagnanus, de statu monach. c. Monachi, nn. 61-64;

prevail against the Trent.[114] The idea of dependent peculium was not "in se" repugnant to the vow of poverty.[115] Had not the Holy See, taking into consideration the circumstances of the case, approved the "Constitutiones Ordinis Sanctae Mariae de Mercede," in which peculium was permitted with the permission of the Superior?[116] And Benedict XIV taught that peculium dependent on the will of the Superior, under certain conditions, was licit.[117] Even Clement VIII seemed to tolerate such peculium in an individual case.[118]

Customs concerning dependent peculia, although contrary to the Tridentine decree and its authentic interpretations, have obtained in many places[119] during the past three hundred years. Nor can these practices be called illegitimate although they do not conform to the text of the Tridentine law.[120] As St. Alphonsus, speaking of the eighteenth century, said: "By reason of custom which has been introduced in nearly all Religious Institutes, at least not reformed, I think the rigor of the Council has been modified today, and it is lawful for Religious to have peculium, with the consent of the Superior."[121] To conclude with Pellizarius, "I dare not condemn a custom tolerated by Pontiffs, Ordinaries and Religious Prelates,

---

114. Cf. Belorgey, *De Consuetudine,* pp. 122 sq. who ably argues that the opinion holding that custom could prevail against the law is the more probable one. Cf. Suarez, *De Legibus,* lib. VII, c. 19, n. 27; Billuart, *De Legibus,* Diss. V, art. 2; Santi, *Praelectiones,* lib. III, de prebend et dignitat. n. 75; Schmalzgrueber, lib. III, tit. 35, n. 14; Castellini, *De electione,* XVI, III, 7, 6. Innocent. XII, *In iniunctio,* 7 dec. 1691, (*Bul. Rom.* XX, pp. 232 sq.); Lezana, I, 1, 6, 56; Salmanticenses, XII, 21, 203; Castro Palao, XVI, 3, 7, 6.

115. Cf. Lombardi, Vol. I, p. 432.

116. D. 3, Caput, De Voto Paupertatis (*Bul. Rom.* XX, p. 518).

117. *De Servorum Dei Beatificatione,* lib. III, c. 41, n. 12; *De Synodo Diocesana,* lib. III, c. 12, n. 21.

118. Cf. Ferraris, *Bibliotheca,* Moniales, II, 69; Piat, I, p. 246.

119. Antonius a Spiritu Sancto, Sect. II, tract. 3, disp. 4, n. 84, p. 127; Bouix, I, p. 517; Piat, I, p. 247; St. Alphonsus, Liguori, IV, c. l, n. 15; Gearin, AER, LXI (1919) 152; and a great many others as may be found in St. Alphonsus-Gaude, Vol. II, pp. 456-457.

120. Schmalzgrueber, lib. III. tit. 25, n. 14; St. Alphonsus, IV, c. l. n. 15; Craisson, *Praelectiones,* n. 2757; Ballerini-Palmieri, IV, t. 9, nn. 115 sq.; Bacoffen, p. 120; Carriere, Vol. I, n. 204; D'Annibale, pars III, n. 504; et multi alii.

121. *Theologia Moralis,* IV, c. l, n. 15.

knowing and consenting, for the avoidance of greater evils."[122]

(e) *Obligations of Bishops Regular*

The obligations of Regulars elevated to the episcopacy, as regards the vow of poverty, continued to be the same, after the Council, i.e., they had the right to acquire property, but only for the Sees, although they had unrestricted administration and use of it,[123] yet as far as possible they must observe their vow in the use of things, as is done by their brethren in the Institutes to which they belong.[124] Benedict XIII went even further and commanded that Cardinals and Bishops Regular must observe evangelical poverty according to the norm of their Institute. "If they contemn or neglect this constitution they are 'ipso facto' suspended from the use of Pontificals,"[125] until receding from their contumacy they merit to obtain from the Holy See a relaxation from the suspension. The same Pontiff revoking previous constitutions of Alexander IV and Clement IV declared that Regulars promoted to the episcopate need permission to take away with them anything other than their breviary and their personal writings.[126]

A Franciscan Bishop in 1864 did quite a favor for the Bishops Regular of our times. The rescript educed from his query was very definite and satisfying. "Bishops Regular are obliged to observe the Rules of their Institute which determine the matter of poverty."[127]

No express legislation was formulated for those Religious, belonging to Congregations, who had been elevated

---

122. *De Monialibus,* c. XLVIII, n. 6.

123. *Monumenta Germanica Historica, Leges,* II, p. 560; Benedict, XIV, *Quaestiones Canonicae et Morales,* Q. CCCXXXIX, Vol. I, pp. 436-437; *Fontes,* n. 238; Barbossa, *Iuris Ecclesiastici Universi, Libri Tres,* I, c. XLIII, nn. 241-243; Pallottini, *Regulares,* VII, n. 60; ASS, I, (1865), 227; *Fontes,* n. 1990.

124. S. C. EE et RR, *Alexien.* 6 maii 1864, (*Fontes,* n. 1990).

125. Const. *Custodes super* 7 martii 1726, §§ 4-6 (*Fontes,* n. 291); cf. etiam, Benedict XIII, const. *Postulat.* 7, martii, 1725, § 5, (*Bul. Rom. Luxemburg;* XIII, p. 145);*Collectanea. S. C. de Prop. Fidei* n. 2152.

126. Cf. Prümmer, *Jus Regularium Speciale,* P. 111, c. 3, art. 1, Q. 120.

127. S. C. EE et RR, *Alexien,* 6 maii, (*Fontes,* n. 1990.)

to the episcopacy. Canonists thought that such Bishops had the same kind of obligation, due allowance being made for the difference of the vows, as had the Bishops Regular.[128]

(*f*) *The Dower*

On September 1, 1604, the Holy See decreed that after the fixed quota of any convent of nuns had been filled, all prospective subjects must deposit at least four hundred ecus (about $400)[129] with the community.[130] What a change of discipline had taken place in this regard during the preceding seven centuries! The seventh eecumenical Council most severely forbade as a species of simony, any exaction for support from candidates of a Religious Community.[131] Abesses guilty of such a forbidden practice were to be ejected from the community and confined in another monastery for penance. A national Council repeated the prohibition.[132] The Lateran III Council also forbade anything to be exacted on entrance into the monastery,[133] as did the Decretals.[134] St. Thomas[135] and St. Bonaventure[136] as well as later theologians[137] advanced the idea that if the money or property is not exacted as a price of admission but rather as sustenance for the subject because the monastery is too poor to support her, such a practice is not illicit.

The Council of Trent in endeavoring to safeguard the liberty of the novice had established that nothing other

128. Cf. Avanzini, ASS, I (1865) 446; Cf. Vermeersch, *Periodica,* I (1905) p. 7.

129. Bizzarri, pp. 241-243; Lucidi, Vol. II, Cap. V, De monialibus, § 5, n. 191.

130. Cf. Boudinhon, "Dower" (*Cath. Ency.*)

131. Cf. C. Nicaea II, (787) c. 19 (Harduin, IV, 498.)

132. C. Francfordensis, (794) c. 16, (Harduin, IV, 906).

133. (1179) c. X, (Mansi XXII, 1051).

134. cc. 8, 19, 25, 30, 40, X *de simonia,* V, 3.

135. *Summa Theologica,* II, II, Quaes. 100, art. 3, n. 4.

136. *In Apologetica contra adversarios FF. Minor,* q. 18. It is a well known fact that the subject of poverty was the dominant theme of discussion during the thirteenth and fourteenth centuries; it was argued as hotly and stubbornly as was the natures of the Savior from the fourth to the sixth century, cf. Harnack, *Dögmengeschichte,* III, p. 388; Balthaser, *Geschichte des Armutsstreites im Franziskanerorden bis zum Konzil von Vienne;* Felder, 457.

137. Cf. Benedict XIV, *De Synodo Diocesana,* XI, 6, 2,; VII, 58, 2;

than the actual expenses of sustenance during the novitiate could be exacted from the novice.[138] However, it had not been the mind of the Council to reprobate the doctrine of St. Thomas and the theologians as can be seen from the decision the Sacred Congregation of Bishops and Regulars gave.[139] Experience having demonstrated that monasteries and convents once wealthy were not infrequently reduced to distress in later years, the Holy See issued the decree concerning dowers.[140]

Numerous decisions were given by the Sacred Congregation for the benefit of communities petitioning for rescripts pertaining to dowers. The dower must be in money and not in real estate,[141] except when a special indult was obtained from the Holy See;[142] nor may it be left in the possession of relatives but must be placed in the hands of honest and capable men, as representatives of the monastery.[143] Before the postulant receives the habit the dower ought to be actually[144] on deposit.[145] Ordinaries must not legislate that they be made the "depositarius" nor may they determine the amount of the dower.[146] Profession having taken place, the money must be placed in the common fund of the convent.[147] It was permissible to defer the Profession beyond a year, if the dower was not available at the proper time[148] or the novice could be

138. Sess. XXV, *de regularibus,* c. XVII; Cf. Suarez, Vol. XV, tract. 7, lib. 5, c. 9, n. 16.

139. Cf. Fagnanus, 111, Non amplius, c. de institutionibus, n. 24, p. 178.

140. Benedict XIV, *De Synodo Diocesana,* XI, 6, 2; VII, 58, 2; Cf. Ferreris, *Moniales,* II, n. 18; Pellizarius, *De Monialibus,* p. 34; Lucidi, *De Monialibus,* § 5, n. 184.

141. S. C. EE et RR. *In Camerien,* 28 martii 1588; *Interamin.* 2 maii 1614, (Lucidi, 1. c. n. 187).

142. S. C. EE et RR, *Brictorien.* 30 maii 1766; 13 iulii 1881 (Lucidi *ibid*).

143. S. C. EE et RR, *Camerien.* 15 martii 1591; *Neapolitana,* 11 maii 1640; 20 ian. 1643, (Ferraris, *Moniales,* nn. 18-20).

144. S. C. EE et RR, *Portugalen.* 6 iul. 1635; *Brundusin.* 15 iun. 1616, (Ferraris, 1. c. nn. 21-23).

145. Cf. Lucidi, 1. c. nn. 187-188.

146. S. C. EE et RR, *Vercellen.* nov. 15, 1606, (Lucidi, 1. c. n. 189).

147. S. C. EE et RR, *Asculana,* 19 ian, 1630, (Lucidi, 1. c. n. 190).

148. S. C. EE et RR, 31 maii 1597, (Ferraris, 1. c. n. 25.).

allowed to make the customary vows.[149] Earlier discipline did not prevent the spending of the dower for the utility of the monastery.[150] However, in the latter part of the eighteenth century, it was an established principle that all dowers of Religious must be invested in safe and stable capital.[151] Very stringent precautions were taken lest the dower be alienated.[152] The dower was not to be paid in instalments but the whole was to be deposited at one time.[153] It was considered an intolerable abuse that a nun should have a testament whereby on her death the dower would revert to her heirs and not to the monastery.[154] Much discussion arose as to which monastery a dower should belong when a nun transferred from one monastery to another. The better solution was always to seek a rescript from the Sacred Congregation of Bishops and Regulars, having stated in the petition anything which ought to be taken into consideration, e.g. peculiar circumstances affecting the case.[155]

(g) *Secularization and vow of poverty.*

It may be noted here that before the Code an indult of secularization obtained from the Holy See did not "ex se" release a Religious from his vow of poverty. Nor did it grant the right to recover possession of the property renounced before Profession. Bizzarri also observed that a special faculty was required to dispose of property by an act, "inter vivos" or "mortis causa", even if the indult had granted perpetual secularization.[156]

---

149. S. C. EE et RR, *Nucerin.* 14 febr. 1635, (Ferraris, 1. c. n. 26).

150. S. C. EE et RR, *Ariminen.* 12 maii 1601; *Ferrarien.* 25 martii 1601, (Lucidi, 1. c. n. 191).

151. S. C. EE et RR, 21 aprilis et 24 nov. 1780 (Lucidi, c. n. 191). n. 191).

152. S. C. EE et RR, *Brixien,* 23 febr. 1603; *Aretina,* 24 martii 1597; *Cremonen,* 27 sept. 1601; *Mediolanen.* 4 aug. 1603 (Lucidi, 1 c. n. 197).

153. S. C. EE et RR, *Faventina,* 13 apr. 1602; *Messanen,* 16 dec. 1617 (Lucidi, 1 c. n. 191).

154. S. C. EE et RR, *Mutinen.* 11 iunii 1627 (Lucidi, 1 c. n. 198).

155. Cf. Lucidi, 1 c. nn. 204-213.

156. Bizzarri, p. 75; *Thesaurus Resolutioum S. C. Concilii,* LXX, 179 (1805); Vecchiotti, *Institutiones Canonicæ,* Vol. I, p. 347.

ARTICLE IV. THE ERA OF THE SIMPLE VOW OF POVERTY.

At the end of the eighteenth century there arose the persecution of Religious in Europe. As early as 1781, the Emperor of Austria abolished many monasteries in his kingdom.[157] In France (1790) 'all Orders and Congregations which were not dedicated to general instruction, works of charity or the promotion of science, were suppressed.[158] The Convention (1792-1795) completed the suppression of the Religious under French rule. Germany soon followed the example of France; in 1802 the civil law there suppressed all Religious in the four provinces across the Rhine[159] and the following year the remaining Institutes suffered a similar fate.[160] In nearly all European countries the same kind of legislation, so disastrous to the Religious Life came to prevail.[161]

The interference of the Belgian civil laws, declaring solemn vows non-existent, and granting to Religious who had professed the solemn vow of poverty, the right to retain dominion and usufruct of private property, as well as to dispose of it by an act "inter vivos" in favor of whomsoever they willed, was the occasion of remarkable indults, from the Holy See. The Sacred Penitentiary on February 18, 1809 granted to French nuns the following indult relative to poverty: "Art. 9, Chaque hospitaliere conservera l'entiere propriete de ses biens et revenus, et le droit de les administer at d'en disposer conformement au code civil. Art. 10. Elle ne pourra, par acte entre vifs, ni y

157. Cf. Jungmann, *Dissertationes Selectæ in Historiam Ecclesiasticam*, VII, p. 418.

158. Cf. Funk, *Manual of Church History*, II, p. 233.

159. Cf. Marx, *Lehrbuch der Kirchengeschichte*, p. 744.

160. Marx, p. 756.

161. Cf. Wouters, *Historiæ Ecclesiasticæ Compendium*, II, pp. 301, 312; Marx, pp. 758-759, "Der angefertigte Plan . . . wurde der Reichsdepuatation . . . zu Regensburg vorgelegt, und sie nahm ihn . . . an in ihrem Reichsdeputationschauptschlusse von 25 Februar 1803 . . . Die Aufhebung der Klöster wurde mit einer Roheit und sakrilegischen Verunehrung des Heiligen durchgeführt, welche jener der französchen Revolutionare kaum nachstand." For Italy cf. Wouters, II, p. 329, Alzog, III, 790. Piontek, 62-64. The older and well known Orders being suppressed and the works of charity such as nursing and teaching being in great demand, associations of pious people under episcopal direction sprang into existence. Many of these developed into Religious communities. They worked so well both for the sanctification of their members and the salvation of souls that

renoncer au profit de sa famille, ni en disposer soit au profit de la congregation, soit en faveur de qui gue ce soit".[162] On December 1, 1820, the Sacred Penitentiary granted to all solemnly professed Religious, of both sexes in the Kingdom of Belgium (which at that time included Holland) the right to acquire, retain, administer and dispose of private property for any pious and honest use, provided this was done with due dependence on their Religious Superiors.[163] It is evident from a subsequent authentic interpretation of July 31, 1878, that this indult conferred a real right to property and not merely an authorization to perform civil acts.[164]

Quite different was the indult granted to the Religious of the United States of America on Dec. 15, 1840. This rescript empowered duly authorized Religious to hold and administer property of their Institute in their own name but these acts were to be valid only in civil law.[165]

As a result of the anti-Religious laws, many Religious were compelled to live separated from their communities. Not infrequently many of these Religious found them-

---

finally the Holy See bid them increase and welcome into the ranks of Religious. Cf. Leo XIII, Const. *Conditæ a Christo,* 8 dec. 1900 (*Fontes,* n. 644); Pius X, motu proprio, *Dei Providentis,* 16 iulii 1906 (*Fontes,* n. 675). Thus at first forbidden and opposed, then tolerated, later praised and finally fully recognized as Religious, the Simple Vow Institutes have come into their own.

162. The same decree was promulgated in parts of Holland on June 22, 1810. Cf. Vermeersch, *De Religiosis,* I, *Supplementum,* VI, p. 79.

163. "S. Paenitentiaria intellegens velle omnino gubernium, ut vetus illud decretum diei 18 Febr. 1809, a regularibus regni Belgii observetur, quo proprietas, possessio et administratio bonorum, quae ad eos pervenerunt, singulis religiosis vel monialibus vindicetur, concedit de expressa auctoritate Apostolica regularibus utriusque sexus iam sollemniter professis, ut ea bona aquierere, retinere et administrare, deque iis in pios honestosque usus disponere possint, non obstante paupertatis voto, dummodo cum debita a Superioribus legitimis dependentia hoc faciant." Bizzarri, p. 739; Vermeersch, *De Religiosis,* I, *Supplementum,* VI, p. 78; De Angelis *Praelectiones,* Vol. II, lib. 3, tit. 35, p. 168; Angelus a SS Corde, *Manuale Iuris Regularium,* Vol. I, pp. 313-314, 318.

164. S. Paenit. 31 iulii 1878 (Vermeersch, *De Religiosis,* I, *Supplementum,* VI, pp. 77-78).

165. S. C. de Propaganda Fide, decr. *Quum in Foederatibus,* 15 dec. 1840, (*Collectanea S. C. de Propaganda Fide,* n. 916 ad 11).

selves distressed for want of funds necessary for sustenance. For such emergencies a rescript could be obtained from the Holy See giving the Religious the right to revoke the act of renunciation of property which had been made just previous to solemn Profession. whenever the beneficiary of that renunciation refused to give the Religious sufficient means of support.[166]

The Sacred Congregation in charge of the affairs of Religious on March 19, 1857 issued an encyclical letter which introduced a notable change of discipline affecting Profession in Orders of men.[167] It ordered that simple vows must be made by the Novice at the completion of the Novitiate. After three years[168] from the day they made profession of the simple vows, Solemn Profession could be made. Some exceptions to the duration of the simple vows could be admitted.[169] Doubts having arisen about the force of this law, Pius IX solved them by declaring that it obliged all Orders of men, as a requisite for the validity of Solemn Profession.[170]

The effects of the newly instituted Profession of simple vows in Orders of men was not stated in the encyclical letter of March 19, 1857.[171] On June 12, 1858, the Dominicans obtained a rescript wherein it was declared that these Religious could (in the sense of must) retain the radical dominion of their property while they were obliged by simple vows. However, the administration, the use and the usufruct of this property must be confided to another person whether physical or moral. Even the Institute could be favored with it if the novice

---

166. Cf. e.g. S. C. EE et RR, 10 martii 1843 (Bizzarri, p. 103).

167. S. C. EE et RR, *Neminem latet*, 19 martii 1857 (*Fontes*, n. 1976, the full text of the document, telling why the change was introduced, may be found in Bizzarri, pp. 853-854 (1885 ed.), or pp. 158-159 in the first edition, or in Vermeersch, *De Religiosis*, II, pp. 332-333).

168. Cf. *Annuario Juris Pontificii*, series XXVI, col. 376.

169. Cf. Piat. I, p. 132; Vermeersch, *De Religiosis*, II, p. 333 (2), p. 375.

170. Pius IX, const. *Ad Universalis*, 7 febr. 1862 (*Fontes*, n. 532); cf. *Annuario Juris Pontificii*, series XVI, col. 376; cf. S. C. EE et RR, *Anagnina*, 6 ferb. 1874 (*Fontes*, n. 2002).

171. Since the Jesuits already had such a practice they were not affected by this document nor the declarations pertaining to it appearing afterwards.

so willed and the Institute was willing to accept the responsibility.[172]

The renunciation of property which the Council of Trent had decreed should be made within the last two months of the novitiate was henceforth to take place within the two months proximate to the expiration of the term of simple vows.[173]

Since March 1, 1839, the Trappists in France had made only simple vows. On December 20, 1861, they were given a rescript defining the obligations of their simple vow of poverty.[174] Above and beyond what the Dominican rescript had stated, this document provided that under certain conditions, a clause could be attached to the provision made for the property of the Religious while he remained obligated by simple vows. This clause could state that the cession of property could be revoked. However, the exercise of this right of revocation was not to be used by the Religious except when the Apostolic See gave permission to perform such an act.

A still later development as regards legislation for the simple vow of poverty was observed in 1882 when the Holy See published the instructions it ordinarily gave when inquiries were made about the obligations arising from the simple vow of poverty. This document repeated substantially the "Trappensium" and added; Whatever property comes to the Religious *after* the first simple Profession, from the title of heredity, must be treated in the same way as the property possessed *before* the first profession. The Superior or Superioress General could give permission to their subjects to dispose of

---

172. S. C. EE et RR, rescr. *Sanctissimus,* 12 iunii 1858 (*Acta Capituli Generalis Ordinis Praedicatorum,* Romæ, 7 iunii 1862, *Constitutiones Ordinis Praedicatorum* (1886), nn. 297, 299, Bizzarri, p. 856); Other Orders also received similar rescripts when they petitioned for them. Cf. Ballay, *Archiv für Katholisches Kirchenrecht,* XVII (1867), p. 34, for a decree of S. C. EE et RR, 16 sept. 1860 pro Congregat. bavaro-benedictina, editum, n. 5; Sleutjes, *Commentarius in Constitutiones Generales Fratrum Minorum,* Vol. I, pp. 436-437, where there is quoted a response given by the S. C. EE et RR, 7 sept. 1866, wherein mention is made of previous decree of July 17, 1858; the Friars Minor and the Capuchins were not permitted to accept the administration use and usufruct of their subject's property, cf. Piat, I, p. 240.

173. Bizzarri, p. 865; *Constitutiones Ordinis Praedicatorum* (1886), n. 305, p. 168.

their property freely by an act "inter vivos" or by testament. The cession of the property ceases when the dominion of the property is transferred, unless an express provision was made to the contrary. Whatever a Professed Religious acquires "ex industria sua" or "intutitu Societatis", he must not reserve to himself but he must place it in the community fund and expended for the common utility of the Society. Those acts which the civil law requires concerning property can be done licitly with only a Superior's permission.[175]

It was not until 1902 that the solemn vow Institutes of women were obliged to make simple profession similar to that prescribed for men in 1857. The decree which made law for the women with solemn vows carried with it regulations concerning the practice of the vow of poverty. This legislation was practically the same as was contained in the encyclical letter of December 30, 1882.[176]

In conclusion, it may be recalled that before the Code there was no general legislation, as such, for the simple vow of poverty professed in Institutes which were either papally or episcopally approved as simple vow Congregations. These Institutes were guided in the matter of poverty by their private legislation. The simple vows of poverty professed in Orders of men also lacked general legislation as such and were guided by rescripts and the private legislation of the respective Institute. The Orders of women alone had general legislation dating from 1902. The promulgation of the Code was a blessing to all Institutes having professions of simple vows.[177]

---

174. S. C. EE et RR, *Trappensium,* 20 dec. 1861 (*Fontes,* n. 1982).

175. S. C. EE et RR, litt. 30 dec. 1882 (*Fontes,* n. 2008).

176. S. C. EE et RR, decr. *Perpensis,* 3 maii 1902 (*Fontes,* n. 2039). The Normæ of 1901, for the Simple Vow Institutes to be founded in the future, was of course not legislation obliging Institutes which were already founded.

177. In 1913, the Sacred Congregation of Religious declared that Religious of solemn and simple vows have not dominion over the manuscripts which they have produced while obligated by vows, so that they may be aliented under any title. Dubium, 13 iulii 1913 (AAS, V [1913], 366).

CHAPTER III.

THE VOW OF POVERTY IN GENERAL.

ALTHOUGH our Divine Savior counselled the practice of poverty, He did not declare in detail just how it was to be observed. He well realized that the multitude of his followers would occupy various stations in life and hence He left the choice of the details in the observance of poverty to the selection of the individual. What is essentially required for the practice of the counsel is the abandonment of all that is superfluous, not that it is absolutely necessary to renounce the ownership of all property, but a person must be content with what is necessary for his own use. Then only is there a real detachment which sufficiently mortifies the love of riches, cuts off vain glory and frees from undue solicitude concerning temporal property.[1] Above and beyond this there may be much variation in the observance of the evangelical counsel. What is true in general concerning the observance of the counsel of poverty is true also of the vows made concerning the observance of the counsel viz. there may be a great variety. Due to the individual conceptions which the founders of Religious Institutes had concerning evangelical poverty as well as the "raison d'etre" of the Institute's existence, there is a difference among the vows of poverty made in Religious Institutes. The novice in the act of Profession, promises God he will observe poverty as it is observed in the Institute he is entering.

The Code legislation while prescribing a general discipline for the observance of the vows of poverty[2] makes due allowance for their individuality. In fact it obliges both Superiors and subjects to observe faithfully and integrally the vow they have professed.[3]

---

1. Vermeersch, "Poverty," (*Cath. Ency.* XII, 324-325). The three obstacles which riches place in the way of perfection are cupidity, vain glory, and excessive solicitude. Cf. St. Thomas, *Summa, Theologica,* II, 2, quaes. 186, art. 8.

2. E.g., Canons 569, 580-583, 593.

3. *"Omnes et singuli religiosi, Superiores aeque ac subditi,*

The vow of poverty, as it is made in Religious Institutes today is well described as a vow whereby the individual promises God the renunciation of exterior property (estimable at a price) which the legislation of the Institute prescribes as the matter of the vow.[4]

ART. I. THE REMOTE MATTER OF THE VOW.

Although the vows of poverty made in Religious Institutes may vary in some things as regards the matter of the vow, yet, in general, it may be said that the remote matter of the vow of poverty consists in external and material things which have money value. This is the common teaching of the authors. Yet the statement must be understood in a modified sense today when there are few things which can not be reduced to a money value.

The industry of a Religious is not considered as the remote matter of the vow and hence if a Religious performed work gratis for another he would not violate his vow of poverty. And if a priest applied Mass gratis for a friend there would be no violation of his vow of poverty. Nor does the vow of poverty embrace, the life, fame, reputation, or health of the Religious. Nor does the Religious, in virtue of his vow of poverty lose his independence as regards his right of choosing, presenting or conferring a benefice.[5] Relics, in themselves are not the matter of the vow of poverty because they are not of money value; when the case enclosing the relic is of practically no value it is sometimes regarded as being outside the matter of the vow by virtue of custom. Yet costly reliquaries are to be considered matter of the vow. The knowledge of a Religious is not comprehended under the vow and hence if he freely gives away an idea, (not a manuscript composed for publication) he does not vio-

---

debent, non solum quæ nuncuparunt vota fideliter integreque servare, sed etiam secundum regulas et constitutiones propriæ religionis vitam componere atque ita ad perfectionem sui status contendere." Canon 593.

4. Cf. Vermeersch, *Theologiæ Moralis, Principia-Responsa-Concilia,* III, n. 125, p. 112.

5. St. Thomas, *Summa, Theologica,* II, 2, quaes. 186, art. 7; Lessius, lib. II, c. 4, n. 26; Lehmkuhl, *Theologia Moralis,* Vol. I, n. 675, p. 371; Laymann, *Theologia Moralis,* lib. IV, tract. 5, c. 7, n. 1; Busembaum, *Medulla Theologiæ Moralis,* lib. IV, c. 1, dub. 4; St. Alphonsus, *Theologia Moralis,* IV, n. 14; La Croix, *Theologia Moralis,* lib. IV, n. 96; Pejska, *Ius Canonicum Religiosorum,* p. 122.

late his vow of poverty, even though the idea could be or was used by the extern for perfecting an invention or the composition of a saleable book.[6]

Are manuscripts to be considered the remote matter of the vow? This is a muchly mooted question. For centuries, the most common opinion of the authors maintained that a Religious had dominion over his manuscripts.[7] This opinion was enshrined in custom[8] which obtained in full vigor down to the twentieth century.[9]

There were two reasons which supported the opinion and the custom. The first reason was: man has a natural right to have and conserve his knowledge. The written expression of that knowledge is intimately connected with the thought itself. Again the manuscript is a means of aiding the memory and thus conserving knowledge. The material used in the composition of the manuscript was too negligible (in comparison with the knowledge re-

6. Schäfer, p. 405; Voltas, CpR, I (1920), 277.

7. Pellizzarius, *Manuale Regularium,* tract. III, c. 5, n. 156; Tract. IV, c. 2, n. 318; St. Alphonsus, IV, n. 14; Antonius a SS Sancto, *Directorium Regularium,* tract. III, disp. 4, nn. 244 sq.; Craisson, *Manuale Totius Iuris Canonici,* n. 2750; *Des Communautes Religieuses a Voeux Simples Legislation Canonique et Civil,* n. 527; Landry, *La Mort Civile des Religieux,* p. 159; Bartsherer-Huber, *Tyrocinium Religiosorum,* p. 276; Kazenberger, *The Book of Life,* p. 152; (quotes Kerckhove, *Commentaria in Generalia Statuta Ordinis S. Francisci Fratrum Minorum,* as holding this opinion probable); *La Regola dei Fratri Minori Breve Commenta ad usu speciale dei novizi e dei nuovi professi,* p. 58; *Instructions on the Vows for the Brothers of the Christian Schools,* n. 237.

8. Bordonus, *De Professione Regulari,* c. V, n. 44; Tamburinius, *De Jure Abbatum,* Tomus, III, disp. 7, quaes, n, n. 8; Diana, *Resolutiones Morales,* Tomus VII, tract. 3, resol. 30 § 1; Petra, *Commentaria ad Constitutiones Apostolicas* Const. XIV, Eugen. IV, sect. 1, n. 13; Cf. Gaude edition of S. Alphonsus, *Theologia Moralis,* vol. II, pp. 456-457, for many other authors.

9. Cf. D'Annibale, *Summula Theologiæ Moralis,* III, n. 504 (35); Marc-Gesterman, *Institutiones,* II, n. 2154; Gury-Ballerini, *Theologia Moralis,* De Stat. Rel. III, n. 156; Ojetti, *Synopsis Rerum Moralium,* III, n. 3086; Appeltern, *Compendium Praelectionum Juris Regularis,* n. 169, quaes. 162; Bucceroni, *Institutiones Theologiæ Moralis,* II, 281; Bargilliat, *Praelectiones Juris Canonici* (1907), II, n. 1153; Aertnys, *Theologia Moralis,* (1906), I, 433; Bonal, *Institutiones Canonicæ,* II, n. 131; Lanslots, *Handbook of Canon Law for Congregations of Women under Simple Vows* (1910), p. 103; Lehmkuhl, *Theologia Moralis,* I, p. 372; Piat, *Praelectiones Iuris Regularis,* I, p. 242; Salsmans, *Periodica,* VII (1914), p. 166; n. 2; Mackee, *Institutiones Iuris Ecclesiastici,* Vol. II, p. 3.

corded) to be considered. Hence, the manuscript was rated as intellectual property and thus not comprehended as matter of the vow of poverty. Although it was produced by the industry of the Religious, its special nature exempted it from the class of material productions.

The second reason supporting the opinion and custom was: during the days of the more ancient authors Religious were not accustomed to receive pecuniary compensation for their manuscripts. Indeed frequently they had to seek a benefactor to bear the expense of printing it.[10] Under such conditions it may be seen how manuscripts remained under the dominion of the author. The custom once established continued to prevail although conditions changed.[11]

Shortly before the promulgation of the Code, the Holy See declared, "ad instar novae legis" that a Religious who had produced a manuscript, intended for publication, while obligated by solemn or simple vows, did not have dominion over it so that he could donate it or alienate it under any title.[12] From this legislation it could not be

10. Cf. Lehmkuhl, *Theologia Moralis,* I, p. 372.

11. Two papal declarations are sometimes alleged in favor the opinion that manuscripts belong to Religious. What Sporer (or rather his continuator, Kazenberger, *Supplem. Decalogi,* c. 2, n. 147) certainly does not substantiate the opinion. Cf. Lehmkuhl, l.c. The second document, Benedict XIII, brev. *Postulat humiliati,* 7 martii 1725, *Bul. Rom.* XX, pp. 129 sq., permitted Regulars promoted to the Episcopacy to take away with them their personal clothing, Breviary and their manuscripts. This latter document may have been intended as an admission that manuscripts were under the dominion of the Religious. Yet it is not a highly conclusive argument.

12. S. C. Rel. resp. datum 15 iunii 1911 (AAS, III [1911], 270): "Quaesitum est ab hac Sacra Congregatione de Religiosis: 1. An Religiosi pertinentes ad Instituta votorum simplicium iisdem teneantur legibus ac Regulares votorum solemnium, quoad *Imprimatur* seu beneplacitum a suis Superioribus expostulandum, quoties aliquod suum manuscriptum in lucem edere cupiunt? 2. An Religiosi, quoties eis a suis Moderatoribus publicatio alicuius manuscripti fuerit interdicta, vel *Imprimatur* denegatum, possint idem manuscriptum alicui typographo tradere, qui illud publicet cum *Imprimatur* Ordinarii loci, suppresso auctoris nomine? Ad. 1. Affirmative. Ad. 2. Negative. Since this response was not entirely to the satisfaction of all (Cf. *Periodica,* VI [1912], 67-68 for an interpretation of the document), the Holy See was petitioned: "An Religiosi tum votorum solemnium, tum votorum simplicium, qui aliquod manuscriptum durantibus votis exaraverunt, eiusdem dominium habeant, ita ut illud donare aut quocumque titulo alienare valeant." Negative. (S. C. Rel. 13 iunii 1913,

rightly concluded that the Religious was thereby deprived of the dominion of all his manuscripts.[13] Salsmans[14] and Ferreres[15] expressly declared after this decision that from the decree it could not be argued that a Religious would sin against either justice or his vow of poverty, if he refused to give his manuscript to the Superior or to send it to the press or merely destroyed it. In other words, the dominion over his manuscript was not taken away from the individual by the decree of the Sacred Congregation. His exercize of that dominion was merely restricted to the extent that he could not alienate his manuscript nor donate it,[16] without authorization from the Superior. As today happens in Institutes of simple vows, the Religious retains the dominion over his property, although he may not donate or alienate it, similarly the decree declared relative to the manuscripts over which the Religious still retains the dominion. The opinion of St. Alphonsus which affirmed manuscripts were not the matter of the vow of poverty remained intrinsically and extrinsically probable.[17]

Besides the opinion of St. Alphonsus which was the most probable opinion there was also the opinion of Passerinus[18] and Rotarius,[19] which merely allowed to Religious the so called, "dominium ad usum suum" and not the

---

AAS, V (1913), 366. The English version of these documents as found in *Roman Documents and Decrees,* IX (1913), 105 is not exact.

13. Salsmans, *Periodica,* VII (1914), 166-167; Ferreres, *Razon y Fe* XXXVII (1913), 246; *Illustracion del Clero* (1914), 154; Besson, *Nouvelle Revue Theologique,* XLV (1914), 709 sq.; Vicenti, *Recentia Instituti,* p. 186; Augustine, III, 305; Choupin, *Nature et Obligations de l'Etat Religieux,* 322-325; Marc-Gesterman, *Institutiones,* II, n. 2154; Genicot-Salsmans, *Institutiones Theologiæ Moralis,* II, n. 92; Arregui, *Summarum Theologiæ Moralis* n. 500; Gearin, *American Ecclesiastical Review,* XLI (1919), 146; Matulewicz, *Constitutiones Cong. Cler. Reg. Marianorum,* n. 224; Cotel-Jombart-McCabe, p. 43 implicitly holds this, as do many other authors.

14. *Periodica,* VII (1914), 167.

15. *Razon y Fe,* XXXVII (1913), 246-247.

16. Cf. Choupin, p. 322.

17. Cf. Choupin, pp. 323-324; Salsmans, *Periodica,* VII (1914), 167. In the Dominican and Franciscan Orders disposal of manuscripts were considered as acts contrary to obedience rather than poverty.

18. *De Hominum Statibus et Officiis, Quaes.* 189, art. 8, n. 184; quaes. 186, art. 7, n. 412.

19. *Theologia Moralis Regularium,* Tomus II, lib. 3, c. 1, punct. 12, n. 2.

"dominum ad alienationem." The propositors of this opinion thought the Religious considered it lawful for the Religious to take his manuscript with him wherever he went without permission of a Superior.[20]

The Code has not changed the previously obtaining problem of the dominion of manuscripts produced by Religious while obligated by the vow of poverty.[21] Hence the old discipline remains untouched. As has been seen, maunscripts, at least from custom,[22] remain under the dominion of the individual Religious. Manuscripts which have been prepared by a Religious after he was professed and which have been intended for publication must not be donated or alienated under any title. As long as the manuscript serves the personal use of the author it remains outside the matter of the vow of poverty.[23] Some reputable authors writing since the Code opine that a Religious would not act against either justice or the vow of poverty if he merely destroyed his manuscript.[24] Yet there are a

---

20. Prümmer, *Ius Regularium Speciale,* Quaes. LXXIV preferred this opinion. Gennari, *Il Monitore Ecclesiastico,* series 3, Vol. V (1913), 264-265, was of a similar mind; he considered the manuscript as belonging to the Institute yet allowing the Religious the personal, although not the venal use of it.

21. Manuscripts not intended for publication and which have no venal value are not the object of dispute, as is evident. Cf. Pejska, p. 123.

22. Raus, "Der heilige Alfons von Liguori die Manuskriptenfrage und die neuesten römischen Entscheidungen," *Theologisch-praktische Quartalschrift,* LXXIV (1921) pp. 367-368; *Institutiones Canonicaæ,* p. 314, counsels following custom and the Constitutions of the Institute as regards the rights over manuscripts produced by Religious.

23. Iglesias-Kazenberger (1926), *Liber vitæ seu Expositio Regulæ S. Francisci,* p. 159; Jansen, *Ordensrecht,* 140; Monthon, *Traite sur L'Etat Religieux,* art. 320; Vermeersch, *Theologiæ Moralis Principia-Responsa-Concilia,* III, n. 126; Augustine, III, p. 305; Arregui, n. 500; Choupin, pp. 322-325; Ferreres, *Compendium Theologiæ Moralis,* n. 211; Sabetti-Barrett, *Compendium Theologiæ Moralis,* p. 537.

24. Genicot-Salsmans, II, n. 92; Arregui, n. 500; Choupin, pp. 322-325. These authors, certainly are logical. Immemorial custom had exempted manuscripts from the matter of the vow; the decision of 1913, as understood in its context, seems to be more a disciplinary measure for the prevention of a Religious publishing his manuscript rather than anything else; "ni fallor," it was in some degree provoked as the result of a controversy between an American Religious and his Superiors over the publication of a manuscript. Nor does the Code

few authors who hold that manuscripts if worthy of a price are wrought by a Religious pertain to the matter of the vow of poverty.[25]

According to the opinion of St. Alphonsus, objects of art which are wrought by a Religious with the intention of retaining them e. g. pictures etc. are acquired by the Institute, especially if they are wrought by a layic who is obliged to give manual service to the community. But if a Religious uses the materials of an extern and produces an object of art with the intention that it belong to the extern, the extern acquires the dominion of the work.[26]

ART. II. PROXIMATE MATTER OF THE VOW

In describing the vow of poverty, it was said that it was a vow whereby the individual renounced property according to the legislation of the Institute.[27] The proximate matter of the vow is concerned with acts performed in relation to what the legislation of the Institute or the common law determines as regards the remote matter of the vow.

The general discipline of the Church and Religious Institutes effects that a Religious professing solemn vows ordinarily becomes incapable of private ownership of property.[28] It is said ordinarily for it is possible to profess a solemn vow and yet be able to own, retain, use and enjoy

---

alter the precedent of centuries as regards the dominion of manuscripts. An exception is, however, to be made concerning the manuscripts which are composed by Religious assigned to writing, for these belong to the Institute as was also held before the Code. Cf. Salsmans, *Periodica,* VII (1914), 167; Ciravegna, *De Paupertate Societatis Jesu,* n. 158 in Ferreres, *Compendium Theologiæ Moralis,* n. 211; Arregui, n. 500; Aertnys-Damien, *Theologia Moralis* (1928), Vol. I, n. 1194; Goyenche, CpR, II (1921), 141.

25. E.g. Biederlack-Führich (1919), p. 185; Fanfani, n. 223; Bargilliat (1923), n. 1250; Arndt, *Die Kirchlichen und weltlichen Rechtsbestimmungen für Orden und Kongregationen,* p. 50; Voltas, CpR, I (1920), 278 considers them as fruit of industry in the sense of canon 580 § 2.

26. *Theologia Moralis,* IV, c. 1, n. 14; Pejska, 124; Biederlack-Führich, pp. 185-186; Genicot-Salsmans, II, n. 92; Vermeersch, *Theologiæ Moralis, etc.,* III, n. 126; David, 130; Augustine, III, 306.

27. The legislation of the Institute will either include the common law prescriptions or have a properly warranted exception from it.

28. Canon 582.

property with permission of a Superior, as happened very often in the last century, and as obtains today in some places in Europe. Moreover, normally, acts placed contrary to the solemn vow of poverty are invalid as well as illicit.[29] It is almost superfluous to remark that whatever is established in common law relative to the vow of poverty applies equally to Religious women professing solemn vows.[30]

The individual Constitutions establish what capacity a Religious professed of a simple vow of poverty has relative to property. Ordinarily these Religious retain the radical dominion of the property possessed before profession, but the use, usufruct, and administration of their property is interdicted to them while they remain obligated by their vows.[31] Acts placed contrary to the simple vow of poverty are ordinarily illicit but not invalid.[32]

The effects of both simple and solemn vows, in relation to Religious and private property both anterior and posterior to Profession will be discussed in detail in the latter part of this dissertation. Moreover, it is beyond our scope to treat all the acts comprehended by the proximate matter of the vows. It will be sufficient here to deal with the more common acts of a Religious in regard to property.

Every Religious knows that the vow of poverty, as made in nearly every Institute, necessitates permission for whatever he may have for his use. Unless permission is possessed, it is unlawful to take, accept, keep, use, borrow, buy, give, exchange, loan, destroy, or use things for a purpose otherwise than that for which they were given. Furthermore to be ignorant of the legislation of the Institute in the matter of poverty will not generally excuse from fault, although inadvertance may excuse.[33] Nevertheless, there are some points in the proximate matter of the vow which merit a few remarks.

It is controverted as to whether a Religious while outside his monastery would violate his vow of poverty if

29. Canon 579.
30. Cf. canon 490.
31. Cf. canons 569, 580 sq.
32. Cf. canon 579.
33. Cf. Da Toratona, *Catechismo della Prima Regola di Sancta Chiara*, p. 141.

without any permission he consumed food and drink furnished by an extern while in the company of the extern. A strongly probable opinion maintains there is no violation of the vow in such a case. It is more a use of something by the owner of it than an act of proprietorship by the Religious.[34] Under the same principle, is to be placed such cases, as, accepting cigars and tobacco to be smoked in the presence of the giver, or while travelling to attend a place of amusement with a friend or relative who gives the treat. To escape scruples it would be better in these cases to presume permission if it can be done.

To accept articles for deposit without any responsibility for the articles, is not an act subject to the vow of poverty. Even though there is responsibility attached to the deposit, (if it is retained merely as a strict deposit) it is not considered to be an act subject to the vow of poverty, according to the common opinion.[35] Yet the Superior would certainly be justified should he prohibit deposits of the latter kind. Justice would be violated by exposing the Institute to responsibility for grave damage when there are wanting proper facilities for protecting valuable deposits.[36]

The concealment of an article estimable at a price lest the Superior take it away from the use of the Religious is an act opposed to the vow of poverty. Yet if permission has been obtained from a higher Superior, it is not contrary to the vow of poverty to conceal the article from a lower Superior; nor is it a violation of the vow of poverty to conceal a thing merely from equals lest they appropriate it during an absence, or a similar motive, e. g. someone ask for it.[37]

May a Religious refuse to accept property without violating his vow of poverty? This question must be

---

34. De Lugo, *De Justitia et Jure,* Dub. III, n. 53; Vermeersch, *Theologiæ Moralis, Principia-Responsa et Concilia,* III, n. 127 d); Genicot-Salsmans, II, n. 93.

35. Aertnys-Damien, *Theologia Moralis* (1928), p. 717; Trienekens, *Vota et Praecepta Regulæ Fratrum Minorum,* p. 36; Genicot-Salsmans, II, n. 93, ad 5.

36. Some Constitutions prohibit the Religious to accept deposits unless express permission is obtained.

37. Da Toratona, p. 140; Genicot-Salsmans, II, n. 93, ad 3; *Annotazione nella Prima Regola Della Madre S. Chiara tradotta in Italiano,* p. 42; Vermeersch *Theologiae Moralis.* III, n. 127, p. 115,

answered only with the proper distinctions. If a Religious with either a solemn or simple vow of poverty refuses to accept property offered to the Institute, the cause of the donation being merely liberality on the part of the donor, there is no violation of the vow nor of justice; if the Institute really needed the property there might be a violation of charity.[38]

The Oblates of Mary Immaculate have an admirable provision in their Constitutions: "Societas nihilominus donationes non accipiet eorum quorum propinqui inopia laborant." cf. n. 188. If a Religious with either a solemn or a simple vow of poverty refuses, what is offered to him from mere liberality, when the donor intends the private convenience of the Religious himself, e. g., a new suit etc., there is no violation of the vow of property. If a Religious with a solemn or a simple vow of poverty performed a mental or physical labor, e.g.: the solution of a canonical problem or a work of handicraft, for a friend, with the intention of bestowing a gratuitous favor, but at the completion of the work, the Religious is offered pecuniary compensation for his work, he may refuse such an offering without violating his vow of poverty. But if the money was accepted, it would by common law belong to the Institute and not to the Individual Religious, if the cause of the offering was the work done. If a Religious with either solemn or simple vows performed work for an extern, under an implied or express contract, e. g., teaching or lecturing, once the work is finished, the Institute has an acquired right to the compensation, and a private Religious is acting contrary to his vow of poverty, if he refuses the remuneration, without proper authorization from his Superior. Yet it would not be an act against the vow of poverty, if he declined to accept the remuneration in person but instructed that it be sent to the Superior. If an inheritance or legacy is willed to a Religious, in a place where the civil laws prescribe that such things belong to the heir or legates before he has accepted them, and the Religious belongs to an Institute which has a right to all property coming to its members, then the Religious

38. Trienekens, p. 37; Vermeersch, l. c. n. 127; David 171; Ferreres, II, n. 213; The Oblates of Mary Immaculate have an admirable provision in their Constitutions: "Societas nihilominus donations non accipiet eorum quorum propinqui inopia laborant." cf. n. 188.

is not at liberty to refuse such property, since the Institute has an acquired right to it; such a refusal would be contrary to the vow of poverty. A Religious with simple vows and capable of acquiring further private property, can without any permission, refuse to accept donations intended for his private capital, as such an act is not opposed to his vow of poverty. If the civil laws establish that an inheritance or legacy belongs to the beneficiary immediately on the death of the testator and before the acceptance of it by the beneficiary, then the inheritance or legacy left to a Religious with simple vows and capable of acquiring private property after profession, belongs to him and constitutes property which he can not abdicate without permission; yet if the civil law determined that the right to property or the property left by will needs the implicit or explicit acceptance of the beneficiary for the completion of the title to it, it does not seem that the vow of poverty professed by a Religious in an Institute permitting its members to acquire private property after profession, obliges him to place an act of acceptance.

Does a Religious with either a simple or solemn vow of poverty generally speaking, act contrary to his vow of poverty, if without a Superior's consent, he asks or receives alms to be distributed for pious purposes? If the person entrusting the alms to the Religious, determines the application of the alms, the act of the Religious is not opposed to the vow of poverty. If the person entrusting the alms to the Religious determines only in general, the kind of charity, e. g., the poor, leaving to the Religious the decision of the particular cases as regards quantity and persons, the Religious does not act against the vow of poverty if he acts in the name of the donor of the alms.[39] However, the Constitutions of an Institute may prohibit such a practice.[40]

Authors teach that a Religious does not offend against his vow of poverty, if unknown to his Superior, he under-

---

39. Sanchez, *In Praecepta Decalogi,* lib. VII, c. 30, n. 4; Suarez, *Opera Omnia* Vol. XV, tract. 7, lib. 8, c. 15, nn. 15-16; Diana, Tomus, VII, tract. 3, respl. 23, n. 2; Prümmer, *Manuale Iuris Canonici,* Quaes. 224; Vermeersch, o. c. n. 127; Schäfer, p. 405; Ballerini-Palmieri, Vol. IV, tract. 9, c. 1, n. 132; Trienekens, p. 36.

40. Cf. e.g., Constitutions of the Discalced Carmelites (1906), c. 3, n. 11.

takes even buying and selling for an extern's utility, when no temporal emolument directly accrues to the Religious from the transaction.[41]

ART. III. PERMISSIONS AND VOW OF POVERTY

In view of their vow of poverty Religious need a legitimate permission from their Superior for the licit performance of acts included in the proximate matter of the vow. This necessity of permission entails no little sacrifice although this fact is not at all times sufficiently appreciated by persons outside the cloister. How often have Religious heard such remarks as: "Religious take the vow but we keep it. A Religious can get whatever he wants by simply asking the Superior for it." Even though it were true that a Religious could get whatever he wanted by simply asking the Superior for it, yet it is not the most pleasant thing in the world to be obliged to ask another for everything he needs or wants. But is it true, Religious can obtain whatever they want for the mere asking? It depends on *what* they ask and *what* they want. To secure what they want they must be very moderate in their requests, and confine them to both the quantity and quality of things which the poverty of the Institute permits to its members.[42]

Furthermore, the permission, in order to be effective is subject to certain conditions.

A permission must first of all be *valid*. The Superior in granting the permission must act within his power. For instance, a Superior could not give permission to a Religious professed of a solemn vow of poverty, to have as his own a sum of money.[43]

A permission is *licit* when it is given for a sufficient reason. Among the licit permissions, as St. Alphonsus teaches, a Superior can grant permission for money to be spent in recreational purposes of an honest character.[44]

---

41. Vermeersch, *De Religiosis,* I, n. 257; De Lugo, *De Justitia et Jure,* Dub. III, n. 155; Trienekens, p. 37; Genicot-Salsmans, II, n. 93 ad 4.

42. Cf. Papi, *Religious in Church Law,* p. 237.

43. This is to be understood apart from those extraordinary cases where Religious enjoy papal indults in this matter.

44. St. Alphonsus-Gaude, IV, c. 1, dub. 4, n. 32; Salmanticensis, Tract XII, De Justitia et Jure, c. 2, n. 94; Laurentius de Peyrenis,

Permissions valid and licit, may be general, particular, express, implicit, or reasonably presumed. A *general* permission is that which is given for a number of cases. Thus in many Institutes Superiors give to their subjects permission to receive, retain and dispose of *small* things, e. g. writing materials etc.[45] Some Institutes require renewal of this permission at stated times.[46] A *particular* permission is that which is granted in an individual instance as the necessity for it arises.

A permission is called *express* if the consent of the Superior is manifested in words or signs and is explicitly meant for an act authorized, not simply for another which contains or supposes it.[47] Permission may be described as *implicit* when the act to be done is not directly allowed, but is contained in another act expressly permitted, either as a means or a consequence, e. g., permission to accept or buy things suitable only for giving away, such as medals, pictures and other pious articles implies permission to give them away.[48] A permission is considered to be *tacit* permission if it results from the silence of a Superior, in virtue of the principle, "Qui tacet consentire videtur".[49] Yet in order that this silence may be equivalent to a permission it is necessary: (1) that the Superior be aware of the matter, for how can he consent to what he does not know?; (2) that the Superior be sufficiently free to manifest his disapproval, if he should desire to dissent.

The so called *presumed* permission also suffices in acts concerning the proximate matter of the vow of poverty. In reality, in the case of the presumed permission, no permission at all has been given, but it is *prudently*[50] judged the permission would be given if it were asked. While implicit and tacit permissions really exist and are evidenced

---

Religiosus Subditus et Praelatus,, Tomus I, quaes. 2, c. 2, § 7; Lessius, *De Justitia et Jure,* lib. II, c. 26, n. 37. Such a permission could even be presumed, cf. Gaude, Vol. II, p. 471.

45. Cf. Kerckhove, *Commentaria in Statuta Generalia Ordinis Sancti Francisci Fratrum Minorum,* cap. 3, § 5, n. 13; Trienekens, p. 38.

46. E.g. the Passionists have to obtain a renewal weekly.

47. Cf. David, pp. 147-148.

48. David, p. 148; Papi, *Religious in Church Law,* p. 242; Genicot-Salsmans, II, n. 94. "Express permission to travel includes implicitly permission to get from the burser the means necessary for the journey."

49. *Regulæ Juris XL.*

either by another permission or the silence of the Superior, the so called presumed permission does not exist since the Superior does not know about it nor grant it. It is based completely on a habitual frame of mind the Superior is supposed to have.[51] Two conditions are requisite for the use of the presumed permission: (1) The Superior cannot be approached and (2) necessity urges the placing of the proprietary act.[52] Nor is it necessary to report a presumed permission to the Superior.[53] Yet if something was acquired which still exists, permission should be obtained for the retention of it,[54] when the Superior can be approached. There is a class of cases which are frequently grouped under the so called presumed permissions. When the Superior can be approached, physically, but on account of human respect, shame, excessive timidity or a similar reason does not dare to approach a Superior, if the subject can presume that the Superior would grant the permission if he were asked, but would object only to the *mode,* the Religious would not sin gravely if grave matter was concerned, however he would not be excused from light sin.[55] It suffices to excuse from grave sin also, if the Religious has only a probable opinion that the Superior

---

50. S.C. EE et RR, *Florentina,* 14 et 24 febr. 1845, ad 5, (*Fontes,* n. 1941).

51. David, p. 151.

52. Suarez, Vol. XV, tract. 7, lib. 8, c. 11, n. 3; Passerinus, *De Hominum Statibus et Officiis,* Quaes. 186, art. 8, n. 121; Rotarius, *Theologia Moralis Regularium,* Tomus, II, lib. 3, c. 1, punct. 5, n. 14; Schmalzgrueber, lib. III, tit. 35, n. 27; Sanchez, *In Praecepta Decalogi,* lib. VII, c. 19, n. 4; Antonius, a SS. Sancto, *Directorum Regularium,* Tract. III, disp, 4, n. 342; Donatus, *Rerum Regularium Praxis Resolutoria, Tomus,* IV, pars. 15, tract. 14, n. 1; Piat, *Praelectiones Iuris Regularis,* I, p. 256.

53. Schäfer, p. 400; Genicot-Salsmans, II, n. 94; David, p. 152; Trienekens, pp. 33-34; Saint-Jure, *The Religious,* Vol. 1, p. 115.

54. Schmalzgrueber, lib. III, tit. 35, n. 27; Sanchez, lib. VII, c. 19, n. 8; De Lugo, Disp. III, n. 128; Suarez, Vol. XV, tract. 7, lib. 8, c. 9, n. 3; Rotarius, Tomus, II, lib. 3, c. 1, punct. 10, n. 4; Biederlack-Führich, p. 194; Aertnys-Damien (1928), I, p. 718 and many others.

55. Passerinus, *De Hominum Statibus. Quaes.* 186, art. 7, n. 131; Suarez, Vol. XV, tract. 7, lib. 8, c. 11, n. 11; Rotarius, Tomus, II, lib. 3, c. 1, punct. 5, n. 15; Pellizarius, tract. IV, c. 2, n. 410; Sanchez, lib. VII, c. 19, n. 5; Schmalzgrueber, lib. III, tit. 35, n. 30; Aertnys-Damien (1928), I, p. 719; Biederlack-Führich, p. 195; Genicot-Salsmans, II, N. 94, pp. 86-87.

would grant permission if he were asked;[56] however, moral certitude is required when there is a case of diminishing, a grave amount of the monastery property.[57] Finally, whenever the Constitutions of an Institute prescribe that the Superior be notified concerning all permissions which are presumed, such an enactment is to be obeyed but not necessarily under penalty of a violation of the vow of poverty.[58]

Permission obtained from a Superior perdures even after he vacates his office, unless he has in some way restricted his permission or his successor revokes it, or the private legislation of the Institute determines otherwise.[59] If a permission was granted for the giving of something to person A, it is not unlawful to give the thing to person B, unless the permission was granted for the person A on account of special reasons.[60] And it is probable that if a permission was obtained by Religious A to give something to Religious B of the same community, Religious B needs no further permission from the Superior to accept it.[61]

When a Religious has asked permission for something which is due to him from the law of nature or the legislation of his Institute, e. g., food or clothing, and this is unjustly denied to him, if there is danger in delay or urgent necessity, and a higher Superior cannot be approached,

---

56. St. Thomas, *Summa,* II, 2, quaes. 32, art. 8, ad 1; Schmalzgrueber, lib. III, tit. 35, n. 31; De Lugo, Disp. III, n. 123; Rotarius, Tomus, II, lib. 3, c. 1, punct. n. 17; Suarez, Vol. XV, tract. 7, lib. 8, c. 11, n. 11; Passerinus, *De Hominum Statibus* Quaes. 186, art. 7, n. 130; Pellizarius, tract. IV, c. 2, n. 411; Sanchez, lib. VII, c. 19, n. 15; Piat, I, p. 257.

57. Suarez, Vol. XV, tract. 7, lib. 8, c. 15, n. 2; Rotarius, Tomus, II, lib. 3, c. 1, punct. 5, n. 18; Passerinus, *De Hominum Statibus,* Quaes. 186, art. 7, n. 131; Donatus, Tomus, IV, pars 15, tract. 14, quaes. 3; Piat. I, p. 257.

58. Antonius a Spiritu Sancto, tract. III, disp. 4, n. 342; Suarez, Vol. XV, tract. 7, lib. 8, c. 11, n. 10; Piat. I, p. 257; Papi, *Religious in Church Law,* p. 242.

59. Piat. I, p. 257; La Croix, lib. IV, n. 115; Aertnys-Damien, I, p. 719; Ferreres, o.c. II, n. 218, ad 15.

60. Pellizarius, tract. IV, c. 2, n. 275; La Croix, lib. IV, n. 119; Piat, I, p. 258; Schäfer, p. 401; Ferreres, *Compendium Theologiae Moralis,* II, n. 218, ad 16.

61. Donatus, Tomus, IV, pars 15, tract. 37, quaes. 7; Pellizarius, tract. IV, c. 2, n. 428; Ferreres, o.c. II, n. 218, ad 17.

the permission of the higher Superior can be presumed and the articles procured.[62]

Should a Religious be travelling and "only passing through" a house of the Institute, his lawful Superior as regards permissions in the matter of poverty is still the Superior of the house at which he is "de familia". Yet if use is to be made of property belonging to the house in which he is a visitor, the permission of the Superior of that house ought to be obtained, since he is in charge of the administration of that property.[63]

ART. IV. NATURE AND GRAVITY OF VIOLATIONS OF THE VOW OF POVERTY

(a) *Different Kinds of Malice in Sins against this Vow.*

Poverty practiced on account of a vow, has the aspect of the virtue or religion, since its object is the worship of God. Every sin opposed to the vow of poverty is necessarily a sin against the virtue of religion in so far as it is the breaking of a promise made to God. And the violations of the public vow of poverty, as made in Religious Institutes, constitute personal sacrileges.[64] Moreover, a Religious commits a sin of injustice as well as a sin against religion, if he disposes of property belonging to the community or any other person, if he acts against the will of its owner. Furthermore, unauthorized proprietary acts relative to property belonging to an ecclesiastical person, such as a Religious Institute or a canonically erected House are also "real" sacrileges.[65]

(b) *Acts of Injustice in Sins against this Vow.*

Unjust proprietary acts committed against property owned by anyone not belonging to the Institute of which the Religious is a member, are to be judged according to the proper principles laid down by moralists. These acts are of such rare occurrence that they do not merit treat-

---

62. Schmalzgrueber, lib. III, tit. 35, n. 35; St. Alphonsus, lib. IV, c. 1, n. 33; Genicot-Salsmans, II, n. 95, p. 88; Aertnys-Damien, I, p. 719.

63. Cf. David, p. 154.

64. Cf. Vermeersch, "Poverty," (*Cath. Ency.* XII, 326); David, 158-159.

65. Cf. David, p. 159. Yet parvity of matter is admitted in violations of the vow of poverty.

ment here. Yet it may be useful to consider briefly, possible violations of justice in regard to property owned by a Religious Institute or community.

In sins which are violations of justice as well as of religion the more commonly received opinion[66] considers a mortal sin to be committed by a Religious when he places a proprietary act which effects a loss to the community equal to that which if stolen by an extern, would constitute a mortal sin of injustice.[67]

Some authors hold that ordinarily, i. e., outside cases where the monastery is reduced to penury, the norm of absolute grave matter applies to unauthorized proprietary acts of a Religious as regards community property.[68] Others consider that relative grave matter is the norm to be used.[69] Yet when this latter norm is employed, the fact that there are many persons bearing the loss (instead of a private individual) must be taken into consideration,[70] except, perhaps, in the case where the monastery is reduced to penury.[71] Hence ordinarily a higher amount of loss is necessary for the constitution of a mortal sin committed against a monastery.[72] Furthermore, since the position

---

66. The opinion of St. Antoninus, *Summa Theologia,* Pars III, tit. 16, c. 1, § 11, nota 2; Ameno, *Opera Omnia,* Pars III, tit. 3, § 2, n. 26; Matthaeucci, *Schola Paupertatis,* tit. II, c. 3, n. 6; Hilarius Paris, *Regula Fratrum Minorum,* n. 1028 apud Piat. I, p. 266, holding that any violation of the vow of poverty, even in the little things constitutes a mortal sin, is obsolete. The theory that a Religious in matters of unauthorized appropriation is to be treated as a son in a family has, since the time of St. Alphonsus, been in disfavor with most moralists.

67. Sanchez, lib. VII, c. 20, n. 3; Diana, tract. *De paupertate religiosa,* resol. 36; Laymann, lib. IV, tract. 5, c. 7, n. 11; De Lugo, *De Iustitia et Iure,* disp. III, n. 110; Gury, II, 159; Konings, n. 1164; Lehmkuhl, I, n. 685; Genicot-Salsmans, II, n. 90; Sabetti-Barrett, p. 539; Ferreres, II, n. 215; Aertnys-Damien (1928), I, n. 1192, ad 2; Papi, *Religious in Church Law,* p. 244 and many others.

68. Elbel, n. 646; Salmanticenses, c. 6, n. 12; Sanchez, VII, c. 20, n. 5; Angelus a SS Corde, n. 275 seem to hold this opinion; among the modern authors, Ballerini-Palmieri, Vol. IV, tract. 9, c. 1, n. 122; Ferreres, II, n. 214, p. 128; Genicot-Salsmans, II, n. 98.

69. Lehmkuhl, I, n. 685; Pejska, p. 134; Arregui, n. 500, ad 3.

70. Cf. Arregui, n. 500; Lehmkuhl, I, n. 685.

71. Antonius a Spiritu Sancto, tract. III, disp. 4, n. 189; Piat, I, p. 267.

72. Schäfer, p. 405 thinks that the monastery is ordinarily to be regarded as a rich person.

of a Religious in a community is different than that of a stranger (although his status may not be equal to that of a son in a family) this fact too must not be overlooked when the relative grave matter norm is employed.

Between ten and fifteen dollars would be considered sufficient to constitute absolute grave matter in sins of theft, according to the opinion of some American moralists occupying professorial positions in prominent seminaries. Yet the text book having the widest circulation states that a person would not err if he considered about thirty-five dollars as the absolute norm.[73] Nor has this latter opinion been regarded as being beyond the realm of probability. If the norm of relative grave matter is used, it would seem that about five dollars, taken from a small and poor community would be sufficient to constitute a grave sin. And it would seem that an ordinary community of active members, could scarcely be rated lower than a private individual moderately wealthy; in which case perhaps eight or ten dollars, everything being considered (inclusive of money values in America today) would be the minimum amount.

The opinion which holds that the absolute norm is to be used can be followed in practice, as well as, the opinion which maintains the relative norm is to be applied.

The "real" sacrilege involved in unauthorized proprietary acts relative to property owned by a Religious Institute, has the same degree of gravity as the sin against justice.[74]

(c) *Gravity of the Sacrilege against the Vow of Poverty.*

The more commonly received opinion among the moralists considers that a mortal sin against the vow of poverty is committed, even though justice is not violated, if a Religious places a proprietary act, which if it were opposed to justice, would constitute a mortal sin.[75] Yet

73. Cf. Sabetti-Barrett (1929), n. 404, p. 369 [Ojetti, *Furtum*, n. 2259; Gury-Ballerini (1907), I, 407; Prümmer, *Manuale Theologiæ* Moralis (1923), II, p. 74; also considered as not improbable amounts higher than ten or fifteen dollars].

74. David, pp. 160, 165.

75. Gury, II, 160; Konings, n. 1164; David, 166; Genicot-Salsmans, II, n. 98; Aertnys-Damien, I, n. 1192, ad 2.

it is not improbable, that in sins of this kind, a greater amount be required than in sins which are opposed to justice as well as the vow of poverty.[76] Vermeersch teaches that a much greater amount is required when the proprietary act is concerned with the property which a Religious owns personally.[77]

In conclusion it must ever be remembered that each Institute has its own vow of poverty. The novice in making Profession, vows poverty according to the legislation of the Institute. This legislation determines for the particular Institute what is the remote and proximate matter of the vow of poverty. Some Constitutions go further and state more or less adequately, what will constitute a grave violation of the vow of poverty. Whatever the legislation of the Institute establishes relative to the vow of poverty must be observed by the members of that Institute, since poverty is vowed not in general but according to the legislation of the particular Institute.

---

76. Elbel, n. 646; Salmanticenses, c. 6, n. 12; Angelus a SS Corde, n. 275.

77. *Theologiæ Moralis, Principia-Concilia,* III, n. 130, ad 3; Papi, *Religious in Church Law,* p. 245.

CHAPTER IV.

THE NOVICE AND THE PRACTICE OF EVANGELICAL POVERTY

SINCE the Novice has not professed a public vow of poverty, he is not required to practice the evangelical counsel with the same obligation as a Religious. However, it is certainly conformable to right reason and the dictates of what is congruous, that a Novice, as a member of an organization (the Novitiate), practicing community life should submit to the discipline therein established. His duties as regards the Common Life and the practice of evangelical poverty will be defined by the novice's regulations or rule book, the novitiate traditions and the directions of his Master. Whatever his Master dictates in the matter of poverty must be obeyed.[1]

During the course of the Novitiate, the property rights of a Novice remain restricted by virtue of canon law. "In novitiatus decursu, si suis beneficiis vel bonis quovis modo novitius renunciaverit eademve obligaverit, renunciatio vel obligatio non solum illicita, sed ipso iure irrita est."[2]

In the earlier days of the Religious Life, it was lawful for a Novice to renounce his property at any time throughout the whole period of his probation.[3] Experience taught that many evils could arise from permitting such liberty. This moved the Council of Trent.[4] to enact that if any renunciation of property was made by a Novice, except within the two months proximate to his profession and with the permission of the bishop or of his vicar, it was ecclesiastically null and void. The Code prescription, in this matter of renunciation of property, differs somewhat from the Tridentine legislation, but

---

1. Cf. 561 § 2.
2. Canon 568: "If, during the Novitiate, a Novice in any way whatever renounces his benefices or his property or encumbers them, such a renunciation or encumbrance is not only illicit but also invalid."
3. Cf. Schmalzgrueber, III, 31, 96.
4. Sess. 25. *De Regularibus,* c. 16.

in so far as it agrees with the old law, it is to be interpreted as the old law was interpreted.[5]

The purpose of the canon is to prevent a candidate in his unschooled fervor from disposing of his property, lest he afterward regret it, if he should be rejected as a subject of the Institute, or, if he should change his mind in the matter of becoming a Religious. If a Novice were permitted to divest himself of his property and benefices or to encumber them, a temptation might urge him to profess his vows, even though he perceived that he was not suited for the Religious Life. Left in the possession of his property, the source of such temptation is removed.[6]

The precept of this canon rests on all Novices of both sexes regardless of whether they are of papally or episcopally approved Institutes. Since the canon says *Novice,* it means only Novice; it must not be extended to Postulants even though they are living in the house of the Novitiate.[7] This was the common and the more probable opinion before the Code,[8] although some weighty pre-Code writers favored the opinion that if a postulant made a renunciation of property," *intutitu ingressus in Religionem*" he could revoke it, should he again resume life outside the Institute.[9] All renunciations made

5. Cf. canon 6, 2°, 3°.

6. Cf. Gearin, AER, LXI (1919), 137.

7. Cf. canons 11, 19; S. C. Concilii, 3 martii 1594 and especially the decision of 18 martii 1598 which declared that the renunciation was valid even if *"animo et proposito religionem ingrediendi facti"* in De Luca-Gallemart, p. 358. Cf. Pallottini, *Regulares,* VII, 35, 36 for many decisions supporting this opinion.

8. Cf. Ferraris, *Novitius,* nn. 37-38; Schmalzgrueber, lib. III, tit. 31, nn. 129 sq.; Petra, *Const. I, Clem. IV,* II, 24, 25; Sanchez, lib. VII, c. 5, n. 2; Donatus, Tomus, II, pars 2, tract. 7, quaes. 20; Passerinus, Quaes. 189, x, *Novit.* 138; Rotarius, Tomus, I, lib. 2, c. 3, punct. 1, n. 3; De Angelis, Vol. II, lib. 3, tit. 31; Leurenius, lib. III, quaes. 1819, n. 2; Pirhing, lib. III, tit. 31, n. 80; Reiffenstuel, lib. III, tit. 31, n. 103 acknowledges this opinion as probable.

9. Cf. Reiffenstuel, lib. III, tit. 31, n. 143; Molina, II, 139, n. 13-14; Lessius, II, 41, 40, 2°; Pignatellus, I, 228, 4 sq.; Pirhing, III, 31, 83; Piat, I, pp. 125-126; De Luca-Gallemart thought that renunciations made *"intutitu ingressus in Religionem"* were to be considered, "tamquam facta in fraudem huius canonis"—C. Trident. Sess. XXV, *de regularibus,* c. 16—and hence "videtur subesse huic dispositioni ex sententia Congregationis," p. 257. Rodericus, II, 48, 8, may also be quoted as favoring this opinion. Larraona, states that in practice donations or renunciations made *"intutitu"* were regarded as hav-

by Postulants are valid and licit in so far as canon 568 is concerned. If the Postulants, in making a renunciation of his property attached a suspensive condition to it, e.g., "if I am professed", then the renunciation is subject to the condition posited.[10]

What is meant by the term "bona"? All property estimable at a price, whether movable or immovable, real or personal, corporeal or incorporeal, e.g., money, bonds, stocks, patents, credits, copyrights, real estate, title deeds or other claims to property, rights to actions against others etc.[11] Inheritances, in those places where the civil law provides that a child is entitled (independent of any acceptance on his part) to a portion of the parental property, belong under the term "bona" of canon 568. But in those places where the civil law requires acceptance to complete the title to the parental property and hence until the acceptance is signified, the potential property right as regards the person concerned is valueless, these inheritances are not to be classed as "bona". Legacies and donations, since the title of acquisition is not complete before their acceptance are not to be grouped among the interdicted "bona." The Novice by repudiating the second mentioned kind of inheritances or a legacy or a donation merely declares that he does not will to acquire them.[12]

The amount of property a Novice owns can not be diminished canonically, in a notable amount.[13] during the course of the novitiate. The gratutitous renunciation or donation of a non-notable part, i.e., considering the gift in the light of all the property the novice owns, is

---

ing been made with the tacit suspensive condition that if the Postulant afterward left the Novitiate, the renunciation could be rescinded (CpR, V [1924)], 224).

10. Larraona, CpR, V (1924), 224 seems to hold that all renunciations of Postulants, if made *"intutitu ingressus in Religionem,"* are at least rescindible, in cases where they return to life outside the cloister. Bakalarczyk, p. 184, assents to this opinion, which has a decision of the S. C. EE et RR supporting it. Vide *Transactionis,* 20 dec. 1878 et 3 aprilis 1879 ad VI, *Acta Sanctæ Sedis,* XII 528, "Donationes vel renunciationes quæ locum habeant ante ingressum in Religionem, sed ipsius ingressus intutitu, non aliter censeri effectum sortiri, nisi sequuta donantis professione." Cf. also, ASS, XII, 584-586.

11. Cf. Gearin, AER, LXI (1919), 137.

12. Cf. Vermeersch, *Periodica,* XIV, pp. 46-47.

13. A third part of the property certainly must be considered a notable amount.

not affected by this canon. Hence, such a donation could be made in favor of friends or relatives or as an alms to the poor, pious places or even to the Institute itself.[14] Wherefore a Master of Novices can permit a Novice to make an offering for Masses to be celebrated for himself or for a friend provided a notable amount of the novice's property is not used for this purpose. Likewise a Master of Novices can give permission to his subjects to purchase small articles of devotion to be used as mementoes for well wishers, and as a means for spreading devotion. Furthermore, if a Novice owned no property on his entrance into the Novitiate, but during its course received a number of small monetary donations not totaling enough to influence in any way his departure from or perseverence in the Religious Institute, the Master of Novices could allow him to spend this money for purposes similar to those just mentioned. The renunciation of a non notable amount of property is justified on the principle of *"parum pro nihilo reputatur"*.[15] However, it is not legitimate to dispose gratuitously of a number of small donations which in the aggregate equal a notable amount of the Novice's property.

Contracts of buying and selling, provided the Novice receives thereby as much as he gives, are not prohibited, since the property of the Novice is not diminished.[16] The

---

14. Cf. Ferraris, *"Novitius,"* n. 42; Sanchez, *In Praecepta Decalogi,* lib. VII, c. 5, n. 22; Passerinus, *De Hominum Statibus et Officiis,* Quaes. 189, x. *Novit.* n. 146; Rotarius, *Theologia Moralis Regularium,* Tomus, I, lib. 2, c. 3, punct. 1, n. 12; Donatus, *Rerum Regularium Praxis Resolutoria,* Tomus II, pars 2, tract. 7, Quaes, 15, n. 1; Bordonus, *De Professione Regulari,* c. XIII, n. 21; Pirhing, *Ius Canonicum,* lib. III, tit. 31, n. 85; Reiffenstuel, lib. III, tit. 31, n. 100; Schmalzgrueber, lib. III, tit. 31, n. 134; Pellizarius, *Manuale Regularium,* Tract. II, c. 8, n. 28; Piat, *Praelectiones Iuris Regularis,* Vol. I, p. 126; Bouix, *Tractatus de Iure Regularium,* Vol. I, p. 584; Gearin, *American Ecclesiastical Review,* LXI (1919), 138.

15. Cf. Schmalzgrueber, lib. III, tit. 31, n. 100.

16. Cf. Suarez, Vol. XV, tr. 7, lib. 5, c. 16, n. 7; Schmalzgrueber, III, 31, 100; Sanchez, VII, 5, 32; Reiffenstuel, III, 31, 140; Pellizarius, II, 9, 17; Ferraris, *Novitius,* n. 36; Rotarius, I, 2, 3, 1, 8; Leurenius, lib. III, quaes. 1819, n. 4; Passerinus, 189, x, *Novit.* 153; Pirhing, III, 31, 87; Bouix, I, 584; Piat, I, 126 and many others. Eichman, *Lehrbuch des Kirchenrechts,* p. 235, remarks that the Novice can make provision for the use and usufruct of his property during the Novitiate, unless the Constitutions of the Institute determine otherwise.

drafting of wills, the adding of codicils and the making of donations "mortis causa" are not to be understood as invalidated by this canon, since these acts do not limit the liberty of the Novice, and they can be revoked at any time during the Novitiate or should the Novice leave the Novitiate.[17] However, donations involving a notable amount of the Novice's property made with conditions such as: "I will give you this if I make my Profession, but if I am rejected in the chapter, or on account of any other reason fail to become a Religious", are to be understood at least as encumbrances to the property of the Novice and hence invalid in virtue of this canon.[18] When the Novice becomes a Religious of simple vows he cannot gratuitously dispose of such property.

In antecedent jurisprudence, it was commonly held that benefices were included in the Tridentine nullification of property renunciations made by Novices.[19] Canon 568 expressly nullifies the renunciation of a benefice,[20] if done during the Novitiate. At the end of the first year dating from Religious Profession a parochial bene-

---

17. Cf. Pallottini, *Regulares,* VII, 28; Pirhing, III, 31, 79; Passerinus, 189, x, *Novit,* 160; Ferraris, *Novitius,* n. 35; Donatus, II, 2, 7, 30, 3; Suarez, XV, 7, 5, 16, 7; Sanchez, VII, 5, 13, sq.; Reiffenstuel, III, 31, 136; Schmalzgrueber, III, 31, 100; Piat, I, 126.

18. Before the Code the opinion was held by many weighty authors that such donations were invalid in virtue of the Tridentine decree. Cf. Reiffenstuel, III, 31, 135; Sanchez, VII, 5, 17, Pirhing, III, 31, 87; Pellizarius, II, 9, 13; Laymann, III, 5, 7, 8; Rotarius, I, 2, 3, 1, 11; Garcia, XI, 9, 19 and 21; and others.

19. Cf. Fagnanus, C. Statuimus, 23, De Regularibus, 19; Petra, *Constit. I, Clem. IV,* II, 18 and 22; Ferraris, *Regulares,* VII, n. 46; Giraldus, II, 171, nota, 1; Suarez, XV, 7, 5, 16, 12; Rotarius, I, 2, 3, 5, 1; Tamberinius, III, 6, 10, 3; Passerinus, 189, x, *Novit.* 155; Donatus, II, 7, 17, 2; Piat. I, 124; De Angelis, II, III, 31, p. 103; Vermeersch, *De Religiosis,* Vol. I, n. 201.

20. *"Beneficium ecclesiasticum est ens juridicum a competente ecclesiastica auctoritate in perpetuum constitutum seu erectum, constans officio sacro et iure percipiendi reditus ex dote officio adnexos."* Canon 1409. *"Licet aliquam cum beneficiis similitudinem praeseferant, in iure tamen beneficii nomine non veniunt*: 1° *Vicariæ paroeciales non in perpetuum erectæ;* 2° *Cappellaniæ laicales, quæ scilicet erectæ non sunt a compentente auctoritate ecclesiastica;* 3° *Coadiutoriæ cum vel sine futura successione;* 4° *Pensiones personales;* 5° *Commenda temporaria, idest concessio redituum alicuius ecclesiæ aut monasterii alicui facta ita ut, eo deficiente, reditus ipsi ad ecclesiam vel monasterium revertantur."* Canon 1412.

fice will automatically become vacant; and at the end of three years dating from Religious Profession the other kinds of benefices become vacant. [21] In the United States the principal kinds of benefices are the episcopal and the parochial. [22]

The encumbrance of a notable part of the Novice's property is not only forbidden but it is also canonically invalid. Hence if the whole or a notable part of the property was mortgaged, except when this is necessary for conserving the estate itself it would be an illegal encumbrance. The placing of the whole or a notable part of the property as a security for some one else, a long term lease or the granting of a lien on it or the loaning of it, is likewise to be considered an encumbrance. Yet, since the encumbrance, in order to come under the injunction of canon 568, must concern at least a notable part of the whole property, acts encumbering merely the rentals from real estate, interest on investments and other similar revenues are not prohibited.[23] Surely transactions concerning the revenues, cannot be presumed so to impair the liberty of the Novice that he would, on this account, feel impelled to profess the vows, even though he were convinced that the Religious Life was no place for him.

To preserve the liberty of the Novice still further and to remove danger of simony, the Code establishes: "§ 1. *Nisi pro alimentis et habitu religioso in constitutionibus vel expressa conventione aliquid in postulatu vel novitiatu ineundo solvendum caveatur, nihil pro impensis postulatus vel novitiatus exigi potest.* §2. *Quae adspirans attulerit et usu consumpta non fuerint, si e religione, non emissa professione, egrediatur, ei restitu-*

---

21. Canon 584. Forced renunciations of benefices in accordance with canon 2149 § 1, are in no way affected by this canon (Vermeersch, *Periodica*, XVIII (1928), pp. 144-145); *Apollinaris*, I (1928), 522.

22. Cf. Golden, *Parochial Benefices in the New Code*, p. 2; Augustine, *"The Canonical and Civil Status of Catholic Parishes in the United States,"* p. 85 relative to pastorates in the United States. The question has arisen whether or not American parochial vicars have benefices. Cf. for the affirmative AER. LXXI, 74-79 and LXXII, 309-312; negative, AER, LXXII, 306-309. The negative is the correct interpretation. Moreover when inquiry is made of the Apostolic Delegate, the reply is in the negative.

23. Cf. Gearin, AER, LXI (1919), 138.

antur." [24] Therefore the payment of expenses for food and clothing during the Novitiate is regulated by dispositions of the Constitutions or an express agreement made in particular cases before the Novitiate begins. If the Constitutions are silent and no express agreement has been made, the Institute cannot later exact anything for expenses. But if a Novice spontaneously gives something for expenses, the donatión seems to be valid and licit;[25] for the Tridentine decree implied that the donation of an amount of property sufficient to cover the expenses of support during the Novitiate would not be enough to constitute the condition which the legislator was endeavoring to remove.[26]

Beyond what the express wording of cánon 570 §2. states we will merely note that if a Novice returns to the world, he must not take the habit with him, but the value of it must be restored to him if he paid for it.[27]

The Code is silent relative to the fruits of the industry of the Novice. In practice, the Novice will agree to perform a specific work or series of works for the Institute. Refusal to obey in a reasonable matter and especially when the work is not of a distracting nature would tend to form an unfavorable opinion of the candidate in the mind of the capitulars. But if a Novice unknown to his Superiors, in a matter concerning which he had no agreement with the Institute, wrought a useful article from his own materials, he would not violate justice if he took

---

24. Canon 570 § 1: "Except the Constitutions or a formal agreement require the payment of a certain sum for food and clothing during the Postulancy or Novitiate, nothing can be exacted to defray the expenses of the Postulancy or the Novitiate. § 2. If the aspirant leaves the Institute without making profession, all that he brought with him to it and has not consumed by use shall be returned to him."

25. Vermeersch, *Periodica,* XIV, p. 47; Bakalarczyk, p. 186.

26. Sess. 25, *De Regularibus,* c. 16; Several pre Code authors considered donations for novitiate expenses legitimate. Cf. Passerinus, 189, x, *Novit.* 148; Pellizarius, II, 8, 28; Rotarius, I, 2, 3, 1, 12; Piat, I, pp. 126, 127; the S. C. EE et RR, *Carmelitarum,* 11 dec. 1789 (*Fontes,* n. 1884), expressly declared that such donations were permissible.

27. Cf. Bouix, I, p. 591; Ferraris, *Novitius,* n. 68; Bakalarczyk, p. 186. *The Constitutions of the Congregation of the Sisters of the Precious Blood,* n. 17, wisely ordain that the Mistress of Novices carefully register everything the candidate brought, so that everything may be returned should the novice leave.

it away with him should he leave the Novitiate and return to the world. In practice, the priest-Novice will form an agreement with the Institute relative to the Masses he will celebrate during the Novitiate. The celebration of Mass in itself may be classed as industry and hence he can agree to celebrate Mass according to the intention of the Master and decline to accept the stipends from the Institute.

If the Novice, having canonically begun his Novitiate, should become so ill that he is considered to be "in articulo mortis", he may be permitted to make his Religious Profession, although the period of his Novitiate is not complete. However, if the Novice should die intestate, from that illness, after making his Religious Profession, the Institute is not entitled to the property of the deceased.[28]

---

28. S. C. Rel. decr. *Iam inde,* 30 dec. 1922, AAS, XV (1923), 156-158; cf. Lopez, *De Novitiatu,* p. 47.

CHAPTER V.

THE SIMPLE VOW OF POVERTY

ARTICLE I. ADMINISTRATION, USE AND USUFRUCT OF THE CAPITAL

(*a*) *Provision*—canon 569 §§ 1, 2

TODAY, "in every Order both of men and of women, and in every Congregation with perpetual vows, the perpetual vows, whether solemn or simple, must be preceded, saving the exception provided for in canon 634, [1]by the profession of simple vows which the Novice on the completion of his Novitiate, shall make in the Novitiate house itself; this Profession is valid for three years, or for a longer period if the subject requires more than three to attain the age prescribed for perpetual Profession, unless the Constitutions require annual professions."[2]

"Ante professionem votorum simplicium sive temporariorum sive perpetuorum novitius debet, ad totum tempus quo simplicibus votis adstringetur, bonorum suorum administrationem cedere cui maluerit et, nisi constitutiones aliud ferant, de eorundem usu et usufructu libere disponere."[3]

In virtue of this section of canon 569, *before the profession of simple vows,* in all Institutes, Orders as well as papal and diocesan Congregations, the Novices who will have property at the moment they make their Pro-

---

1. "If a person who has made profession of solemn or of simple perpetual vows joins another Institute with solemn vows or with simple perpetual vows, he must, after the Novitiate, omit the temporary profession spoken of in canon 574, and make profession of solemn vows or of simple perpetual vows according to the Institute, or he must return to the former Institute; the Superior, however, has the right to prolong the period of probation, but not beyond one year after the completion of the Novitiate." Canon 634.

2. Canon 574, § 1. "The legitimate Superior can prolong this period but not beyond a second term of three years, the Religious meanwhile renewing the temporary profession." Canon 574, § 2.

3. Canon 569 § 1. "Before the Profession of simple vows

fession, must fulfill the precept therein expressed. The obligation rests only on those Novices having property which would prove of use to him should he leave the Institute after Profession. The exact time for the performance of the obligation is not precisely prescribed. The phrase, "ante professionem", suggests the last weeks of the novitiate. [4] The obligation of the canon begins to urge when the Novice becomes morally certain that he will make his Profession.[5]

In the preceding paragraph it was remarked that Novices who have property are obliged to cede the administration and dispose of the use and usufruct of their property. But what must be considered property? Assuredly money, bonds, stocks, real estate and the like must be comprehended under the term property. But what about credits, rights to actions and other things of a similar nature? The legislator certainly did not intend that the person now a Novice, (and who later will be a Religious) should, as a Religious, administer these things. A Novice, now in the possession of such things, must place them in the care of a second party to be administered for him; of their nature, they have no usufrust, and hence he is not obliged to dispose of their usufruct. In some places the civil law determines that each child is entitled, apart from his acceptance of it, to a share in the parental property at the death of the parent. In virtue of this civil legislation the Novice has something which he could not validly dispose of during the course of the Novitiate. In the treatment of the preceding canon it was classed among the property of the Novice. From the nature of this thing, it cannot have its administration nor a use or usufruct of it entrusted to another person. Hence the Novice is not obliged to cede its administration nor dispose of its use and usufruct. The canon imposes no

---

whether temporary or perpetual, the Novice must cede, for the whole period during which he will be bound by simple vows, the administration of his property to whomsoever he wishes, and dispose freely of its use and usufruct, except the Constitutions determine otherwise."

4. Cf. Schäfer, p. 313, nota 8; The Council of Trent, Sess. XXV, *de Regularibus*, c. 16, had required this renunciation to be made during the last two months of the Novitiate.

5. Cf. Schäfer, p. 317. The *"Constitutions of the Sisters of St. Joseph of Peace,"* page 35, wisely dictate that the obligation is to be fulfilled "before going into retreat" for Profession.

obligation relative to the use, usufruct and administration of (a) inheritances to come after Profession from parents in those places where the child is not entitled to a part of the parental property apart from his acceptance; (b) inheritances to come after Profession from relatives and friends; (c) legacies and donations by which property may be acquired after Profession. The three classes of property just mentioned are not now among the Novices' property; they are property "in spe"; the Novice has not even a right to them, much less the ability to entrust their use, usufruct and administration to another. Yet he could, at this time, declare his will, in these matters, relative to the things "in spe".

The phrase *"whether temporary or perpetual"* has been the subject of diverse interpretation. Larraona[6] would have it understood to mean: in every Institute, before the *first* simple Profession, whether of *temporary* vows, according to the *general* law of canon 574 § 1, or of *perpetual* vows in those Institutes which (in virtue of their *private* legislation approved or received from the Holy See) make *perpetual* vows immediately after the completion of the novitiate,[7] the Novice must cede the administration and dispose of the use and usufruct of his property. This seems to be the most probable opinion.[8] Another interpretation is given by Prummer,[9] who declares that the phrase is to be understood: ordinarily the cession of the administration, etc., must be done before the profession of *temporary* vows; however, when a Religious professed of *perpetual* simple vows, transfers to another Institute and makes a new novitiate, this cession of the administration, etc., is done before the Profession of the perpetual vows,[10] made in the new Institute immediately after the completion of the novitiate.[11]

6. Cf. CpR, I (1920), 335.

7. E.g. the Jesuits and the Madames of the Sacred Heart. Cf. Vermeersch, *Periodica,* X (1922), p. (13).

8. Cf. Maroto, CpR, I (1920), 168; Goyeneche, CpR, II (1921), 145; CpR, III (1922), 58; Bakalarczyk, p. 188; Chelodi, *Ius De Personis,* p. 449; Vermeersch, *Periodica,* X (1922), p. (13); Schäfer, pp. 314-315.

9. *Manuale Iuris Canonici,* Q. 212, pp. 279-280.

10. Cf. canon 634.

11. This opinion does not lack probability. Cf. Larraona, CpR, I (1920), 336; Bakalarczyk, p. 188; Goyeneche, CpR, II (1921), 145; Vermeersch, *Periodica,* X (1922), p. (13).

A third interpretation of the phrase is given by Blat,[12] who concentrating his attention on the phrase, "ad totum tempus quo simplicibus votis adstringetur", contends that before each profession, *temporary and perpetual* the cession of the administration, etc., must be done, either implicitly if no change is to be made in the provision, or with authorization, if a change is to be made.[13] This opinion of Blat does not find favor with some of the authors who even go out of their way to declare that they do not consider this opinion solidly probable.[14]

The text enacts that *the Novice must cede . . . for the whole period during which he will be bound by simple vows.*. This phrase alludes to the span of time from the first profession of temporary vows until the Religious is no longer juridically a Religious of simple vows whether the cessation of simple vows is occasioned by death, solemn Profession or by departure from Religion. It is the intention of the law that there should be no delay in making the next Profession after the period of the temporary vows has elapsed.[15] A slight delay after the expiration of temporary vows, before perpetual vows are professed would not be considered a juridical interruption of the period during which the Religious is bound by simple vows.[16] Hence the cession of the administration, etc., made before the first temporary Profession must not be changed after that Profession without the proper permission.

In order that the Religious may not be distracted by the cares of administering his property, canon 569 § 1 prescribes that *the novice must cede the administration of his property to whomsoever he choses.* Do these words mean that the Novice must abdicate the *right* to administrate his property or are they to be understood in the sense that the canon requires merely the actual possession

---

12. *Commentarium Textus Codicis Iuris Canonici,* Liber II, p. 550. He maintained the same opinion in his edition of 1921, p. 625.

13. Cf. Fanfani, p. 294. Lanslots holds the same opinion as Fanfani. Cf. Lanslots (1919), p. 104.

14. Cf. Chelodi, *Ius de Personis,* p. 449 (3); Larraona, CpR, I (1920), 336; Bakalarczyk, p. 188.

15. Cf. Papi, *Religious in Church Law,* p. 253.

16. Larraona, CpR, I (1920), 337.

of the property to be transferred to a second person, physical or moral, with the understanding that the property is at least to be kept intact? Certainly the latter interpretation of the text would if translated into practice attain the "ratio" of the law, viz., remove from the Religious the distraction of caring for his property while he is bound by simple vows and at the same time secure the preservation of his property so that it would be readily available in case the Religious for any reason would become released of his simple vows and resume secular life. If the *right* to administrate his property was really abdicated for the period he remained bound by simple vows any act of administration he might perform would be not only illicit but invalid; assuredly that act is legally null, if it is performed when the power to act legally is in the hands of another; yet canon 579 declares that acts contrary to simple vows are to be illicit but not invalid unless it be otherwise formally expressed. Nowhere in the Code nor in authentic interpretations is it expressed that acts contrary to the simple vow of poverty are invalid. Moreover, if the *right* of administering his property were abdicated, how could the cession of administration be revoked during the time the Religious is obligated by simple vows?[17] Hence it may be concluded that the administration of his property is committed to another only as an agent acting for a principal who retains the *right* or *ius administrandi;* of course this right is restricted by his vow of poverty which requires that he exercise no act of administration of his own property without the permission of the proper Superior.[18]

The question may be asked: whether a Novice, who according to the civil law is a minor and as a minor before the civil law lacks the legal capacity to administrate his own property[19] is obliged by canon 569 § 1 to trans-

17. Cf. Canon 568. The *Normæ* of 1901 permitted that the cession contain a clause to the effect that it could be revoked. Cf. Art. 116-117.

18. To place an act of administration *in one's own name* is an an act of proprietorship forbidden by the vow of poverty unless the proper permissioin has been obtained. To place an act of administration *in the name of another* is an act of industry subject to the vow of obedience.

19. In the United States no such law exists. A novice who is a minor before the civil law can administrate his property; but any

fer the administration of his property to another? A civil law impediment of any kind e.g. age, is not of itself sufficient to excuse from the obligation of this canon, provided the obligation could be fulfilled privately or by a private document effective in canon law. However in the question proposed, since the Novice has not the administration of the property to cede to another, the canon does not oblige; moreover the purpose of the canon is already attained. When the Religious arrives at his majority, the cession of the administration must be done according to canon 569 § 2 or in virtue of 580 § 3.[20]

The Novice is at liberty to entrust the administration of his property to whomsoever he pleases, even to the Institute. [21] As regards the mode of conveyance of the administration, the Code does not expressly prescribe anything.[22] The Novice could simply pass the property to a relative or friend with an agreement that it is to be returned to the owner immediately whenever it is demanded; who will declare that the Code expressly obliges sometimes used in civil law as evidences of contract.[23] e.g., witnesses and a document drafted in the presence of a public notary? If the Novice can be reasonably sure that such a

---

contract or agreement he may make before his majority is voidable. Cf. Tiffany, pp. 307-309. In Italy a minor is inhabile as regards making a contract. Art. *Codice Civile* 1106; Cocchi VI, p. 405.

20. Cf. Larraona, CpR, II (1921), 113-114.

21. *Before* Profession: the Novice can cede the administration and dispose of the use and usufruct, in whole or in part, to the Institute, providing the Institute will accept it. (The Constitutions of the Friars Minor expressly declare that the administration, use and usufruct are not to be entrusted to the Order. Innocentii XI, Const. *"Solicitudo,"* 20 nov. 1679, *Monumenta Selecta Juris Regularis*, p. 62, *Constitutiones* (1922), n. 77). *After* Profession: there is no canon prohibiting the Religious of simple vows to cede the administration and dispose of the use and usufruct of property acquired after Profession. *But* if an arrangement has been made concerning the property received before or after Profession, it can not be licitly modified in favor of the Institute, if the modification concerns a notable part of the whole property the Religious owns.

22. The "Normae of 1901" had declared *"Dispositio de usu et usufructu et designatio administratoris, de quibus supra, fieri possunt per actum sive publicum sive privatum."*.. Art. 118.

23. In American Civil Law the witnesses and seals, etc., are evidences of contract and not the contract itself. Cf. Bouvier, I, pp. 424-429.

transaction is safe, the prescription of canon 569 § 1 is fulfilled. Of course the legislator did not intend that the property the Novice now entrusts to an administrator should be unreasonably exposed to loss or diminution. The very least that could be expected of the administrator is that he conserve the property intact. Ordinarily, the office of administrator would comprise such acts as rendering the property productive by leases, loans or investments or the like. It certainly would be safer and more prudent to have the act of cession of the administration regulated by a duly evidenced civil instrument drafted by a competent lawyer. Experience frequently proves the wisdom of such procedure. Still there is no strict obligation to do this. Nor is there any obligation whatever to confide the administration of *all* the property to one person. The Novice is at liberty to distribute the administration of his property among several persons. [24] It might even be adviseable to have an expert administrate each kind of property, e.g., a reliable brokerage firm to manage the stocks, a banker to direct the investments, a lawyer to handle the leases, loans and collect the rentals.

In confiding the administration of the property to one or several persons he can cede the administration "carte blanche" for the period he remains professed of simple vows or he can condition the cession according to his prudent judgment. It certainly would be well to determine the scope of the administrator's activity at least along general lines. In the terms of cession it may be stipulated that the administrator render an account of his office periodically to a person named by the Novice.[25] Nor is there any canonical prohibition about agreements for a salary for the administrator's services.

A civil formulary used in transferring the administration need not necessarily contain the words "as long as I remain a member of X Institute". Such a clause, if unrestricted, might prove troublesome should a Religious, after Profession desire to change administrators, e.g., if he discovered the administrator to be incapable, negligent

---

24. The *Normæ* of 1901, Art. 115, permitted this. Cf. Vermeersch, *De Religiosis,* Vol. I, Supplementum X, n. 70, p. 143.

25. Cf. Papi, *Religious in Church Law,* p. 252.

or dishonest. For be it remembered that although it is the intention of the Church that the cession remain in force as long as the individual is restricted by simple vows, it is also the intention of the Church that the cession be revocable for any good cause,[26] the Superior's permission alone being required according to canon 580 § 3. In the United States it would be a better arrangement to insert a clause in the formulary, similar to this: "This power of agent shall continue in force until revoked by me through written notice served upon my said agent". Of course, the Religious must not exercise this revocation or change his administrator without due canonical permission.[27]

A sample formulary for the appointing of an administrator or agent is given in the third volume of Augustine's Commentary. It is canonically correct and civilly exact:

BE IT KNOWN, THAT I.................... of the ....do hereby appoint and empower .... to be my sufficient and lawful attorney, to receive and collect all rents, interest or income now or hereafter coming to me from any real or personal property owned by me, or in which I have any right or title, and wherever situate, and to do and transact and accomplish all things whatsoever in the premises as fully to all intents and purposes as I, if present, might or could do, hereby ratifying and confirming all that my said attorney shall do in the premises by virtue hereof; and I also authorize and empower my said agent and attorney to use and apply the said income or any part thereof to the following uses and purposes:

....

This power of attorney shall continue to be in force until revoked by notice in writing served on my said agent and attorney.

WITNESS my hand and seal this..........day of................19...

....

26. Cf. *Normæ* of 1901, Art. 116-117.

27. If the sale of property is to be done by the administrator,

Some Institutes provide formulas for the convenience of their members when they are about to cede the administration or dispose of the use and usufruct of their property. A stock form for the drafting of a last will or testament is also supplied sometimes. These instruments are not intended by the Institutes as restrictives on the liberty of the Novice but are merely matters of convenience. And in view of the fact, that printed formula are so vulnerable and so readily broken, a Novice might well refrain from using such an instrument in drafting his testament.

Not only must the Novice cede the administration of his property to another but he must also *dispose freely of its use and usufruct;* for the legislator does not will that the Religious hold and enjoy in his immediate possession the property over which he retains dominion. Yet it must be noticed that the term "*disponere*" is used in the text and not "*dare*".

The question may be asked whether a Novice may dispose of the usufruct so that it accumulates to his capital, provided the Constitutions of an Institute do not expressly prohibit such a practice? Certainly there is nothing to the contrary stated in the canon. Before the Code many authors in their interpretation of the simple vow of poverty were misled by a piece of rescript appearing in several periodicals.[28] The same was found incorporated in the *Collectanea S. Congregationis de Propaganda Fide,*[29] and is now to be found in the same form in the *Fontes Codicis Iuris Canonici.*[30] We refer to the response of the Sacred Congregation of Bishops and Regulars dated November 21, 1902. "*Se possa un religioso prima della professore disporre che i frutti del suo capitale accumulino al capitale stesso? Respondendum censuit: Negative.*" If the whole text of that response had been given in its context, an entirely different interpretation would have been attainable. Research in the archives

---

since the property is not "ecclesiastical property," the permission of the Holy See is not required. Cf. Papi, *Religious in Church Law,* p. 253.

28. *Analecta Ecclesiastica,* XII (1904), 248; *Revue Theologique Francais,* IX (1904), 396; *Il Monitore Ecclesiastico,* XVI (1904), 252; *Periodica,* I (1905), 122.

29. N. 2151.

30. N. 2041.

revealed that the document was a fragment of a response given to a procurator general who had petitioned the Holy See to have it declare, or better, enact, that the subjects of his Institute be prohibited to dispose of the usufruct of their property so that it accumulated to the capital thereof.[31] Since this decision is the mainstay of the argumentation opposed to the interpretation which permitted the disposal of the usufruct to the increase of the capital the contrary opinion is to be considered the true one.[32] Why should the Procurator General have asked to have prohibited what was already prohibited? To those who object that a Religious would thus enrich himself and this would prove a temptation to quit the Institute, it may be rejoined that the Code permits wealthy Novices to retain, in fact, demands that they retain their property; and would the temptation be any greater in its species than that arising from an inheritance coming to a Religious from a wealthy relative—a possibility which the Code favors, in canon 580 § 1.[33] In fact many Institutes have the practice of permitting the accumulation of revenues to the increase of the capital.[34]

Very important is the phrase, *"nisi constitutiones aliud ferant"*. On October 16th, 1919, the Pontifical Commission for the Interpretation of the Code authentically declared:" *"Constitutiones ante promulgationem Codicis approbatae servandae sunt sive novitiis adimant ius disponendi de usu et usufructu suorum bonorum, sive hoc ius limitent, seu praefiniant"*. [35] Hence if it is evident the *Constitutions approved before the* Code do not permit

31. Cf. Battandier, *Guide canonique pour les constitutions des Instituts a voeux simples,* Edito VI (1923), p. 186.

32. Battandier, *Guide Canonique pour les Constitutions des Instituts a voeux simples,* pp. 186-187; Kinane, p. 470; Fanfani, p. 248; Chelodi, *Jus de Personis,* p. 449, (4); Vermeersch, *Periodica,* X (1922), (14); Gearin, AER, LXI (1919), 141; Biederlack-Führich, p. 182; *Catechism of the Vows,* p. 185; Prummer, *Manuale Iuris Canonici,* p. 285, n. 2; Papi, *Religious in Church Law,* p. 254; Cocchi, VI, p. 166.

33. Cf. Gearin, *American Ecclesiastical Review,* LXI (1919), 141.

34. Cf. Vermeersch, *Periodica,* X (1922), p. (14); Schäfer, p. 315.

35. Cf. AAS, XI (1919), 478; *Repertorium Juridicum Ecclesiasticum,* n. 66; *Jus Pontificium,* III (1923), 68; Cimetier, *Pour etudier le Code de Droit Canonique,* p. 95.

the Novice to dispose freely of the use and the usufruct of his property or if the Constitutions clearly limit the right to dispose of the use and usufruct such legislation must be obeyed.[36]

If the *Constitutiones approved since the promulgation of the Code* restrict the liberty of the Novice, then such legislation obliges as priviledged private law.[37] Even if such Constitutions prohibit the capitalization of the usufruct,[38] it is not unlawful to specify in the cession of the administration, that a portion of the usufruct is to be devoted to the salary of the administrator, the insurance fees taxes or repairs of the property.[39] If the Constitutions prescribe that the usufruct must be given away, it is allowable for the Novice to instruct the administrator to accumulate the revenues until there will be formed a fund sufficient to constitute a burse for the education of a student or an endowment of a bed for a hospital, etc. In such cases the usufruct is really given away and the intention of the lawgiver attained.

If the Novice cedes the administration and disposes of the use and usufruct by means of a document, may he retain such an instrument in his possession? Surely there is no prohibition in the Code concerning this matter. Nor does the spirit of the law require that it be placed with another. If there is no Constitutional or other Institutional legislation to the contrary, it is licit to keep such a document in the possession of the Religious whom it

36. In this regard Maroto quotes the Redemptorist Constitutions, art. 271: "non licere subditis, de bonorum suorum usufructu disponere nisi in favorem coniunctorum, ad quartum usque consanguinitatis gradum inclusive, de iure canonico aut usque ad quartum gradum affinitatis, non tamen spiritualis; aut in beneficium Congregationis; aut pro Missis, in beneficium animæ propriæ, aut coniunctorum"; vel etiam, "de licentia tamen Rectoris Maioris vel Provincialis, ad determinatum aliquod opus pium in favorem tertii." Cf. Pontifical Decree of June 6, 1880, apud Maroto, CpR, I (1920), 168.

37. In the new Constitutions of the Calced Carmelites, n. 42 (not yet pontifically approved), it is ordained that one-half of the use and usufruct of the Novice's property must be given to the Order, the other half may be freely given to whomsoever the Novice may choose.

38. Cf. *Constitutiones Congregationis Clericorum Regularium Marianorum, sub titulo Immaculatæ Conceptionis Beatissimæ Virginis Mariæ,* Romæ, 1927 (not yet approved), n. 224.

39. Cf. Vermeersch, *Periodica* I (1905), 122; David, 124; Gearin, AER, LXI (1919), 141.

concerns; however, the Novice can have it retained in the archives of the Novitiate or any other place that seems suitable or convenient to him.

"Ea cessio ac dispositio, si praetermissa fuerit ob defectum bonorum et haec postea supervenerint, aut si facta fuerit et postea alia bona quovis titulo obvenerint, fiat aut iteretur secundum normas § I statutas, non obstante simplici professione emissa."[40]

This paragraph of the canon applies to the same class of individuals who were obliged to satisfy the obligation of the first part of the canon. If the Novice had no property when the other Novices fulfilled the precept of § 1 of this canon, but received property before Profession, he must cede the administration of it etc. before Profession. Or if a Novice made provision for the administration etc. of the property he already had, and other property comes to him before profession, then he must provide for this new property as he did for the old. The same is true of property received after Profession, e.g., when property accrues to the Religious from the credits, rights to actions, inheritances from relatives or friends, legacies or donations. If the Novice omitted to fulfill the mandate of § 1 through forgetfulness, carelessness or for any other such reason, he is obliged to supply the omission after Profession, since the precept is *"ad urgendam obligationem et non ad finiendam obligationem"*. No permission from any Superior is needed for the performance of the acts prescribed by this section of the canon, in so far as the common law is concerned.[41] However, if individual Constitutions prescribe that the Superior be informed of the transaction, such legislation would oblige.[42]

---

40. "If the Novice, because he possessed no property, omitted to make this cession and disposition and if subsequently property came into his possession, or if after making the provision, he becomes under whatever title the possessor of other property, he must make provision, according to the regulations of § I, for the newly acquired property, even if he has already made simple Profession."

41. Cf. Prümmer, p. 280; Blat, n. 638, p. 626; David, p. 134; Kinane, p. 470.

42. Cf. *Constitutions Soeurs de la Charite de L'Hospital General de Montreal Dites Communement "Soeurs Grises,"* n. 64.

(*b*) *Modification*—Canon 580 § 3

"Cessionem vel dispositionem de qua in canon 569 § 2, professus mutare potest non quidem proprio arbitrio, nisi constitutiones id sinant, sed de supremi Moderatoris licentia, aut si de monialibus agatur, de licentia Ordinarii loci et, si monasterium regularibus obnoxium sit, Superioris regularis, dummodo mutatio, saltem de notabili bonorum parte, non fiat in favorem religionis; per discessum autem a religione eiusmodi cessio ac dispositio habere vim desint."[43]

Canon 580 § 3 is well placed amid the legislation pertaining to Religious Profession. Yet in treating the Vow of Poverty apart from the rest of the Code, it seems preferable to comment on 580 § 3 immediately after 569 § 2 in order to retain unity of subject matter.

Regardless of whether the cession of the administration or the disposal of the use and usufruct of the property was made immediately before simple Profession or during the period the Religious remains bound by simple vows, these provisions *can be changed.* This canonical right to modify the previous arrangement however will avail little, if in fact, such a modification is impossible. Hence the importance of inserting provisory clauses in the agreements made concerning these three proprietary acts, so that they can in fact and if necessary, by aid of civil law, be altered or revoked, "ad nutum".

Be it noted that the canon is worded: "*professus mutare potest.* What if the cession of the administration, as regards the whole or only a part of the property, *ceases* by the death of the administrator or his unsolicited resignation? What if the usuarius or the usufructuarius dies or for any reason abdicates his privilege? It can not be truly said that either canon 569 nor 580 § 3 covers this exigency. Assuredly the obligation of canon 569 §§ 1, 2 is already fulfilled. Canon 580 § 3 regulates the ac-

---

43. As regards the cession or disposition of property treated of in canon 569, § 2, the professed Religious can modify the arrangement, not, however, of his own free choice except the Constitutions allow it, but with the permission of the Superior-General or, in the case of nuns, of the local Ordinary, and if the monastery be subject to Regulars, of the Regular Superior; the modification, however, must not be made, at least for a notable part of the property, in favor of the Institute; in case of withdrawal from the Institute, this cession and disposition ceases to have effect."

tion whereby the Religious terminates or alters the previous arrangements and inaugurates a new one. In the cases proposed the previous arrangement ceases; the professed Religious does not change it. The Code has no express legislation for such a case, and hence recourse must be had to the suppletory law of canon 20. In canon 20 it is declared that if no legislation can be found to cover expressly a certain matter, the norm must be taken from law covering similar circumstances, etc. But the Novice or the Religious mentioned in canon 569 §§ 1, 2 is in circumstances similar to the Religious who again has the actual administration or use or usufruct of his property in his possession. Hence the norm that must be followed must be taken from canon 569 § 2. Therefore, in virtue of canons 20 and 569 the Religious must again cede the administration or dispose of the usu or usufruct of his property. Since the Novice or the Religious mentioned in canon 569 needed no permission to perform the acts prescribed, neither does the Religious who has had the administration or the use or the usufruct thrust back upon him. In the nature of things why should a person obliged by the Holy See to do something have to obtain the permission of a Religious Superior before he could licitly act? Of course if the Constitutions of an Institute or a Papal rescript[44] required a consent or otherwise restricted the liberty of the Religious in the performance of his obligation, he must conform to this special regulation.[45] If the Novice or the Religious in making the first cession of the

---

44. If the Holy See required the consent of a Superior, then the case is different. The Order of Friars Minor had a rescript from the Sacred Congregation of Religious declaring that when the office of administrator of the property of their simple vow Religious became vacant, the consent of the Local Superior was required before the administration could be ceded to another. This declaration concerned a decree given to this Order on July 17, 1858, wherein was defined the obligation of the simple vow of poverty which is made prior to solemn Profession. Cf. Sleutjes, I, pp. 436-437.

45. When the Sacred Congregation of Religious solved a case of a usufruct, it declared that at the death of the usufructuarius the usufruct, *"ad proprietarium redeat, ita ut hic pro suo arbitrio possit iterum disponere.* "No permission was necessary before the performance of his obligation to again dispose of the usufruct. The decision was an interpretation of the Passionist Constitutions which contained legislation similar to that found today in the Code. Cf. S. C. EE et RR, *"Romana,"* 15 septembris, 1837, ad 2 (Bizzarri (1885), pp. 74-75).

administration or in the disposition of the use or usufruct of his property had attached a clause providing for the substitution of another to the office of administrator, or the occupancy of the use or the usufruct in the event of the death or the unsolicited resignation of the person first designated, there would not occur this difficulty about the lacuna in the Code. Certainly it would not be out of place to suggest to the Novice or the Religious that he provide for a substitute against such a vacancy; however the Code does not oblige him to make such provision at the time he fulfills the obligation of canon 569.

A modification of the provision for the administration or the use or the usufruct may be made by the Religious *but not of his own free choice unless the Constitutions allow it.* Some Constitutions formed before the last half of the nineteenth century[46] granted to the Religious the right to change, in a greater or lesser degree, after Profession, the arrangements he had made concerning his property. Hence, should the Constitutions of such an Institute permit the Religious to perform such an act without any authorization from a Superior, such private legislation could be followed. Undoubtedly, such an act is an exercise of proprietary power; yet it is not the only exercise of proprietary power authorized by the Code.[47] What if the Constitutions approved before the Code determine that the permission of the Provincial or the Local Superior suffices for the performance of such an act? If attention is paid only to the locution of the canon, the Code makes no exception for this case. Moreover canon 6, 1° declares; "Leges quaelibet, sive universales sive particulares, praescriptis huius Codicis oppositae, abrogantur, nisi de particularibus legibus aliud expresse caveatur." Furthermore canon 489 enacts: "Regulae et particulares constitutiones singularum religionum, canonibus huius Codicis non contrariae vim suam servant; quae vero eisdem opponuntur, abrogatae sunt." Hence it would appear at first sight that the Constitutions declaring the permission of a Provincial or a Local Superior is necessary and suffices, are abrogated.[48] Yet, in view of the fact that

46. Larraona, CpR, II (1921), pp. 42-43.
47. E.g. canon 569 § 2.
48. Cf. Larraona, "De paupertate simplici," *Commentarium pro Religiosis,* II (1921), 43.

canon 580 § 3 makes an express exception for cases in which Constitutions declare that the Religious may make changes as regards the cession and disposal *without any permission,* it seems unlikely that the legislator willed to abrogate Constitutions when they required *some permission* viz. that of the Provincial or Local Superior.[49] There does not seem to be real opposition[50] between the enactment of canon 580 § 3 and the Constitutions which declare that the permission of the Provincial or that of the Local Superior suffices. Canonical equity[51] considered in relation to canon 580 § 3 and the legislation of the Constitutions declaring the permission of the Provincial or Local Superior is necessary and sufficient for the change of the cession or disposal, also suggests that the legislation of such Constitutions is not abrogated. It is at least probable that in the case proposed, the permission of the Provincial or the Local Superior continues to be sufficient.

Except when the Constitutions approved before the Code provide otherwise *the permission of the Superior General* is required in order to modify the arrangement the Religious has made for his property. In other words, the Superior General alone of all the Superiors has the power to give the necessary permission. Yet he can delegate that power. As regards distant provinces, it may be even advisable to invest the Provincial of such provinces with delegated power; and in those cases, where there is only one house, in a distant country, the Local Superior might well be delegated, for instances requiring immediate attention. If no such delegation exists and a case of urgent necessity arises, the General's permission may be presumed.[52]

What if the administrator of the property of the Religious proves dishonest or incapable? Is the permission of the Moderator General necessary before the unworthy person may be removed? It can not be urged that either

---

49. Cf. Periodica, X (1922), pp. (12)-(13); Schäfer, p. 343.

50. In a decision of the Sacra Romana Rota (AAS, V [1913], 223 sq.) contrariety ("opposition and contrariety are considered on a parity by the legislator"), is used synonymously with incompatibility. For argumentation on this point consult, Neuberger, *Canon* 6, pp. 36 ff.

51. Cf. D'Angelo, "De Aequitate in Codice Iuris Canonici," *Periodica,* XVI (1927), 220* sq.; *Apollinaris,* I (1928), 374 sq.

52. Cf. Vermeersch, *Epitome,* I, p. 164.

canon 569 or 580 § 3 obliges the Religious to change the administrator; of course in practice the Religious will want to change the administrator. Since the act of discharging the first and appointing the second administrator is subject matter for the vow of poverty, some kind of permission is needed.[53]

The legislator does not want the property of the Religious to be damaged or lost through the fault of the administrator; the reason for the law requiring the appointment of an administrator was precisely that the property of the Religious be preserved. It is also clear that a change necessitated by a supervening contingency affecting the end of the law is different from a change desired on account of a necessity exterior to the end of the law, or a change desired without any necessity at all being present. It is worthy of note that the Order of Friars Minor had a rescript declaring the obligation of legislation similar to the Code in the cases where the administrator was discovered to be dishonest or incapable in his trust. A copy of the rescript is given in full as it is not readily accessible. "Il Ministro generale di tutto l'Ordine de' Minori con venerazione profonda e pari umilità, supplice implora dalla S. V. la dichiarazione di'seguenti dubbii . . . III. In forza del Decreto del 17 Luglio 1858 permettendosi ai professi di voti semplici retinere il domino radicale de 'loro beni, si prescrive non ostante ai medesimi di affidarne l'administrazione a chi piu loro aggrada *prima* di venire all'atto dei voti semplici. Morendo pertanto l'administratore gia designato o redendosi questi incapace od infedele nell'administrazione dei beni; sarà lecito ai medesimi sostituirgli un altro anche dopo la professione dei voti semplici?" "Ex Aud. a SSmi habita ab infra D. Secretario S. Congnis Eporum et Regularium sub die 7 septembris 1886 . . . Quo vero ad quaesitum sub numero III. Eadem Sanctitas Sua respondi mandavit"; "Affirmative de consensu Superioris localis." Romae

A Card. Quaglia Praef.
S. Svigliati, Secret."[54]

53. In discussing the problem of the administration left vacant and the necessity of appointing another to succeed to the office of administrator, we pointed out that since the legislator obliged the Religioius to appoint another administrator, the act of appointing that administrator needed no permission from a Superior of the Institute, unless positive legislation required it.

From the wording of this rescript, it seems that it is the norm for other Institutes also, although it directly obliged only the Institute that received it. It is probable that in cases where the administrator is discovered to be dishonest or incapable, the permission of the local Superior suffices for the performance of the proprietary act of appointing another administrator in place of the first: "*ubi eadem est ratio, ibi eadem debet esse iuris dispositio*".

In the case of nuns is a phrase that here comprehends those Order members, who have not yet professed solemn vows, but only the simple vows preparatory to the solemn profession, which will be made when the canonical term for the simple vows' duration has expired. All nuns of this kind must have the permission of the Ordinary of the place before they may change the provision previously made relative to their property. If a community of nuns is subject to the jurisdiction of a Regular Superior, a nun desiring to change the administrator or the usuarius or usufructuarius of her property must get two permissions for such an act; one from the Local Ordinary and the other from the Regular Superior. Some nuns who normally would profess solemn vows[55] and who by their Constitutions are subject to Regulars, by virtue of special legislation still in force in some countries, e.g., the United States[56] or France[57] or Belgium[58] make only simple vows and are not under the jurisdiction of a Regular Superior; hence they

54. "Ex *Archivo Procuræ Generalis Ordinis Fratrum Minorum,* Regestum a die Julii 1862 ad diem 26 Aprilis 1869 (in dorso tomo XVIII), pp. 262-263." Sleutjes, pp. 436-437.

55. Canon 488, 7°.

56. Cf. S. C. de Prop. Fidei, 30 septembris 1864 (*Acta et Decreta Concilii Plenarii Baltimorensiis* II, n. 419, pp. 215-217), where it is stated that the vows of all female Religious are simple, with the exception of the Visitandine convents of Georgetown, Mobile, St. Louis, Baltimore and Kaskaskia. The convent at Kaskaskia has ceased to be a community of solemn vows. It is not out of place here to note that the Visitandines never were subject to a Regular Superior. Cf. Vermeersch, *Periodica,* XII (1924), p. 79. Today the Carmelite nuns at Philadelphia profess solemn vows by virtue of a decree received from the S. C. de prop, Fidei, 10 iunii, 1902 (*Decretum,* n. 49, 877).

57. "excepti Nicensi et Sabaudia," (Cf. Maroto, CpR, I (1920), 262-263; CpR, IV (1923), 163, (1).

58. S. C. de Rel. 13 maii, 1910 (AAS, XI [1919], 240), ibid. 23, iunii, 1923, AAS, XV (1923), 357; Maroto, CpR, IV (1923), 330, n. IX.

need only the one permission from the Ordinary of the place.[59]

Who may be considered the local Ordinary from whom the nuns just mentioned must obtain permission? If the Religious house is situated: (a) *in a diocese;* when the See is not impeded or vacant, the permission may be obtained from the bishop of the diocese[60] or the Vicar General or from one of the Vicars General if there are more than one in the diocese.[61] The Religious is free to seek the permission from any one of these prelates. But it is well to remember: "A favor denied by the Vicar General and later obtained from the Bishop, without mention of the refusal, is invalid; a favor denied by the Bishop cannot validly be obtained by asking the Vicar General without the Bishop's consent, even if mention of the refusal is made."[62] The Soverign Pontiff, for weighty and special reasons sometimes entrusts a canonically established diocese to an Apostolic Administrator even while the Bishop remains in the diocese.[63] When the diocese is ruled by an Apostolic Administrator (unless instructions are issued contrarywise)[64] his permission should be sought[65] and not that of the Bishop or his Vicar General because their power is suspended.[66] *When the See is impeded,* i. e. "when the proper Bishop is unable to communicate with his diocesans even by letters whether this be due to imprisonment, relegation, exile (as obtains in Mexico today) or his own physical or mental disability,[67] the administration of the diocese passes into the hands of the Vicar General or any other priest chosen by the Bishop who may even delegate several for such purposes, not indeed 'in solidum,' but successively."[68] When this obtains, it is evident that the person the Bishop has appointed is to be approached for the requisite permission. *When the*

59. Cf. Vermeersch, *Periodica,* X (1922), p. (14).
60. Canon 198 § 2.
61. Cf. canon 366 §§ 1, 3; Boiux, *Tractatus de Judiciis Ecclesiasticis,* I, pp. 411 sq.
62. Canon 44, § 2; translation by Augustine, I, 133.
63. Canon 312.
64. Cf. canon 314.
65. Canon 315.
66. Canon 316.
67. Cf. Klekotka, p. 157; canon 429.
68. Canon 429; Klekotka, p. 157; Blat, II, n. 473, p. 463.

See becomes vacant, by the death, resignation, transfer or removal of the Bishop, the person, who legitimately administers the See until the next Bishop assumes his office, alone can grant the permission.[69]

(b) *in an exempt territory,* i. e. belonging to no diocese (e.g., at Belmont, North Carolina, in the United States)[70] and ruled by an Abbot or Prelate Nullius[71] the permission of that Abbot or Prelate is to be sought. If his office *becomes vacant,* an incumbent deputed according to canon 432 sq. will take charge;[72] if office of Abbot or Prelate Nullius *becomes impeded,* the administration of it will be occupied according to canon 429. In these two exigencies, the nuns are to seek permission from the temporary administrator.

(c) *in missionary places* governed by Vicars or Prefects Apostolic[73] the permission is to be sought from the Vicar or Prefect of the place. In case the Vicar or Prefect *ceases in his* office[74] or if his jurisdiction *is impeded*[75] the Pro Vicar or Pro Prefect[76] is to be petitioned for permission in case a nun desires to change the administrator or usuarius or usufructuarius, of her property.

Close attention should be paid to the phrase: *"dummodo mutatio, saltem de notabili bonorum parte, non fiat*

---

69. In the cases of resignation or deposition from office, the Holy See usually provides the substitute; even in cases of death and transfer, the Holy See sometimes designates the administrator. When the Holy See does not so act, the Cathedral Chapter will elect a Vicar Capitular (canon 432), whose permissioin is to be sought until the next Bishop of the diocese begins to exercise his jurisdiction. In the United States, the office of electing the administrator of the diocese "sede vacante," belongs to the diocesan consultors; but where there are less than five consultors in the diocese when the bishop dies, the Metropolitan or Senior Suffragan Bishop with the approbation of the Delegate appoints the administrator, whose permission is to be sought in the dioceses of the United States. Cf. S. C. Consistorialis, decr. 22 febr. 1919 (AAS, XI [1919], 75-76). Klekotka pp. 162-163 for information about the special decree in this matter obtained from the Sacred Consistorial Congregation February 22, 1919.

70. Cf. Augustine, II, 332.

71. Canon 319; Cf. Augustine, *The Rights and Duties of Ordinaries,* 79.

72. Canon 327.

73. Canon 293.

74. Canon 309 § 2.

75. Cf. canon 429 §1.

76. Canon 309 § 1; Cf. Jarre, *Antonianum,* III (1928), 321 sq.

in favorem religionis." The Code does not prohibit a Novice to entrust (immediately before Profession) the administration of the whole of his property to the Institute if the Novice so desires and the Institute accepts the office. The whole of the use and the usufruct may also be conferred upon the Institute, by the novice, under the same conditions as we have just mentioned concerning the administration. If, after Profession, the simple vow Religious receives the whole or the greater part of his property, the administration, use or usufruct of it, may likewise be conferred upon the Institute.[77] Immediately before Profession the Novice may leave all his property by way of testament to the Institute;[78] nor is it prohibited that a Religious of simple vows, having obtained due permission to change his will, should favor the Institute with his property, in the new or altered will.[79] Yet the Code prohibits the Religious to entrust the Institute with the administration of a notable part of his property or to confer the use or the usufruct of a notable part[80] in favor of the Institute[81] after permission has been obtained to modify the previous arrangement made concerning these matters.[82]

Should the Religious *depart from the Institute, the provision* made for the administration, the use and the usufruct of his property canonically *ceases.* As has been remarked before, the owner of the property concerned would do well, if in fulfilling the precept of canon 569 §§ 1, 2, he took care that he could come into full possession of his property, immediately, should he leave the Insti-

77. Canon 569 §§1, 2.

78. Canon 569 § 3.

79. Canon 583, 2°.

80. A third of the total property is certainly notable; Cf. Prümmer, *Manuale Iuris Canonici,* p. 270; Chelodi, *Ius de Personis,* p. 457; David, *The Religious State,* pp. 136-137; Cocchi, *De Religiosis,* i.e. lib. II, *De Personis,* pars II, n. 80, p. 167. Vermeersch, *Epitome,* I, p. 433; thinks that oftentimes a fourth will constitute a notable part.

81. The Constitutions of the Friars Minor, n. 79 expressly prohibit the changing of the provision of the administration or the use or the usufruct in favor of the Institute. Cf. Ilg, p. 36.

82. Larraona explains, that if by entrusting the administration to the Institute, the Religious is favored and not the Institute, then, the Code does not here limit the liberty of the Religious in again providing for the administration of his property. Cf. CpR, II (1921), 44, 1°.

tute. By "discessum", is understood a legitimate departure effected after the expiration of temporary vows[83] or by an indult of secularization[84] or by dismissal in accordance with canons 646-672. Neither the apostate nor the fugitive from Religion can licitly administer his property nor enter upon the use and usufruct of it;[85] as the action of these individuals does not constitute a canonical "discessus".

Is the canonical "transitus"[86] of a Religious from one Institute to another a canonical "discessus" as intended by the legislator in canon 580 § 3? This question is here agitated only in so far as it concerns the "transitus" of simple vow Religious to an Institute in which he will profess simple vows at the conclusion of the novitiate.[87] Further, the "transitus" of the Religious is treated here only in so far as it affects the cession and disposal, prescribed in canon 569 §§ 1-2 and regulated by 580 § 3. The wording of canon 580 § 3 is clear: "per discessum autem a religione eiusmodi cessio ac dispositio habere vim desinit."[88] Yet in recalling the wording of canon 580 § 3, it must be remembered at the same time that the cession and disposal transacted while a member of the first Institute was to endure "ad totum tempus quo simplicibus votis adstringetur",[89] except a change was effected in virtue of the legislation in the preceding part of canon 580 § 3. Now how is this "transitus" to be regarded in rela-

---

83. "Those who have made profession of temporary vows may, when the term of the vows has expired, freely leave the Institute; likewise, the Institute, for just and reasonable motives, can exclude the Religious from renewing the temporary vows or from making profession of perpetual vows, not however because of ill-health except it be clearly proved that the Religious before Profession, had fraudently hidden or dissimulated the illness." Canon 637.

84. Cf. canon 640, § 2.

85. Canon 645 § 1.

86. Cf. canons 632-636.

87. The Religious professed of solemn vows passing to a simple vow Institute has no property to which a cession of administration and disposal of use and usufruct adheres. The Religious passing to an Institute in which he must profess solemn vows at the completion of the Novitiate will make final disposition concerning his property within the two months proximate to solemn Profession.

88. "a religione" can mean only, "from the Institute" as may be readily seen by referring to canon 488 proemium and 1°.

89. Cf. canon 569 § 1.

tion to the legislation of 569 §§ 1-2 and 580 § 3? No one will dispute the intention of the law in canon 569 §§ 1-2, viz. to liberate the Religious "for the whole period during which he will be bound by simple vows", from solicitude and distraction about the property he owns and at the same time provide for the preservation of the property, against the event of the return of the Religious to the world. Undoubtedly, the intention of the law in canon 580 § 3, is to provide for necessary changes that become imperative; yet to guard the Religious from desiring to change the previous provision concerning his property without a sufficient reason and thus give occasion for unnecessary distraction, the consent and permission of the Moderator General—a person required to have prudence for such matters—was placed as a requisite condition for the modification of the previous provision. Now, consider the case of the Novice-Religious[90] passing to another Institute: the maintenance of his property has already been secured; and the distraction concerning the cession and the disposal has already been minimized; why should the law declare that in the case of such a Religious, the arrangement he has made, (concerning the administration, the use and usufruct) for the whole period he will be obliged by simple vows, must suddenly come to an end at the moment he finishes the act of Profession in the second Institute? Supposing that the previous provision made does cease: then the administration the use and the usufruct returns to the Religious having dominion, again to be ceded and disposed, in virtue of the legislator's enactment in canon 569 §§ 1-2. What motive could the legislator have, in terminating the first arrangement and then obliging the Religious immediately to do again what has been undone, by virtue of canon 580 § 3?: this is the question to be answered by the person who interprets the "transitus" of canons 632-636 as a "discessus" of canon 580 § 3, which can not be divorced from canon 569 §§ 1-2. It is preferable to think that the cession and disposal made in virtue of canon 569 §§ 1-2 endures as long as the Religious remains obligated by simple vows. Certainly the canonical obligation not to change the cession and disposal except in accordance with canon 580 § 3, endures up till the moment the sec-

90. Canon 633 § 1.

ond Profession is made; for until that moment the Religious is not transferred from the first Institute. At the instant of Profession also the Religious is still obligated by the simple vows of the first Institute. The next moment after Profession in the second Institute, the Religious is still obliged by simple vows—those of the second Institute; since the second Profession, the right and obligations of the Religious, as regards the cession of the administration and the disposal of the use and the usufruct of his property, are determined by the Constitutions of the second Institute. Before, during and after the "transitus", the Religious remained obligated by simple vows. It is not to be thought that the "transitus" of canons 632-636 is to be regarded as a "discessus" of canon 580 § 3.[91] Hence, the cession and disposal do not cease at the moment of the second Profession; nor is the Religious obliged to make a new cession and disposal; nor can the cession and disposal licitly be changed, except in accordance with the prescription of canon 580 § 3.[92]

ARTICLE II. OWNERSHIP

(*a*) *The capacity to own—canon 580 § 1*

"Quilibet professus a votis simplicibus, sive perpetuis sive temporariis, nisi aliud in constitutionibus cautum sit, conservat proprietatem bonorum suorum et capacitatem alia bona acquirendi salvis quae in canon 569 praescripta sunt."[93]

This legislation applies to *all those who have made profession of simple vows whether perpetual or temporary.* Hence, members of Orders who have made only simple profession[94] as well as members of Papal and Diocesan

91. Cf. Goyeneche, CpR, II (1921), 145.

92. For other solutions see: Goyeneche, CpR, II (1921), 144-146; Prümmer, *Manuale Iuris Canonici,* Q. 212, pp. 279-280.

93. "All those who have made profession of simple vows, whether perpetual or temporary, except the Constitutions declare otherwise, retain the proprietorship of their property and the capacity to acquire other property, the prescription of canon 569 remaining in force." 580 § 1.

94. Cf. canon 574; Blat, II, n. 651.

Congregations are subject to canon 580 § 1.[95] The distinction between the simple vow ordinarily made in a Congregation and that made in an Order before solemn profession consists in the legal ability to alienate property. The simple vow of poverty made in an Order entails inhability to validly alienate property except within the two months proximate to solemn Profession.[96] Whereas, the vow of poverty made in a Congregation ordinarily renders acts of alienation only illicit.[97] The vow of poverty made in an Order and that made in a Congregation are alike in the fact that both admit the retention of ownership and the acquirement of other property during the existence of the simple vow.[98]

Religious of simple vows retain *the proprietorship* of their property. The term "proprietas" conveys a more exact idea of the intention the legislator had in formulating the canon than would the more ancient term "dominium." "Proprietas" expresses the sum total of all proprietary rights as it exists in a passive, inert or static state. Whereas, "dominium" expresses the idea of the sum total of proprietary rights, as it exists in an active, dynamic or operative state.[99] Most authors in their definitions of "proprietas" or "dominium" are substantially correct. A highly technical and most exact definition is given by D'Angelo but it is not so apt for our purpose.[100] For practical purposes "proprietas" as used in canon 580 § 1 might be defined as the complete right to have external property as one's own, except when prohibited by law. It is complete, because this right comprehends in itself all other forms of proprietary rights such as to use, loan, exchange, administrate, etc. Simple profession does not deprive the Religious of the right of proprietorship, except the Consti-

95. Larroana CpR, II (1921), 12 (1), remarks that the lay brothers in some Orders which do not permit these Religious to ever make solemn profession, are likened to members of Congregations as regards the vow of poverty.

96. Cf. canon 581 § 1.

97. Cf. canon 579.

98. Cf. Larraona, CpR, II (1921), Schafer, p. 341.

99. Cf. D'Angelo, *Ius Digestorum,* Tomus, II, Vol. I, De iuribus realibus, p. 15.

100. "Proprietas est nexus iuris privati quo res, ut pertinentia personæ, huius (personæ) voluntati subiicitur in omnibus quæ prohibita non sint a iure publico vel a concursu alieni iuris." Cf. o. c. pp. 26-27.

tutions of the Institute determine otherwise. If the Constitutions of the Institute are silent, then it is a corrolary of this canon that should a simply vowed Religious die intestate, his property belongs to his heirs "ab intestato" and not the Institute;[101] the dowry excepted, since this (even though the vows professed are only temporary) belongs to the Institute by virtue of an express prescript of canon law.[102] In other parts of the dissertation are treated the restrictions canon law places on the exercise of the right of proprietorship possessed by Religious of simple vows.

Not only does the Code permit the Religious of simple vows to retain the proprietorship of their property but it also declares that they retain *the capacity to acquire* other private property unless the Constitutions determine otherwise. Beyond allowing the Constitutions to restrict the capacity to acquire, the Code makes no restriction other than that contained in the second section of this canon, viz. "Whatever the Religious acquires by his industry or in respect of his Institute, belongs to the Institute." Hence as far as the common law is concerned, a Religious can acquire private property by inheritance, legacy, donation, payment of debts, settlement of law claims, etc. Moreover, since the Code gives permission to acquire other property for the augmentation or foundation of capital, no other permission is necessary as regards property acquired for this purpose,[103] unless the Constitutions of the Institute determine otherwise.[104]

The concession of the legislator in allowing the Constitutions of the Institutes to remain in force as regards the retention of ownership of private property and the capacity to acquire other property, is stated in the phrase: *"nisi aliud in constitutionibus cautum sit."* As is evident, this phrase refers to the Constitutions already in effect before the Code began to function. Furthermore, this phrase grants concession to the Constitutions only in so far as they affect *the capacity* to retain and *the capacity* to acquire

101. Cf. S. C. EE et RR, 6 iunii 1836 ad IV, Bizzarri, p. 71; Larraona, CpR, II (1921), p. 12; Schäfer, p. 342.

102. Canon 548.

103. Augustine, III, p. 278; Papi, *Religious in Church Law*, p. 256 (probably); *Religious Profession*, pp. 53-54 (probably).

104. Some Constitutions require permission, e.g., *Costituzioni Delle Suore Terziaie figlie di S. Francesco*, n. 46.

further property. By this phrase, the Code does not "canonize" those parts of Constitutions (which having already admitted the capacity of the Religious to acquire property for himself) then legislate, that whatever property the Religious acquires for himself, must be given to the Superior for the common welfare of the Institute, the Province or the House in which he lives. Such legislation as this latter, is opposed to the Code for (a) canon 583 speaking of members of Congregations declares that they: "may not abdicate gratuitously the dominion of their property by a voluntary deed of conveyance" and (b) canon 581 § 1 declares concerning simple vow members (who will profess solemn vows) of Orders:[105] "Not, except within sixty days preceding the solemn Profession, can the professed of simple vows validly renounce his property, but within this time he must, saving special indults from the Holy See, renounce in favor of whomsoever he wishes all the property which he actually possesses, on condition of his profession subsequently taking place." Hence, it may be seen that such donations for members of Congregations are illicit and for members of Orders[106] are invalid.[107] When the Constitutions of an Institute clearly deprive the Religious of the capacity to own or acquire property, such legislation enjoys the concession of the Code. For the sake of example, if the Jesuit Constitutions were not revised, the old Constitutions, declaring that the Formed Coadjutors of the Society were incapable of private ownership, would remain effective.[108] This example would be a clear case of Constitutions *depriving* a Religious of capacity to own or acquire. There are other instances of Constitutions merely *limiting* the capacity to acquire, e.g., the Constitutions of the Society of Mary declare that all *personal* donations are to be refused and prescribe that presents offered are to be accepted only for the community or the chapel.[109]

---

105. Cf. canon 574.
106. Canon 574.
107. Cf. Papi, *Religious in Church Law,* pp. 255-256.
108. *"Constitutiones,"* p. 6, c. 2, n. 12; cf. Schmalzgruber, lib. III, tit. 35, n. 6; Bucceroni, n. 285.
109. Cf. *Constitutions of the Society of Mary,* Chapter III; the newly approved *Constitutions of the Sisters of Mercy,* n. 32, declare that presents are to be considered for the use of the community and not the receiver even though given by relatives.

The admonition: *"salvis quae in canon 569 praescripta sunt,"* seems to have been added for the sake of security. Section one of canon 580 declares that unless the Constitutions determine otherwise, the simply vowed Religious can acquire private property after profession. In order that there might not be any misunderstanding concerning this property the phrase "salvis, etc.," ordains that the property acquired after profession must be treated the same as the property possessed before profession, viz., the administration, use and usufruct must be entrusted to someone else, according to the norm of canon 569 §§ 1, 2.[110]

(*b*) *The capacity to acquire, restricted—canon 580 § 2*

"Quidquid autem industria sua vel intuitu religionis acquirit religione acquirit."[111]

(*a*) *Property accruing from industry*

Historically considered, the principle of canon law concerning the industry of Religious, here enunciated as general law, for all simple vow Religious, takes its origin from the very dawn of community life in Christian monasticism.[112] Intrinsically considered, this principle arises from the contract implicitly made by Religious Profession, whereby the Religious gives the fruits of his labor, in return for the temporal care bestowed upon him by the Institute. Acts placed contrary to this principle are not only opposed to the virtue of religion, as violations of the vow of poverty, but are also violations of justice. Furthermore, such acts are canonically invalid.[113] It is corrolary of this principle that should a Religious leave his Institute at the expiration of temporary vows or after obtaining an indult of secular-

110. Cf. Chelodi, *Ius de Personis,* p. 456, n. 274; Larraona, CpR, II (1921), 13.

111. "But whatever the Religious acquires by his own industry or in respect of his Institute, belongs to the Institute." canon 580 § 2.

112. Cf. Cassian, *Institutes,* IV, c. 14; Zoega, *Catologus Codicum Copticorum Manuscriptorum,* N. CCIV et N CCXII.

113. Cf. David, p. 128.

114. Canon 643 § 1. Of course a female Religious is entitled to the restoration of her dowry, minus the interest that accrued to it. Cf. canon 551 § 1. If a Religious is only exclaustrated he remains obligated by his vow of poverty. He is entitled to use as much money, etc., as he needs for his support but whatever he acquires "ex industria sua" belongs to the Institute.

ization or by apostatizing from Religion, he has no right to compensation for services, the art, the labor, the ministry, etc., which were produced by his industry;[114] and it may be of interest to the Religious of the United States to know that the Supreme Court indirectly recognizes the corrolary of this canon.[115]

It can not be denied that the pecuniary compensation accepted for services performed by a Religious, e.g., emoluments from preaching, teaching, nursing, royalties from publications, etc., belong to the Institute. As a general principle it can be accepted that whatever arises from labor mental or physical, or the exercise of art or a profession belongs to the Institute. We have already seen the exception to this rule as regards manuscripts. As regards paintings or sculptures and the like, if an immemorial custom which cannot be prudently removed obtains to the effect that such productions belong to the artificer, then as long as the custom remains, the article belongs to the Religious. However, if the article was sold by the Religious, the principle of this canon would function, in favor of the Institute.

What if a Religious, without any permission from his Superior celebrates Mass gratis for a friend? If the Religious, in making his Profession, as a part of the contract implied in Profession, had tacitly agreed that all his Masses would be celebrated for a stipend whenever possible—the stipend always to belong to the Institute, then in virtue of this contract, the Religious acts unjustly when he celebrates Mass gratis.[116] If that Religious instead of celebrating Mass gratis for a friend, celebrates Mass for a "generous stipend" rather than the intention assigned by the Superior and then disposes of the money, without any permission, he offends against the vow of poverty as well as the virtue of justice. If a Religious, according to the Constitutions of the Institute or custom, etc., was entitled to a "free" Mass, i.e., to celebrate Mass for any intention he pleased but never for a stipend unless a special permission had been accorded to him for this, acts contrary to the condition attached to the "free" Mass, he does not act

115. Cf. Order of St. Benedict v Steinhauser 234 U. S. 640; *Fortnightly Review,* XXI (1914) pp. 268-269; 418-419; Cf. Brown, p. 131.

116. Cf. Vermeersch, *Epitome,* I, n. 683; Schäfer, p. 344.

against justice but obedience. However, since the stipend arose from the industry of the Religious, it belongs to the Institute.

We must here take cognizance of a document appearing in volume XIV of the Acta Apostolicae Sedis.[117]

"Circa pecunias religiosis obvenientes occasione servitii militaris praestiti tempore belli.

"DUBIA

"Sacrae Congregationi Religiosorum Sodalium negotiis praepositae, sequentia dubia pro opportuna solutione subiecta fuere:

"I. Utrum religiosi sollemniter professi ad tenorem iuris communis quidquam pecuniarum, quae illis occasione servitii militaris durante bello praestiti obvenerunt, vel obvenient, iure sibi retinere valeant, vel potius eas omnes suo Ordini refundere teneantur.

"II. Utrum religiosi sollemniter quidem professi, sed ex indulto apostolico post professionem nihilominus capaces adquirendi, quidquam pecuniarum, de quibus in primo dubio, suas facere valeant absque assensu et licentia expressa sui Superioris maioris.

"III. Utrum religiosi simpliciter professi, sive in perpetuum sive ad tempus, quorum constitutiones excludunt post professionem omnem ulteriorem acquisitionem bonorum temporalium, teneantur dictas pecunias omnes suae religioni tradere.

"IV. Utrum religiosi quomodocumque simpliciter professi in perpetuum vel ad tempus, sive in Ordine sive in Congregatione, quorum constitutiones non obstant, de pecuniis *titulo stipendii* (*le solde*) acceptis quidquam suum facere valeant — vel potius quidquid post eorum dimissionem ex exercitu superfuerit, respectivae religioni tradere teneantur.

"V. Utrum pensio-vitalitia data ob mutilationem vel debilitationem in bello perpessam religiosis simpliciter professis, vel iis de quibus in canon 673 § 1, aut demum iis quorum vota vel promissa suspensa manebant, pertineant ad respectivam Religionem aut Societatem.

"VI. Utrum emolumenta pecuniaria, ob decus militare (*la médaille militaire, la croix de la légion d'honneur*)

117. Cf. pp. 196-197.

in bello reportatum obvenientia, pertineant ad ex-milites aut potius ad Religionem.

"VII. Utrum retributio singulis militibus in actu eorum dimissionis tributa tanquam sollemne publicae gratitudinis signum (*le prime de la démobilisation*), pertineat ad Religionem.

"VIII. Utrum qui de pecuniis occasione belli perceptis contra superiores resolutiones iam disposuerint etiam in favorem tertii, teneantur ad restitutionem.

"Porro Eminentissimi Patres in plenario coetu ad Vaticanum habitio die 24 Februarii 1922, re mature perpensa, ad proposita dubia respondendum censuerunt:

"Ad I. *Negative* ad 1^{am} partem; affirmative ad 2^{am}.

"Ad II. *Negative.*

"Ad III. *Affirmative,* quoad religiosos qui tempore servitii militaris votis legati erant; *negative,* quoad ceteros.

"Ad IV. Si agatur de iis qui tempore servitii militaris votis adstricti erant: *negative* ad 1^{am} partem, *affirmative* ad 2^{am}; si vero de iis quorum vota cessarunt, *affirmative* ad 1^{am} partem; quoad alteram vero: aequam compensationem suae Religioni tradant.

"Ad V. Quoad religiosos tempore servitii militaris votis obstrictos: pertinet ad Religionem; quoad ceteros: pertinet ad personam, quae tamen tenetur eam suo Instituto tradere quamdiu in eo permaneat.

"Ad VI. *Negative* ad 1^{am} partem; *affirmative* ad 2^{am}, nisi de iis agatur qui votis non erant obstricti tempore belli.

"Ad VII. *Affirmative;* nisi tempore belli votis ligati mimime fuerint.

"Ad VIII. *Affirmative;* nisi religiosus ex permissione Superioris, rationabiliter praesumpta, egerit.

"Facta autem praemissis relatione SSmo D.N.Pio Div. Prov. Pp. XI ab infrascripto P.Secretario S.Congregationis, in audientia habita die 25 Febrarii 1922, Sanctitas Sua resolutionem EE.Patrum approbare et confirmare dignata est.

"Datum Romae, ex Secretaria S.Congregationis de Religiosis, die 16 Martii 1922.

"Th. Card. Valfrè de Bonzo, *Praefectus.*
"Maurus M. Serafini, Ab.O.S.B. *Secretarius.*"

1. The interpretation of this document

This document directly concerns the money received by Religious on the occasion of military services rendered during War. It makes no mention of the source of the doubts proposed in the plenary session of the Congregation. Its subscription declares that the decisions of the Congregation were approved and confirmed in an audience with the Pope. Evidently, the Congregation intends the decisions to apply to all Religious receiving money on the occasion of war. Beyond the subjects of the response and the matters to which it refers, it has no *direct* obligatory force.

Since the first two solutions deal with solemn vow Religious cognizance of them will be taken only in the commentary on solemn vows. The third solution was undoubtedly based on the "ex industria sua" principle of canon 580: the same is true of the fourth solution; even though the industry itself was of a nature not expressly contemplated when Profession was made; it might be added to, that if the soldier-Religious had acquired money from illicit acts it should be considered as belonging to the Institute from the title "ex industria sua."[118]

But what about the fifth solution? This decision was not based on the "ex industria sua" principle[119] as Cange asserts.[120] Rather, it was based on principles of equity.[121] As Goyeneche well observes concerning pensions: "*Dantur sane non agenti sed patienti, infortuno non industriae.*"[122] Military service was the *occasion* of the pension being awarded. *Multilation* or *debility* arising from the occasion of military service was the *cause* of the compensation being given. Since the Institute to which the Religious belongs

118. Cf. Periodica, XI (1923), 35; Schäfer, p. 403.

119. Cf. Goyeneche, CpR, IV (1923), 37; CpR, I (1920), 342.

120. *Le Code de Droit Canonique,* II, p. 100. Vermeersch *Periodica,* XI (1923), 36, uses the vague expression: "quia pensio debetur propter professi industriam, late sumptam, ideo fructibus industriae assimilata videtur." Schäfer, p. 403, appears to agree with Vermeersch.

121. Cf. *Il Monitore Ecclesiastico,* Quarta Serie, Vol. IV (1922) 143; *Jus Pontificium,* II (1922), 60; Goyeneche, *Commentarium pro Religiosis,* IV (1923), 37; *ibid,* I (1920), 342.

122. CpR, I (1920), 342.

is obliged to maintain the injured Religious[123] it is but equitable that the Institute become entitled to the pension.[124]

The sixth solution decided that the emolument attached to such military honors as "le médaille militaire," la croix de la légion d'honneur" belonged to the Institute of which the Religious was a member. Undoubtedly the norm of "ex industria sua" was the guiding principle of the Congregation.[125] The military award can be considered as the fruit of industry understood in a wide sense. True it does not arise from a stipulated contract. Yet such an award is possible only because the government of the nation has enacted, that whenever a soldier has been observed to give distinguished service, or to display extraordinary diligence in the discharge of his duty, he is to receive a special reward. In other words the same government that grants the "stipendium" for *ordinary* service, also grants an extraordinary reward for *extraordinary* service. Placed the condition that the soldier be cited for bravery, etc., then he will receive the reward of his extraordinary service. Since the fruits of industry belong to the Institute and not to the Religious, it is not hard to understand why the Sacred Congregation formulated the sixth solution in the document now under discussion.

The seventh solution, viz., that concerning the first demobilization award, also can be considered as arising from the industry principle[126] provided that we use that principle in its widest sense. The bonus was granted as a sign of gratitude for the service rendered during the war. It was intended as a help to the soldier during the period immediately following his discharge from the service when he had not yet secured means of support in civil life.

The eighth solution was based on the principles of justice as may be readily seen. Very apposite is the re-

---

123. Canon 647 § 2, 2°.

124. Persons who were not Religious at the time of their injury but who became Religious later, are obliged to give to the Institute their allowance as long as they remain Religious. If these individuals abandon the Institute, they are able to enter upon their pension.

125. Cf. Vermeersch, *Periodica,* XI (1923), 37; Cange, o.c. II, p. 100; *Jus Pontificium,* 11 (1922), 60; Creusen, *Nouvelle Revue Theologique,* XLIX (1922), 373-374; *Il Monitore Ecclesiastico,* ut supra, IV (1922), 143-144.

126. Cf. *Il Monitore Ecclesiastico* Quarta serie, Vol. IV (1922) p. 144; *Jus Pontificium,* II (1922), 60; Schäfer, p. 404; Vermeersch, *Periodica,* XI (1923), 37.

mark of Creusen when he says: "Ajoutons toutes les dépenses ou aumones faites avec une entière bonne foi et l'impossibilité pour un grand nombre de restituer le bien, peut-etre injustement dépensé. Le champ ouvert à l'indulgence des Superieurs pour effacer le passé ne sera probablement pas très étendu et leur bonté n'hésitera pas à s'y exercer."[127]

2. Its further application

Are these responses to be used as norms in deciding similar cases? Goyeneche is the only author (of the writings here available) who makes a direct and absolute statement in this matter. He says: "Licet responsiones commentatae argumentum particulare afficiant, maximum habent momentum, quia demonstrant criterium S. C. Religisorum in interpretatione vis voti paupertatis simplicis, quod, prout in Codice, videretur nimis cedere favori religiosi, dum S. Congregatio iura Religionis sarta tectaque docet habenda."[128] Vermeersch in the recent edition of his moral theology work[129] says *"si normam sumamus responsionum,"* etc. Such diction does not convey the idea that this illustrious author was certain the responses must be taken as the norm in all analagous cases. It is also significant, that the most recent edition of the *"Epitome Iuris Canonici,"* by Vermeersch-Creusen, entirely omits the responses, as a norm for the interpretation of the "ex industria sua" principle. Certainly, the document does not expressly state, that it is intended for analagous cases also. Most authors who have written since the promulgation of the responses do not use the document as interpretation of similar cases. Cange, professor at the "Grand Seminaire de Rodez" declares, that it seems to him the Sacred Congregation gave the responses in view of the particular circumstances, and did not wish to give a norm obligatory for analagous cases occurring thereafter.[130] Hence it can be concluded it is not evident that the responses given by the Sacred Congregation of Religious on

---

127. Cf. *Nouvelle Revue Theologique,* XLIX (1922), 377.
128. CpR, IV (1923), 39.
129. *Principia-Responsa-Concilia Theologiae Moralis,* III, p. 112. p. 112.
130. Cf. Cange, *Le Code de Droit Canonique,* II, p. 100; Bastien, *"Directoire Canonique,"* 3 ed. n. 596.

March 16, 1922, were intended as the norm for all analogous cases.

There can be little doubt that the first four responses, even though they were not intended to be the guiding principle for similar cases, can without doubt be applied in similar cases. Yet, there can be considerable doubt about applying the fifth response to analagous cases. For example: a Religious, while on a journey to a mission became the victim of a railroad accident and on that account was given an amount of money as compensation for injuries he sustained. Certainly, that money received by the Religious does not belong to the Institute from the title "ex industria sua." Undoubtedly, equity would dictate that the Religious obtain permission from the Holy See to give that money to the Institute, since the Institute must support the Religious.

The sixth response rests sufficiently upon the principle "ex industria sua" to warrant its use in analagous cases. It might find its application should a Religious receive a medal for bravery in the discharge of duty. Not so long ago in New York a Sister saved the life of one of her charges who had fallen in the Hudson River; if the Sister placed the reward in the Religious community fund, it could scarcely be called an illegitimate disposal of property; similarly a Religious priest, a chaplain to the fire department saved a man's life at the peril of his own; if he placed the monetary recognition of his bravery, in the Religious community fund, it could scarcely be called illicit.

The seventh response is also sufficiently based upon the "ex industria sua principle" to warrant its use in similar cases. For example, if a priest-Religious at the conclusion of a retreat to the laity is presented with a purse by the people, *from a motive of gratitude,* that money should be placed in the common fund. It not infrequently happens that on the occasion of services rendered to the diocesan clergy, e.g., a mission or Sunday work, an extra amount of money is given to the Religious priest. Supposing that the pastor as the Religious is leaving, hands to him an envelope saying "This is for your Superior" and then extending a bank note remarks, "This is for yourself." From the will of the donor the bank note is intended only for the Religious and not for the Institute. Nor is it an extraordinary occurrence for a pastor to say: "Unless you can keep it for yourself, give it back to me, as I don't want you to hand it to your Superior." Although the donation followed an exercise of industry, the title to it arose from the will of the pastor which expressly excluded the Institute. The motive of gratitude to the individual Religious is frequently not present as far as the donation is concerned. Ordinarily the donation is motivated by mere priestly benevolence towards a brother priest.

(*b*) *Donations "intutitu religionis"*

The Institute is entitled not only to the fruits of the industry of the individual Religious but also to whatever he receives "*intutitu religionis.*" Whenever the intention of the donor is to benefit the Institute and not the individual Religious, then a donation is made "intutitu religionis." The intention of the donor may be known by express declaration in word or equivalently by the mode or circumstances of the donation. This is the meaning of the phrase, "intutitu religionis" which the Sacred Congregation of Religious formerly referred to in the terms "intutitu Societatis"[131] and "intutitu instituti."[132] The correlative of this term is "intutitu personae." A donation is made "intutitu personae" when the intention of the donor is to benefit only the Religious individual. An evident case of the former might occur during a mission, if an admirer of the work of a certain Institute made a donation to a priest whom he never knew personally; such a donation, without a doubt belongs to the Institute. A case of the latter would occur, should a Sister receive a donation from a parent, friend or relative on her feast day;[133] such a donation belongs not to the Institute but to the Religious.[134] Another clear case of "intutitu personae" donation would be that of the gifts showered upon a newly ordained priest by relatives and friends of the occasion of his first Mass.

In practice it often happens that the Religious is uncertain as to whether the donation was given "intutitu re-

131. S. C. EE et RR, litt. 30 dec. 1882 (*Fontes,* n. 2008).

132. *Normae,* 28 iunni, 1901.

133. Cf. Papi, *Religious Profession,* pp. 58-59.

134. Here it is assumed that the Constitutions of the Institute do not restrict the capacity of the Religious to own and to acquire private property after Profession.

ligionis," or "intutitu personae" or from another title or even a combination of titles. The case of the teaching Sister celebrating the silver jubilee of her profession may serve as an example. On this occasion the Sister receives many gifts of money. The motives behind the gifts may be of several kinds, e.g., personal affection or friendship, gratitude for the labor of teaching, a desire to help the Sisters using this occasion as a graceful opportunity, or the mere fact that the jubilee is an occasion when conventionalities dictate that a gift should be bestowed upon a personal acquaintance, viz., an occasion similar in character to Christmas, a graduation or wedding. It would seem that whenever the *motive* cause of the gift was affection or friendship or the observance of a conventionality, even though there may have been an *impulsive* cause such as a desire to help a worthy public institution, the donation belongs to the Sister. But if gratitude, or desire to help a worthy cause or to honor the Religious State[135] was the *motive* cause and affection or friendship were mere *impulsive* causes, then the donation belongs to the Institute.

What if a Religious doubts whether the donation was made to him or to the Institute? Religious, as pastors or Rectors of churches must be guided by canon 1536 § 1: "Nisi contrarium probetur, praesumendum ea quae donantur rectoribus ecclesiarum, etiam religiosorum, esse ecclesiae donata." However, canon 1536 § 1 is to be their norm only as regards donations made to them in their official capacity.[136] It is not their norm for doubts concerning the ownership of other kinds of donations, viz., those received in their non-official capacity; these latter doubts are to be solved according to the principles of moral the-

---

135. Cf. Papi, *Religious in Church Law,* p. 256; Vermeersch, *Epitome,* Vol. I, p. 434, c; Pejska, p. 130; Woywood, n. 488; Larraona, CpR, II (1921), 41.

136. Whatever property is given to a Religious pastor "intuitu paroeciæ" which he governs, belongs to the parish; other property may be acquired by him in the same way and under the same conditions as other Religious. Notwithstanding his vow of poverty, the pastor is allowed to accept, collect and administer alms offered in any manner for the benefit of the parishoners, or for Catholic schools or pious institutions joined to the parish. He may, according to his prudent judgment distribute alms in conformity with the intention of their donors; the Superior of the pastor has the right of vigilance over this activity. Canon 630.

ology taking into consideration the circumstances attending the donation and the principles of canon 580 §§ 1, 2. This latter norm applies to all other Religious, except those who have an official capacity similar to that of a pastor or Rector of a Church. In so far as a Religious holds an office similar to the Rector of a church, he must be guided by canon 1536 § 1 as regards donations received under conditions similar to a Rector of a church acting in his official capacity.[137]

If a Religious is created a cardinal or elected a bishop, either residential or titular or acquires any other dignity outside his Institute he is not released from his vow of poverty.[138] But if a Religious belongs to an Institute wherein the right to have and acquire property is not lost with Profession, he recovers the administration, use and usufruct of the property he owns and becomes in this regard like a Prelate without Religious Vows. He can also acquire property like a Prelate who is not a Religious. Of course whatever he acquires other than from the title "intutitu personae" must be used according to the will of the donors.[139] If the Religious belongs to an Institute wherein the members lose the right of owning property, after he attains such a dignity, he may retain the administration use and usufruct of the property he thereafter acquires, during the actual exercise of the dignity. If the Religious becomes a Residential bishop, vicar or prefect apostolic, the ownership of the property he acquires, belongs to the diocese, vicariate or prefecture apostolic. If the dignity the Religious acquires is a titular bishopric, the

---

137. Canon 20. Canon 1536 § 1 must be considered in the light of the source from which it was drawn. (Cf. Supremum Signaturæ Apostolicæ Tribunal, *De Manila,* 6 apr. 1920, AAS, XII [1920] 258; Leo XIII, const. *Romanos Pontifices* 8 maii 1881, AAS, II [1910] 267 sq.; Leo XIII, const. *Appendix-Romanos Pontifices,* 1 ian. 1910, AAS, VIII [1916] 296; Hilling, "*Interpretatio Codicis Iuris Canonici,* p. 101, n. s.), and the interpretation given to it by the "Tribunal Supremum Apostolicæ Signaturæ (AAS, XII [1920] 258 sq.), if it is to be properly understood.

138. Cf. Canon 627. Hence as regards the things which he has for his private use, he must observe the poverty of his Institute, in so far as he judges the observance of the poverty of his Institute to be compatible with his dignity. Cf. Prümmer, *Manuale Iuris Canonici,* p. 330; Pejska, p. 180; Augustine, III, p. 357; Vermeersch, *Epitome,* Vol. I, p. 476.

139. Canon 628.

property accruing to him belongs to the Institute, Province or House according to the specifications of the Constitutions of his Institute; hence that moral person may claim the property he possessed at the time of his death. What about Cardinals who are members of an Institute in which it is not permitted that the members as individuals own property? By virtue of a special privilege, they can dispose of the revenues of their benefices even by testament.[140] The sacred furnishings and all other objects devoted permanently to divine worship in the possession of a deceased cardinal who had his domicile in the city of Rome, though he was a suburbicarian bishop or an abbot nullius, becomes the property of the Papal sacristy, no matter by what kind of revenue they were acquired, unless he had donated or willed them to some church, public oratory, pious place or to an ecclesiastical or religious person. Excepted from this latter category are his rings and pectoral crosses, even those with sacred relics.[141] However, it is to be desired that the Cardinal who wants to use his right to donate or will his sacred furnishings, should leave at least part of them to the churches of which he has the title, administration or "commenda."[142] As regards the other property a cardinal Religious may acquire, e.g., personal donations, etc., it is not very clear that he may will them.[143] Prummer[144] and Vermeersch[145] do not restrict the right of the cardinal as regards the disposal of this property.

ARTICLE III. DISPOSAL OF PROPERTY DURING THE LIFETIME OF SIMPLE VOW RELIGIOUS

Abdication of property by members of Congregations

During the century just passed, antagonistic governments in Europe confiscated the property of Religious In-

140. Canon 239 § 1, n. 19; Prümmer, *Manuale Iuris Canonici,* p. 330; Vermeersch, *Epitome,* Vol. I, p. 476; Woywod, Vol. I, p. 274.

141. Canon 1298; Woywod, Vol. II, p. 78.

142. Canon 1298; Woywod, II, pp. 78-79.

143. Fanfani, p. 474 thinks it probable that they belong to his Institute. It is true he speaks here of a member of an Order, for he distinguishes between an Institute capable of owning property, and one that is not; he declares that in the former case the property probably belongs to the Order; in the latter case, it belongs to the Holy See. Yet the principle he uses expresses his opinion on this matter.

144. *Manuale Iuris Canonici,* p. 330.

stitutes and dispersed the Religious who thus suddenly found themselves without proper means of support. What happened then can occur again. Thus the practicality of the legislation of canon 583, 1° is observed even though the Religious never become released from the simple vows he has professed. And should a member of a Congregation abandon the Institute, this legislation provides for his maintenance on his return to the world. It is the purpose of canon 583, 1° to maintain intact the property of the Religious against such untoward exigencies.

As is evident from the wording of the text, this canon was formulated for *members of Congregations.* It applies to members of diocesan as well as papal Institutes. Members of these Institutes, whether they are professed of temporary or perpetual vows are subjects of this law. It does not apply to members of Orders as mentioned in canon 574.[147] However, members of Orders, such as lay brothers, who never will profess solemn vows should observe the norm of this canon, if they are permitted to own property after the profession of simple vows. Since the Code has no express precept for them in this matter, the norm is to be found in this canon, by virtue of canon 20.[148] Should a Religious of a Congregation transfer to another Institute, during his second Novitiate, he remains obliged by his simple vows[149] and is not considered a Novice in every sense of the term. Since he is still a professed Religious, he is obliged by this canon rather than canon 568[150]; hence a renunciation of property by him would be illicit but not invalid.

The subjects of this canon are prohibited to abdicate *the dominion of their property.* If this legislation would be interpreted aright, it would be well to view for a moment the mind of the Church, as regards this matter, in the days before the Code. The Holy See published in

145. *Epitome,* Vol. I, p. 476.

146. Canon 583—"Those who have made profession of simple vows in any religious Congregation: 1° May not gratuitously abdicate the dominion over their property by a voluntary deed of conveyance."

147. These Religious are governed by canon 581 which declares invalid any renunciation of property made except within the two months proximate to solemn profession.

148. Cf. Larraona, CpR, II (1921), 72, n. 2; Schäfer, p. 346; Blat, II, pp. 645-646; Chelodi, p. 457.

149. Cf. canon 633 § 1.

1901, the "Normae" it was wont to follow in the approbation of new Congregations of simple vows. Article 119 of this document declared: "Professae retinent dominium radicale bonorum suorum; immo ipsis prohibetur se abdicare hoc dominio radicali ante professionem votorum perpetuorum per actus inter vivos." Article 121 declared: "Ut sorores in perpetuum professae licite se spoliare possint dominio radicali omnium bonorum suorum per actus inter vivos, requiritur licentia Apostolicae Sedis." As may be readily observed, the "Normae" *absolutely* prohibited Religious of only *temporary vows* to abdicate their property by an act "inter vivos."[151] Whereas, article 121 merely declared that Religious professed of *perpetual vows* needed the permission of the Holy See in order to licitly abdicate the radical dominion *of all their property*. Moreover, the Sacred Congregation of Religious, in the new redaction of the Constitutions of the *Handmaids of Mary* approved the following article: "Hechos los votos perpetuos necesitaran las Hermanas licencia de la S. Sede para desposeerse por actos inter vivos de la propiedad de todos sus bienes *cuando ellos sean de alguna consideracion*."[152]

It is now to be noted that canon 583, 1° makes no distinction between Religious professed of temporary vows and those professed of perpetual vows. The form of the Code legislation resembles the prohibition of article 119 in the "Normae" and hence it seems that the Holy See does not want any Religious to notably decrease the private property they own and much less does it want the Religious to dispose of the whole of their property.

What if a Religious of *temporary* vows desires to abdicate the dominion of his property? Before the Code, Ferreres states, the Sacred Congregation of Religious, *never* granted such a permission to Religious of temporary vows, when the petition concerned the *whole property* of the Religious; and only *rarely* was permission conceded for the abdication of *a part* of the property, even when serious reasons urged such a permission.[153] The reason for such a rigid attitude on the part of the Holy See is quite apparent. A Religious with only temporary vows may want to

150. Cf. Larraona, CpR, II (1921), 71.
151. Art. 119.
152. Cf. Larraona, CpR, II (1921), 74.
153. *Las Religiosas,* n. 525.

leave the Institute at the expiration of these vows, an occurrence that is by no means rare. Again, since a Religious with only temporary vows is still on probation, the Institute not infrequently decides to refuse the Religious authorization to profess the perpetual vows of the Institute. The legislation concerning the abdication of the capital a Religious owns prevents imprudent disposal of property. Hence, in the event of departure from the Religious Life, the person concerned can resume secular life in his former social status; again, this legislation assures greater liberty to the Religious when the time aarrives for the renewal of temporary vows or the profession of perpetual vows, for if he did not have the property he owned on his entrance into Religion, there might be the temptation to assume the new vows rather than return to the world impoverished. Hence it would seem that after the Code, permission from the Holy See will not be granted for the abdication of *all* the property owned by Religious with temporary vows. If such a Religious desires to abdicate a notable *part* of the property he owns, it is seriously to be doubted whether the Holy See will grant permission for such an act.

What if a Religious with *perpetual* vows desires to abdicate the dominion of his capital whether in whole or in part? It is true that before the Code, permission for the abdication of the *whole* of the property owned was sometimes granted. It is also true, that if a perpetually professed Religious desired to abdicate the dominion of only a *part* of his property, the permission for such an act was not so difficult to obtain as may be seen from the fact that the papally approved Constitutions of some Institutes authorized their Superior General to grant such permissions.[154] But the Code in expressing the new law uses diction similar to that contained in Article 119 of the "Normae," viz., it declares without qualification, that the abdication of dominion over property owned by simple vow Religious is unlawful; it does not even suggest the possibility of permission being granted for such abdication

154. Cf. "*Constitutiones et Regulæ Congregationis Missionarium Oblatorum Sanctissimæ et Immaculatæ Virginis Mariæ* (1910), n. 191; also the Constitutions of the Missionaries of the Most Sacred Heart of Jesus, n. 52; the Constitutions of the Society of the Divine Word (1910), n. 71 (cf. Larraona, CpR, II [1921] 76).

either in whole or in part. Furthermore it is of interest to note that the newly revised Constitutions of the Institutes with simple vows no longer have a phrase permitting the Superior General to grant permission for the abidcation of even a part of the property owned by the Religious.[155] In fact most of the newly revised Constitutions are scarcely more than a paraphrase of the Code legislation in this matter.

There certainly is reason for the attitude of the Holy See as regards the abdication of property by these Religious. Undoubtedly, Religious professed or perpetual vows are older and and hence may be more prudent as regards the disposal of their property. However, it is by no means a rare occurrence for circumstances to develop either from within or from without the Institute, causing the Religious with perpetual vows to obtain a dispensation from their vows; hence the practicality of their retention of the dominion of the property they may have or may acquire. Furthermore, a misfit Religious is more apt to seek a return to the secular life if he has property than if he is penniless or has very little property.

Everything being considered, it seems clear, that as long as the reason for the law obtains in a given case, perpetually professed Religious will not receive permission for the abdication of either the whole of a notable part of the property they own.[156] Yet, in cases where there is little or no danger of the Religious being in need or reduced circumstances should he leave the Institute, especially in cases of Religious well advanced in years, it is hard to believe that permission would not be granted by the Holy See for the abdication of a *part* of the property owned.[157]

Although the canon prohibits the abdication of the dominion of the property owned by the subjects of this canon, yet the prohibition extends only to the *gratuitous* abdication by means of an act "inter vivos." A gratuitous

---

155. Even the Oblates of Mary Immaculate find that their revised Constitutions no longer have the clause permitting the General to grant permission for the abdication of a part of the property owned by the perpetually professed. cf. *"Constitutiones et Regulæ Congregationis Missionarium Oblatorum Sanctissimæ et Immaculatæ Virginis Mariæ"* (1928), n. 178; the same is true of, *"Constitutiones Societatis Verbi Divini,* (1922), n. 79, 5°, p. 36.

156. Cf. Larraona, CpR, II (1921), 75, 3°, 5°.

157. Cf. Larraona, CpR, II (1921), 75, 6°.

abdication would be a gift, the cancelling of a debt and other acts of a similar nature. Nor does the prohibition extend to small alms and the bestowal of things of minor moment on friends, relatives or pious causes, as long as such donations in no way affect the end intended by the law.[158] However, such donations should not be of such frequency that they constitute a notable diminution of the capital.[159] The basis for this opinion about donations of minor moment is the fact that the Tridentine decree[160] relative to the invalidity of donations made by Novices was interpreted in this fashion[161]: and surely that law was subject to stricter interpretation than is canon 583, 1°. However, such donations are not to be made without permission, at least reasonably presumed,[162] since they are acts of proprietorship restricted by the vow of poverty.

Moreover, since the canon says *gratuitous*, authors declare that the canon does not prohibit abdication of property "titulo oneroso." This latter form of abdication, although not prohibited by this canon, must not be thought to be permissible on this account. Onerous abdications of property such as buying, selling, loaning, leasing, etc., are acts of administration and as such, must be regulated in accordance with canons 569 §§ 1, 2 and 580 § 3.

Furthermore, since the canon specifies gratuitous abdication, "titulo gratioso" by an act *"inter vivos,"* acts of abdication, "mortis causa" are not prohibited by this legislation. Hence, if a Religious, professed before the Code began to operate, belongs to a Congregation which did not oblige its members to make a will, has received property since May 19, 1918, he may donate that property "mortis causa" to anyone he pleases, merely a Superior's permission being required; yet the administration, use and usufruct of that property during his life time must be provided for. As regards Religious professed since the Code

158. Cf. Chelodi, p. 457, n. 3; Larraona CpR, II (1921), 73 sq.; Augustine, III, 158; Gearin, AER, LXI (1919), 148; Papi, *Religious Profession,* 64. Jansen, p. 138, n. 6.

159. Cf. Larraona, CpR, II (1921), 74-75.

160. Sess. XXV, *De Regularibus,* c. 16.

161. Vermmersch, *De Religiosis,* I, n. 201; Bouix, *Tractatus de Iure Regularium,* I, p. 585.

162. Papi, *Religious Profession,* 64-65.

began to operate, they must remember that while canon 583, 1° does not expressly prohibit donations "mortis causa," yet the second section of that canon prohibits a change in the will made in accordance with canon 569 § 3, viz., concerning the property possessed at the time of profession and that which might be afterwards acquired. While it is true that a donation "mortis causa" is not a testament yet such a donation, when made after the testament, amounts to a *direct* change of the disposition already made concerning the property in the testament.[163] Therefore, in order licitly to make a donation "mortis causa," after profession, the prescription of canon 583, 2° must be observed.[164]

ARTICLE IV. DISPOSITION OF PROPERTY AFTER DEATH

(*a*) *Formation of the Will—canon 569 § 3*

We have already seen how canon law regulates the possessions of a simple vow Religious during his lifetime. We now approach the question of the disposal of those possessions after his death. This section of canon 569 declares that before the first Religious Profession the novice must draught an instrument technically known as a will or testament. It must state the last will of the Religious relative to all the property he owns at his death. This enactment of canon law safeguards the liberty of the person concerned as regards the disposal of his property after death and at the same time minimizes the danger of disedifying litigation arising from a Religious with simple vows dying intestate.

---

163. Cf. Larraona, CpR, II (1921), 105; Schäfer, p. 346.

164. The civil law of the United States and England permit donations "mortis causa." Some Codes do not acknowledge or formally exclude such donations. cf. *Codice Civile* (Italy) art. 1050; *Code Civil* (France and Belgium) art. 893; Mexico, art. 2601; Netherlands, art. 1701. Others liken it to a legacy, *Manuale del Codice Civile Generale Austriaco* § 956; Germany, art. 2301; Spain, art. 620; Portugal, art. 1457; Peru, art. 628. vide. Vermeersch, *Principia-Responsa-Concilia Theologiæ Moralis,* II, p. 386.

165. Canon 569 § 3.—"In every Religious Congregation the Novice, before making profession of temporary vows, shall freely dispose by will of all the property he actually possesses or may subsequently possess."

"Novitius in Congregatione religiosa ante professionem votorum temporariorum testamentum de bonis praesentibus vel forte obventuris libere condat."[165]

This section of the canon directly obliges only members of Religious Congregations whether papal or diocesan. It is a precept and not merely an instruction or a counsel.[166] This is strongly evidenced in a decision concerning the common law given to the General of the Redemptorists—a decision which gives no little weight to our opinion.[167] Are members of those Orders, which in some countries do not make solemn vows (due to an indult of the Holy See, granted on account of the extraordinary circumstances obtaining in those countries) obliged to follow the prescript of canon 569 § 3?[168] Creusen considers these Relig-

---

166. Lijdsman, "Der neue Kodex und das Testament der Ordensleute" *Theologisch-praktische Quartalschrift,* LXXIII (1920), 337-338; Battandier, p. 188; Balmes, p. 131; Fanfani, p. 228; Catechism of the Vows, n. 161; Larraona, CpR, II (1921), 104; Brandys, *Kirchliches Rechtsbuch,* p. 33; Stadtmüller, *Das neue Ordensrecht,* n. 254; Ferreres, *Institutiones Canonicae,* I, n. 871 (c); Creusen, *Religieux et Religieuses* n. 21; Tischpert, *Religious Profession,* p. 29.

167. "SSmus Dominus Noster Benedictus P. P. XV, referente infrascripto Cardinali Praefecto Sacrae Congregationis Negotiis Religiosorum Sodalium praepositae, ad praecavendam quamcumque dubitationem aut controversiam, quae in Congregatione SSmi Redemptoris, a sancto Alphonso Maria de Ligorio fundata, occasione Codicis Iuris Canonici conditionem et vim voti paupertatis oriri possent, ad dubium a Rmo P. Patritio Murray propositum ea quae sequuntur respondenum mandavit:

1. Sodales Congregationis SSmi Redemptoris, etiam in posterum in omnibus tenentur Decreto, die 31 aug. 1909, ab hac S. Congregatione dato.

2. Qui tamen, postquam Codex Iuris Canonici vim obligationis habere inceperit, id est a die decima nona mensis maii huius anni 1918, professionem in eadem Congregatione emissuri sunt:

a. debebunt ad normam can. 569 § 3 condere testamentum, quod mutare non poterunt nisi secundum dispositionem canon 583, 2°;

b. prohibentur per actum inter vivos dominium suorum bonorum titulo gratioso abdicare secundum praescripta can 583, 1°. Contrariis quibuscumque minime non obstantibus.

Datum Romae, ex audientia SSmi. diei maii, 1918.

J. Card. Tonti, Praefectus

Adulphus Episcopus Caniopitan, Secretarius."

Lijdsman, *Theologisch-praktische Quartalschrift,* LXXIII (1920), 337.

118. E.g. the Religious of St. John of God, in France, Cf. Goyeneche, CpR, II (1921), 46-47.

ious to be obliged only by their Constitutions and their Apostolic indult.[169] However, there is here a juridical analogy; there is no express precept for such Religious in the Code on the matter of making wills, etc. Yet, canon 20 declares: "Si certa de re desit expressum praescriptum legis, sive generalis sive particularis, norma summenda est, nisi agatur de poenis applicandis, a legibus latis in similibus." Hence the Religious of the Order of Saint John of God, in France[170] as well as others in a similar position must follow the norm prescribed in canon 569 § 3. According to the present discipline of the Church, members of Orders must first profess simple vows preparatory to the profession of solemn vows.[171] The Novices in Orders, under ordinary conditions, are not obliged by canon 569 § 3. However, it is at least permissible as far as the Code is concerned, and even advisable for such novices to make a will.[172] Such an instrument will be nullified in practice by solemn profession; yet should the Religious die while he is obligated by simple vows, a last will certainly ought to prove serviceable.

Since the canon says *"novitius,"* it does not oblige those who made their Profession before the Code went into effect. For canon 10 declares: "Leges respiciunt futura, non praeterita, nisi nominatim in eis de praeteritis caveatur." Included in this exemption are the Religious who were professed during the vacation of the Code, i.e., from May 27, 1917, to May 19, 1918, since the law did not yet begin to oblige. Such Religious may make a will

---

169. *Religieux et Religieuses,* p. 160; *Periodica,* X (1922), p. (56).

170. Cfr. Larraona, Cpr, II (1921), 72.

171. "In quolibet Ordine tam virorum quam mulierum et in qualibet Congregatione quæ vota perpetua habeat, novitius post expletum novitiatum, in ipsa noviatiatus domo debet votis perpetuis, sive solemnibus sive simplicibus, praemittere, salvo praescripto can. 634, votorum simplicium professionem ad triennium valituram, vel ad longius tempus, si aetas ad perpetuam professionem requisita longius distet, nisi constitutiones exigant annuales professiones." § 2. "Hoc tempus, legitimus Superior potest, renovata a religioso temporaria professione, prorogare, non tamen ultra aliud triennium". canon 574.

172. Cf. Jombart, *Nouvelle Revue Theologique,* LI (1925). 276-277; Chelodi, p. 450, nota 1; Vermeersch, *Epitome,* I, p. 417 Bakalarczyk, p. 190; Larraona, CpR, II (1921), 89; Schafer, p. 319;
Bakalarczyk, p. 190; Larraona, CpR, II (1921), 89; Schäfer, p. 319;

if they so desire, but they are not obliged to do so.[173] However, if for any reason a Religious professed since the Code became effective has not made a will, he is obliged to do so now.[174] From the purpose of the law, it is seen that it obliges, "ad urgendam obligationem et non ad finiendam obligationem." The obligation to make a will begins when the Novice becomes morally certain that he will be professed. Perhaps the best time for the observance of this precept is immediately before the retreat for Profession begins. If for any reason it is not made before that time, and even if the will was not made before the ceremony of Profession, the omission must be supplied as soon as possible.

It is the mind of the legislator that the Novice *freely dispose by will of all the property he possesses or may subsequently possess.* The term *"libere"* is to be understood in the sense that the Novice is to be unrestricted by any one or in any way, in determining to whom the property is to be bequeathed. However, the law requires that the mode of conveyance be a *testament.*

All authors are agreed that a civilly valid testament should be drafted if this can be done. However there is a well balanced controversy relative to the obligation of the law, if the Novice is incapable of making a civilly valid will.

Larraona and others prefer the opinion that when a will would be civilly invalid, the Novice is not obliged by the canon to draft a will which would be valid only canonically.[175] Larraona maintains that the law is satisfied only by a civilly valid will. If it is not possible to make such a will, then there is no obligation to make any will until it is possible to make a civilly valid will. For example: if the civil law will not recognize a testament except the testator is twenty-one years of age, the person who is now a Novice does not have to make a testament until he becomes twenty-one years of age; if civil statutes will not

173. Cf. Larraona, CpR, V (1924), 57.

174. Cf. Blat, II, p. 626; Fanfani, p. 228; Vermeersch, *Epitome,* I, p. 418; Gearin, AER, LXI (1919), 143; Larraona, CpR, II (1921), 8; Schäfer, p. 318.

175. Larraona, CpR, II (1921), 10 and nota (3); Bakalarczyk, p. 192; Chelodi, p. 450 nota (2); Ramos, CpR, III (1922), 32; Jardi, n. 518; Choupin, pp. 285-286; Goyeneche, CpR, V (1924), 441; Cf. David, pp. 130-131.

recognize as valid a will made concerning property which will be acquired only in the future, there is no obligation to make a testament concerning this property until the property is acquired. Larraona even goes so far as to state that he does not believe the obligation of canon 569 § 3 is fulfilled when a testament valid only canonically is made.[176]

Vermeersch and others contend that if valid civil testament can not be made, a testament only canonically valid must be draughted;[177] and after Profession it should be validated whenever this becomes possible, without any changes being made. It certainly would be difficult to explain how a legislator who knew that frequently Novices would be minors before the civil law and thus incapable of the full exercise of liberty as regards the formation of a testament, would yet formulate an unqualified law for them if he intended only a civilly valid will to be drafted. The legislator stated the law without distinction and where the law does not distinguish neither must we distinguish. Moreover, when the General of the Redemptorists petitioned the Pontifical Commission for the Interpretation of the Code as to whether the Novice would have to make a will even though it would be civilly invalid, the Commission gave an affirmative reply.[178]

---

176. CpR, II (1921), 10 nota (3); CpR, II (1921, 105.

177. Vermeersch, *Epitome,* I pp. 417-418; Blat, II, p. 636; De Meester, p. 446; Schäfer, p. 318; Bastien, n. 239; Balmes, p. 130; Battandier, p. 189; Gearin, AER, LXI (1919), 143; Woywod, n. 492; Creusen, *Religieux et Religieuxes,* p. 161; Papi,*Religious in Church Law,* p. 252; Fanfani, p. 228; Beijersbergen, *Nederlandsche kath. stemmen,* XXI, (1921), 340 nota (3). Cf. Bakalarczyk,*De Novitiatu,* p. 192.

178. The rescript from the Commission has not been published, yet the general of this Institute communicated the tenor of it a Circular Letter, n. 56 of April 12th, 1919. The pertinent sections of this letter are as follows: "II. Tria quaesita proposueram Commissioni ad interpretandum novum Codicem institutae, Responsionem tandem accepi, Quam hic describo, etsi, ut arbitror, ab ipsa Sede Apostolica aliquando evulgabitur.
I . . . .
II . . . . . .
III. "Testamentum, de quo Codex quo in can. 569 § 3, conficiendum est, etiam si ex lege civili invalidum sit, et tum quoque si novitius non habeat bona praesentia, sed tantum forte obventura juxta Decr. "Ut tollatur", no. 3. Sed curandum est ut, cumprimum fieri poterit, testamentutm etiam ex lege civili vim habeat, nulla tamen in eo mutata

Modern civil legislation relative to the age requirement in the matter of making a valid testament is as follows: Twenty-one years of age is required in England,[179] British Columbia,[180] Manatoba,[181] Nova Scotia,[182] Ontario,[183] and Quebec.[184] In the United States the age necessary for the making of a will depends entirely on Statutes.[185] In most states twenty-one years of age is required.[186] In some states eighteen years of age suffices.[187] In Georgia fourteen

dispositione nisi secundum canonem 583, 2°." The "Ut tollatur" here mentioned is a Decree relative to the manner in which members of the Institute may increase their patrimony or acquire new property.

179. Sec. 1, Vict, c. 26, § 7; *Cyclopedia of Law and Procedure,* Vol. XL, p. 999; Bouvier, III, p. 3458.

180. *The Revised Statutes of British Columbia* (1924) Vol. III, chap. 274, 5.

181. *The Revised Statutes of Manitoba* (1902), vol. III, c. 174, p. 2643.

182. *Revised Statutes of Nova Scotia,* (1923) Vol. II, Chap. 146, sect. 4, p. 1227.

183. *Revised Statutes of Ontario,* (1927), Vol. II, Chap. 149, n. 10, p. 1476.

184. *Code Civil de la Province de Quebec,* § § 831, 833. *The Civil Code of Lower Canada* §§ 831, 833, declares 21 years is required for making a testament.

185. *Cyclopedia of Law and Procedure,* Vol. XL, pp. 997.

186. Alaska, *Compiled Laws of the Territory of Alaska* (1913), § 563; Arizona, *The Revised Statutes of Arizona* (1913) Civil Code, § 1204; Delaware, *Revised Statutes of the State of Delaware* (1915), § 3240; Florida, *The Compiled General Laws of Florida* (1927) § 5457; Indiana, *Annotated Indiana Statutes* (1926) § 3449; Iowa, *Code of Iowa* (1927), § 11846; Kansas, *Revised Statutes of Kansas* (1923) § 22-201; Maine, *The Revised Statutes of the State of Maine,* (1917), Chap. 79, p. 1120; Massachusetts, *The General Laws of the Commonwealth of Massachusetts,* (1921), Chap. 191, sect. 1; Michigan, *The Compiled Laws of the State of Michigan* (1915), (11817) sect. 1, 2; Minnesota, *Mason's Minnesota Statutes* (1927), § 8735; Mississippi, *Annotated Mississippi Code,* (1927), § 3566; Nebraska, *Compiled Statutes of the State of Nebraska* (1922), § 1241; New Hampshire, *The Public Laws of the State of New Hampshire,* Vol. II, Chap. 297, 1, p. 1201; New Jersey, *Compiled Statutes of New Jersey* (1910), Vol. IV, p. 5862, 4; New Mexico, *New Mexico Statutes Annotated* (1915) § 5857; North Carolina, *Consolidated Statutes of N. Carolina* (1920), § 4128; Ohio, *Throckmorton's Annotated Code of Ohio* (1929), § 10503; Pennsylvania, *Digest of Pennsylvania Statute Law* (1920), § 8307; South Carolina, *Code of Laws of S. Carolina* (1922), (5335), § 1; Tennessee, *Shannon's Code* (1918), § 3895; Texas, *Complete Texas Statutes* (1928) § 8281; Vermont, *General Laws,* (1917), § 3200; Wyoming, *Wyoming Compiled Statutes* (1920), § 6667.

187. California, *The Codes of California,* The Civil Code (1919),

years of age suffices.[188] And in Louisiana sixteen years of age is required.[189] Males of twenty-one and females of eighteen years are capable of making a will in other places in the United States.[190] Some states admit testamentary capacity of a part of the property owned, when the person is not yet twenty-one years old.[191] Eighteen years complete is required in Italy,[192] Nicaragua,[193] Argentina, Peru, Brazil, and Venezuela.[194] In France and Belgium a person must be twenty-one years of age complete before he can dispose of all his property; but at the age of sixteen years complete, a person can dispose of one-half his property:[195] at eighteen years complete, a person can validly make a will.

---

§ 1270; Connecticut, *The General Statutes of Connecticut* (1918),§ 4941; Hawaiian Islands, *Revised Laws of Hawaii* (1925), § 3317; Idaho, *The Compiled Statutes of Idaho* (1919), § 7808; Montana, *The Revised Codes of Montana,* The Civil Code (1921), § 6974; Nevada, *Revised Laws of Nevada* 1912), § 6202; North Dakota, *The Compiled Laws of the State of North Dakota* (1913), § 5640; Oklahoma, *Compiled Statutes of Oklahoma* (1921), § 11221; South Dakota, *The South Dakota Revised Code* (1919), § 604; Utah, *The Compiled Laws of the State of Utah* (1917, § 6311;

188. *Code* (1926). § § 3838-3839.

189. *Revised Code* (1870) art. 1477.

190. District of Columbia, *District of Columbia Code* (1924), Sect. 1625; Illinois, *Revised Statutes of the State of Illinois* (1927), Chap. 148, p. 2503, § 1; Maryland, *The Annotated Code of the Public General Laws of Maryland* (1924), art. 93, p. 2986, § 331; Missouri, *The Revised Statutes of the State of Missouri* (1919), Sec. 505 [males of 18 years can devise only realty]. In Wisconsin only a married woman of 18 years can make a will. *Wisconsin Statutes* (1927), § 233.01 and § 233.05.

191. Persons of 18 years may dispose of personal property by will, though they cannot dispose of real property by will until they are twenty-one years of age. Alabama, *Alabama Code of* 1928 § 10577, 10582; Arkansas, *A Digest of the Statutes of Arkansas,* (1919), § § 10492, 10493; Missouri, *Revised Statutes* (1919), Sect, 505; New York, *Cahill's Consolidated Laws of New York* (1923), Chap. 13, § 16; Oregon, *Oregon Laws* (1920), § § 10092-10093; Rhode Island, *General Laws of Rhode Island* (1923), § 4992 and § 4995; Virginia, *The Code of Virginia* (1924), § 5228; West Virginia, *West Virginia Code* (1916) pp. 968, 973; Persons of 17 years can dispose of personality by will in Colorado, *Compiled Laws* (1921), § 5184.

192. *Codice Civile,* art. 763, 1°.

193. *Codigo Civil de la Republica de Nicaragua* (1904), § 1029; Eighteen years is required for the solemn testament in Equador, *Codigo Civil de la Republica de Ecuador* (1889), art. 1002.

794. Goyeneche, CpR, V (1924) 441.

195. *Code Civil,* (ed. 1921) art. 904 and art. 488; *Les Codes Belges* ed. (1925) Code Civil, art. 904 and art. 488.

In Austria, minors (not "impuberes" who are incapable of making a testament), before they become of age can make a testament nuncupatively before a judge, who must ascertain that the person is not acting under duress.[196] Sixteen years suffices if the testament is made before a judge in Germany.[197] Fourteen years suffices in Spain,[198] Portugal,[199] Panama,[200] Porto Rico,[201] Columbia, Mexico,[202] San Salvador.[203] Males of fourteen and females of twelve may make a testament in Bolivia.[204]

Then, too, the testament only canonically valid could prove useful. Should a Religious die, having made a testament that was not valid civilly but only canonically, his wishes relative to the disposal of his property after death, are more likely to be fulfilled than if he died intestate. In the supposition, that the heirs appointed in the canonical will are exactly those who would have succeeded to the property in virtue of intestacy, then such a will, from the standpoint of transference of property serves no purpose. But, if the Novice has stipulated in the canonical will, that Masses should be offered for the repose of his soul, or that his property should be devoted to a pious or charitable cause, then such a will would be of service. Such a will would have to be executed according to its specifications. If the heirs who were entitled by civil law to succeed to the property, under the title of the civil intestacy of the diseased, respected the intention of the diseased and complied with his last wishes as expressed in the canonical will, the practicality of a merely canonical will is demonstrated.[205]

---

196. *Grotze Aüsgabe* (1922), § 569, Cf. 573 for other legislation relative to the wills of Religious.

197. *Bürgerliches Gesetzbuch nebst Genführungsgesetz* (1927), § 2228.

198. Goyeneche, CpR, V (1924) 441;

199. *Code Civil Portugaise* (1868) § 1764.

200. *Codigo Civil Republica de Panama* (1917), art. 695.

201. *Compilation of the Revised Statutes and Codes of Porto Rico* (1913) (3749), Sec. 671;

202. Goyeneche, CpR, V (1924), 441.

203. *Codigo Civil de la Republica de el Salvador,* art. 1002. Age of Puberty suffices in Chili, *Codigo Civil de la Republica de Chili* (1912), art. 1005; Columbia, *Codigo Civil Colombiano* (1923), art. 1061.

204. *Codigo Civil* (1910), § 459. In Uraguay, 12 years suffices, Goyeneche, CpR, V (1924), 441.

Although there is a dispute about *the time* when a will must be made, the authors are agreed that a civilly valid will should be draughted whenever this is possible. Hence it will not be out of place to make a few suggestions concerning the drafting of wills in the United States.

"An unobjectionable will is extremely difficult to draw. It is the work of a skilled legal draughtsman, and unless an emergency is prohibitive none but such should be called upon to act."[206] Knowledge of a few general principles may be found helpful in case of emergency.

Any person of sound mind, if he has attained full age may devise his property.[207] If not of full age, personality may be disposed of by will but not realty. The instrument should state that it is the last will of the testator. However, it is not necessary, in every state, for the witnesses to learn from the testator that the will he is making is the last.[208] A mark may be made in the place of the signature, if from any cause a testator is incapable of writing his name. A codicil will not invalidate a last testament but will simply modify it and it is worthy of note, that while there can be but one last testament, there can be many codicils.[209]

---

205. If the heirs according to the civil law refused to fulfill the last wishes of the Religious, when the canonical testator left his property to a *moral person* of canon law (Cf. Noldin, II, n. 555; Vromant, p. 168;) they should be admonished of their obligation. (canon 1513 § 2); if they still refuse, the Church, while recognizing the validity of the canonical will of the Religious (cf. c. 11, *de testam.* X, III, 26; S. C. EE et RR, 16 martii 1900; S. Poenit. 10, ian, 1902 in *Collectanea S. C. de Prop. Fide,* n. 2099) is not averse to a compromise with the heirs rather than have disedifying litigation. Cf. D'Annibale, II, 3ed. n. 339; Retzbach, p. 13; Doheny, p. 90. The Sacred Poenitentiary will grant a compromise for the internal forum. Cf. Cocchi, VI, p. 372; Nor is such a compromise difficult to obtain. Cf. Genicot-Salsmans, I, n. 675; Cocchi, VI, p. 372; Doheny, p. 90. The Sacred Congregation of the Council grants compositions for the external forum. canon 250 § 2.

206. Hall, p. 222. "It is a common saying amongst lawyers that the man who makes his own will is the special benefactor of the legal profession." Dillon, *Bequests for Masses,* p. 5.

207. Swinburn, *Wills,* Book, I, Part II.

208. In the following states it is necessary that the witnesses be told by the testator that the will is the last one: Arkansas, California, Idaho, Louisiana, Montana, New Jersey, New York, North Dakota, Oklahoma, South Dakota, and Utah.

209. Cf. Hall, p. 222.

All states require that there be at least two witnesses. In Connecticut, Georgia, Maine, Massachusetts, New Hampshire, South Carolina and Vermont, three witnesses are required.[210] In most states the witnesses are expressly required to sign the will, although it is not necessary that they do so in joint presence, except in Louisiana, South Carolina, New Mexico, Utah, Vermont and Wisconsin.[211] "The date is likewise essential, but it is not necessary that the date given shall be that upon which the paper was in fact written."[212]

Because of the complexities and difficulties of American Laws on the question of charities, great care should be taken in formulating divises to the Church and especially in establishing bequests for Masses. Such gifts are recognized as valid charities but can easily be contested if not made in the proper legal form.[213] The beneficiary of a devise or bequest must not be left uncertain. Not a few bequests for Masses have been held void because of the uncertainty of the object and the lack of a definite person entitled to the benefit of the trust to appeal to the services of the court.[214] For the sake of ready reference two forms of bequests for Masses are quoted from Dillon who made a study of this subject. The first example is that which could be used if it is desired "to create a perpetual annuity (whether consisting of rents or profits of real estate or of interest on money invested)":

"I bequeath the sum of $...... to A. B. upon trust to invest the same in etc. (give directions, if any, as to mode of investment) and to pay the interest, dividends or income thereof to the Rev. C. D., the pastor of the Catholic Church of ...., on ...... street, in the city of ...., and to his successors in the office of pastor, of said ...... church, and in case the Rev. C. D. shall pre-

210. Hall, pp. 223-225.

211. Doheny, p. 92.

212. Doheny, p. 92. *In re Vance,* 174, Cal. 122, 162, Pac. 103, L. R. A. 1917 C. 479.

213. Zollman, *American Law of Charities,* p. 180; Doheny, p. 94.

214. Fetorazzi v St. Joseph's Catholic Church of Mobile (1894), 104 Ala. 327, 18, So. 394, L. R. A. 360; Shanahan v Kelly (1903), 88, Minn. 92 N. W. 948; McHugh v McCole (1897), 97, Wis. 166, 72 N. W. 631, 65 Am. St. Rep. 106, 40 L. R. A. 274; Cf. Doheny, p. 93; Dillon, p. 33; Keller, *Mass Stipends,* p. 123.

decease me, then upon trust to pay said interest, dividends or income to the pastor at the time of my death of said Church of ......, and his successors in said Pastorate, and I make this bequest upon the condition that the said Rev. C. D., or other, the Pastor to whom said interest, dividends or income may be payable under the trust hereinbefore expressed, will say or cause to be said in each year as many Masses for the repose of my soul and for the repose of the souls of ...... as would, according to the rules and usages of such Church, for the time being, be said in return for a donation of the amount which may be paid to such pastor during such year under the trust aforesaid, such Masses to be said in public in said Church of ......, being a place of public worship, and said church to be open to the public during the celebration of said Masses, and all persons who desire to worship during said Masses to be admitted for that purpose."[215]

The second example can be used when it is not desired to create a trust:

"I hereby bequeath to the Rev. A. B. pastor of ...... Catholic Church, on ...... street, in the city of ......, the sum of $......, and in case the said Rev. A. B. shall predecease me, then I bequeath said sum of $...... to the pastor of said ...... Church at the time of my death. I request that the said Rev. A. B., or other such Pastor at the time of my death as aforesaid, will of his charity say or cause to be said as many Masses for the repose of my soul and the souls of ...... as, according to the rules and usages of said ...... Church would be said in return for a donation of the amount of the legacy hereby given to said A. B., or other, the Pastor of said church as aforesaid, but I do not desire by this request to create any trust or legally enforceable obligation for the saying of said Masses, as this bequest is intended to be absolute in law and equity to the individual use and benefit of the legatee."[216]

It cannot be too strongly urged that a man well versed in the technicalities of will drafting be employed in formulating testaments.[217]

215. Dillon, pp. 55-56; Concerning the acceptance of such a foundation of Masses, vide Miller, *Founded Masses*, pp. 24 ff.

216. Dillon, p. 58.

217. Cf. Tanquery, *Synopsis Theologiae Moralis*, Vol. III, p. *24. for many helpful suggestions concerning wills.

(b) *Alteration of the Will—canon 583, 2°*

"Professis a votis simplicibus in Congregationibus religiosis non licet:

2° Testamentum conditum ad normam canon 569 § 3 mutare sine licentia Sanctae Sedis, vel, si res urgeat nec tempus suppetat ad eam recurrendi, sine licentia Superioris maioris aut, si nec ille adiri possit, localis."[218]

Those who have made Profession of simple vows in any Religious Congregation: may not alter the will made according to the terms of canon 569 §3. The ambitus of this legislation is the same as that of canon 569 § 3. In virtue of this legislation a Religious professed in a Congregation would act illicitly although not invalidly,[219] if he altered his testament without having first obtained permission of the Holy See to do it.[220] The same is true also concerning a Religious of an Order, in those places, where due to an Apostolic indult, the members of the Institute make only simple vows.[221] If a member of an Order, forseeing the possibility of his death, before he could be solemnly professed, had made a testament immediately before he made temporary simple profession, does he need permission from the Holy See, in order to change that testament? Larraona is of the opinion that should such a question arise, in practice, the norm stated in can 583, 2° would have to be applied. It certainly would be unlawful for a Religious to make an entirely new will abrogating the

---

218. "Those who have made Profession of simple vows in any Religious Congregation:

219. Canon 579.

220. A petition for such permission should be addressed to the Congregatio Negotiis Religisorum Sodalium Praeposita. The address of this congregation is: "Palazzo della Cancellaria Apostolica" (Cf. *Official Catholic Directory* (1928), p. [4]. A formula that could be used is the following:
Beatissime Pater:

N. N. sacerdos (clericus, frater, laicus, soror,) professus (professa) . . . in Congregatione . . (in Provincia . . . in domo . . .) ad pedes S. V. provolutus (humiliter veniam petit, secundum can. 583, 2°, mutandi suum testamentum, quod propter . . . etc.

221. Cf. Goyeneche, CpR, II (1921), 47.

2° May not alter the will made according to the terms of canon 569 § 3, without the permission of the Holy See, or, if the case be urgent and time does not admit of recourse to the Holy See, without the permission of the higher Superior, or, if recourse cannot be had to him either, without the permission of the Local Superior."

previous one, unless the permission of the Holy See was first obtained.[222] Moreover, since the testament was made concerning all the property then possessed or thereafter acquired, the addition of a codicil after profession or the bestowal of a donation "mortis causa" after profession is to be regarded as a direct alteration of the testament in the sense of this canon. However, if a Religious, on account of serious reason desires to dispose of the capital he owns, he needs only permission to dispose of the capital: for although the testament is *indirectly* altered by the disposal of the property he has already willed, this change does not require a special permission of the Holy See.[223]

A mere declaration, by a more complete statement of what was already contained in either the canonical or the civil testament is not to be considered a change in the sense of this canon. By way of example: a Religious would not need permission (a) to clarify the meaning of certain dispositions made in the will, or (b) to facilitate the transfer of the property, or (c) to secure its validity of the document by supplying a civil law requirement which had been overlooked when the will had been drafted.[224] And, of course, the civil ratification of a canonical will is not to be understood as a change necessitating permission of the Holy See. But, if in the civil ratification *important* changes relative to the disposition of the property are made, the permission of the Holy See is required. However, since the law requires permission from the highest authority to make changes in the testament the Holy See is to be petitioned only for important changes, for *"de minimis non curat praetor."*[224] Yet, if many small changes were made at different times to avoid the trouble of writing to Rome, this would amount to "fraus legis" and would be illegitimate. Permission from a Superior of the Institute would be required, to make even the small changes of which we have just made mention.

Should the beneficiary of the testament die before the Religious testator, must permission be sought from the Holy See before a new testament can be licitly drafted?

---

222. Cf. Larraona, CpR, II (1921, 105 *Normæ of* 1901, art. 122, *"Sorores professae tum ad faciendum, tum ad mutandum testamentum indigent venia Apostolicae Sedis."*

223. Cf. Larraona, CpR, II (1921), 105, (5).

224. Cf. Schäfer, p. 346.

Assuming that in the testament there was no provision for such an occurrence, there is no necessity of recourse to the Holy See for the drafting a second testament.[224] It is certainly the mind of the Holy See that the simple vow Religious should not die intestate, otherwise canon 569 § 3 and canon 583, 2° would not be in existence. Who will say that the Religious whose sole beneficiary has died before him is free to omit the drafting another testament? Whence the obligation to make a new will except from the law? If the legislator obliges a Religious to make another will, why should the Religious seek permission from him to do what he is already obliged to do?[227] If the lawgiver himself obliges a Religious to make a will, certainly no permission of a Superior of the Institute is required.

It is the mind of the legislator that whenever there arises a matter which ordinarily requires the permission of the Holy See but which *on account of the urgency* of the particular case and the fact that *time does not admit of recourse to* the Sacred Congregation of Religious, permission should be sought from the higher Superior; if this latter is also impossible the permission of the local Superior should be obtained. By the higher Superior is to be understood the Moderator General of the Institute; and in his absence, his vicar, whether " a iure," i.e., the person whom the constitutions of the Institute designate, or the individual who has received special delegation "ad tempus."[228] The Provincial too is a higher Superior. If the Provincial is absent from the province, e.g., at the time of a General Chapter, etc., the permission of his substitute should be obtained if possible. If, the case is so urgent that there is no time to have recourse to either the General or Provincial or their delegates when they are absent, the permission of the local Superior must be sought. If the local Superior is absent, then the permission of his delegate should be obtained. In the extreme case of a Religious dying outside the monastery, e.g., at a sanitorium or hospital for incurables or for contagious diseases, the permis-

225. Cf. David, p. 132.

226. This is an exception to the general statement made concerning the drafting a new will and finds it justification in the reasons attending such a case.

227. Cf. David, p. 132.

228. Cf. canon 488, 8°.

sion of the proper Superior could be presumed, when none of those Superiors could be approached and time does not admit of a delay.

Although this canon was not directly formulated for Orders, if members (under the circumstances mentioned previously in the treatment of this canon) of such Institutes having made a testament desire to alter it, they must seek permission for such an act according to the norm of canon 583, 2°.[229] In the case of Monks and Monastic Congregations, it is the Abbot of the monastery whose permission is first to be sought, when the Holy See can not be approached. As Schafer well observes[230] the power of the local Abbot in a Monastic Congregation frequently exceeds the amount of power possessed by a Provincial and is equal in many things to that of a Moderator General in other kinds of Institutes. Although canon 488, 8° mentions the Abbot Primate and the Superior of a Monastic Congregation before the Abbot of an independent monastery, yet canon 501 § 3 declares: "Abbas Primas et Superior Congregationis monasticae non habent omnem potestatem et iurisdictionem quam ius commune tribuit Superioribus maioribus, sed eorum potestas et iurisdictio desumenda est ex propriis constitutionibus et ex peculiaribus Sanctae Sedis decretis firmo praescripto canon 655, 1594, § 4." Relative to the Abbot Primate of the "black" Benedictines, it is to be noted that he has no jurisdiction over the Monks, outside of that which he enjoys in St. Anselm's College in Rome.[231]

229. Cf. canon 20.

230. Cf. p. 38, e).

231. Certainly the Apostolic letter *"Summum semper"* of July 12, 1893 (Cf. *Fontes*, n. 619 or *Acta Leo XIII*, Vol. XIII, pp. 207-212) did not give him jurisdiction except as abbot of S. Anselm's in Rome. Cf. also S. C. EE et RR, 16 sept. 1893 (AkkR, LXX [1893] 204 sq. And Augustine who has read the rescripts given in this matter since then, viz. S. C. EE et RR. 31, ian. 1902; 2 dec. 1906; 21 dec. 1907; Pius X, 30 maii, 1908 declares: "he has no jurisdiction over the single congregations or abbeys or over the various abbots or members." Cf. Augustine, III, pp. 112-113.

CHAPTER VI.

THE SOLEMN VOW OF POVERTY

ARTICLE I. THE RENUNCIATION OF PROPERTY BEFORE SOLEMN PROFESSION—CANON 581

THE Religious Life had been practiced for over a thousand years in the Western Church when the Council of Trent convened. The history of these centuries was full of practical lessons which served good purpose when the prelates of the Council formulated the new legislation for Religious. How often had it happened at the completion of the term of the novitiate, a youth, who had divested himself of his property, when faced with the dilemma of becoming a Religious against his will and judgment or returning to the world in straightened circumstances, had chosen the former to the detriment of his own soul and the harm of the community arising from the fervorless life of a discontented member?

In order to protect inexperienced youth from an imprudent disposal of his property and thereby safeguard the liberty of the Novice[1] a wise and beneficent decree was formulated by the Council. Treating of the property of the Novice, the Council of Trent decreed: "No renunciation made or obligation assumed, even though under oath or in favor of any pious object whatsoever, shall be valid, unless it is made with the permission of the bishop or his vicar, within the two months nearest Profession, and it shall not be understood otherwise as having any effect unless the Profession followed thereupon: but if done in any other manner, even with the express renunciation of

1. Cf. Pellizarius, *Manuale Regularium,* Tract, II, c. 9, n. 7; Miranda, *Manuale Praelatorum Regularium,* Tomus I, quaes. 23, art. 1; Passerinus, *De Hominum Statibus et Officiis,* Quaes. 189, art. x, *Novit* n. 130; Rotarius, *Theologia Moralis Regularium* Tomus, I, lib. 2, c. 3, p. 1, n. 2, p. 94; Donatus,*Rerum Regularium Praxis Resolutoria,* Tomus, II, p. 2, tract. 7, quaes. 5, n. 1; Molina, *De Justitia et Jure,* Tract. II, disp. 139, n. 13; apud Piat, *Praelectiones Juris Regularis,* Vol. I. p. 122, n. 2; De Brabandere, *Compendium Juris Canonici et Canonico-Civilis,* Vol. I, p. 418; Wernz,*Jus Decretalium,* III, p. 312.

this privilege, even if under oath, it shall be invalid and of no effect. . . . Before the Profession of the Novice, whether male or female, nothing shall be given to the monastery out of the property of the Novice, either by the parents relatives or guardians, under any pretext whatever, except for food and clothing, during the time they are under probation, lest (the said Novice), be unable to leave on this account, that the monastery is in possession of the whole or the greater part of his substance and he is not able to recover it easily if he should leave. The Holy Synod commands under pain of anathema on the givers and the receivers lest in any way this be done and that everything that was theirs be restored to those who leave before profession. In order that this may be properly observed, the bishop shall use if necessary ecclesiastical censures."[2]

A change, as regards the time, when the renunciation of property was to be made in Orders of men was effected towards the latter part of the past century. In an encyclical letter of March 19, 1857, the Holy See enacted that the Novices in Orders of men must profess simple vows at the termination of their Novitiate. After three years from the date of simple Profession, solemn vows could be made.[3] Doubts having arisen as to when the renunciation of property was to be made, the Sacred Congregation of Bishops and Regulars declared: "Sanctitas Sua Apostolica auctoritate statuit renunciationem, quam in citato capite 16 Sess. XXV, *De Regularibus,* Concilium Tridentinum respicit, pro professis votorum simplicium locum habere infra duos menses proximos ante professionem votorum solemnium.

2. Sess. 25, *De Regularibus,* c. 16. The Jesuits were expressly exempted from this legislation.

3. S. C. EE et RR, litt. ency. *"Neminem latet,"* 19 martii 1857, *Fontes,* n. 1976; Bizzarri, pp. 853 sq. Cf. Pius IX, const. *"Ad universalis"*, 7 feb. 1862, *Fontes,* n. 532; Acta Pii IX, vol. III, pp. 417-420; Bizzarri, pp. 862 sq.; Pii IX, decr. *"Sanctissimus,"* 12 iunii, 1858, n. 1, Bizzarri, p. 856, Vermeersch,*De Religiosis,* Vol. II, p. 354; S. C. EE et RR, declaratio, 20 ian, 1860, n. 3, Bizzarri, p. 860; Vermeersch, *De Religiosis,* Vol. II, p. 356; S. C. EE et RR, responsio 20 iulii, 1860, Bizzarri, pp. 858-859; Bizzarri, p. 859; Vermeersch, *De Religiosis,* Vol. II, pp. 356-357; Pii IX, declaratio, 7 feb, 1862, n. 4, Bizzarri, pp. 861-862; Vermeersch, *De Religiosis,* Vol. II, pp. 357-358; S. C. EE et RR, declaratio 16 aug. 1866, Bizzarri, p. 866 S. C. Rel, decr. 1 ian. 1911, n. 4, AAS, III (1911) 30-31; S. C. Rel. decr. 3 maii 1914, n. 1, ASS, VI (1914) p. 229.

Contrariis quibuscumque non obstantibus."[4] The decree "Perpensis" of May 31, 1902,[5] extended to Orders of women, "iuxta congruum modum" the legislation which had been given to Orders of men.[6] The ecclesiastical law which now regulates the renunciation of property before solemn Profession is contained in canon 581.

"Professus a votis simplicibus antea nequit valide, sed intra sexaginta dies ante professionem solemnem, salvis peculiaribus indultis a Sancta Sede concessis, debet omnibus bonis quae actu habet, sui maluerit, sub conditione secuturae professionis, renunciare.

§ 2. Secuta professione, ea omnia statim fiant quae necessaria sunt ut renuntiatio etiam iure civili effectum sonsequatur."[7]

According to the present discipline of the Church, "In every Order both of men and of women," the solemn Profession, "must be preceded, saving the exception provided for in canon 634,[8] by the Profession of simple vows which the Novice, on the completion of his Novitiate, shall make in the Novitiate house itself; this Profession is valid for three years, or for a longer period if the subject requires more than three years to attain the age prescribed for perpetual Profession, unless the Constitutions require annual

---

4. Bizzarri, p. 865; Piat, I, pp. 128-129; *Analecta Juris Pontificii,* Series VII, col. 1990.

5. S. C. EE et RR, decr. *Perpensis* 31 maii 1902, nn. 1, 2, 11,*Fontes,* n. 2039; S. C. EE et RR, responsio, 30 iulii 1909, AAS, I, (1909) 699-700.

6. Since September 30, 1864, the Visitandine nuns of Georgetown Baltimore, St. Louis, Mobile and Elfin Dale, Missouri in the United States of America had been required to profess simple vows for five years, at the completion of their Novitiate. At the end of that time they could profess solemn vows. cf. S. C. EE et RR, litt. 30 sept. 1864, n. 3, *Fontes,* n. 1995.

7. Canon 581, § 1. "Not, except within sixty days preceding the solemn Profession, can the professed of simple vows validly renounce his property, but within this time he must ,saving indults from the Holy See, renounce in favor of whomsoever he wishes all the property which he actually possesses, on condition of his Profession subsequently taking place.

§ 2. The Profession having been made, the necessary measures must be immediately taken to ensure that the renunciation be effective according to the civil law."

8. "If a person who has made profession of solemn vows or of simple perpetual vows joins another Institute with solemn vows or with simple perpetual vows, he must, after the Novitiate, omit the

Professions. The legitimate Superior can prolong this period but not beyond a second term of three years, the Religious meanwhile renewing the temporary Profession."[9]

Except within sixty days preceding the solemn Profession the professed of simple vows cannot validly renounce his property. How is this time to be computed? According to the pre-Code canonists the time was to be computed from moment to moment.[10] There was no dispute about this among the authors.[11] Some even declared that the Sacred Congregation of the Council had thus declared upon this mode of computation.[12] However, canon 31 declares clearly that time in the Code must be reckoned according to the norm specified in canons 32-36, inclusive, unless a different method of computing time is expressly provided.[13] In canon 581 there is no express provision as to how the time is to be reckoned. But canon 34 § 3, 3° prescribes that when the "terminus a quo" is expressly or implicitly determined and that point does not coincide with the beginning of the day, the first day is not counted. This enactment covers the matter contained in canon 581. Hence it is the norm to be used. Thus if the solemn Profession is due on the afternoon of a May 31st, the act of renunciation should be made between the midnight beginning April 1st and the moment of Profession.

If the solemn Profession happens to be deferred, the renunciation made within the sixty days immediately preceding the time when the solemn Profession should have occurred, remains valid. Thus was the old law commonly interpreted.[14] Moreover, if the renunciation is not made

---

temporary Profession spoken of in canon 574, and make Profession of solemn vows according to the Institute, or he must return to the former Institute; the Superior, however, has the right to prolong the period of probation, but not beyond one year after the completion of the Novitiate." canon 634.

9. Canon 574 § § 1, 2.

10. Wernz, III, p. 313, n. (282); Piat, I, p. 585; Ferraris, *Novitiatus*, n. 81; cf. etiam, Lopez, p. 44.

11. cf. Bouix, I, p. 585.

12. Cf. Barbossa, *Collectanea Doctorum in Concilium Tridentinum,* Sess. XXV, c. 16, n. 36; Donatus,*Rerum Regularium Praxis Resolutoria,* Tomus, II, pars, 2, tract. 7, quaes. 9, n. 3; Wernz, *Ius Decretalium,* Vol. III, p. 313, (282), Pallottini refers to many more ancient decisions, cf. *Regulares,* VII, nn. 5-6.

13. Cf. Toso, *Commentarium Minora ad Codicem Juris Canonici,* p. 100.

within the sixty days immediately preceding the time when the solemn Profession should have occurred and the Profession is deferred, the renunciation may be validly made within the sixty days immediately preceding the time when the Profession actually occurs.[15] It is scarcely necessary to observe that the time mentioned in this canon is "tempus continuum"[16] and not "tempus utile," since the latter is not to be presumed,[17] especially when there is an antecedent practice to the contrary.

The subjects of this canon *must* renounce all his property before solemn Profession. The legislator obliges the Religious to perform the act prescribed and hence he is not free to omit it.[18] Nor is permission required from anyone in order to licitly perform the renunciation. Formerly the law required the obtainment of permission from the Ordinary of the place or his Vicar[19] under penalty of invalidity.[20] The silence of the Code is here a positive

---

14. "The Sacred Congregation of the Council thus declared; cf. Pallottini, *Regulares,* VII. 33 sq.; Schmalzgrueber, lib. III, tit. 31; nn. 106 sq.; Donatus, Tomus, II, pars. 2, tract. 7, quaes. 10, n. 1 sq.; Pellizarius, tract. II, c. 9, n. 42; Passerinus, Quaes. 189, art. x, *Novit,* n. 166; Sanchez, *In Praecepta Decalogi,* lib. VII, c. 5, n. 82; Barbossa, *Collectanea Doctorum in Concilium Tridentinum,* Sess. XXV, *De Regular.* c. 16, n. 37; Petra, *Const. I Clem. IV,* sect. II, n. 11; Antonius a Spiritu Sancto, tract. III, disp. 2, n. 162; Rotarius, Tomus, I, lib. 2, c. 3, punct. 2, n. 5; Bouix, I. pp. 585-586; Ferraris, *Novitiatus,* n. 83; vide Piat. I, p. 129 for other authors. cf. canon 6, 2°, 3°; Augustine, III, p. 282.

15. Cf. S. C. Concillii, 21 aug. 1627; 10 et 24 ian. 1660 apud Pallottini, *Regulares,* VII, nn. 8, 33; De Franchis-Pasqualigi, p. 497; Rotarius, Tomus, I, lib. 2, c. 3, punct, 2, n. 5; Tamburinius, *De Jure Abbatum,* Tomus, IV, disp. 4, quaes. 10, n. 6; Bordonus, *Variae Resolutiones,* resol. LX, n. 12; Piat, I, p. 129, Appeltern, quaes. 82; canon 6, 3°; Nueberger, 79; Ferreres, *Las Religiosas,* n. 468; Ferreres, *Institutiones Canonicae,* I, p. 404.

16. Cf. canon 35.

17. Antonelli, lib. I, c. 2; Maroto, *Institutiones Iuris Canonici,* pp. 284-285; Cicognani, *Commentarium in Primum Librum Codicis,* p. 200.

18. Cf. Kinane, *Irish Ecclesiastical Record,* Vol. XII (1918), 476.

19. Concilium Tridentinum, Sess. 25, *de regularibus* c. 16.

20. Cf. Schmalzgrueber, lib. III, tit. 104, n. 3; Tamburinius, tom. III, disp. 6, quaes. 10, n. 1; Sanchez, *In Praecepta Decalogi,* lib. VII, c. 5. n. 77; Barbossa, *De Officio et Potestate Episcopi,* Pars, III, alleg. 90, n. 10; Bordonus, *De Professione Regulari,* Cap. XII, n. 23, 1 (a); Passerinus, Quaes. 189, art x *Novit.* n. 163; Piat, I, p. 128.

silence.[21] *"Legislator quod voluit expressit, quod noluit tacuit."*

The canon enacts that the Religious must *renounce* all his property in favor of whomsoever he wishes. This renunciation means the abdication of the dominion of the property he owns.[22] This should be done by an outright donation[23] and not by a donation "mortis causa" or a testament as these latter would not fulfill the precept of the canon.[24] Although the property must be renounced the Religious is at liberty to favor any one he pleases with it.

Once the renunciation has been made, it can not be revoked arbitrarily by the Religious before profession. The canon does not declare this, it is true. But certainly such an act would be an exercise of proprietorship necessitating a permission of some kind. The older canonists taught that the renunciation could not be revoked by a subject intending to remain in Religion.[25] Some authors assert that the Sacred Congregation of the Council so decided.[26] However, if the renunciation had been made with a condition that it could be revoked before Profession, even though the person renouncing the property intended to remain in Religion, a revocation could be made.[27]

---

21. Cf. Blat, II, n. 652. Moreover canon II states "Irritantes aut inhabilitantes eae tantum leges habendae sunt, quibus aut actum esse nullum aut inhabilem esse personam expresse vel equivalenter statuitur."

22. Cf. Augustine, III, p. 282.

23. Cf. Gearin, *American Ecclesiastical Review,* LXI (1919), 149.

24. Cf. Larraona, CpR, II (1921) 9, n. (1) who speaks there only of a testament but the same principle holds for a donation "mortis causa"; Papi *Religious Profession,* p. 67.

25. Cf. Rotarius, Tomus, I, lib. 2, c. 3, punct. 2, n. 2; Sanchez, *In Praecepta Decalogi,* lib. VII, c. 5. n. 58; Molina, *De Iustitia et Iure,* Tomus, II, disp. 2, con. 7; Schmalzgrueber, lib. III, tit. 31, n. 120; Passerinus, Quaes. 189, art. x,*Novit.* n. 175; Pellizarius, tract. II, c. 9, n. 52; Tamburinius, Tomus III, disp. 6, quaes. 10, n. 4; Petra, *Const. I, Clem. IV,* sect. II, n. 93; Pirhing, lib. III, tit. 31, n. 92; Donatus, Tomus, II, pars 2, tract. 7, quaes. 34, n. 1; Bouix, I, p. 587; Piat. I, p. 130; Vermeersch, *De Religiosis,* I, p. 131, n. 202; Ballerini-Palmieri, t. 3, tract. 8, p. 3, c. 3, n. 738.

26. Cf. Diana, *Resolutiones Morales,* Pars V, resol. 55, tract. 2; Rotarius Tomus, I, lib. 2, c. 3, punct. 2, n. 2; Donatus, Tomus, II, pars 2, tract. 7, quaes. 34, n. 1; Piat. I, p. 130.

27. Cf. Rotarius, ut supra.

The text makes an exception for Religious having *an indult from the Holy See.* Such an indult obtains for some Religious in Belgium and Holland.[28] By virtue of this indult, the Religious, although solemnly professed, are able to retain the property they owned before profession and to acquire other property after profession; they can administrate their property and even dispose of the dominion of it. However, these proprietary acts may be performed licitly only when permission is obtained from the Religious Superior.[29] Vermeersch affirms that the mind of the Holy See as regards the indult is that it be used only for extraordinary cases, especially for the avoidance of civil difficulties.[30]

All property that constitutes the remote matter of the vow of poverty and which the Religious *actually owns* before solemn profession must be renounced. Can a Religious also renounce in favor of whomsoever he pleases the property that will come to him after profession? Property that may come to the Religious after profession may be classed as: (a) that to which he now has a *certain right,* especially parental inheritances in those places where children are necessary heirs;[31] (b) that to which he has *no right* but only a more or less founded *hope.* Concerning the former class of property, it was commonly held before the Code that this property could be renounced.[32] In fact it was practiced in at least some Institutes.[33] From general

28. Vermeersch, *Epitome,* I, p. 436; Cocchi, lib. II, pars 2, pp. 167-168; Goyeneche, CpR, II (1921), 46-47; Aertnys-Damien, I, n. 1190, p. 713.

29. Vermeersch, *Epitome,* I. p. 436; De Meester, Vol. II, p. 370; Maroto, CpR, V (1924) 388; Creusen, *Religieux et Religieuses,* p. 198; Chelodi, *Ius de Personis,* p. 457; Bouuaert-Simenon, *Manuale Iuris Canonici,* n. 657, nota 2; Goyeneche, CpR, VIII (1927), 121.

30. *Epitome,* I, p. 436.

31. "Under the laws that are fairly generally followed in the States of the American Union, children have no vested right in the goods and property of the parents, but at most a hope that the parents will give them a share in their goods by last will. There is a right of inheritance of the children in case of intestacy of the father, but whether that right will ever give them anything depends on a contingency which may never happen—that is, the death of their father without a will." (Woywod, I, p. 241.)

32. Rotarius, Tomus, I, lib. 2, c. 3, punct. 3, n. 10; Antonius a Spiritu Sancto, tract. 3, disp. 3, n. 170; Pellizarius, *Tractatus de Monialibus,* c. 2, n. 67; Vermeersch, *De Religiosis,* I, p. 130;

33. Cf. S. C. EE et RR, 16 sept. 1885, *Fontes,* n. 2011; *Nouv-*

canonical principles[34] it may be concluded that the former discipline may be still practiced.[35] But what about the second class of property, viz., that had only "in spe," e.g., inheritances or legacies which possibly may be willed to him? It seems that today there is a distinction to be made between inheritances and legacies which rest on a well founded hope and those which lack a solid foundation. An example of a well founded hope would be that of a child who has always been a credit and a solace to his parents; according to the law of the land, the child is not a necessary heir; yet it is solidly probable the parents will leave at least something of the property owned by them in favor of the child; the possibility of that child, in relation to a parental inheritance or legacy is such that in America it would be estimable at a price; it is something which the child has and could dispose of without much difficulty for a monetary consideration; there are also other examples of well founded hopes estimable at a price: It would seem that the hope concerning this kind of legacy or inheritance, etc., could be considered among the property which the Religious actually has and hence could be renounced.[36] Inheritances and legacies which do not have a solid foundation in relation to the Religious at the time of his profession can not be renounced.[37]

It is to be noticed that the renunciation is *conditioned* by the canon, viz., *that the solemn profession actually occur.* Hence if a Religious should die before solemn pro-

---

elle Revue Theologique, XXII (1890), 28; *Analecta Iuris Pontificii,* IX (1867) col. 785; Vermeersch, *De Religiosis,* II, p. 326. nota 1; Sleutjes, I, p. 129; Trienekens, p. 27; *Acta Ordinis Minorum,* IV (1885) p. 146.

34. Cf. canon 6, 2°, 4°.

35. Vermeersch, *Epitome,* I, n. 685, p. 436; Larraona, CpR, I (1920) 79-80, 183; Chelodi, *Ius de Personis,* p. 457, nota 7; Fanfani, *De Iure Religiosorum,* p. 298; cf. "*Regula et Constitutiones Generales Fratrum Minorum*" (1922) n. 89; "*Constitutiones Fratrum Sacri Ordinis Praedicatorum* (1925) n. 115.

36. Cf. Fanfani, n. 261, pp. 297-298. Before the Code, De Lugo, *Responsa Moralia,* t. 8, lib. IV, disp. 5, n. 9, made no such distinction. After the Code. Larraona, CpR, I (1920) 79-80, 183; Blat, II, n. p. 644; Chelodi, *Ius de Personis,* p. 457, nota 7: Schäfer, p. 349 make no such distinction.

37. Vermeersch, *Epitome,* I, n. 685; Larraona, CpR, I (1920), 79-80, 182; Chelodi, *Ius de Personis,* p. 457, nota 7; Fanfani, pp. 297-298; Blat, II, n. 652, p. 644; Schäfer, p. 349,

fession, his property would go to the beneficiaries of his will or the heirs "ab intestato." If the Religious should abandon the Religious Life before profession according to the canon the renunciation would be invalid since the condition therein placed was not fulfilled. If the ceremony of solemn profession was performed but the profession happened to be invalid, the renunciation is also invalid.[38]

At the moment of solemn profession the renunciation immediately becomes operative in canon law and in conscience. Since difficulties could arise if the renunciation was not considered valid in civil law, the canon prescribes that after the profession has been made, "the necessary measures must be immediately taken to ensure that the renunciation be effective also according to the civil law." It may not be out of place to here observe that if the civil law will not recognize the validity of the renunciation made by the Religious, e.g., on account of minor age, etc., this does not militate against the obligation imposed by canon 581. An act binding in ecclesiastical law and in conscience must be placed. Nor will the Religious be able to modify the canonical disposition when he becomes able to perform a valid civil act.[39]

What becomes of the property of the Religious who failed to renounce his property? Provided he had not made, previous to his entrance into Religion, donations contingent on solemn Profession, whatever property he had owned is acquired by the Institute,[40] if it is capable of acquiring property,[41] or if the Institute has no contrary

---

38. Cf. S, C. Concilii, *Bononien,* 3 ian, 1733, *Thesaurus* Tomus VI (1733-1734) pp. 289-290; Schmalzgrueber, lib. III, tit. 31, n. 113; Sanchez, *In Praecepta Decalogi,* lib. VII, c. 5, n. 55; Barbossa, *Ius Ecclesiasticum Universum,* lib. I, c. 42, n. 238; S. C. Rel. 30 iulii 1909 (AAS, I [1909], 699-700); canon 6, 2°, 4°.

39. S. C. EE et RR, 16 sept. 1885, *Fontes,* n. 2011; Larraona, CpR, I (1920) 372, II (1921) 10.

40. Wernz, III, n. 650, (371); Pallottini, *Regulares,* VII. n. 34; Pirhing, lib. III. tit. 26, nn. 57 sq.; ibid. III, tit. 27, nn. 33 sq.; Schmalzgrueber, lib. III, tit. 35, n. 7; Suarez, Tomus XV, lib. 2, c. 12, nn. 9 sq.; lib. 6, c. 2, n. 8; lib. 8, c. 7, nn. 10, 16; Piat, I, p. 132; Appeltern, Q. 84 Vermeersch, *Epitome,* I, n. 685, p. 436; Biederlack-Führich, p. 179 (probably). Cf. *Constitutiones Fratrum Sacri Ordinis Praedicatorum* (1925) n. 131. Ferreres, *Compendium Theologiae Moralis.* II, p. 122.

41. E.g. the Friars Minor and the Capuchins ordinarily are

regulation in this regard.[42] If the act of renunciation has been omitted before solemn Profession and the solemnly professed Religious desires to perform an act of renunciation, he should obtain an indult from the Holy See.[43] Yet it is noteworthy that a number of the indults granted for such a purpose, required that the property be disposed of in the name of the convent,[44] or, if the Order was incapable of having property, in the name of the Holy See.[45]

ARTICLE II. ACQUISITION OF PROPERTY AFTER SOLEMN PROFESSION—CANON 582

"Post solemnem professionem, salvis pariter peculiaribus Apostolicae Sedis indultis, omnia bona quae quovis modo obveniunt regulari:

1° In Ordine capaci possidendi, cedunt Ordini vel provinciae vel domui secundum constitutiones;

2° In Ordine incapaci, acquiruntur Sanctae Sedi in proprietatem."[46]

The canon declares that whatever property a Regular may acquire in any way, after solemn profession, does not belong to him. Of course, this is to be understood only

---

incapable; but in some places there is an indult permitting them to acquire property.

42. Some Religious Orders, e. g. the Jesuits have special regulations to the effect that this property is to go to the heirs "ab intestato". Cf. Ferreres, *Compendium Theologiae Moralis,* II, p. 122; *Institutum Societatis Jesu,* Vol. II,*Examen et Constitutiones, Decreta Congregationum Generalium, Formulae Congregationum,* P. VI, C. 2, n. 12; Greg. XIII, const. *Ascendente Domino,* 25 maii 1584 § 11, *Fontes,* n. 153; Greg. XIII, const. *Quanto fructuosius,* 1 feb. 1583, § 3, *Fontes,* n. 150; Lessius, *De Iustitia et Iure,* lib. II, c. 41, d. 10, nn. 81, 86; Molina, *De Iustitia et Iure,* tract. II, disp. n. 5; De Lugo, *De Iustitia et Iure* disp. III, nn. 189, 212; Sanchez, *In Praecepta Decalogi,* lib. VII, c. 12, n. 1.

43. Cf. Pallottini, *Regulares,* VII, nn. 48 sq.; Piat, I, p. 132.

44. *Analecta Juris Pontificii,* IX (1867) col. 784, n. III; Piat, I, p. 132.

45. *Analecta Juris Pontificii,* IX (1867) col. 788, n. IV; Piat, I, p. 132.

46. "After solemn Profession, likewise without prejudice to special indults of the Apostolic See, all the property which comes in whatever manner to a Regular:

1°. In an Order capable of ownership, goes to the Order, to the province, or to the house, according to the Constitutions;

2°. In an Order incapable or ownership, it becomes the property of the Holy See." canon 583.

of things which constitute the matter of the vow of poverty. The principle stated in this canon has been acknowledged without dispute so long, and has been understood so well, that the annotators of the Code did not deem it worth while to indicate its sources.

At the moment the Religious becomes solemnly professed, he looses all capability to be and to act as owner of property,[47] in his own behalf and in his own name. Nor can a Religious Superior confer such power upon him.[48] However, it is within the competency of the Holy See to confer upon a solemnly professed Religious the power to exercise full dominion over property in his own name, with dependence upon a Religious Superior for only the liciety of his acts. In the past there are many examples of such action on the part of the Holy See.[49] A classic instance of such an indult obtained by an individual is that of St. Francis Borgia who did not abdicate the temporalities he had as Duke of Gandia until four years after his solemn Profession.[50] During the last century indults to own and acquire property in their own name and to administrate and dispose of the same, with due dependence on Superiors, were granted collectively to the Religious of Orders in parts of Europe.[51] Indults given by the

---

47. C. I, 3, 54 (56); N. V, 4-5; N. CXXIII, 38; cc. 7, 8, 9, C. XIX, q. 3; cc. 10-11, C. XII, q. 1; c. 7, X, *de officio iudicis ordinarii,* I, 31; cc. 2, 4, 6, X, *de statu monachorum et canonicorum regularium,* III, 35; c. 2, X, *de testamentis et ultimis voluntatibus,* III, 26; c. 14, X, *de regularibus et transeuntibus ad religionem,* III, 31; Conc. Trident. sess. XXV, *de regularibus,* c. 2; Clemens VIII, decr. *Nullus omnino,* 25 iulii 1599, *Fontes,* n. 187; S. C. Rel. resp. 16 martii 1922, AAS, XIV (1922), 196-197.

48. Conc. Trident. sess. XXV, c. 2; Clem. VIII, decr. *Nullus omnino* 25 iulii 1599, *Fontes,* n. 187.

49. Cf. Ballerini-Palmieri, Vol. IV, p. 55.

50. Cf. Ballerini-Palmieri, Vol. IV, p. 55.

51. S. Poenitentiaria, responsa, 28 nov. 1818, Carriere, *De Iustitia et Iure,* Pars I, sect. I, cap. 4, n. 214; S. Poenitentiaria, responsum, 1 dec. 1820, Vermeersch, *De Religiosis,* Vol. II, p. 463; Leo XIII, indultum, 31 iulii 1878, Vermeersch, *De Religiosis,* Vol. I, Supplementum, VI, pp. 77-79. S. C. EE et RR, indultum, 23 iun. 1880, *Collectio Instructionum et declarationum SS. Rom. Congregationum pro Italiae Regularibus suppressis,* Part 14, n. 11, p. 41 apud Piat. I, 239; S. C. EE et RR, indultum 1 maii 1883, Appendix in *Collectio,* p. 48, apud Piat, I, p. 239.

Holy See were not revoked by canon 582 and are still enjoyed.[52]

Although the solemnly professed Religious loses the right to acquire property for himself and in his own name, he does not become incapable of acquiring property for his Order,[53] if the Institute is able to own property. In the days when a Religious remained a member of one community throughout his Religious Life, it was the universal principle that, "whatever a monk acquired, he acquires for the monastery." Later, when other Institutes arose, organizing the local houses into provinces and the provinces into an Order, so that a Religious could change his membership from one House to another, the old principle was applied in the sense that whatever a Religious acquired, he acquired for his Order according to its regulations.[54] The law obtaining in this matter today merely declares that the property acquired by a Religious after solemn profession goes to the Order, Province or House according to the directions of the Constitutions of the Institute. Thus is regulated the ownership, of the property of a Religious who has failed to renounce his property prior to solemn profession, of inheritances and legacies coming to solemnly professed Religious, the copyrights and patents accruing from the industry of the Religious.[55] But whatever a solemnly professed Religious acquires in his capacity as a pastor or rector of a church, must be presumed to have

---

52. Cf. Vermeersch, *Epitome,* I, p. 436; Creusen, *Religieux et Religieuses,* p. 198; Chelodi, *Ius de Personis,* p. 457; De Meester, Vol. II, p. 370; Maroto, CpR, V (1924), 388; Bouuaert-Simenon, *Manuale Iuris Canonici,* n. 657, nota 2; Goyeneche, CpR, VIII (1927) 121.

53. C. I, 3, 54, (56); N. V, 4-5; N. CXXIII, 38; cc. 7, 8, 9, C. XIX, q. 3; cc. 10-11, C. XII, q. 1; c. 7, X, *de officio iudicis ordinarii,* I, 31; c. 8 *de probationibus* II, 19; cc. 2, 4, 6, X,*de statu monachorum et canonicorum regularium,* III, 35; c. 2, X, *de testamentis et ultimis voluntatibus,* III, 26; c. 14, X, *de regularibus et transeuntibus ad religionem,* III, 31; Conc. Trident, sess. XXV,*de regularibus,* c. 2; Clem. VIII, decr. *Nullus omnino* 25 iulii 1599, *Fontes* n. 187; S. C. *EE et RR, Zamoren.* 15 ian. 1897, *Fontes,* n. 2032, S. C. Rel. resp. 16 martii 1922, AAS, XIV (1922), 196-197; Wernz, III, pp. 331-332.

54. Cf. Wernz, III, p. 332; Papi, *Religious Profession,* 71-74.

55. The Dominican Constitutions (1925) n. 1139 establish that inheritances coming to Religious after solemn Profession belong to the Province, as do also, the fruits of industry of the Provincial. Cf. Larraona, CpR, I (1920), 80-81.

been given to the church, unless the contrary is proven.[56] The old principle *"Quidquid monachus acquirit, monasterio acquirit"* is out of place in these circumstances.[57] The principle stated in canon 1636 § 1 will obtain when solemnly professed are placed in similar circumstances, e.g., in charge of a hospital, etc.[58]

It sometimes happens that in order to acquire property for the Institute, it becomes necessary for a Religious to act civilly in his own name. Some authors have claimed that in order a Religious professed of solemn vows may be able to act licitly permission of the Holy See is necessary.[59] However, there is declaration from the Sacred Congregation of Religious to the effect that only the permission of a Religious Superior is necessary for a Religious to act merely civilly in his own name. This authentic document puts an end to the controversy and merits to be given here in full with its petition, since it did not appear in the Acta Apostolicae Sedis.[60]

"Beatissime Pater: Saepe contingit ut religiosis feminis bona aut iura obveniant haereditate et aliis titulis. Horum occasione multi actus dominii sunt ponendi, ex natura rei vel ex lege civili necessarii: acceptare, dividere, permutare, alienare. In his etiam casibus consultius est aliquid renuntiare, aequa compensatione accepta. Demum aliquando valde utile et prope necessarium est quae habent bona alienare, ut pretium impendatur in titulos frugiferos tutos et facilioris administrationes. Votum autem, maxime solemne, paupertatis obstat quominus ea omnia, aut eorum aliquod, fiat sine licentia Sedis Apostolicae. Unde incom-

---

56. Canon 1636 § 1.

57. Cf. Supremum Signaturae Apostolicae Tribunal, acta tribunalium, *De Manila,* 6 aprilis, 1920, AAS, XII (1920), 258.

58. Cf. canon 20.

59. Cf. De Angelis, *Praelectiones Iuris Canonici,* lib. III, tit. 35, n. 4, pp. 167-168; Wernz, *Ius Decretalium,* III, n. 278, p. 293; Ferreres, *Institutiones Canonicae,* I, n. 878, IV, c); Mach-Ferreres, *Tesoro del Sacerdote,* Vol. II (1920) n. 595; *Compendium Theologiæ Moralis,* II, p. 123, c); *Monitore Ecclesiastico,* Quarta Serie, Vol. V (1923), 117.

60. Ferreres, *Razon y Fe,* LXIV (1921), 103; Manucci, *Il Monitore Ecclesiastico* Quarta Serie, Vol. V (1923), 155 now assent to the view so ably demonstrated by Maroto, *De licentia requisita ad hoc ut Religiosus votorum solemnium possit proprietatis in foro civili nomine proprio exercere,* CpR, I (1923), 266-272; V (1924), 10-20; 94-998; 270-277; 378-389.

moda frequentia sequuntur, et sumptus non exigui. Ut igitur in sanctimonialium favorem molestiae vitentur, simul expensis parcatur, Archiepiscopus Valentinus postulat humiliter habituales facultates cum illis super voto paupertatis dispensandi in singulis casibus, ubi sufficientes rationes adesse existimaverit, quatenus illae voto, etiam solemni, non obstante, actus dominii valide et licite ponere possunt ex natura rei aut ex lege civili necessarios: (1°) Ad acquirenda bona et iura, cum aliis gratuitis titulis, tum maxime haereditate, legato aut donatione; (2°) Ad ea, dum acquiruntur, dividenda, permutanda, vendenda, vel etiam, aequa accepta compensatione, renuntianda: (3°) Ad alienanda bona et iura quae forsan habeant, ut pretium invertatur in alias res frugiferas tutas et facilioris administrationis.

"Rescript: Ex Secretaria S. Congr. de Religiosis. N. 716/20. Romae, 3 Februarii 1921. — Ill,me ac Rv.me Domine. Haec S. Congregatio, mature perpensis precibus, quibus ab Amplitudine Tua quaedam habituales facultates implorabantur circa actus dominii a religiosis feminis ponendos, atque attentis omnibus ad rem facientibus, rescribendum censuit, prout rescribit: Unaquaeque monialis, de consensu suae Antistitae, peragere potest actus legales seu civiles. Bona quaecumque monialibus tum modo haereditario tum donatione obvenientia, monasterio cedunt. Quod attinet vero ad venditionem, alienationem, etc., procedatur ad normam iuris.

"Haec a me significanda erant Amplitudini Tuae, cui fausta omnia adprecor a Domino. Addictissimus—Maurus M. Serafini Ab. O. S. B., Secretarius.

"Ill.mo ac Rv.mo Ordinario Valentino."[61]

Whatever property comes, after solemn Profession, to a member of an Institute *which is incapable of ownership* belongs to the Holy See.[62] On account of the fact that the Church is not the State religion, it has no recognition as a legal personality capable of holding property. As a sovereign Power, a political and ecclesiastical State, the Holy See can acquire the right to hold property only by a

---

61. From CpR, V (1924), 276

62. Since the Council of Trent (vide Sess. XXV *de regularibus*, c. 3 there are only two Institutes incapable of ownership, viz., the Order of Friars Minor and the Capuchin Order.

treaty with the United States Government.[63] As a private civil corporation, the Holy See can hold property.[64] Hence, in the United States proper, the Friars Minor and Capuchins should incorporate, either as a corporation sole or aggregate, in order that there may be no legal difficulties about the civil acquirement of property coming to their members.[65] For individual members of these Institutes permission of their Religious Superior suffices for the performance of proprietary acts which have only civil effect.[66] In some of the territorial possessions of the United States the corporate personality of the Holy See is recognized.[67] This is due to the international obligation on the part of the United States to permit the continuance of the "status quo" already obtaining in the territories where the Church enjoyed legal personality and unrestricted proprietary rights.[68] Obviously, the Capuchins and the Friars Minor in the possessions of the United States are free from the inconveniencies of their brethren in the States proper.

Provided a Religious Order, Province or House is duly incorporated according to the civil laws of the state, the solemn vow of poverty with its attendent effects will be recognized by the civil law of the United States. This was evidenced in the case of Father Wirth. In 1887, Augustin Wirth, transferred his stability from the Benedictine Archabbey of St. Vincent, in which he had professed his vows, to the Abbey of St. Mary in Newark, N. J. At the time of his death, December 19, 1901, Father Wirth was living after the manner of a secular priest in Springfield, Minn. From the royalties on the books he had published and his exercise of the ministry there had accumu-

---

63. Bonacum v Murphy 71 Neb. 463; Zollman, p. 47; Bartlett, p. 30; Baart, p. 14.

64. Zollman, pp. 47 ff; Badii, p. 580.

65. Some Capuchins in the United States have an indult granted for ten years, permitting the local Superiors to acquire property civilly for the Holy See. At least one Province of the Friars Minor has an indult allowing property to be civilly acquired by the Province.

66. Cf. Goyeneche, CpR, VII (1926) 39-40.

67. Santos v Holy Roman Catholic Church, 212 (U. S.) 463; Treaty Art. VIII. cited in Ponce v Roman Catholic Church, 210 (U. S.) 296. Bouvier, III, 2974; Lincoln, p. 669.

68. Ponce v Roman Catholic Church, 210 (U. S.) 296; Brown, *The Canonical Juristic Personality with Special Reference to its Status in the United States of America,* 116.

lated a considerable amount of money. The Order of St. Benedict of New Jersey, as a corporation chartered in that state, claimed that Father Wirth, as a member of that corporation had resigned all his proprietary rights when he had made his vows and hence the estate of the deceased belonged to the Abbey of St. Mary. The court held that the contract included in the vow of poverty was a valid contract. By it all that Father Wirth had acquired during his life as monk belonged to the Order of St. Benedict. Father Wirth had never formally severed relations with the abbey to which he belonged. Hence though the title of the property stood in the name of the deceased, yet it belonged to the monastery and not to the relatives of the dead priest.[69]

---

69. Order of St. Benedict of New Jersey v Steinhauser, 179 Fed. (Minn.) 137; Order of St. Benedict v Steinhauser 234, (U. S.) 640; Cf. Brown, 131; Lincoln, 172-173; *Fortnightly Review,* XXI (1914) 268-269; 418-419.

CHAPTER VII.

THE COMMON LIFE

ARTICLE I. OBSERVANCE OF THE COMMON LIFE—CANON 594

The ideal of a sort of Christian socialism was the aim of the founders of Religious Orders.[1] According to their concept of the Common Life, not only were their followers to live together according to a definite plan of exercises but they were to have no concern for personal aggrandizement as regards temporalities. The Institutes would supply from the common property everything necessary for the use of the individuals belonging to the society. In return- the individual should place completely at the disposal of the community all the property he acquired after he became a full fledged member of it. In the use of temporalities all would be entitled to share equally, everything being considered.

Admittedly it is a beautiful ideal and well calculated to be helpful for the advancement of a soul in Christian perfection. It removes solicitude and anxiety concerning maintenance throughout life. Since all temporalities are owned by the Institute or the Holy See and since no one is to fare better than his brother in the use of temporalities, everything being considered that ought to be considered, temptation to obtain such things, with all the disturbance occasioned by selfish efforts in this regard are minimized, and thus the Religious is enabled to concentrate all his energies and attention upon God and His Work. No wonder that the founders of the Religious Institutes desired the Common Life to be perfectly observed in their communities.[2]

---

1. St. Francis of Assisi of course did not want even the community to have the ownership of property.

2. Cf. Concilium Vaticanum, *De Vita Communi,* Collectio Lacensis, Vol. VII, coll, 675-676. The term " vita communis" in canon 594, certainly comprehends the notion stressed in this article.

Due to the nature of simple vows[3] and the greater possibility of return to secular life, as well as the political and social conditions prevailing when most Congregations arose[4], viz. the possibility that civil governments might disband the communities and leave their members without the maintenance which would be theirs under normal conditions, the concept of the Common Life among these Religious, generally speaking, was modified. The difference, in the Common Life, as it applies respectively to Religious with simple vows and those with solemn vows, generally speaking, consists in the permittance of the former to retain the ownership of the property they had before simple profession and the ability to acquire private property for their capital, after profession.[5]

The actualization of the ideal of the Common Life, as it obtains respectively in the cases of simple and solemn vows constitutes the Common Life which is prescribed in Canon 594.[6]

"In quavis religione vita communis accurate ab omnibus servetur etiam in iis quae ad victum, ad vestitum et ad supellectilem pertinent."[7]

In every Religious Institute all must observe carefully the Common Life. Obviously, both Orders and Congregations, of women[8] as well as men, are obliged by this canon. Moreover, all members of these Institutes, Superiors as well as subjects must practice the Common Life.[9] Nevertheless, since customs prevailing against the Common Life are not expressly reprobated, immemorial and

---

3. Cf. Greg. XIII, const. *Ascendente Domino,* § 7, 25 maii 1594, *Fontes,* n. 153; Lugo, disp. 3, n. 89; Aertnys-Damien, n. 1191.

4. Aertnys-Damien, n. 1191; Vermeersch, *Epitome,* n. 684. b).

5. The limitations placed by the Code and the Constitutions of the respective Institutes, of course, being understood here.

6. The Common Life does not pertain to the essence of the Religious State. Cf. St. Thomas, 2, 2, q. 186, art. 5, ad 3; Cappello, *De Visitatione,* Vol. II, c. 9, sect. 2, n. 1, p. 376; Lombardi, Vol. I, p. 432; Cf. Vromant, "Obligatio Vitae Communis", *Periodica,* XVIII, (1929) p. 25* and Fanfani, n. 300 for idea of "vita communis".

7. Canon 594 § 1. "In every Religious Institute, all must carefully observe the Common Life, even in matters of food, clothing, and furniture.

8. Canon 490.

9. Cf. Clem. VIII, decr. *Nullus omnino,* §§ 2-4, 25 iulii 1599, *Fontes,* n. 187.

centenary customs may be tolerated if in the judgment of the Ordinary they cannot be prudently abolished, considering the persons and places concerned.[10] Nor does the canon destroy the indults or privileges which individuals or organizations enjoyed previous to the Code.[11]

The legislator intends that the Common Life be practiced, *even in matters of food, clothing, and furniture.* From the date of Religious Profession, the Institute has a strict obligation to provide the necessities of the Religious,[12] with maternal care.[13] These temporalities are to be supplied from the common fund.[14] As regards travelling that is to be undertaken, in the performance of the work of the Institute, all are to have the same quality of accomodations.[15]

Certainly in the matter of food and drink all should share alike.[16] Distinctions in these matters breed discontent and are a source of temptation to violate the Common Life. The Decretals expressly prohibited practices whereby the Superior with a few of the Religious dined outside the common refectory, partaking of food denied to the rest of the brethren.[17] Nor should individual Religious be allowed, at least as a practice, to receive from externs, quantities of Epicurean delicacies, and liqueurs for their personal use, for this is opposed to the Common Life.[18] But it is not illegitimate for the sick, whether Superiors

---

10. Canon 5. The Vatican Council, *De Vita Communi* was also considerate of customs well nigh ineradicable.

11. Canon 4.

12. Conc. Trident. Sess. XXV *de regularibus,* c. 2; Clem. VIII, decr. *Nullus omnino,* § 3, 25 iulii 1599, *Fontes,* n. 187; *Normae* (1901) art. 127-128.

13. Cf. Schäfer, p. 408.

14. Clem. VIII. decr. *Nullus omnino,* § 3, 25 iulii 1599, *Fontes,* n. 187; Concilium Vaticanun, *De Vita Communi,* Collectio Lacensis, Vol. VII, col. 677; Pejska, p. 130.

15. S. C. EE et RR, decr. 22 augusti 1814, n. X, (*Fontes,* n. 1893).

16. Cf. Clem. VIII. decr, *Nullus omnino,* § 4 25, iulii 1599, *Fontes,* n. 187. S. C. EE et RR, decr. 22 augusti 1814, n. X,*Fontes,* n. 1893.

17. c. 6, X, *de statu monachorum et canonicorum regularium,* III, 35..

18. Cf. Clem. VII, decr. *Nullus omnino* § 4, 25 iulii 1599 (*Fontes,* n. 187). Cf. Aertnys-Damien, *Theologia Moralis,* Vol. I, n. 1200, p. 720.

or subjects, to have special attention[19] as regards diet. Decretal Law expressly declared in favor of such consideration.[20] In the matter of medical treatment and health trips all should be favored alike in similar sicknesses;[21] for instance, when the doctor prescribes for an ordinary Religious, a month or two at Miami or a boat trip to Bermuda these restoratives should not be denied to him, if it has been demonstrated already by the example of Superiors and "distingue" members of the Institute, that such health builders are not foreign to the spirit of the Institute. It may be well to recall what the Holy See has decreed as regards Religious in the time of sickness; viz. nothing should be wanting which will assist in the recovery of health.[22]

The Common Life requires that the community supply the Religious with clothing.[23] In the past during sieges of extraordinary poverty clothing was sometimes obtained from externs; this led to practices which gradually undermined the Common Life as regards clothing, esby the Religious. It is the community's duty to supply the clothing and when practices obtain to the contrary i. e. when the Religious either are expected or required to procure from externs their clothing or the means of purchasing it, grave disorders in Religious Discipline usually follow. The Common Life, the hedge protecting the

---

19. Choupin-Gautrelet,*Nature et Obligations de l'Etat Religieux,* p. 391; Papi, *Religious in Church Law,* p. 40; Gearin, *American Ecclesiastical Review,* LXI (1919), 151; Augustine, III, p. 304.

20. c. 6. X, *de statu monachorum et canonicorum regularium,* III, 35.

21. S. C. EE et RR, decr. 22 augusti 1814, § X, *Fontes,* n. 1893.

22. Innocentii XII seu S. C. super Disciplina Regulari, decr. *Sanctissimus,* n. 5, 18 iulii 1695, *Bul. Capuccinorum,* VI, 456 § 9; *Bul. Ord. Praed,* VII, 362 § 9; *Bullarii Romani editio Luxemburgensis,* Tomus VII, p. 295, apud Vermeersch, *De Religiosis,* Vol. II, pp. 322-323, referred to by the Concilium Vaticanum, *De Vita Communi,* Collectio Lacensis, Vol. VII, col. 676: "Studeant vero praecipue ut ea omnia quae tam ad victum et vestitum quam ad reliquas vitae necessitates pertinent, singulis Religiosis prompte subministrentur, ac praesertim aegritudinis tempore nihil alicui desit quod ad sanitatem recuperandam pertineat." Cf. Cappello, *De Visitatione,* Vol. II, c. 9, Sect. 2, p. 378.

23. Cf. Clem. VIII, decr. *Nullus omnino* § 3, 25 iulii 1599, *Fontes,* n. 187; *Normae* (1901) art, 127; Concilium Vaticanum, *De Vita Communi,* Collectio Lacensis. Vol. VII, col. 677.

observance of evangelical poverty,[24] is also broken down, when such illicit practices as permitting Religious with wealthy contacts, to accept from this source clothing above and beyond the quantity and quality allowed by the standard of the Institute.[25] Another destructive influence on the Common Life is that of the Superior whose exhortations to bear the standard (of the Common Life and poverty) aloft and untarnished, are deafened by his personal example in the matter of clothing. There is of course a greater ambitus for abuse in non-Catholic countries where the street clothing of male Religious is similar to that in vogue among the diocesan clergy.

It may be remarked that it is permissible to keep personal clothing separate from the supply room, provided the Superior will authorize such a practice and his control over the use of it is recognized.[26] Reasons of sanitation dictate such a practice,[27] especially when there are members of the community laboring under corporal infirmity.

All the Religious, Superiors as well as subjects, should practice the Common Life as regards furniture. The rooms should be supplied with the same quantity and quality of furnishings. However, furniture, instruments and books etcetera which are necessary and useful for the proper discharge of an office such as a professor are not to be considered departures from the Common Life.[28]

"Quidquid a religiosis, etiam a Superioribus, acquiritur ad normam canon 580 § 2, et canon 582, n. 1, bonis domus, provinciae vel religionis admisceatur, et pecunia quaelibet omneque tituli in capsa communi deponantur."[29]

---

24. Cf. Aertnys-Damien, *Theologia Moralis* (1928) Vol. I, n. 1198, p. 719; Pejska, p. 129.

25. Canon 594 § 3.

26. *Normae* (1901) art, 127; The Philadelphia Foundation of the Sisters of St. Francis by their Consitiutions (1915) n. 55 are permitted to have their personal clothing kept separate but in a common room.

27. Battandier, *Guide Canonique pour les Constitutions des Instituts a Voeux Simples,* n. 229, p. 197; Gearin, *American Ecclesiastical Review,* LXI (1919) 151.

28. Cf. Vermeersch, *Epitome,* Vol. I, n. 696.

29. "Whatever is acquired by the Religious, including the Superiors, according to the terms of canon 580 § 2 and canon 582, n. 1, must be incorporated in the goods of the house, or of the province, or of the Institute; and all the money and *titles* (tituli) shall be deposited in the common safe." canon 594 § 2.

Canon 580 § 2 declares that all the property a Religious with simple vows acquires by his industry or in respect of his Institute belongs to the Institute.[30] And canon 582, 1° declares that whatever property a Regular acquires after solemn Profession belongs to the Order, Province or House of which he is a member.[31] Canon 594 § 2 declares *how* the money and other property acquired by the Religious according to the terms of canons 580 § 2 and 582, 1° is to be possessed.

Whatever property, belonging to the province, Institute, house, is acquired by any Religious, must be incorporated in the goods of that moral person. The legislator does not want individual Religious as such, to retain property beyond what the Common Life of the Institute permits. All money and titles to property must be kept in the common depositary of the moral person to whom it belongs. Of course this latter does not mean that there is to be only one place of deposit. In America the money, stocks, bonds, deeds, letters of exchange and other negotiables, such as promisory notes, checks, copyrights, patents etc., could be kept in one or several banks in the name of the corporation which civilly represents the Institute Province or House.

(*a*) *Designated Gifts*

Donations made to a community through an individual Religious may be unqualified or they may be given for a specific purpose. Unqualified donations are to be possessed in the same way as the fruits of industry. But what about designated gifts? By a designated gift is to be understood a donation which is given with a condition determined by the donor, viz. it must be used for a specified person or purpose.[32] If such a donation is bestowed on an Institute, Province, or canonically erected House, the

30. Whatever else he acquires belongs to himself, (Chelodi, *Ius de Personis,* p. 457) unless the Constitutions of the Institute provide otherwise, (580 § 1).

31. Except indults have provided otherwise; the Holy See owns whatever comes to a solemnly professed member of an Institute incapable of owning property. Canon 582.

32. Cf. Bernardini, *American Ecclesiastical Review,* LXXIX (1928) 16.

donation becomes ecclesiastical property.[33] Moreover, since it is given for a pious cause,[34] it is subject to all the restrictions which Canon Law places for the protection of the fulfillment of the intention of the donor. Before the Code the Holy See declared: "Postulat enim imprimis *ius naturale et divinum;* jubent canonicae, civelesque ipsae leges; pluribus denique in locis studiose commendat Sacrosancta Synodus Tridentina, ut voluntates fidelium, *facultates suas in pias causas donantium* vel relinquentium, *diligentissime impleantur,* et *in eos precise usus iuxta modum conditionesque* iis benevisas, *pecunia* inde obventa insumatur ad quos destinati fuit, *neque in alios convertatur, etsi meliores utiloresque* videantur; si secus fieret, fidelium voluntates, quae pro lege habendae sunt, fraudarentur, ipsique, magno cum Ecclesiae detrimento, a piis huiusmodi largitionibus retraherentur. Quibus vero pro eorum munere administratio bonorum seu pecuniarum huius concredita est, ii nullis laboribus et difficultatibus deterrendi eam omnem diligentiam in hisce omnibus adhibentes, quam prudens ac probus paterfamilias adhibere solet in rebus suis."[35] The principles enunciated in this important Instruction have been substantially incorporated in the Code.[36] Canon 1514 declares that the will of the Faithful, who give their property by donation "inter vivos" or "mortis causa" or leave it by testament, to a pious cause, is to be fulfilled most diligently, even in reference to the manner of administration and the application of the property.[37]

---

33. Canon 1497 § 1. Cf. D'Annibale, *Summula Theologiae Moralis,* Vol. III, n. 77; Vermeersch,*Periodica,* VI (1913) p. 327. Institutes, Provinces, and canonically erected Houses are, of course, moral persons capable of owning property, cc. 536, 582; Cf. Stutz, *Der Geist des Codex iuris Canonici,* p. 203.

34. A cause is pious whenever it is in favor of religion or Christian virtue. Cf. Bernardini, AER, LXXIX (1928) 19; Nebreda, CpR, VII (1926) 114; Cocchi, VI, n. 189, p. 386; Vermeersch, *Epitome,* Vol. II, n. 834; Vromant, n. 147, p. 159; Fanfani, n. 176; Nebreda, *De Loci Ordinariorum iuribus circa pia legata donationesve tum religiosis tum eorum ecclesiis etiam paroecialibus facta,* p. 19.

35. S. C. de Prop. Fide, Instructio a. 1807, *Collectanea,* n. 689. Italics are not in the original.

36. Bernardini, AER, LXXIX (1928) 20.

37. *"Voluntates fidelium facultates suas in pias causas donantium vel relinquentium, sive per actum inter vivos, sive per actum mortis causa, diligentissime impleantur etiam circa modum administrationis*

Whenever such gifts are accepted for a definite purpose or person, the Superior is strictly obliged in conscience to fulfill the condition attached to that donation. He may not arbitrarily change the designation. Only the donors and the Holy See for a just cause[38] and necessary reason, can substantially change the designation of pious causes.[39]

(*b*) *Peculium*

Superiors, acting as such, alone should retain property of the moral person whom they represent. As private Religious, the Superiors, should not retain any property of the Institute beyond what is permitted to the other Religious by the Common Life of the Institute. In other words this canon prohibits peculium.[40] Peculium as it

---

et erogationis bonorum, salvo praescripto can. 1515 § 3." Canon 1514.

38. Cf. S. C. de Prop. Fidei, instructio, a. 1807, n. 689; "This is in virtue of the supreme and universal power of the Holy See in such matters, as recognized by moral theologians and indicated by Canon 1499 § 2." cf. Bernardini, AER, LXXIX (1928) 22;

39. Beranardini, AER, LXXIX (1928) 22

40. In Roman Law, Ulpian, as quoted by Justinian thus defined it: "Peculium dictum est quasi pusilla pecunia sive patrimonium pusillum," D. 15, 1, 5, 3; Tubero, as Celsus remarks, explained peculium, as that which, with the permission of his Master, a slave possessed, separate from the property of which he had to give an account, cf. D. 15, 1, 5, 4. From early times it had been customary to entrust to slaves a peculium. Sons too received such a fund from the head of the family. This came to be known as the "peculium profectitium." cf. Buckland, p. 279. Whatever accrued from that fund belonged to the head of the family, and not to the son or slave, D. 41, 2, 44, 1; (Beseler, *Bietrage zür Kritik der römischen Rechtsquellen,* IV, 61 sq. is too ruthless here). For throughout the days of Republican Roman Law both son and slave were not capable of owning property, G. II, 86, Baviera, *Fontes Iuris Romani Antejustiniani,* p. 53; Cogliolo, *Fonti del Diritto Romano,* p. 112, G. II, 87. Baviera, p. 54, Cogliolo, 123; G. III, 163, Baviera, p. 115, Cogliolo, p. 281; Poste-Whittuck, pp. 40 ff; Leage, pp. 78-79; Sherman, II, p. 95; Buckland, p. 279. Nor was the concept of this kind of peculium altered even by Justinian, I, 2, 9, 1; D. 41, 1, 10, 1; I, 2, 9, 3; C. 6, 61, 6; Muirhead, 417. At the time of Augustus or Titus, sons of families who were soldiers were allowed to hold as their own, the pay received from military service. Paul, *Sententiæ,* 3, 4a, 3, Cogliolo, p. 431; D. 49, 17, 11. This was called "peculium castrense," Sherman, II, 97, Buckland, p. 279. It also included whatever, the son received as the result of his military service, e.g., spoils. Constantine extended the same privilege to money received as a State official, C. Th. 6, 35, 15; C. 12, 30, 1; Mackensie,

applies to Religious may be described as: Property, belonging to the community, but separated from the common property, for the private convenience of an individual, beyond what his present moral necessity requires.[41] In the past, where peculium existed, it arose from three main sources. For instance, persons with property were professed with the understanding that after profession the community would own the property but the individual concerned would have the use of it for his food, clothing, furniture, etc. Another practice was that whereby Religious obtained from externs property for the monastery but the use of it was to be retained by the individual who had acquired it. Again another usage was that whereby the community distributed to the members of the community a fund from which the clothing, food or furniture etc., were procured.[42]

Before the Council of Trent, according to the opinion of some authors[43] it is probable that when the jurisdiction of the Superior was acknowledged over the peculium, the practice was not illicit according to common law. However, the decree of the Council of Trent and the subsequent declarations of the Holy See made illicit, by common law, all practices whereby property estimable at a price and belonging to the community was separated from the common fund for the convenience of an individual be-

---

p. 127. Another kind of peculium was that known as "adventitium." Constantine provided that a son could own the property his mother had willed to him, C. Th. 8, 18, 15; C. 6, 60, 1; Ortolan-Prichard-Nasmith, pp. 393-394. Successive emperors extended this privilege to other acquisitions of property, C. Th. 8, 18. Finally Justinian decreed that the son could own all the peculium except the "profectitium," I, 2, 9, 1; C. 6, 61, 6.

41. Cf. Vermeersch, *De Religiosis,* Vol. I, p. 178.

42. Concillium Auscitanum (1308) cc. 4-5, (Harduin, *Acta Conciliorum et Epistulæ, Decretales ac Constitutiones Summorum Pontifficum,* Vol. VII, col. 1282-1283; Clem. VIII, decr. *Nullus omnino,* § 2, 25 iulii 1599, *Fontes,* n. 187; Fagnanus, I, n. lib. III, De statu monachorum, c. Monachi n. 1 sq.; Lambermond, *Der Armutsgedanke des Hl. Dominikus und Seines Ordens,* p. 51: "Ein anderes Beispiel sehen wir im Leben des hl. Thomas von Aquin der jedes Jahr dem Konvente eine "pitantia" stiftete zum Feste der hl. Agnes, aus Dankbarkeit fur erlangete Heilung."

43. Concina, *Disciplina Apostolico-Monastica,* Diss. I, c. 12, n. 2; Schmalzgruber, lib. III, tit. 35, n. 12; Wernz, Vol. III, p. 334, n. (380); Suarez, Vol. XV, tract. 7, lib. 8, c. 14, n. 3; Bouix, Vol. I, p. 515.

yond what his present moral necessity required, even though the property was obtained from the Superior whose jurisdiction over it was acknowledged at all times.[44] Canon 594 § 2 also renders such practices illicit.[45]

As peculium is to be classed: (a) money which is kept separate from the common fund, to be used *exclusively* for the needs of a particular Religious, whether these needs are food, clothing, furniture, etc.[46] even though the money is deposited with the Superior and even if the separation is only "on the books".[47] (b) the property which a Religious must acquire in those communities wherein only food is given to the Religious, each individual being required to procure clothing for himself, (because the fruit of industry is not incorporated in the funds of the monastery but is administered by an individual for his own use).[48] (c) annuities, etc., bestowed on a community, with the agreement that the property must be used *exclusively* for the wants of an individual member of the community.[49]

---

44. Concil. Trident. Sess. XXV *de regularibus*, c. 2; Clem. VIII, decr. *Nullus omnino*, §§ 2-4, 25 iulii 1599, *Fontes*, n. 187; S. C. EE et RR, *Nullius Mercatelli*, 24 iun. 1579, *Fontes*, n. 1358; *Hispaniarum*, 25 ian. 1591, *Fontes*, n. 1438; *Messanen.* 1 martii 1595, *Fontes*, n. 1534; *Ordinis B. M. V. de Mercede*, 9 ian. 1601, *Fontes*, n. 1598; decr. 22 aug. 1814, n. X, *Fontes*, n. 1893; *Florentina*, 14 et 21 febr. 1586 ad 1-3, *Fontes*, n. 1941; litt. 30 dec. 1882, *Fontes*, n. 2008; S. C. Concilli, 4 iulii 1602-12 ian. 1613—apud Wernz, Vol. III, p. 334; Cf. Giraldi, I, sect. 555; Ferraris, *Votum*, II, n. 45; *Moniales*, II, n. 64; *Legatum*, II, n. 91; Reiffenstuel, lib. III, tit. 35, n. 6; Schmalzgrueber, lib. III, tit. 35, n. 14; De Angelis, II, lib. 3, tit. 35, pp. 158 sq.

45. Raus, *Institutiones*, p. 316; Vermeersch, *Epitome*, Vol. I, n. 696; Egger, *Das Neue Ordensrecht*, zu. 242, p. 36; David, *The Religious State*, p. 143; Gearin, AER, LXI (1919) 152; Schäfer, *De Religiosis*, p. 409; Balmes, *Religieux a Voeux Simples*, p. 169, n. (2); Monthon, *Traite sur L'Etat Religieux*, n. 319, p. 405.

46. Cf. Sleutjes, I, p. 401.

47. Cf. Vermeersch, *De Religiosis*, Vol. I, n. 276. P. Vincent Caraffa declared that in the Society of Jesus permissions in such matters given by Superiors would be invalid; *Constitutiones Societatis Divini Salvatoris* c. VII, n. 33 has similar enactment; vide *Constitutiones Societatis Verbi Divini*, (1922) n. 79, 30, p. 36.

48. Vermeersch, *De Religiosis*, Vol. I, n. 276.

49. Vermeersch, *De Religiosis*, Vol. I, n. 278, p. 180; But if a fund or property is given to a community, to be fused with the common property, so that it can be used for the welfare of the community, yet at the same time there exist an understanding that the Superior see to it that a definite Religious is never to want for the

Vermeersch teaches that canon 594 does not prohibit Religious engaged in an Apostolic Life to hold a small amount of money, such as is necessary for daily travel in the city.[50] He justifies this practice not on the fact of necessity but on an application of the principle, "parum pro nihilo reputatur". Another great authority on the Religious Life, although engaged in a different field than Vermeersch remarks: "Under existing conditions of society and civilization it is in practice necessary that Religious stationed, for whatever reason, outside of a monastery and out of the conditions of conventual life must have some kind of allowance for their personal expenses; and if a monk is living, even in a monastery in a large city, he can not go about without some money in his pocket for tram car and underground railway fares and he can not be asking for a few pence every time he goes out".[51]

Today, at least in the cities of the United States, it is morally necessary for Religious engaged in Apostolic work, especially for those who dress after the style of diocesan clergymen when out of the House, to have a small amount of money on their person when they go out. It is true that this moral necessity could, theoretically speaking, be supplied by an express permission obtained "toties quoties". But, it is also true, that theoretically speaking, it would be (taking only one view of the matter) more meritorious for a Religious to obtain permission "toties quoties" for the little things of frequent necessity e. g. ink,

---

things which the Common Life of the Institute admits, this is not prohibited. Cf. S. C. EE et RR, *Nullius Mercatelli,* 24 iun, 1579, *Fontes,* n. 1358; *Hispaniarum,* 25 ian. 1591; *Fontes,* n. 1438; *Messanen,* 1 martii 1595; *Fontes,* n. 1534; decr. 22 aug. 1814, n. X; *Fontes,* n. 1893; Cf. Schmalzgruber, lib. III, tit. 35, nn. 15-17; Wernz, Vol. III, p. 335, n. (384); Vermeersch, Vol. I, n. 278; Some authors hold that when a Religious is transferred from one monastery to another, such a fund or property goes with him. Cf. De Luca, *De Regularibus* Disc. 57, n. 19; Petra, Tomus, IV, ad Const. V, Benedict XII, sec. 2, n. 60; Bouix, II, p. 525; Piat, I, p. 247 q. 7; Passerinus, Tomus, I, p. 186, art. 7, n. 325 sq.; Suarez, tract, 7, lib. 8, c. 14, n. 14; Vermeersch, *De Religiosis,* Vol. I, p. 180; Biederlack-Führich, n. 111, p. 191, (1); Wernz, II, p. 335; Goyeneche, CpR, I (1920) 341.

50. Vermeersch, *Epitome,* I, n. 696, pp. 448-449: "Non ideo tamen vetantur religiosi vitæ apostolicæ tenere modicam pecuniam—si qua, ad cotidiana itinera per civitatem fuerit necessaria—de qua valet istud: parum pro nihilo reputatur."

51. Butler, *Benedictine Monachism,* p. 153.

shoe strings, collar buttons, etcetera. Yet in most Institutes, there is to be found the practice of general permission for these things because (taking a broad view of the matter) it is a better arrangement, everything being considered. The Common Life does not suffer thereby nor is the vow of poverty nor its spirit injured by the practice. What is better, from a broad and practical standpoint, for the little necessities of frequent occurence *in the House* would also be better from a practical and broad standpoint for the little necessities of frequent occurence *outside the House*. A similar practice, under the present state of affairs in cities in America, is morally necessary for those engaged in Apostolic work.

From the history of Religious Institutes we know that when Religious were denied what was morally necessary, the difficulty was overcome by obtaining illicitly what was needed. Human nature has not changed. We have the authority of Vermeersch that it is not peculium for a Religious engaged in Apostolic work to have a small amount of money for the little necessities occuring outside the monastery in cities.[52] Of course it is understood that the money be had with permission from the Superior who retains the capacity to revoke or modify the permission. Thus it would in no way constitute a violation of the vow of poverty. Nor would the spirit of poverty be injured. Certainly it would act as a preventative against violations of the vow of poverty in small matters. It may not be feasable that this be practiced by young student Religious and others having a similar status, who leave the House only occasionally.[53]

---

52. The principle of "parum pro nihilo reputatur" as he applies it can correctly be applied or extended to other Religious having frequent need of being outside the monastery in the city.

53. As regards students in the House of Studies of clerical Institutes, canon 587 § 2 declares that they can not be promoted to Orders if the perfect Common Life does not flourish in that House. The practice of peculium is what is usually meant by the perfect Common Life. But, as Vermeersch states his opinion, a small amount of money held by those who daily go into the city is not peculium. That is why, it is stated, that it may not be feasible, rather than, student Religious must not be permitted to have such a practice.

The Council of Trent forbade all kinds of peculium at least according to the more probable opinion. After the declarations from the Holy See, especially during the latter part of the fifteenth and during the early sixteenth centuries, it was evident that the Holy See had prohibited peculium. Yet it was possible for custom to prevail, in the course of time, against the Tridentine decree.[54] What could happen did happen.[55] The Holy See even approved Constitutions in which the practice of peculium was regulated.[56]

The regulations concerning the practice of peculium vary in the teachings of authors and in the approved Constitutions, and pronouncements of the Holy See. The pre-Code Dominican Constitutions required that the peculium be had with at least the presumed permission of the Superior; and dependent on his will; the amount must be moderate in quantity relative to the quality of persons, places and times; excessive amounts, not in accord with the state of poverty are to be incorporated with the common

54. Cf. Belorgey, *De Consuetudine,* pp. 122 sq. who ably argues that the opinion holding that custom could prevail against the law of the Council or Trent is the more probable one. Cf. Suarez, *De Legibus,* lib. VII, c. 19, n. 21 (Oecumenical Councils in general), Billuart, *De Legibus, Diss.* V, art. 2; *Praelectiones,* lib. III, de praebend. et dignitat, n. 75; Wernz, III, 334. Biederlack *Zeitschrift für Theologie,* (1892) 438-471-608-658 apud Abbeloos, *De Consuetudine,* pp. 147-148.

55. Benedict XIV, *De Servorum Dei Beatificatione,* lib. III, c. 41, n. 12; *De Synodo Diocesana,* lib. III, c. 12, n. 21; Schmalzgruber, lib. III, tit. 35, n. 14; St. Alphonsus, IV, n. 15; Melot, p. 49; Bouix, I, p. 517; Piat, I, p. 247; Craisson, *Des Communautes Religieuses a Voeux Simples,* p. 272 (tolerated usage); *Manuale Iuris Canonici,* n. 2757; Ballerini-Palmieri, lib. IV, t. 9, n. 115; Slater, I, p. 652; n. 4; Carriere, I, n. 204; D'Annibale, pars III, n. 504; Vermeersch, *De Religiosis,* Vol. I, p. 181; *Analecta Juris Pontificii,* LXXXII, col. 955; Bachofen, p. 120; Biederlack, *Archiv für Katholiches Kirchenrecht,* XXXIX (1899) p. 179; Lehmkuhl, Vol. I, n. 680; Genicot (1902) I, p. 105; Chelodi, *Ius de Personis,* p. 461, n. (4); Concilium Vaticanum, "De Vita Communi," *Collectio Lacensis,* Vol. VII, coll. 675-676.

56. Cf. *Constitutiones Ordinis S. Mariæ de Mercede,* dist. 3, c. De Voto Paupertatis (*Bul. Rom.* XX, pp. 232 sq.); Innocent XII, *Pastoralis officii* 21 iunii 1695 (*Bul. Rom.* XX, p. 690; *Constitutiones S. Ordinis Praedicatorum* (1886) D. I, c. XV, dec. 7, nn. 312 sq.; *Constitutiones Urbanæ Fratrum Minorum Conventualium ad breviorem methodum redactæ* (1894) p. 65, c. IV, t. 2, n. 2; Cf. Bouix, II, p. 518; Ferraris, *Moniales,* art. II, n. 69.

fund; it is to be expended with at least the implicit permission of the Superior and used for laudable purposes; moreover it must be kept on deposit with the convent, except minor sums which will be spent in a brief time; it must actually be on deposit and not merely on paper.[57] Other Institutes had regulations less complete and different. Some of the authors are more exacting in the regulations they prescribe for the licit use of peculium. Where centenary or immemorial custom obtains in any Institute as regards peculium, it may be tolerated if the Ordinary prudently judge that it cannot be removed.[58] But if circumstances are favorable, so that the custom can prudently be abolished, it should be done.[59] Yet it is to be remembered that the Holy See has declared that where a Religious did not profess his vows according to the Common Life, as it obtained before the Code, he was not to be forced by Superiors to lead the strict Common Life.[60]

Religious must not only posses things in common but the furniture which they have for their use according to the Common Life must be conformable to the poverty that a Religious professes:

> "Religiosorum supellex paupertati conveniat quam professi sunt."[67]

This part of the canon refers to the Common Life, in so far as it regulates the quantity and quality of the furniture which the Religious may have for their use in the Common Life. Not only must Religious practice poverty,

---

57. *Constitutiones* (1886) D. I, c. XV, dec. 7, nn. 316 sq.; Aertnys-Damien (1928) n. 1201 lays down similar conditions for the use of peculium.

58. Canon 5; Cf. Raus, *Institutiones*, p. 316; Gearin, AER, LXI (1919) 152; Biederlack-Führich (1919), p. 189. Where peculium is allowed by indult, obtained before the Code, it can continue in force after the Code, canon 4; cf. S. C. EE et RR, 22 apr. 1851, *Fontes*, n. 1859; Cf. Lombardi, I, p. 432.

59. Cf. Fanfani, n. 225, Dubium, I; Schäfer, p. 409.

60. Innocent XII, decr. *Sanctissimus*, 18 iul. 1695, *Bullarii Romanii editio Luxemburgensis, Tomus* VII, p. 295; *Bullarium Ordinis Fratrum Minorum S. Francisci Capuccinorum*, VI, 455-456; *Bullarium Ordinis Praedicatorum*, VII, 632; S. C. EE et RR declaratio, 1 oct. 1852, Bizzarri, p. 853; Vermeersch, *De Religiosis*, Vol. II, p. 304; Cf. Cappello, *De Visitatione*, II, p. 376.

61. "The furniture of the Religious must be in accordance with the poverty of which they make profession." Canon 594 § 3.

in the sense that they do not own anything they have for their use (since they can use only what the Institute owns) but their furniture must be in conformity with the poverty which they vow.[64]

ARTICLE II. PUNISHMENT FOR VIOLATIONS OF THE COMMON LIFE—CANON 2389

"Religiosi legem vitae communis constitutionibus praescriptae in re notabili violantes, graviter moneantur et, emendatione non secuta, puniantur etiam privatione vocis activae et passivae et si Superiores sint, etiam officii."[63]

This canon applies to all Religious Institutes.[64] It is a preceptive canon imposing a strict obligation, that members of Religious Institutes, without exception, be punished for violating the Common Life. Such a punishment for the violation of the Common Life is not surprising when the history of the Religious State is recalled.

The object of this canon must be a delict, as the heading of Title XVII of Book V Part III declares.[65] A delict in ecclesiastical law is an external and morally imputable violation of a law to which there is annexed a canonical sanction at least an indeterminate one.[66] The Church takes cognizance of a delict of the Religious in so far as it can disturb the social order of the Institute.[67] It is almost superfluous to remark that the culprit must be considered guilty of a theologically grave sin before he is amenable

---

62. Cf. Clem. VIII, decr. *Nullus omnino,* §§ 3, 16, 25 iul. 1599, *Fontes,* n. 187; *Normæ* (1901) art. 128.

63. Canon 2389.—"Religious who violate in a notable matter the law of the Common Life prescribed by the Constitutions, must be seriously admonished, and if no amendment follows, punished even by the privation of active and passive voice, and if Superiors, of office also."

64. It applies also to clerical Societies in so far as they practice the Common Life, even though they do not profess vows (Pontifical Commission for the Interpretation of the Code, 2-3 iunii 1918, AAS, X (1918), 347).

65. *"a rubro ad nigrum valet illatio,* Cf. Maroto, *Institutiones,* n. 167; Ayrinhac, *General Legislation in the New Code of Canon Law,* p. 82.

66. Canon 2195.

67. Lega, *De Delictis et Poenis,* p. 41; Chelodi, *Ius Poenale,* pp. 134-135. Cf. Vidal, "Notio Delicti in Jure Codicis," *Jus Pontificium,* II (1922) 99-100.

to the sanction of canon 2389.[68] Circumstances which excuse from mortal sin, excuse from the sanction attached by common law for the violation of the law of Common Life prescribed by the Constitutions of an Institute.[69] Yet a Religious must prove he is not gravely culpable in his action in order to be excused from the sanction to the law of Common Life.[70] For the Fifth Book of the Code ordains that whenever a law has been violated externally the offender is presumed to have acted with malice until the contrary is proven.[71]

The canon declares that violators of the law of *Common Life* prescribed by the Constitutions of an Institute must be gravely warned. Decretal and Tridentine legislation[72] established penalties only against the contumacious retainer of "community property".[73]

The Decretal Law was worded: "Monachi non pretio recipiantur in monasterio, nec peculium permittantur habere . . . Qui vero peculium habuerit, nisi ab abbate fuerit ei pro iniuncta administratione permissum, a communione removeatur altaris, et qui in extremis cum peculio inventus fuerit, et digne non paenituerit, nec oblatio pro eo fiat nec inter fratres accipiat sepulturam; quod etiam de universis religiosis praecipimus observari."[74] The Tridentine read: "Nemini igitur regularium, tam virorum quam mulierum, liceat bona immobilia vel mobilia, cuiuscun que qualitatis fuerint, etiam quovis modo ab iis acquisita, tanquam propria aut etiam nomine conventus possidere vel tenere; sed statim ea superiori tradantur conventuique incorporentur. Nec deinceps liceat superioribus bona stab-

68. Cf. Vermeersch, *Epitome,* Vol. III, n. 383; Salucci, *Il Diritto Penale,* p. 2, n. 2; Vermeersch, *Theologiæ Moralis.* Vol. II, n. 536: Baart, *Legal Formulary,* p. 427; Noval, "De ratione corrigendi," *Jus Pontificium,* III (1923) 36-37.

69. Cf. canon 2218 § 2.

70. Cf. canon 2218 § 2.

71. Cf. canon 2200 § 2.

72. Cc. 2, 4, X, *de statu monachorum et canonicorum regularium,* III, 35; Conc. Trident., Sess. XXV, *de regularibus,* c. 2.

73. Reiffenstuel, lib. III, tit. 35, n. 21; Castropalao, Tract. XVI, disp. 3, c. 24, punct. 4; Schmalzgrueber, lib. III, tit. 35, n. 40, 2; Sanchez, lib. VII, c. 20, nn. 11 et 13; Passerinus, Quaes. 186, art. 8, n. 565; Donatus, Tomus IV pars 15, tract. 52, quaes. 13; Rotarius, Tomus, II, lib. 3, c. 1, punct. 18, n. 10.

74. c. 2, X, *de statu monachorum et canonicorum regularium* III, 35; Cf. same argument in chapters 4 and 6 of this title.

ilia alicui regulari concedere, etiam ad usufructum vel usum, administrationem aut commendam. Administratio autem bonorum monasteriorum seu conventuum ad solos officiales eorundem, ad nutum superiorum amovibiles, pertineat. Mobilium vero usum ita superiores permittant, ut eorum supellex statui paupertatis quam professi sunt, conveniat, nihilque superflui in ea sit, nihil etiam quod sit necessarium iis denegetur. *Quod si quis aliter quicquam tenere deprehensus aut convictus fuerit,* in biennio activa et passiva voce privatus sit, atque etiam iuxta suae regulae et ordinis constitutiones puniatur."[75] This decree was so interpreted that although a Religious was convicted of having accepted or having spent money or given away property without permission he was not subject to the above mentioned penalty unless he was convicted of having retained such things.[76] Is canon 2389 to be interpreted as a mere paraphrase of the former law or is it to be considered a new law? Assuredly the phraseology differs appreciably from the former law. Now the text of canon 2389, since it is penal legislation, must be interpreted strictly. "*Leges quae poenam statuunt . . . strictae subsunt interpretatione*".[77] Strict interpretation clings to the text and pays due regard to the mind of the legislator but mitigates the rigor of the law as far as the "ratio legis" will permit (Augustine, I, p. 98). To restrict, "Religious who violate in a notable matter the law of Common Life prescribed by the Constitutions" to such a degree that it is to be understood as "the obstinate retention of a notable amount of illicit peculia", would scarcely be clinging to the text. Unless we are mistaken, canon 2389 must be understood as sanctioning whatever the Constitutions of the Institutes prescribe relative to the "Common Life".[78]

Only violations of the common life *as prescribed by the constitutions* are amenable to the application of the

75. Sess. XXV, *de regularibus,* c. 2. Italics are not present in the document itself.

76. Cf. Piat, I, p. 269; Schmalzgrueber, lib. III, tit. 35, n. 40, 2; Sanchez, *In Praecepta Decalogi,* lib. VII, c. 20, nn. 11 et 13; Passerinus, Quaes. 186, art. 8, n. 565; Rotarius, II, 3, 1, 18, 10; Donatus, Tomus IV, pars. 15, tract. 52, quaes. 13; Reiffenstuel, lib. III, tit. 35, n. 21.

77. Canon 19.

78. Pejska, p. 135; Sole, p. 392; Eichman, *Das Sträfrecht des Codex Juris Canonici,* p. 218.

penal treatment prescribed by canon 2389. Or course, if in the not-yet-revised Constitutions of an Institute, there is legislation, relative to the common life, contrary to the Code, it is abrogated and hence it violation is not punishable in virtue of canon 2389. And where customs immemorial, which cannot be removed prudently, obtain against the Constitutions of an Institute, acts placed in conformity with these customs are not to be construed as delicts subject to the aforementioned canon. Nor are actions of individual Religious in possession of an indult exempting them from the Common Life of their Institute to be reckoned as violations of the prescribed Common Life.

Not all violations of the Constitutions in the matter of the Common Life are to be punished by virtue of canon 2389 but only those which must be considered *"in re notabili"*. Hence such violations as are not notable are not subject matter of this canon. But what constitutes notable matter? If the Constitutions expressly determine notable matter, the norm is clear for such an Institute. Whatever is noted in the Constitutions as prohibited under the pain of the graver penalties may also be considered notable matter.[79] e. g. In the Dominican Constitutions (ed. 1925, "Si quis rem sibi collatam, in materia gravi receperit, de his quae prohibentur recipi. Si quis rem, in materia gravi sibi, collatam celaverit, quem B. Augustinus furti judicio dicit esse condemnandum. Si quis pecuniam in materia gravi expenderit sine permissione vel furtum notabile commiserit." n. 1116. The common and received opinion in an Institute as to what would constitute a mortal sin against the vow of poverty may also be used as a guide; and "a fortiori," if the Constitutions determine what is a mortal sin against the vow of poverty; e.g., the Constitutions of the Congregations of the Immaculate Heart of Mary declare: "Generally speaking the same quantity that suffices to make theft a mortal sin also makes an infringement of the vow of poverty a mortal sin", n. 57.[80] To determine in all cases, just what constitutes a delict, considered from the aspect of notable matter, is indeed a very difficult task. There can be some egregious

79. Cf. Pejska, p. 135.
80. Cf. Calced Carmelite Constitutions, art. 270.

violations of the Common Life easily judged as notable violations, e.g., theft of an amount of money even beyond the absolutely grave matter required by the moralists for a mortal sin of theft. In those cases where the notability of matter is not evident so that it can be readily doubted the offending Religious is aware of the quality of the offense brotherly charity would dictate that the offender be unofficially advised before a Superior resorts to the grave canonical admonition.[81]

If the fact of the commission of a delict against the Common Life is neither notorious nor certain but has become known from rumor and public talk or by denunciation or a cursory investigation made by the Ordinary, or by any other way, a special investigation, called in law, inquisition, must be made before summoning the supposed offender to court in order to ascertain whether and what reason there is in the imputation.[82] The investigation should proceed according to the norm prescribed by canons 1940-1946 inclusively, which may be summarized roughly; usually the Ordinary will appoint a delegate to make the investigation; the delegate must be bound to maintain secrecy about his work and faithfully fulfill his commission; no action is to be taken on (a) the mere denunciation of a manifest enemy or that of a person of ill fame, or (b) from anonymous letters if they lack the qualities necessary to make the contents at least probable; every caution must be taken lest rumor of the crime be spread and the good name of anyone be jeopardized; the inquisitor may consult or obtain help from people acquainted with the accused or accusers or with the case in general; the number of persons to be interogated is not determined; witnesses should be placed under oath to tell the truth and maintain secrecy about the investigation; the procedure for examing witnesses is much the same as that prescribed by canons 1771-1781.

If the investigation reveals that it is ony probable that a delict was committed, the Ordinary *may* give a canonical admonition,[83] but he is not obliged to do so in virtue of

81. Cf. Lega, De *Judiciis,* IV, 183; Chelodi, *Ius Poenale,* p. 69.

82. Cf. canon 1939 § 1; 658 § 2 and canon 20; cf. Michalicka, p. 35; cf. Droste-Messmer, p. 146.

83. Cf. canon 2307; Lega, *"De Judiciis,"* IV, 183, 278 sq.; Chelodi, *"Ius Poenale,"* p. 67; Augustine, VIII. 267.

canon 2389. Nor would an admonition thus given suffice for the one prescribed before the infliction of deprivation of active and passive voice or the removal of a Superior from office. Canon 2389 expressly declares that an admonition must be given to a Religious who has been guilty of a delict; until the fact of the delict is certainly established juridically, the monition of 2389 is not to be given. An admonition given before it is juridically certain that the delict against the common life was committed, is not given in virtue of canon 2389; and a Religious has a right to be admonished in virtue of canon 2389, before the penalty therein prescribed, e. g. deprivation of active and passive voice or the removal of a Superior from office is inflicted.

But if the investigation reveals that a delict has been committed and has not been prescribed, then a canonical admonition *must* be given. The proofs of the commission of the delict should be such as would move a prudent man. Sufficient proofs can be had from the confession of the delict, authentic documents, or from the deposition of two witnesses worthy of faith (if strengthened by an oath). Notorious facts, i. e. publicly known or committed in such circumstances that they cannot be concealed by any artifice or be excused by any legal assumption or circumstantial evidence[84] need no proof.[85]

The canon prescribes that when a Religious has been guilty of the delict therein described he must be *admonished gravely,* "graviter moneantur". Canon 2309 § 1 declares that admonitions be either public or secret. Before the Code, the admonitions now known as public and private were called legal and paternal respectively.[86] The paternal admonition was to be given by the Ordinary in an informal way, so that the person warned could see plainly that the admonition proceeded from the Ordinary acting not as a judge but wholly as a father, who

84. Cf. canon 2197, 1°.

85. Cf. canon 1747, 1°.

86. Cf. S. C. EE et RR, instructio, 11 iunii 1880, n. 6 *Fontes,* 2005; S. C. de Prop Fide, instructio, *Cum magnopere,* n. 6, 1884, *Acta et Decreta Concilii Plenarii Baltimorensis Tertii,* pp. 287-288; Chelodi, *Ius Poenale,* p. 69.

acts in all kindness and paternal goodness.[87] In other words the paternal admonition should be done secretly, charitably and prudently by the Ordinary acting as a father rather than a judge.[88] The paternal admonition was described by Wernz: "Inter proceduras contra reum violationis legis ecclesiasticae, quae veri processus criminalis rationem non habent, simplicissima et mitissima et antiquissima est *monitio paterna.*"[89] If the legislator had intended the secret admonition in canon 2389 he would have used a more appropriate expression than "graviter moneantur." Hence it seems that the legislator intended a public admonition.

In clerical exempt Institutes, the public admonition should be given by the immediate major Superior personally or through another person acting under his authorization.[90] Institutes which have no Superiors juridically capable of administering a canonical admonition should have the Local Ordinary act in their behalf or their Regular Superior if they are subject to an Order.[97] The admonition may be inflicted outside the court of the Ordinary whether he acts personally or through an intermediary provided it is certain that a delict has been committed.[92] Whenever the Ordinary gives a mandate for an admonition, it is generally given to the one who had conducted the inquiry, because he is in a better position to give it on account of his acquaintance with the case.[93]

---

87. Cf. Droste-Messmer, p. 150; Smith, *The New Procedure in Criminal and Disciplinary Causes of Ecclesiastics in the United States,* pp. 132-133.

88. Cf. *Analecta Juris Pontificii,* XIX, col. 1102; Smith, *Elements of Ecclesiastical Law,* III, p. 60.

89. Vol. VI, n. 254, p. 259.

90. Cf. canons 20 and 559.

91. Cf. canons 20 and 647 § 1.

92. Canon 1933 § 4.

93. Cf. Michalicka, p. 53.

94. Cf. canons 1719 and 2143 § 1 and the instruction of the S. C. EE et RR, 11 iunii 1880, n. 14; *Fontes,* n. 2005. "Qui impedit quominus monitio ad se perveniat, habeatur pro monito," canon 2143 et canon 20; The receipt for the letter should be inserted in the acts. Cf. Augustine, VIII, 268, (6); Cf. etiam Droste-Messmer, p. 151. Theodorus, *Manuale Practicum Iuris Disciplinaris et Criminalis Regularium,* p. 61 gives a practical suggestion for the form of the admonition. Cf. Michalicka, p. 64; Smith, *Elements of Ecclesiastical Law,* p. 60.

95. Cf. canon 2309 § 2.

The public admonition, when given orally, is in the presence of a notary acting as such or two witnesses; when given by letter it should be a registered one and a record kept to show that the letter was juridically received,[94] and an abstract of its contents placed in a document.[95]

If the admonished Religious fails to amend and this fact has been ascertained by another canonical investigation, he must be punished, since the canon is preceptive.[96] A Religious may be considered not to have amended if after having been admonished he is guilty of another delict or perseveres in the same one. But if the Religious by his exterior conduct manifests that he has properly repented of his delict and a long interval transpires before he again becomes guilty of the same delict, another admonition should be given before the preceptive penalty of canon 2389 is inflicted.

The penalty of this canon is "ferendae sententiae". If the Religious does not amend he must be punished. Yet the punishment ought to be in due proportion to the delinquency. Account ought to be taken of the fault itself, the scandal given and the injury caused. As regards the fault itself, several elements are to be duly weighed: (a) the objective element viz. the nature and gravity of the constitution violated. (b) the subjective element viz. the age, sex, instruction, state of mind under which the delinquent was laboring when the delict occurred; (c) the circumstances which may lessen or increase the imputability; the purpose of the action, the time and place in which it was done; the influence of passion or grave fear by which the Religious may have been affected.[97]

The salutary principle. "*In poenis benignior est interpretatio facienda*"[98] should never be lost out of sight in the application of penalties. The judge or the Superior may even abstain from inflicting the penalty, if he sees that the offender has perfectly amended and repaired the scandal he may have given or if he perceives that the culprit is already punished sufficiently.[99] If there are attenuating circumstances connected with the case notably diminish-

---

96. Cf. canon 2223 § 3, 1°, 2°, 3°.

97. Cf. canon 2218 § 1; Ayrinhac, *Penal Legislation in the New Code of Canon Law*, p. 57.

98. Canon 2219 § 1.

99. Canon 2223 § 3, 2°.

ing the imputability or the Religious has reformed, the penalty may be diminished.[100] It is also left to the prudence of the judge or the Superior to delay the infliction of the penalty until a more opportune time, if it is foreseen that greater evils may follow from a too hasty punishment of the delinquent.[101]

Previous to the Code, authors taught that the penalty of privation of active and passive voice was not incurred before the sentence of the judge.[102] The length of time during which the Religious is to be deprived of voting power should be proportioned to the gravity of the delict. It may be remembered that the Council of Trent stipulated two years.[103]

When the Religious doubts whether the penalty inflicted on him was canonically just: (a) if the Ordinary acted in virtue of his administrative power in the application of the penalty, there is admitted recourse to the next higher Ordinary or the Sacred Congregation of Religious:[104] recourse usually has only devolutive effect and hence the penalty must be observed in both fora pending the awaited decision of the higher authority:[105] (b) if the Ordinary acted in virtue of his judiciary power there is had an appeal from the sentence with suspensive effect[106] except when the judge orders the provisory execution of the sentence.[107]

100. Canon 2223 § 3, 3°.

101. Canon 2223 § 3, 1°.

102. Cf. Castropalao, *Opera Omnia,* tract. XVI, disp. 3, c. 24, 4; Donatus, *Rerum Regularium Praxis Resolutoria,* Tomus IV, pars. 15, tract. 52, p. 5; Passerinus, *De Hominum Statibus et Officiis,* Quaes. 186, art. 8, n. 569; Pellizarius, *De Monialibus, Tractatio,* c. IV, n. 61; Rotarius, *Theologica Moralis Regularium,* Tomus, II, lib. 3, c. 1, punct, 18, n. 5; Schmalzgrueber, *Ius Ecclesiasticum Universum,* lib. III, tit. 35, n. 40, 1; Sanchez, *In Praecepta Decalogi,* lib. VII, c. 20, n. 13; Piat, *Praelectiones Iuris Regularis,* Vol. I, p. 269.

103. Sess. XXV, *de regularibus,* c. 2.

104. Cf. canons 2219 § 2 et 251; the Constitutions of the Friars Minor are excellent on this point. vide n. 363.

105. Cf. canon 2219 § 2.

106. Canon 1889 § 2.

107. Cf. canon 1917 § 2.

INDEX

D

Universitas Catholica Americae

WASHINGTON, D. C.

FACULTAS JURIS CANONICI

1929

No. 54

DEUS LUX MEA

THESES

QUAS

AD DOCTORATUS GRADUM

IN

UTROQUE IURE

APUD UNIVERSITATEM CATHOLICAM AMERICAE

CONSEQUENDUM
PUBLICE PROPUGNABIT

SIDONIUS JOSEPH TURNER

SACERDOS
CONGREGATIONIS PASSIONIS

IURIS UTRIUSQUE LICENTIATUS

HORA IX A. M. DIE XXV MAII A. D. MCMXXIX

JUS ROMANUM

I. Jus Civile.
II. Jus Gentium.
III. De evolutione juris.
IV. De juris consultis.
V. Jus Respondendi.
VI. Constitutio, "Tanta".
VII. De interpolationibus.
VIII. Criteria interpolationes cognoscendi.
IX. Summum ius, summa iniuria.
X. Vim vi repelere licet.
XI. De persona.
XII. De statu libertatis.
XIII. De statu familiae.
XIV. De patria potestate.
XV. De capitis deminutione.
XVI. De cura.
XVII. De tutela.
XVIII. De adoptione.
XIX. De iure proprietatis in genere.
XX. De possessione.
XXI. Iura in re aliena.
XXII. De successione universali.
XXIII. De successione particulari.
XXV. Lex Falcidia.
XXVI. De obligationibus.
XXVII. De contractu.
XXVIII. De stipulatione.
XXIX. Legis Actiones.
XXX. Actiones in factum.
XXXI. Actiones ficititiae.
XXXII. Lex Aebutia.
XXXIII. Cognitio extra ordinem.
XXXIV. Lex Julia de Adulteriis.
XXXV. De Episcopali audientia.

JUS CANONICUM

XXXVI. De relatione inter Ecclesiam et Statum.
XXXVII. De dissertatione.
XXXVIII. De historia Juris Canonici.

XXXIX.	De canonibus introductoriis	Canones	1-7
XL.	De legibus ecclesiasticis.	Canones	8-24
XLI.	De consuetudine.	Canones	25-30
XLII.	De temporis supputatione.	Canones	31-35
XLIII.	De rescriptis.	Canones	36-63
XLIV.	De privilegiis.	Canones	63-79
XLV.	De dispensationibus.	Canones	80-86
XLVI.	De personis in genere.	Canones	87-107

LXXXI.	De ordinariis Apostolicae Sedis tribunalibus.	Canones 1597-1605
LXXXII.	De personis ad disceptationem iudicialem admittendis et de modo confectionis et conservationis actorum.	Canones 1640-1645
LXXXIII.	De actore et reo convento.	Canones 1646-1654
LXXXIV.	De procuratoribus ad lites et advocatis.	Canones 1655-1666
LXXXV.	De testibus et attestationibus.	Canones 1754-1791
LXXXVI.	De peritis.	Canones 1792-1805
LXXXVII.	De probatione per instrumenta.	Canones 1812-1824
LXXXVIII.	De sententia.	Canones 1868-1877
LXXXIX.	De inqusitione.	Canones 1939-1946
XC.	De causis matrimonialibus.	Canones 1960-1992
XCI.	De modo procedendi in remotione parochorum inamovibilium.	Canones 2147-2156
XCII.	De modo procedendi in remotione parochorum amovibilium.	Canones 2157-2161
XCIII.	De modo procedendi in translatione parochorum.	Canones 2162-2167
XCIV.	De modo procedendi contra clericos non residentes.	Canones 2168-2175
XCV.	De modo procedendi contra clericos concubinarios.	Canones 2176-2181
XCVI.	De natura delicti eiusque divisione	Canones 2195-2198
XCVII.	De poenis in genere.	Canones 2214-2240
XCVIII.	De poenis medicinalibus seu de censuris.	Canones 2241-2285
XCIX.	De poenis vindicativis communibus.	Canones 2291-2297
C.	De delictis contra obligationes proprias status clericalis et religiosi.	Canones 2376-2389

Vidit Facultas Iuris Canonici:

PHILIPPUS BERNARDINI, S.T.D., J.U.D., *Decanus.*
LUDOVICUS MOTRY, S.T.D., J.C.D., *a Secretis.*
VALENTINE SCHAAF, O.F.M., J.C.D.
FRANCISCUS LARDONE, S.T.D., J.U.D.

Vidit Rector Magnificus Universitatis:

JAMES H. RYAN, S.T.D., Ph.D., LL.D.

BIOGRAPHICAL NOTE

Sidney Joseph Turner was born at Cambridge, Mass., November 24, 1899. Having finished his elementary and secondary education, he entered the novitiate of the Congregation of the Passion, at Pittsburgh, Pa., September, 1918. After his religious profession, October 19, 1919, he made his philosophical and theological studies at the Passionist Retreats of Dunkirk, N. Y., Scranton, Pa., and Union City, N. J. He was ordained to the priesthood, February 27, 1926, and in September of that year he matriculated in the School of Canon Law at the Catholic University of America as a candidate for the degree of Doctor of Both Laws, attending lectures, in addition to the prescribed course of that school, he attended courses in International Law and Papal Diplomacy.

CATHOLIC UNIVERSITY OF AMERICA

Canon Law Studies

(SCHOOL OF SACRED SCIENCES)

1. Freriks, Rev. Celestine A., C.PP.S., J.C.D., Religious Congregations in Their External Relations, 121 pp., 1916.

2. Galliher, Rev. Daniel M., O.P., J.C.D., Canonical Elections, 117 pp., 1917.

3. Borkowski, Rev. Aurelius L., O.F.M., J.C.D., De Confraternitatibus Ecclesiasticis, 136 pp., 1918.

4. Castillo, Rev. Cayo, J.C.D., Disertacion Historico-canonica sobre la Potestad del Cabildo en Sede Vacante o Impedida del Vicario Capitular, 99 pp., 1919 (1918).

5. Kubelbeck, Rev. William J., S.T.B., J.C.D., The Sacred Penitentiaria and its Relations to Faculties of Ordinaries and Priests, 129 pp., 1918.

6. Petrovits, Rev. Joseph J. C., S.T.D., J.C.D., The New Church Law on Matrimony, X-461 pp., 1919.

7. Hickey, Rev. John J., S.T.B., J.C.D., Irregularities and Simple Impediments in the New Code of Canon Law, 100 pp., 1920.

8. Klekotka, Rev. Peter J., S.T.B., J.C.D., Diocesan Consultors, 179 pp., 1920.

9. Wannenmacher, Rev. Francis, J.C.D., The Evidence in Ecclesiastical Procedure Affecting the Marriage Bond, 1920. (Not Printed.)

10. Golden, Rev. Henry Francis, J.C.D., Parochial Benefices in the New Code, IV-119 pp., 1921. (Printed 1925.)

11. Koudelka, Rev. Charles J., J.C.D., Pastors, Their Rights and Duties According to the New Code of Canon Law, 211 pp., 1921.

12. MELO, REV. ANTONIUS, O.F.M., J.C.D., De Exemptione Regularium, X-188 pp., 1921.

13. SCHAAF, REV. VALENTINE THEODORE, O.F.M., S.T.B., J.C.D., The Cloister, X-180 pp., 1921.

14. BURKE, REV. THOMAS JOSEPH, S.T.B., J.C.D., Competence in Ecclesiastical Tribunals, IV-117 pp., 1922.

15. LEECH, REV. GEORGE LEO, J.C.D., A Comparative Study of the Constitution "Apostolicae Sedis" and the "Codex Juris Canonici," 179 pp., 1922.

16. MOTRY, REV. HUBERT LOUIS, S.T.D., J.C.D., Diocesan Faculties according to the Code of Canon Law, II-167 pp., 1922.

17. MURPHY, REV. GEORGE LAWRENCE, J.C.D., Delinquencies and Penalties in the Administration and Reception of the Sacraments, IV-121 pp., 1923.

18. O'REILLY, REV. JOHN ANTHONY, S.T.B., J.C.D., Ecclesiastical Sepulture in the New Code of Canon Law, II-129 pp., 1923.

19. MICHALICKA, REV. WENCESLAS CYRILL, O.S.B., J.C.D., Judicial Procedure in Dismissal of Clerical Exempt Religious, 107 pp., 1923.

(SCHOOL OF CANON LAW)

20. DARGIN, REV. EDWARD VINCENT, S.T.D., J.C.D., Reserved Cases According to the Code of Canon Law, IV-103 pp., 1924.

21. GODFREY, REV. JOHN A., S.T.B., J.C.D., The Right of Patronage According to the Code of Canon Law, 153 pp., 1924.

22. HAGEDORN, REV. FRANCIS EDWARD, J.C.D., General Legislation on Indulgences, II-154 pp., 1924.

23. KING, REV. JAMES IGNATIUS, J.C.D., The Administration of the Sacraments to Dying Non-Catholics, V-141 pp., 1924.

24. WINSLOW, REV. FRANCIS JOSEPH, A.F.M., J.C.D., Vicars and Prefects Apostolic, IV-149 pp., 1924.

25. CORREA, REV. JOSE SERVELION, S.T.L., J.C.D., La Potesdad Legislativa de la Iglesia Catolica, IV-127 pp., 1925.

26. DUGAN, REV. HENRY FRANCIS, M.A., J.C.D., The Judiciary Department of the Diocesan Curia, 87 pp., 1925.

27. KELLER, REV. CHARLES FREDERICK, S.T.B., J.C.D., Mass Stipends, 167 pp., 1925.

28. PASCHANG, REV. JOHN LINUS, J.C.D., The Sacramentals According to the Code of Canon Law, 129 pp., 1925.

29. PIONTEK, REV. CYRILLUS, O.F.M., S.T.B., J.C.D., De Indulto Exclaustrationis necnon Saecularizationis, XIII-289 pp., 1925.

30. KEARNEY, REV. RICHARD JOSEPH, S.T.B., J.C.D., Sponsors at Baptism According to the Code of Canon Law, IV-127 pp., 1925.

31. BARTLETT, REV. CHESTER JOSEPH, A.M., LL.B., J.C.D., The Tenure of Parochial Property in the United States of America, V-108 pp., 1926.

32. KILKER, REV. ADRIAN JEROME, J.C.D., Extreme Unction, V-425 pp., 1926.

33. McCORMICK, REV. ROBERT EMMET, J.C.D., Confessors of Religious, VIII-266 pp., 1926.

34. MILLER, REV. NEWTON THOMAS, J.C.D., Founded Masses According to the Code of Canon Law, VII-93 pp., 1926.

35. ROELKER, REV. EDWARD G., S.T.D., J.C.D., Principles of Privilege According to the Code of Canon Law, XI-166 pp., 1926.

36. BAKALARCZYK, REV. RICHARDUS, M.I.C., J.U.D., De Novitiatu, VIII-208 pp., 1927.

37. PIZZUTI, REV. LAWRENCE, O.F.M., J.U.L., De Parochis religiosis, 1927. (Not Printed.)

38. BLILEY, REV. NICHOLAS MARTIN, O.S.B., J.C.D., Altars According to the Code of Canon Law, XIX-132 pp., 1927.

39. BROWN, BRENDAN FRANCIS, A.B., LL.M., J.U.D., The Canonical Juristic Personality with Special Reference to its Status in the United States of America, V-212 pp., 1927.

40. CAVANAUGH, REV. WILLIAM THOMAS, C.P., J.U.D., The Reservation of the Blessed Sacrament, VIII-101 pp., 1927.

41. Doheny, Rev. William J., C.S.C., A.B., J.U.D., Church Property: Modes of Acquisition, X-118 pp., 1927.

42. Feldhaus, Rev. Aloysius H., C.PP.S., J.C.D., Oratories, IX-141 pp., 1927.

43. Kelly, Rev. James Patrick, A.B., J.C.D., The Jurisdiction of the Simple Confessor, X-208 pp., 1927.

44. Neuberger, Rev. Nicholas J.,J.C.D., Canon 6 or the Relation of the Codex Juris Canonici to the Preceding Legislation, V-95 pp., 1927.

45. O'Keeffe, Rev. Gerald Michael, J.C.D., Matrimonial Dispensations, Powers of Bishops, Priests, and Confessors, VIII-232 pp., 1927.

46. Quigley, Rev. Joseph A. M., A.B., J.C.D., Condemned Societies, 139 pp., 1927.

47. Zaplotnik, Rev. Ioannes Leo, J.C.D., De Vicariis Foraneis, X-142 pp., 1927.

48. Duskie, Rev. John Aloysius, A.B., J.C.D., The Canonical Status of the Orientals in the United States, VIII-196 pp., 1928.

49. Hyland, Rev. Francis Edward, J.C.D., Excommunication, its Nature, Historical Development and Effects, VIII-181 pp., 1928.

50. Reinmann, Rev. Gerald Joseph, O.M.C., J.C.D., The Third Order Secular of St. Francis, 201 pp., 1928.

51. Schenk, Rev. Francis J., J.C.L., The Matrimonial Impediments of Mixed Religion and Disparity of Cult, pp., 1928.

52. Coady, Rev. John Joseph, A.M., S.T.D., J.U.L., The Appointment of Pastors, 1929.

53. Kay, Rev. Thomas Henry, J.C.L., Competence in Matrimonial Procedure, 1929.

54. Turner, Rev. Sidney Joseph, C.P., J.U.L., The Vow of Poverty, 1929.

55. Kearney, Rev. Raymond A., A.B., S.T.D., J.C.L., The Principles of Delegation, 1929.

www.ingramcontent.com/pod-product-compliance
Lightning Source LLC
LaVergne TN
LVHW050253080826
844660LV00012B/629

* 9 7 8 0 8 1 3 2 2 2 4 3 1 *